Computer Supported Cooperative Work

T0205362

For other titles published in this series, go to
http://www.springer.com/series/2861

Ina Wagner • Tone Bratteteig • Dagny Stuedahl
Editors

Exploring Digital Design

Multi-Disciplinary Design Practices

Ⓐ Springer

Editors
Ina Wagner
Vienna University of Technology
Austria
ina.wagner@tuwien.ac.at

Tone Bratteteig
Department of Informatics
University of Oslo
Norway
tone@ifi.uio.no

Dagny Stuedahl
Department of Media and Communication
University of Oslo
Norway
dagny.stuedahl@intermedia.uio.no

Computer Supported Cooperative Work   ISSN 1431-1496
ISBN 978-1-4471-2584-6   ISBN 978-1-84996-223-0 (eBook)
DOI 10.1007/978-1-84996-223-0
Springer London Dordrecht Heidelberg New York

British Library Cataloguing in Publication Data
A catalogue record for this book is available from the British Library

Printed on acid-free paper

Springer is part of Springer Science+Business Media (www.springer.com)

Preface

Digital design is an important element of our lives. We live with designed environments filled with designed things: systems, media and all sorts of artefacts. Many of these are digital or partly digital. In order to understand contemporary society and culture it is important to study digital designs and how they are weaved into our daily practices. It is, however, just as important to understand the processes of digital design that bring about these digital elements in our lives. This book: *Exploring Digital Design*, presents a research-oriented view on design, and explores how to analyze design in digital domains. It takes a closer look at the diverse disciplinary sources of the current discourses about digital design, paying special attention to the humanities exploring how they can enrich a design discourse currently dominated by design professionals and philosophers.

This book is based on collaboration between three departments at the University of Oslo: the interdisciplinary research centre InterMedia, the Department of Informatics, and the Department of Media and Communication. The book was initiated as part of a multidisciplinary research network *Competence and Media Convergence (CMC)* at the University of Oslo, bringing together researchers from these departments and also many disciplines to do research on IT in a socio-cultural context. In 2006 a new strategic research initiative on *Digital Design* at the University of Oslo was begun, involving researchers from these three partners. The book has been a major collaborative project for the *Digital Design* initiative, and Professor Ina Wagner, Vienna University of Technology, was engaged as an editor, leading the process of making a book. Our first thanks go to the departments and research initiatives that initiated the book and its projects, in particular to CMC's Trond Eilif Hauge and InterMedia's then centre leader Sten Ludvigsen. Thanks also to The Department of Informatics for funding the finalizing of the book.

The writing of the book has been an exploratory journey. We decided to write one part of the book collaboratively and the decision was taken quite early on; this book should not be 'just' a collection of individual contributions but should present the results of mutual learning. However, we also wanted the book to give space to individual contributions that demonstrate how different approaches can enrich digital design research. The writing together (no surprise) revealed that we represent different understandings of digital design. More importantly, however, is that we have experienced the differences as essential for our ambition to explore and move our original disciplinary positions toward more open and complex understandings of digital design. The difficulty of opening up to other approaches while not losing your own perspective is not untypical of multidisciplinary projects. We, the authors of this book, have different and mixed academic backgrounds: informatics, information systems, pedagogy, cultural anthropology, discourse analysis, linguistics, semiotics, new media studies and literary theory, among others. Given this diversity, the process of sharing, exploring and establishing a shared experience is by necessity a long-term project.

Collaborating in the making of this book has been full of challenges. The texts went through many iterations, and the process of re-visiting positions, of re-ordering and re-writing arguments, gave rise to discoveries and rich discussions. So did the joint analysis of examples of digital design projects, which are present throughout the book. We are happy to have been involved in this adventure. And we are happy to have had other researchers with us on the journey, researchers that contributed but did not stay throughout the process, in particular Anders Mørch and Synne Skjulstad from InterMedia, and Anne Lise Wullum from Media and Communication Studies. In addition, Ole Smørdal and Anders Kluge from InterMedia and Jens Kaasbøll from Informatics participated in our first discussions. Towards the end, Erik Stolterman, University of Umeå and University of Indiana, and Joan Greenbaum, City University of New York, read through parts of the manuscript and gave valuable comments. Heather Owen gave the text a round of thorough language editing. Christina Mörtberg made the indexing and together with Annelise Harnesk the finishing editing. Our Springer contacts, Rebecca Mowat, Helen Desmond, Beverley Ford, and Natasha Harding, have been extremely supportive and patient. Thank you to all!

October 2009, Oslo
the authors

Contents

Part 1

A Common Ground

Part 1

A Common Ground

1

Researching Digital Design

Dagny Stuedahl, Andrew Morrison,
Christina Mörtberg, and Tone Bratteteig

The emerging field of digital design research is heterogeneous, encompassing a multiplicity of practices, theories and methods. One source of this heterogeneity is that design as a concept takes different meanings in the context of different design practices, be it the design of software, urban spaces, web pages or industrial products; as does 'the digital' when integrated within different types of design. Another source of heterogeneity is the variety of research traditions, theories and methodologies that meet in digital design research. This book explores the multiplicity and heterogeneity of 'digital things', design practices, and (inter) disciplinary approaches.

In this introductory chapter we seek to map out the positions we come from and how we try to confront and combine them. In many respects, digital design research emerges in a space between several well-established design disciplines related to the digital. In taking up the emerging and dynamic qualities and aspects of digital design, we draw on selected perspectives from informatics, science and technology studies, and 'new media', and communication studies.

The viewpoint we bring from informatics is firmly anchored in Participatory Design (PD) and Computer Supported Cooperative Work (CSCW) which, from their beginnings, focused on how digital technologies become embedded in human practices – situated use. This not only challenges the engineering approach to design but also the traditional focus on the product of design. The humanities bring to digital design research their interest in understanding how the digital shapes cultural modes and means of expression. Several developments strengthen the connections between these perspectives, each of which has its own history of inter-disciplinarity. One concerns the 'naturalization' of digital technologies in society and culture, which makes it impossible to isolate digital design from the larger socio-cultural context in which it occurs. Connected to this is the fact that the 'users' and uses of digital design have changed – from professionals in different work environments and computing specialists to the broad range of people engaging in 'social computing', gaming, art, as well as applications that support citizens' participation in their communities. Finally, the technologies studied in digital design research are emerging and further evolve with use. This makes it necessary to pay attention to how social and cultural aspects are inscribed in the technologies.

I. Wagner et al. (eds.), *Exploring Digital Design: Multi-Disciplinary Design Practices*,
Computer Supported Cooperative Work, DOI 10.1007/978-1-84996-223-0_1,
© Springer-Verlag London Limited 2010

The design research presented in this book is grounded in a set of interdisciplinary research projects. Some of these engage with technology design, some are centred on understanding user experiences, while others focus on the development of design-related theories. These projects provide the main material for the book. Their diversity illustrates the diversity of digital design research. Their discussion from multiple disciplinary perspectives provides means of understanding better the meeting points and differences between approaches (Fig. 1.1).

Fig. 1.1 Digital designs span a variety of situated practices and uses. From *top left to right*: Location-based simulations with smart phones; children producing their own 'readings' of cultural historical museum; investigation of design of tangible user interfaces; and children testing a mobile hospital system prototype in a real-life setting

One of the projects we discuss is about participatory design, which aims at designing a mobile system to allow severely ill children to report symptoms and problems to the clinicians. Another project explores rhetoric and the concept of genre to design for location-based simulations, cartography and encyclopaedic information. A third project, also participatory in its approach, focuses on the design of mixed reality tools and a tangible user interface in support of collaborative urban planning. Two projects engage in and reflect on 'communication design', involving museum visitors in exhibitions with mobile telephones and social media; utilizing digital technologies in a dance performance.

In *Exploring Digital Design* we ask how we can frame and unpack our multiple understandings of digital tools and environments and the practices and expressions that digital technologies enable. What is the nature of the knowledge about the digital that our perspectives can build? How can practice-based research from humanities and informatics conjoin (and diverge) in the practices and analyses of digital design? Are our findings different from those of other, related fields, such as visual design or urban planning, and in which ways do our specific theoretical and methodological approaches contribute to this? What are the relationships between modes of knowing and analysis drawn from the insights and practices of, respectively, designers and researchers? Do the conceptual and methodological encounters we undertake in this book open up fruitful theoretical and methodological venues, and, if yes, how can these be taken further into new digital design (research) projects?

The collection of chapters in this book is geared towards a multidisciplinary audience of researchers and designers. For researchers, it offers a range of approaches, concepts and methods for inquiry into digital design. For designers, it reveals some of the ways in which design research into the digital may be framed theoretically and carried out in practice. The book also has, as a core readership, graduate students in various disciplines, emphasizing distinctions between and connections across disciplinary domains that take time to get to know deeply and use in research.

The book has two main parts. The first looks into research practices, theoretical frameworks and a diversity of methods. The second examines specific topics and cases that involve both digital design products and processes. The title *Exploring Digital Design* highlights the importance we place on transgressing disciplinary boundaries and relations in reforming digital design research. When mapping out our disciplinary homes and the multiplicity of our approaches, confronting and combining, we realize that it is impossible and maybe even not desirable to 'speak in one voice'. Our research into digital design presents and argues for perspectives that are positioned at the margins of many disciplines as well as in between them. Our basic groundings in informatics and the humanities are themselves interdisciplinary positions within these disciplinary frameworks.

Perspectives on Research into Digital Design

The role of the digital in societal daily life, the possibilities of participation and the access to information that today's digital technologies represent, is no longer only about the use of a computer or a well-defined artefact. It is about participating in society, it is about marking and tagging, manipulating and interacting, creating and enjoying – and it is about being connected in informational and communicational relations. The digital comes into being through human and social agency, even where the computational may be designed for automation or for system-generated configurations. We argue that the 'digital' itself has to be understood as design material, as concretized layers of abstractions and representations, which are part of material and discursive practices (see Chapter 2).

Digital design calls for an expanded concept of design, as working with the digital is different from other forms of designing. The digital opens up a discussion between research approaches grounded in technological design and in socio-cultural and humanistic inquiries. This is not entirely new. Twenty years ago the Scandinavian tradition had already located design in the larger social, cultural, political context of use (Nygaard 1986, 1996), inviting practitioners from different disciplines to provide insights into the design and use of digital artefacts, systems, and media. Also, connections between informatics and the humanities have a long history. Linguistics, semiotics and philosophy of language are important in developing programming languages, while sociolinguistics and, for example, Speech Act Theory have played a role in the development of computer support for collaboration (Flores et al. 1988; Winograd 1979).

In this book we strive to take a step further. On the one hand, we do so by looking at digital design through the lens of a broader range of research traditions relevant to the understanding of design practice and the situated use of digital designs (see Chapter 3). On the other hand, we move from 'classical' studies of systems design in support of specific work practices to emerging fields of digital design.

This also calls for a reframing of the notion of use, shifting attention from a narrow concept of product use to the context and practices of use. Design is a situated social practice, and the designed artefacts can only be fully understood in use. Taking into account the evolving and often-participatory character of digital designs, we even have to consider designing for *design after design,* the design that users carry out in use (Ehn 2007; Telier et al. (forthcoming)). We can also look at situated use as where the idea behind the artefact and the reality of use meet.

The explorations in digital design also lead us to revisit the political and ethical issues that receive attention at the meeting ground between informatics and the critical social sciences. The commitment of Participatory Design (PD) to enhancing users' autonomy implies the responsibility to design in ways that enables people to understand the systems they are part of, and puts an emphasis on transparency and critique as parts of digital design (van der Velden et al. 2009). The political and ethical sides of PD resonate with political art, which seeks to express elements of provocation as well as reflection. This focus on autonomy and political analysis characterizes the multidisciplinary areas of PD and Computer Supported Cooperative Work (CSCW), where researchers and designers question the technology from a deep understanding of the context, in which it will be integrated (Bjerknes and Bratteteig 1988; Bowers et al. 1995; Luff and Heath 1998). Researchers in digital design need to understand a range of design practices, sometimes even participate as designers in the practices they research (Bjerknes and Bratteteig 1987).

Research in CSCW is concerned with how understandings of material practices can inform design (Schmidt and Bannon 1992; Randall et al. 2007). Both use and design are studied as collaborative practices, and the empirical and theoretical studies of such practices constitute the basis for designing better computer support for work (see Chapter 4). Research in PD involves users as co-designers in the design process as a way to design artefacts and systems that the users themselves consider of benefit to their activities (Ehn 1989; Bjerknes and Bratteteig 1995). Participation in the design process has been seen as a strategy for giving users more power of decision in design, and a range of methods for PD has been developed

(Greenbaum and Kyng 1991; Bødker et al. 2004). As technology changes, so does technology design and use. PD and CSCW change when the technology opens up for new kinds of functions and interactions and when the use contexts reach beyond work contexts to include other social arenas. Hence, PD has been extended to new fields, yielding creative design ideas for ubiquitous computing, embodied interaction, mobility, and conviviality (Wagner et al. 2009).

These commitments are unfortunately still not a mainstream view in informatics. However, many of the inventions in informatics stem from stretching the technology to meet the wishes and needs of the real world. Understanding the contextual complexities opens up a whole range of new design ideas. We have to add here that foundational to PD and CSCW is a deep commitment to socially embedding technologies in human practice and that both fields of research make use of a diversity of social science methods, among them ethnography. There is a strong overlap with the humanities here, which will also be made visible in the book.

Humanistic and socio-cultural approaches to the digital represent a variety of perspectives and theories, partly interdisciplinary and partly with a strong disciplinary history. In this book we draw on New Media Studies and Cultural Studies that partly embed Science and Technology Studies (STS) perspectives, emphasizing connections to performance and electronic art. Moving on from an early concern with media and communication, especially literary hypertext (Landow 1992) and aesthetics, humanists have questioned the relation between humans and computer interfaces based on concepts such as meaning making, mediation, identity, and related historical and philosophical connections. Scholars in the humanities have joined colleagues from other domains in building interdisciplinary design perspectives where attention is given to new 'textual' environments (Hayles 1999; Bolter 2001; Skjulstad 2007), the design and analysis of environments that transverse mode, time and space (e.g. Lemke 2002, 2005), as well as multimodal discourses related to the digital (Morrison 2010). This has included tropes and genres of gaming (Corneliussen and Walker 2008), mixed reality artistic expressions (Birringer 2002; Hansen 2006; Morrison et al. 2009), and performance (Schiller 2006). There is a bulk of studies on identity, youth and digitally mediated communication – online and via mobile devices, including the so-called social media (Lundby 2009). The humanities also engage in research on designing digital conceptual tools for mediated meaning making in museums (Pierroux 2008), digital environments for experiences and engagement with cultural heritage (Stuedahl 2009), as well as discursive and communicative digital environments (Morrison 2010). An additional area where such connections are being made is in the uptake of digital technologies in practices and studies of literacy and learning, where digital discourses are seen as both learning and communication design (see, e.g. Morrison 2003).

The new media environments are no longer restricted to 'texts' and 'screens' but involve physical artefacts and the human body within physical space, as well as their connections to the digital. This means a shift from written and spoken text to other modes of expression and perception and requires the development of methods of multimodal analysis (Morrison 2010). At the same time, we notice changing understandings of the role of form that require a distributed aesthetics, which deals with the endless relaying of practices and experiences that are related to the digital. This gives us an understanding of mediations as based on loops of dispersal instead of singular 'end use' of information. We therefore need to talk about formations rather than form related to the media we study (Munster and Lovink 2005). These formations include processes of social network formations, which obviously challenge the classical, individual ways of thinking in the humanities (Andersen 2005).

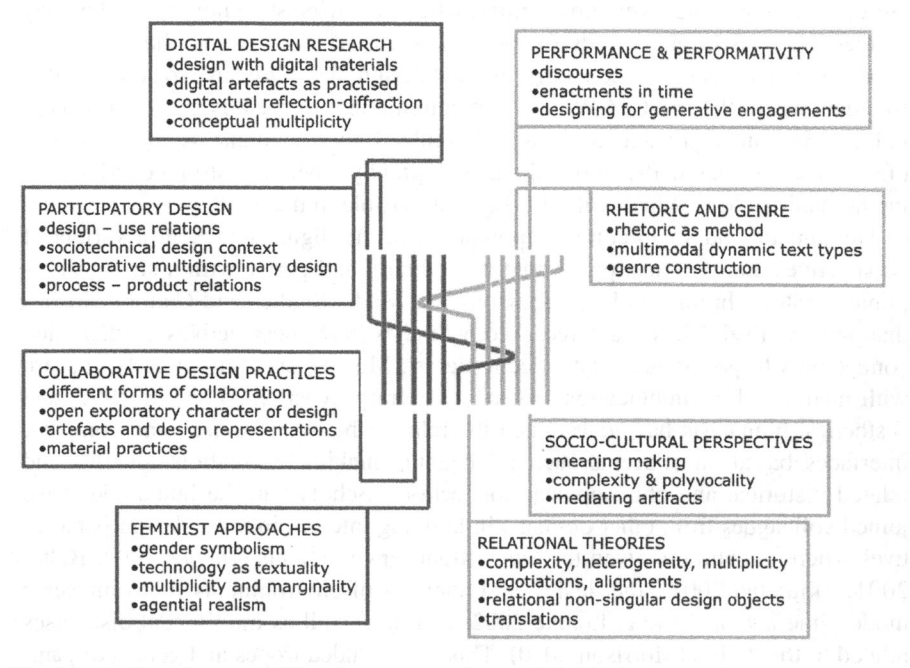

Fig. 1.2 Outline of our multidisciplinary approaches to digital design research

These works in 'new media studies', multimodal discourse and performance, have not been widely cited in digital design research, nor have they often been accessed in reference to digital design established in CSCW and PD. This is one of the connections we try to shape in this book.

While the objects of study do not differ so much from those undertaken from a PD and CSCW perspective, there is a difference in focus and epistemological grounding. A humanist approach to understanding these new media environments spans design issues like information architecture, web design, structure, and aesthetic functions to the dynamics of mediated communication, the interplay between using and producing, with a focus on articulation and interpretation. It is especially in the contact zones between humanistic views and technology studies that digital design research shows the potential of humanistic inquiry, and the ways an already complex multidisciplinarity can open out to further complementarity and reflexivity through new design practices and their critiques.

The various views we propose in this book point to different layers and methods of analysis that the complexity of digital products demands (see Fig. 1.2). The illustration is suggested as an overview for our readers to navigate with and between the concepts and practices on which we build. This is not an invitation to eclecticism, and we argue for considering the epistemological and ontological bases when trying to merge and mix different theories and approaches.

These perspectives will be presented in more depth throughout the book, in particular in Chapters 2–4, where readers can find more references to core literature.

Reflexivity in Multidisciplinary Design Research

From an anthropologist's point of view, Hastrup (2005) points to design being traditionally defined as belonging to creative approaches to knowledge construction in arts. She emphasizes that, as knowledge in general can be understood in multiple ways, we also can understand design knowledge as created in different ways. Hence, there are a variety of possibilities to connect design and research. Within CSCW research there is an ongoing debate about ethnography and how it contributes to design, and if studies of work and technology can be considered design research. A similar discussion needs to be conducted in the humanities.

Knowledge construction in design and design research can be approached in multiple ways, and the question of what we know should be tightly connected with questions of how we know it. Reflexivity in research is a must when it comes to the kind of multidisciplinary projects we consider in this book. The different research traditions we build on represent different views on what we know, what we can know, and how we know it. Here, we briefly discuss if and how such multidisciplinary reflexivity can be anchored in digital design.

We start with noting that reflexivity differs from the notion of reflection, which is used in design studies. The seminal work of Schön (1983, 1987), in which he described design as a reflective process, serves as a starting point. Schön distinguished between reflection-in-action: part of the action ('thinking on our feet'), and reflection-on-action: after the action, and developed an epistemology of reflective practice. Reflection-on-practice, Schön states, yields a critical view on how the designer's own tacit understanding may have affected the design work. Several of the design research approaches presented in this book have long traditions with this kind of reflection. PD research, for example, emphasizes discussions about how alternative and even conflicting views among users and designers are voiced and given power. This includes reflection on the political and ethical premises for so doing, as well as on the practical and emotional constraints such a practice meets (Bjerknes and Bratteteig 1987, 1988).

The humanities traditionally pay attention to the past rather than present and future events. The temporal and spatial detachment of the researcher and the studied object results in after-the-fact reflection, not unlike reflection-on-action. Liestøl (2003) introduces the notion of pre-reflection, indicating two steps of reflection:

reflection related to the process of modifying and reflection related to the reception of the modified. These two reflective steps define the details of a humanistic reflective process and help humanists discuss the practice of reflexivity in digital design research. Reflexive explorations in the humanities consider, for example, the notion of culture, on which digital designs and their analysis are based. They include a critical reflection on the grounding of research in semiotics and different discourse theories.

The distinction between reflection and reflexivity is relevant for understanding the encounters of multiple disciplines that this book explores. Reflection focuses on understanding the assumptions, biases, and perspectives that underlie the research, and it is such self-inspection that a 'reflective practitioner' of research or design is expected to undertake. But reflection requires moving a step further from this reflected positionality of the researcher in order to make his/her self-invisibility visible (Haraway 1997). Reflexivity, goes beyond self-vision, and includes epistemological questions and contextual conditions of understanding that are at work, and how these are rooted in practices of collaboration and negotiation, as well as in decisions affecting the exclusion and inclusion of perspectives. Weber (2003: ix) states that reflexive researchers consider 'the interplay between the research methods they have a propensity to employ in their work and the sort of theories they build to account for the phenomena that are in their focus'.

This book attempts a reflexive exploration of the diversity of approaches to digital design research that we seek to confront and combine. The intention of this book has not been to generate a synthesized, grand and unified theory of (digital) design. The authors have different and mixed academic backgrounds: informatics, information systems, pedagogy, anthropology, discourse analysis, linguistics, semiotics (new) media studies and literary theory, among others. We strongly believe that this diversity is a strength when moving into critical and reflective analysis of digital design and its contexts of construction and use. None of the perspectives or theories put forward in this book claims priority over others. The fact that our research is grounded in different epistemological traditions has been one of the main challenges in writing collaboratively.

Outline of the Book

The book has two main parts. In the first part, we discuss how changes in technology inform digital design research practices, methods and theories. These descriptions of change provide a background for engaging in multidisciplinary dialogues aimed at developing a better conceptual grip on the relations and meetings within and between disciplinary views. A considerable collaborative composition and multidisciplinary authorship stands behind this first part of the book.

In Chapter 2, 'Research Practices in Digital Design', we discuss changes in design research practices that are related to the digital. By presenting four different design cases, the chapter demonstrates how research by designing is explored in relation to several practical design challenges, involving different design objectives and disciplinary perspectives. The chapter describes the PD approach used for the design of a mobile interaction device for seriously ill children in hospitals. The second case covers the design of a novel interface for embodied and tangible interaction that weaves together the technical and human activity. The third case concerns the design of a multi-level interface as part of a multidisciplinary research project in choreography, digital media and learning. The fourth case takes up children's interactions with mobile phones in a cultural historical museum setting with a focus on social media. The last part of the chapter introduces some concepts from design research that we find useful for describing design practices.

In Chapter 3, 'Analytical Perspectives', we provide an overview of selected theories and approaches to digital design research that may be applied in inquiry into its emergent and multidisciplinary character. We outline and explain key concepts and their relevance for understanding digital design practice, drawing on CSCW, informatics, the humanities, the social sciences and their different traditions. The chapter argues that, while we may draw on accepted disciplinary knowledge, digital technology-enhanced design and its contexts, uses and communicative potentials are in need of further theorizing that integrates the interplay of theory and practice. Each of the main sections moves to connect, but also extend, a general design research literature and to do so with respect to already-mapped areas in which digital design is researched. Aspects of the perspectives that are presented in this chapter are taken up and further contextualized and explored in the second part of the book.

Methodological perspectives in digital design are discussed in Chapter 4, entitled 'Methods that Matter in Digital Design Research'. These methodological perspectives are grounded in the conceptual analysis, construction, and reflection undertaken in the previous chapters. In this chapter we describe design methods from a range of disciplinary origins, and we show how they can be applied to digital design, combining them in novel ways. Concrete examples from projects are given for each of the methods so as to enable readers to understand how, and with what results, they have been used in different contexts. Again, elements of these methods are taken up in the second part of the book.

In the second part of the book, we have assembled a set of individual contributions that have been written to illustrate selected aspects of digital design research. Several of the chapters are co-authored, reflecting the arguments for multidisciplinarity outlined above. All the contributions explore the connection between research and practice in the field of digital design. We offer these chapters as instances of our own grapplings with emerging fields and complex design problems. They are also reflexive takes on research methods in digital design research.

In Chapter 5, entitled 'A Matter of Digital Materiality', Tone Bratteteig discusses understandings of digital material and its implications for designing and building digital artefacts and systems. Bratteteig discusses software and hardware as materials for design, and argues that the digital has characteristics that influence the design process as well as the tools used in the design. The chapter proposes some basic properties of digital electronic systems, and examines their consequences for the possibilities and limitations of digital design. The chapter discusses how the digital also characterizes digital design results, artefacts, systems and media, and how conceptualizations of the digital enhance our understanding of our digital environment. Finally, these views are taken back to the design process, to reflect on how the digital material influences the design process.

Relations between genre and design are discussed by Gunnar Liestøl in Chapter 6, 'On Mobility, Localization and the Possibility of Digital Genre Design'. This chapter concerns a potential convergence of mobility, broadband and positioning technologies. Genre design is suggested as a possible method, based on a model of genre constitution (and change), including the context of situation and formal and substantive features that are informed by studies in rhetoric, now transposed to digital design through the notion of *inventio* or heuretics. A prototype of such an approach is presented with respect to web-based learning and the media types that offered means for building digital genres. This is connected to the convergence of cartography and the changing character of encyclopaedias and travel guides. The chapter closes with examples of the suggested genre of 'situated simulations', referring to a Viking ship excavation and burial mound, and an ancient Greek battle site. Both explorations indicate the importance of sketching and creativity in the ongoing design of digital genres informed by theories and textual and communicative legacies in the humanities.

In Chapter 7, 'Unreal Estate: Digital Design and Mediation in Marketing Urban Residency', Andrew Morrison and Synne Skjulstad venture into one of the intriguing yet elusive qualities of the digital: it is 'immaterial' but has textual materiality that is a critical part of the design for engaged participation. The authors unpack the term 'unreal estate', one they have coined to refer to hyperreal digital simulation on the web that markets new urban residency. Digital tools are used to design new apartments, to market them and to mediate their sale and circulation, as part of the wider digital cultural industries. These digital simulations are generated to project and market these as-yet-unbuilt properties. The online texts are examples of digitally designed and mediated persuasive discourse that, from a communication design view, connects textual aspects to mediated use. The researchers discuss this in terms of tertiary artefacts drawn from Activity Theory, multimodal discourse theory, textual analysis and social semiotics, while yet placing considerably more weight on the digital. The chapter contributes a communication design perspective to the under-researched area of digital branding and online advertising.

Matters of designing for discursive performativity are addressed in Chapter 8, 'Whisperings in the Undergrowth: Communication Design, Online Social Networking and Discursive Performativity', by Andrew Morrison, Even Westvang and Simen Skogsrud. This chapter concerns the design and analysis of the emerging domain of digital design and communication related to social software. The chapter is itself a rhetorical experiment. It is co-compiled by a researcher and two designers with a long history of collaboration in different settings related to digital design. The text toggles between expository, analytic discourse, contextual descriptions, screen grabs and quotations. The chapter situates the development and iterative designing of a calendaring and social networking software application called

Underskog for use in a capital city. Theories from applied linguistics and post-structuralist discourse studies are connected to the practice of programmer-designers, and situated within a sociocultural approach to digital design and 'new media'. The chapter demonstrates that digitally mediated communication is itself an emergent partner of design for digitally mediated meaning making.

Digital design also encourages a focus on sustainability and long-term perspectives in design. This is discussed by Christina Mörtberg, Dagny Stuedahl and Pirjo Elovaara in Chapter 9, 'Designing for Sustainable Ways of Living with Technologies'. With a focus on standards, formats and routines, the chapter discusses social and cultural aspects of sustainable design and use of digital technologies. The chapter builds on Donna Haraway's actor-network theory, formulated in the shape of a cat's cradle, in discussions of examples from research projects related to a municipal accounts department and a cultural heritage reconstruction. These projects are analysed in order to unfold different layers of social and cultural sustainability as a design principle that can be applied. The projects also relate sustainability to design and use. The chapter argues that social and cultural aspects of traditions and values play a role for standards surviving in the long term by addressing the question: How can we anchor social and cultural sustainability as a principle inside design practice?

The last chapter, 'Epilogue: A Multidisciplinary Take on Design' is added as an afterthought of the book's two parts: the inter- and multidisciplinary Part I aiming to build a common ground across and beyond our disciplinary starting points, and Part II where we illustrate how deep disciplinary knowledge offers new insights to the transdisciplinary field of digital design. We are particularly proud that this book combines humanities and informatics in new ways and thus moves digital design research forward.

We have entitled the book *Exploring Digital Design*. The title refers to our view that research into digital design needs to acknowledge established practices and be open to importing new concepts and methods. Appreciating the close relations between design and design research, digital design research also takes on its own logic as design and research processes unfold. We expect that readers find things they know but also new arguments, some text that is easy and some that offers challenges, obvious points and more intricate arguments. Above all, we hope that our readers will appreciate the diversity and multiperspectival reasoning that we suggest for research exploring digital design.

References

Andersen, P.B. (2005). Activity-based design. *European Journal of Information Systems archive*, 15(1), 9–25.
Birringer, J. (2002). Dance and media technologies. *PAJ: A Journal of Performance and Art* Jan 2002 (PAJ 70), 24 (1), 84–93.
Bjerknes, G., & Bratteteig, T. (1987). Florence in wonderland. System development with nurses. In G. Bjerknes, P. Ehn & M. Kyng (Eds.), *Computers and democracy. A Scandinavian challenge* (pp. 279–296). Aldershot: Avebury.
Bjerknes, G., & Bratteteig, T. (1988). The memoirs of two survivors— or evaluation of a computer system for cooperative work. In I. Greif (Ed.), *Proceedings of the 1988 ACM conference*

on computer-supported cooperative work, Portland, Oregon, USA (pp. 167–177). New York: ACM.

Bjerknes, G., & Bratteteig, T. (1995). User participation and democracy. A discussion of Scandinavian research on systems development. *Scandinavian Journal of Information Systems*, 7(1), 73–98.

Bolter, J.D. (2001). *Writing space: Computers, hypertext, and the remediation of print*. Mahwah, N.J: Lawrence Erlbaum.

Bowers, J., Button, G., & Sharrock, W. (1995). Workflow from within and without: technology and cooperative work on the print industry shopfloor. In H. Marmolin, Y. Sundblad & K. Schmidt (Eds.), *Proceedings of the fourth conference on European conference on computer-supported cooperative work (ECSCW '95)*, Stockholm, Sweden (pp. 51–66). Norwell, MA: Kluwer.

Bødker, K., Kensing, F., & Simonsen, J. (2004). *Participatory IT design: Designing for business and workplace realities*. Cambridge, MA: MIT Press.

Corneliussen, H. G., & Walker J. (Eds. 2008). *Digital culture, play, and adentity: A world of warcraft reader*. Cambridge, MA: MIT Press.

Ehn, P. (1989). *Work-oriented design of computer artifacts*. Hillsdale, N J: Lawrence Erlbaum.

Ehn, P. (2007). Design av alla? [Design by all?]. In S. Ilstedt Hjelm (Ed.), *Under ytan [Under the surface]* (pp. 76–95). Stockholm: Raster Förlag.

Flores, F.; Graves; M., Hartfield, B., & Winograd, T. (1988). Computer systems and the design of organizational interaction. *Transactions on Office Information Systems*, 6 (1–2), 153–172.

Greenbaum, J., & Kyng, M. (Eds.). (1991). *Design at work: Cooperative design of computer systems*. Hillsdale, NJ: Lawrence Erlbaum.

Hansen, M. B.N. (2006). Embodiment: the machinic and the human. *Theory, Culture & Society*, 23 (2-3), 297–306.

Haraway, D. J. (1997). *Modest_witness@second_millenium. Female man©_meets_ oncomouse™: Feminism and technoscience*. New York and London: Routledge.

Hastrup, K. (2005): *Designforskning: Mellem materialitet og socialitet*. Center for Designforskning, Copenhagen, Art Academy Architectural Highschool, September 2005.

Hayles. C. (1999). *How we became posthuman: Virtual bodies in cybernetics, literature and informatics*. Chicago: University of Chicago Press.

Landow, G. P. (1992). *Hypertext: The convergence of contemporary critical theory and technology*. Baltimore MD: The Johns Hopkins University Press.

Lemke, J. (2002). Travels in hypermodality. *Visual Communication*, 1 (3), 229–325.

Lemke, J. (2005). Place, pace & meaning: Multimedia chronotopes. In S. Norris & R. Jones (Eds.), *Discourse in action: Introducing mediated discourse analysis* (pp. 110–112). Routledge: London.

Liestøl, G. (2003). Gameplay — from synthesis to analysis (and vice versa). Topics of construction and interpretation in digital media. In G. Liestøl, A. Morrison & T. Rasmussen (Eds.), *Digital media revisited. Theoretical and conceptual innovations in digital domains* (pp. 389–413). Cambridge, MA: MIT Press.

Luff, P., & Heath, C. (1998). Mobility in collaboration. In I. Greif (Ed.), *Proceedings of the 1988 ACM conference on computer-supported cooperative work*, Portland, Oregon, USA (pp. 305–331). New York: ACM.

Lundby, K. (Ed., 2008). *Digital storytelling, mediatized stories: Self-representation in New Media*. New York: Peter Lang.

Morrison, A. (2003). From oracy to electracies: Hypernarrative, place and multimodal discourses in learning. In G. Liestøl, A. Morrison & T. Rasmussen (Eds.), *Digital media revisited: Theoretical and conceptual innovation in digital domains* (pp. 115–154). Cambridge, MA: MIT Press

Morrison, A. (2010). Composing multiply: Multimodal mediating artifacts, scopes of articulation and matters of alignment. In A. Morrison (Ed.), *Inside multimodal composition*. Cresskill NJ: Hampton Press.

Morrison, A., Andersson, G., Brečević, R., & Skjulstad, S. (2009). Disquiet in the plasma. *Digital Creativity*, 20 (1–2), 3–20.

Munster, A., & Lovink, G. (2005). Theses on distributed aesthetics. Or, what a network is not. *Fibreculture Journal*, Issue 7. Available on http://journal.fibreculture.org/issue7/issue7_munster_lovink.html

Nygaard, K. (1986). Program Development as a Social Activity. In *Information processing 86: proceedings of the IFIP 10th world computer congress*, Dublin, Ireland (pp. 189-198). Amsterdam: North-Holland.

Nygaard, K. (1996). "Those Were the Days"? Or "Herioc Times Are Here Again"?, IRIS Opening speech 10. August 1996, *Scandinavian Journal of Information Systems*, 8 (2), 91–108.

Pierroux, P. (2008) Extending meaning from museum visits through the use of wikis and mobile blogging. In *Proceedings international perspectives in the learning sciences (ICLS 2008)*, Utrecht, The Netherlands, June 24–28 (9–11.)

Randall, D.W., Harper, R., & Rouncefield, M. (2007). *Fieldwork for design: Theory and practice*. London: Springer.

Schiller, G. (2006). Kinaesthetic traces across material forms: Stretching the screen's stage. In S. Broadhurst & J. Machon (Eds.), *Performance and technology: Practices of verbal embodiment and interactivity* (pp. 100–111). Basingstoke: Palgrave Macmillan.

Schmidt, K., & L. Bannon (1992). Taking CSCW seriously. Supporting articulation work. *Computer Supported Cooperative Work: The Journal of Collaborative Computing*, 1(1), 7–40.

Schön, D (1983). *The reflective practitioner. How professionals think in action*. New York: Basic Books.

Schön, D. (1987). *Educating the reflective practitioner*. San Francisco: Jossey-Bass.

Skjulstad, S. (2007). Communication design and motion graphics on the web. In *Journal of Media Practice*, 8(3), 359–378. doi: 10.1386/jmpr.8.3.359_1

Stuedahl, D. (2009). Digital Cultural Heritage Engagement - A New Research Field for Ethnology. *Ethnologia Scandinavica*. 39, 67–81.

Telier, A. (T. Binder, P. Ehn, G. De Michelis, G. Jacucci, P. Linde, & I. Wagner). (forthcoming). *Design things*. Cambridge, MA: MIT Press.

van der Velden, M., Bratteteig, T., Finken, S., & Mörtberg, C. (2009). Autonomy and automation in an information society for all. In J. Molka-Danielsen (Ed.), *Proceedings of the 32nd information systems research seminar in Scandinavia, IRIS 32, Inclusive Design*, Molde University College, Molde, Norway, August 9–12, 2009. ISBN 978-82-7962-120-1.

Wagner, I., Basile, M., Ehrenstrasser, L. Maquil, V., Terrn, J.-J., & Wagner, M. (2009). Supporting community engagement in the city: urban planning in the MR-tent. In J. M. Carroll (Ed.), *Proceedings of the fourth international conference on communities and technologies (C&T '09)*, University Park, PA, USA (pp. 185–194). New York: ACM.

Weber, R. (2003). The reflexive researcher. Editors comment, *MIS Quarterly*, 27 (4), v–xi.

Winograd, T. (1979). Beyond programming languages. *Communications of the ACM*, 22(7), 391–401.

2

Research Practices in Digital Design

Tone Bratteteig, Ina Wagner, Andrew Morrison,
Dagny Stuedahl, and Christina Mörtberg

In the twenty-first century, we are literally surrounded by digital things and things that turn out to be digital – or have some digital parts or are parts of a larger system in which there are digital elements. We carry around mobile phones and watches; many also have additional music players, PDAs or PCs. We live in houses filled with digital networks and artefacts; we depend on infrastructures that are partly digital and have digital systems attached to them; we use public and private services that are digital, are based on digital infrastructures and have other digital systems attached to them; and we experience embedded, ubiquitous computing as we live in digitally enhanced environments that support our activities with or without our conscious control. The digital layer(s) in the world constitute a real world.

Just as the diversity of digital things is so large, so too is design research varied. It includes a whole range of approaches that require skill and expertise, innovation and critical reflection. Inquiries into the use of digital work tools (Thoresen 1997; Gasser 1986) require different methods than investigating how teenagers shape their identities through text messaging (Ito 2003; Prøitz 2007). Studying the usability of a web site (Nielsen 1999), suggests a different approach than discussing what makes a social software application work successfully (see Chapter 7). Design of accounting systems is very different from designing ubiquitous environments for elderly people for home care. Variety and complexity are one of the main characteristics of digital design practices and their research. Digital design research embraces the diversity of design processes and products by inviting a greater variety of research about the digital. The design research in this book includes studies of design processes and products, people, and things, in which the digital play a crucial role. The analyses come from a broad range of disciplinary and interdisciplinary positions aiming to weave a braid that transcends the individual positions and to help us see the emerging changes.

We start our journey into practices in digital design research by describing our understandings of digital design and how we research these phenomena. Our aim is to communicate how and why a multidisciplinary approach is helpful for understanding and doing digital design. The chapter starts with four different stories from our own research, each of which illustrates aspects that we think

I. Wagner et al. (eds.), *Exploring Digital Design: Multi-Disciplinary Design Practices,*
Computer Supported Cooperative Work, DOI 10.1007/978-1-84996-223-0_2,
© Springer-Verlag London Limited 2010

are particularly salient for digital design research and points to new challenges for design as well as for the research. The section following these stories discusses more theoretically and methodologically digital design and digital design research.

Evolving Practices in Digital Design Research

Digital design is about making of digital artefacts in which the digital is a crucial characteristic. Focusing on the digital does not help us in limiting what things to include here: digital technology ranges from nanotechnology to large satellite infrastructure systems. The digital appears as representations and automata, and as instantaneously and ubiquitously distributed (see Chapter 5). Digital design hence refers to the planning and shaping of such digital representations, computer programs and distributed systems – but also to the shaping of visions about how these properties will be beneficial and important in our lives. Digital design is about the digital, but also about how the digital is embedded in our visions about a better life – as well as in the lived life of users.

The practices in digital design research are evolving as the elements of these practices change. Practices are not only what people do, and which objects are involved; we also need to understand the relations between people and objects in the processes of creating, communicating, knowing, and contextualizing involved in design and design research. In the following, we discuss aspects of design that we see as crucial to understanding digital design research practices: design as a collaborative activity that sometimes involves a large network of actors (client, investor, specialists of all sorts, and more); the multidisciplinarity of design work, which influences the ways designers express, represent, and communicate an evolving design concept; the role of artefacts and materials; the diversity of material practices which shape the design object, their historical-cultural roots and specificity; and the multiplicity of the design object itself, its changing representations in different media, and how it gets translated/transformed in the process of design.

This section presents four cases that tell about four different research practices in which digital design is an important element. They illuminate some of the challenges in digital design research that directly stem from new aspects of digital technologies and how these are translated as well as socially and culturally embedded.

Participatory Design of a Mobile Information Device

Most information systems are designed to be used by many users for different purposes, introducing the risk that those who register information are not the same people who make use of it, resulting in an uneven benefit from using the system and producing poor data quality and frustrated users (Grudin 1988). The story in this section is about a successful multi-user system: an information system that allows patients to report their symptoms on a mobile device when entering the hospital, before consulting a doctor. The *Choice* system was a success, and the hospital wanted to develop a similar system for child patients. Children are, however, different from adults in several ways. For example, small children cannot read and write and do not understand abstract information well. A project was initiated, aimed at designing a '*children's Choice*' system for children with cancer (Ruland et al. 2006, 2007, 2008, Andersen et al. 2005). The project was considered a success, and children in the hospital now use the new system.

The story in this section aims to illustrate some of the challenges and difficulties in the process of designing the '*children's Choice*' system. We focus on some of the issues concerned with designing a multi-user system in which many different interest groups and their relations need to be handled so as to balance the benefits for the various users (see Grudin 1988). We particularly emphasize challenges concerned with the making of a participatory design (PD) process; here even participatory design with children (see Druin 1999a, b; Hutchinson et al. 2003; Iversen and Nielsen 2003; Dindler et al. 2005). The 'children's Choice' system had the additional challenge of having seriously ill children as their future users.

Fig. 2.1 Workshop with children designing the children's Choice (With permission from C. Ruland)

Participatory Design (PD) concerns ways of involving users in the designing of the artefact or system that they will (have to) use (cf. Chapter 1). The users provide knowledge that makes it easier to solve the right problem in the right way. Scandinavian PD acknowledges that users and user groups do not always agree on either problems or solutions, and emphasizes collaboration on developing and negotiating common design visions.

The *children's Choice* system was developed as a PD process, as the adult *Choice* system had been. The project management decided that the demands of the attention and time from the children with cancer could conflict with their illness and decided that children from a nearby school should represent them in the design process. Two groups of six children of 9 and 11 years, respectively, were engaged in the design project. They were picked up after school once a week and brought to the hospital for a 2-hour workshop, before being returned to school.

Each week included a participatory design workshops aimed at creating ideas for the design of the system and its interface. Each workshop had a theme and a goal set by the project leader, and the sequence of themes was designed to refine the design ideas and work out parts of the design visions in more detail. Each workshop included researchers, developers and a group of children. Up to three researchers watched and interacted with the children during the workshop, and each session was videotaped (which meant that there were almost as many adults as children in the workshops!).

In order to get the children to focus on representing very sick children, each workshop started with a scenario about a sick child – sick in a way that was possible for the children to identify with: breaking a leg, having the flu, falling down from a tree. The scenario ended with a task (design a start page, the main way of navigating, the vocabulary, etc.), and the children then went to work in a somewhat school-like way.

The first workshop was more of a warm-up exercise, but then there started a series of workshops focused on designing an information system that the hospitalized girl from the scenario would like to have. After an introductory scenario, the children sat together in groups drawing screen layouts, discussing what they would need to give information about (see Fig. 2.1).

Fig. 2.2 Suggestion for screen sequence using ready-made screen (With permission from C. Ruland)

The next two workshops followed up these design ideas. At this point, several screen layouts and screen elements drawn by a professional designer were brought to the table (Fig. 2.2 right). All the children took advantage of the ready-made figures and included them in their designs, even replacing their own drawings with the ready-made ones (Fig. 2.2).

The ready-made suggestions were based on ideas and navigation metaphors that had been proposed by the children in the second workshop session, such as sailing from problem island to problem island, climbing in a tree where each branch is dedicated to a particular problem, or drawing a cartoon-like body where body parts could be revealed. The groups of children chose different starting points depending on their age (maturity level). The younger ones seemed to pick the figures they liked (e.g., pink and shiny), worrying less about the logic – or so it seemed to the adult observer. The older children were just as concerned about how they would feel – afraid or angry – as they were about symptoms like a hurting stomach. One of the girls knew a person with cancer, and her story and evaluations both contributed greatly to the design and added a sense of realism to the discussions, which was not present in the other groups.

Table 2.1 Suggestions for concepts for describing symptoms: adult categories and children's descriptions of symptoms fitting to those categories

Physical problem	Cry a lot (own suggestion)	Tired	Sleep during the day
	Bleed nose-blood		Easily tired
	Broken leg		Don't manage anything
	Wounds on the skin		Cannot read
Head pain	Head ache	Emotions	Afraid
	Dizzy		Nightmares
Vomiting	Pain in the belly		Embarrassed
	Vomit		Angry
	Nausea		Miss family and friends
	Phlegm in my mouth		Feel sorry
	Things smell bad/ unpleasant		Cry a lot
	Nose feels tight		Irritated
	Cough	Medication problems	Can't take my medicine
	Warm or sweat		Don't want to play with others
Mouth problems	Dry in the mouth		Shivering hands
	Pain in the mouth		Difficult to walk
	Don't manage to eat	Medication problems	Can't take my medicine
			Disgusting to take medicine

The fourth workshop did not add much to the designs, so the fifth workshop therefore moved on to conceptual design. The children were asked to help test and group translations of medical terms into terms that children would use to talk about their symptoms.

A list of terms had been suggested by the hospital researchers and written on post-it notes before the session. The discussion took place in front of a big sheet of paper on the wall. The categorization of the symptoms surprised the adult researchers by the fact that the children mixed physical and emotional symptoms and did not make any distinction between the degrees of seriousness of the symptoms (Table 2.1) This categorization became an interesting occasion for discussing the children's experiences of being ill; between the children, as well as between the children and the researchers. It gave insight into a different logic concerned with the close relations between physical and emotional pain, and with a different way of sorting body parts and their symptoms.

The last workshop aimed at trying out a tablet computer prototype. The prototype was developed by Master students from the University of Oslo (Moe 2006; Sending 2006). The basic metaphor was a cage where the dinosaur Dino could get help from Dr. Spino (Fig. 2.3 right).

The prototype was not fully developed, but at least one path into the cage was ready to test. The children tested the prototypes in a hospital bed (Fig. 2.3, left and middle). The nurse researcher played a small scenario to help the child in the bed to play the role of a sick child and thus get a feeling for how the prototype would feel in a realistic setting.

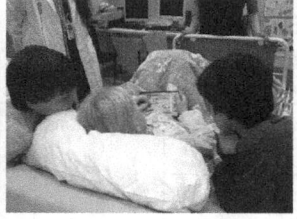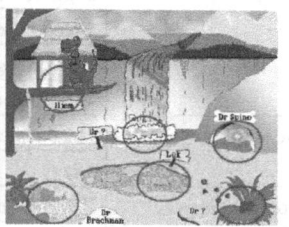

Fig. 2.3 Testing the Dr. Spino prototype from a hospital bed (With permission from C. Ruland)

The children found the prototype interesting, but, having tried it in a bed, they decided that it seemed more like a toy than a system you would use to report serious problems. They also tried the *Choice* system (for adult patients), and concluded that they liked that one better, even if it was more difficult to understand.

Lying in bed and having a scenario played out by the bedside added seriousness to the children's discussions, which had not been there before, but for the input of the girl whose friend has cancer. The children felt that the user interaction should fit the situation, and that a game-like interface did not feel right in a hospital setting. However, from the position of a bed, they commented on features like weight and shape of the terminal that would be relevant in a real use situation.

The *'children's Choice'* system was further developed by hospital developers and tested on a group of employees' children, and on children with cancer (Moe 2006; Sending 2006). The system was finished and introduced as the *Sisom* system: 'si som' in Norwegian translates to 'tell as is' (Fig. 2.4). The system is now used in the hospital (Ruland 2008).

Fig. 2.4 The *Sisom* system: examples of pages (Images from www.rikshospitalet.no. With permission from C. Ruland)

The *Sisom* project illustrates several challenges to PD. Although the project explored a new area for a new type of technology – a mobile patient information system – the *Sisom* system needed to function as a work tool for the doctors and nurses. This double goal made it more difficult for the children as a weaker group to get their opinions heard in the design discussions. The question about which interests get to dominate the overall design is particularly tricky when several different interest group have to use the same system (Bjerknes and Bratteteig 1995). In the *Sisom* project the most important interest groups were children, nurses and medical doctors but doctors and children were represented through others. The tight structure of the *Sisom* project workshops contributed to giving the children a limited role in the design: the workshops acted as inspirational sources for the designers rather than as discussions opening up for very different design ideas. The children's ideas were fitted into a logic based in the profession of the information receivers. The children's choices were limited with respect to both the overall solution and the details of it – and even the setting of the problem to be solved. The doctors' and nurses' needs for information defined the scope of the project and therefore limited the possibilities for maintaining an openness in the design that enabled the (sick) children to discuss how they could communicate with doctors and nurses – or even others – by means of ICTs.

The *Sisom* project demonstrated that the concepts and logics of different interest groups may be very different: the translations and categorizations of medical health problems using child language and child logic revealed different interpretations of pain and of physical-psychological relations.

The different user groups exercised power with respect to the design process very differently. Children generally have a weak position as an interest group, particularly in a situation where medical doctors and nurses are allies in their interests in designing a good working tool. They also claim – like many other groups, e.g. cancer researchers, parents – to represent the children even better than they can do themselves in the design process. In addition, the healthy children were not really able to represent the sick children. The girl with a friend with cancer was the most empathetic. However, the children represented children very well and the experienced nurses and doctors used their knowledge to develop a 'persona' of a sick child (see Cooper 1999), and also arranged interviews with children who had recovered from cancer to test the system.

The *Sisom* project (like the *Choice* project) chose a mobile terminal as its information device. The mobile terminal seemed to have been chosen as a genre rather than from a wish to utilize the mobility of the device: the *Sisom* system is to be used in the hospital as information registration before seeing the doctor, at a particular place. However, a mobile system is useful not only when the user is mobile but also when the user is more or less immobile and cannot easily move to and from a stationary system. Even though mobile terminals have been around for many years, there are still a number of challenges in their design. Designing information services for mobile terminals must address challenges concerned with mobility: the terminal needs to be effortlessly moved – small, lightweight, powerful – and to be supported by an infrastructure that enables its operation. A mobile service is obviously a part of a larger system, and the system must work in order for it to add value to the service. The mobile terminal is often a personal device; when used in public places the distinction between private and public gets blurred. And the size of the mobile terminal poses severe constraints on the interaction, on input and output: the screen is small, any buttons need to be small – making them larger makes it necessary to introduce structure (hierarchical levels or modes) and hence new challenges for designing the presentation of that structural logic (Gutwin and Fedak 2004; Baudisch 2006; Moggridge 2007).

Participatory design is difficult to do (Bratteteig 2004a; Jansson 2007; Hardenborg 2007). In a hospital context it is easy to recognize that the many different users (workers and clients) have very different interests that may be difficult to balance or negotiate. It is also relatively easy to see how the technical systems are aligned with economics and legislation for the health-care sector, and also allied with medicine and medical professionals. The organization of work in health care is a result of earlier negotiations about distributions of tasks and power. Digital systems and artefacts may challenge this order – which makes digital design a political process – and add to the reasons for choosing PD approaches.

Involving children or other 'weak' groups (like elderly, physically handicapped) poses even more challenges to the participation and the representation of users (Marti 2006; Wu et al. 2004). Information systems that are being used for many purposes, by many different user groups, pose challenges as to who will have their logic represented in the overall design (Bjerknes and Bratteteig 1995; van der Velden et al. 2009). The complexity of the design increases as the system is public and private, a tool and a toy, and even a part of the user's identity. Participatory design with 'difficult' users is particularly challenging: users who cannot make their own voice heard and users who speak for others – or claim to be speaking for others. Mobile terminals challenge information systems development by crossing social arenas (work, leisure, school) and therefore also represent a multitude of systems in one – in which the user may take very different roles (Kanstrup et al. 2008; Lee and Bichard 2008). Participatory design with a distributed community of users (Naghsh et al. 2008) poses further challenges to any ambitions to collaborate about design. Today, digital design is distributed and fragmented – as is participation in design (Bratteteig 2004b).

Designing Digital Environments

While the first example was about designing a game-like mobile application, the second example looks into novel interfaces, highlighting some challenges for interaction design. There is a growing interest in interfaces and interactions that involve all our senses, such as sound and tactile input/output, as well as material representations other than screens, like state-changes in objects similar to colour change in traffic lights. With their notion of 'ambient media', Ishii and Ullmer (1997) pioneered this development, designing for making invisible processes in the virtual world visible in the real world. Visible here means noticeable in an ambient way, through (changes of) light, sound, smell, and movement. Early examples were sound of rain, or water ripples projected onto the ceiling, representing the activity of a distant loved one; or 'active wallpaper' – patterns of illuminated projected patches – as indicators of low or high activity. In parallel, designers engaged in tangible interface designs that enable sound and motion interaction, based on gestural performances or physical objects (Ishii and Ullmer 1997; Ullmer and Ishii 2000; Larssen 2004; Loke et al. 2005). Further examples can be found in wearable computing (Farringdon et al. 1999), body-sensor networking (Yang 2006) and pervasive computing, including tracking of everyday interactions with wireless sensors (Tapia et al. 2004) and with RFID-tagged environments (Philipose et al. 2004). Ishii's weather bottles (Ishii et al. 2001) is a nice example of how the experiments with new technical possibilities for ways of interacting with a digital object can be utilized to address a new user: his mother – combining several different design research practices.

Design researchers as well as design practitioners have taken up the notion of embodied interaction introduced by Dourish (2001). The concept addresses how a situation must be considered as a whole. Meaning is created in the use of shared objects, and social interaction is related to how we engage in spaces and with artefacts. In this interplay the body has a central role; in many ways the body can be seen as the medium for 'having a world'. In this perspective Hornecker (2005) provides a definition of tangible interaction that expands human-computer interaction (HCI):

> Tangible interaction is not restricted to controlling digital data and includes tangible appliances or the remote control of real devices. Because it focuses on designing the interaction

(instead of the interface), resulting systems tend less to imitate interaction with screen-based GUIs (as does placing and moving tokens) and exploit the richness of embodied action [...]. Interaction with 'interactive spaces' by walking on sensorized floors or by simply moving in space further extends our perspective on 'tangible' interaction (Hornecker 2005: 225).

This aspect of embodied interaction is gaining relevance in view of attempts of using tangible computing or mixed reality for art and entertainment (Benford et al. 2006; Hämäläinen et al. 2005), in work and educational settings (Bannon et al. 2005; Ciolfi and Bannon 2005), as well as in urban renewal (Maquil et al. 2007). Multimodal interfaces are designed in fields as varied as dance performance, art installations, urban planning, and 3D worlds. Novel applications embed monitoring in interactive and engaging artefacts designed for recreational, tangible, and affective interaction.

The novel interfaces that emerge in the framework of embodied interaction pose challenges for interaction design, on the conceptual and technical level. Although the term 'interactive' is debated with respect to the role of the computer system as an active partner in the interaction (Jensen 1998), it becomes meaningful if we reserve it for the design of options for human activity when it becomes interwoven with technology. This requires developing sensitivities to issues such as the choice of material, enabling embodied interaction, facilitating collaboration, rich and easily understandable interaction, and so forth. The more so, as means of interaction have been extended from classical devices to gestures, body movements, and physical objects (tokens). Interaction is understood as a process with experienced qualities, embedded in social and cultural contexts. In the foreground is not the interaction itself (its technicality) but how to design the interaction (how to, for example, integrate movement and touch), as well as to design interaction styles (expressivity, diversity) before designing the product itself. The challenges involved in designing interactions include the selection of material, as its emotional significance and symbolism is relevant for how people interact with it; as are the aesthetics and economy of movement (Oritsland and Buur 2000). Interaction design has strong aesthetic and emotional, experience-based aspects: 'A user may choose to work with a product despite it being difficult to use, because it is challenging, seductive, playful, surprising, memorable or rewarding, resulting in enjoyment of the experience' (Djajadiningrat et al. 2000: 132).

Tangible user interfaces are among the novel digital designs attracting the attention of designers and researchers, but very few applications have been designed with a view on real life work situations. Some of the challenges connected to designing tangible user interfaces are highlighted by Maquil et al. (2007, 2008). They describe a tangible user interface – the *ColorTable* – designed to support groups of urban planners and diverse stakeholders in collaboratively envisioning urban change, using a set of mixed-reality technologies. Among the challenges were: how to support users in the collaborative creation of mixed-reality configurations; how to make use of material and spatial properties in designing both, physical interface, as well as multiple and simultaneous interactions; how to handle the complexity of urban projects while keeping interfaces and interactions simple and transparent.

The *ColorTable* is set up in the centre of the mixed reality tent (The MR-Tent) and provides a bird's eye view of the site. It presents a collaborative planning and discussion space – users are motivated to share their ideas and visions by moving coloured tokens of different shapes and colours on the table. The tangible user interface uses computer vision-based tracking from an overhead camera to detect the positions, shapes, colours and sizes of the objects on the table. Users can move and turn existing objects, while an overhead video projection onto the table provides interactive feedback. This table view is composed of several layers, combining real and virtual elements, forming a common interaction space. A physical map representing the urban site is placed on the table to define the scale of the interaction. For the workshop we prepared two maps of different scales that can be exchanged.

The *ColorTable* uses multiple interactive views to convey and encourage the urban design process. Inside the MR Tent, two large screens show perspective views of the urban site. The views are alternatively fed by a live video stream from a remote controlled camera, a panorama image prepared previously, and a direct view seen through a half transparent screen. These vertical screens show perspective views as seen by a pedestrian, while the horizontal surface (table) shows an overhead view inspired by maps. In order to navigate within the panorama, users can change the orientation of the viewpoint with a rotating disk (Fig. 2.5).

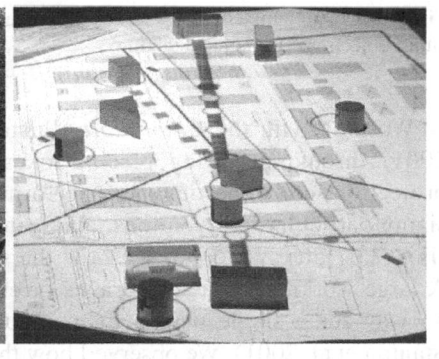

Fig. 2.5 Overview of *ColorTable* application

This is a rather complex set-up that combines different material, virtual and spatial components:

- A round table with physical maps of different scale and a set of tokens, as well as projected traces of participants' interventions (rectangles for objects, moving dots along paths for flows).
- Tokens of different size, shape, material and colour representing different visual and sound content, as well as activities, such as setting paths, defining land use, moving the hearing position, and erasing.
- 'Content cards' with a thumbnail of the visual object, whether it is a 2D or a 3D object, information on associated sound files, and barcode.

- A multi-layered interaction space consisting of a tent mounted on the site of an urban project, round table and two projection screens showing the constructed scene against the backgrounds.

The *ColorTable* went through several cycles of evaluation-feedback-redesign (and is still work-in-progress), which were organized in the form of participatory workshops in the context of real urban planning projects, with architect-planners and other specialists as well as concerned citizens as participants.

Fig. 2.6 Creating mixed reality scenes (here seen in the video-augmented view) through manipulating objects, gesturing, and talking

Working with the *ColorTable* illustrates embodied interaction (cf. Dourish 2001): through gesturing, placing tokens, rotating the table or sketching on the projection screen, participants 'perform' a mixed reality configuration, emphasizing particular interventions, and bringing an expressive element into a scene (Fig. 2.6, left). We could see how the size and shape of the table are relevant. A large working space encourages or even enforces collaboration since there is no way for a single person to manipulate all objects (Patten and Ishii 2000; Stanton et al. 2001). We observed how the round shape of the table, together with the possibility of rotating the viewpoint, was highly conducive to people gathering around and interacting. Also the spatial arrangement of table and the associated workspaces is crucial for collaboration to happen smoothly. In general, all the material and devices needed should be within reach but not in the way.

The size and materiality (haptic quality) of the colour objects clearly influences the way participants interacted with them and how they actively engage in building a scene. As one of the participants in one of the workshops we organized expressed it: 'I have the impression that everyone has their own object placed on the table and everyone identifies himself with his colour and his bench, and I have the impression that all of us negotiate projecting ourselves into the object'.

What we observed is a good example of haptic directness (Fig. 2.7). Haptic directness provides an isomorphism between manipulation and result (Hornecker and Buur 2006): we can watch the effects of our activities while performing

Fig. 2.7 Haptic directness – handling colour tokens

them – it enables simultaneous interaction. The colour objects are easy to understand, invite participation, and are sufficiently neutral so as not to privilege particular perspectives on an urban project. Expert and non-expert users can use them alike. We could also see that the context of urban planning poses specific requirements concerning spatial interaction. Users perform embodied interactions in several dimensions – placing colour objects on the paper map, switching viewpoint and panorama, and at the same time viewing the changes on the projection screen. Mapping these distributed interactions in different scales is a complex task.

Tangible user interfaces as part of new digital designs offer attractive solutions, in particular for collaboratives of users performing tasks or small projects in an expressive way. In her analysis of tangible user interfaces, Hornecker (2005) presents a framework for encouraging collaboration through tangible manipulation, spatial interaction, embodied facilitation, and expressive representation. Hornecker talks of embodied constraints as subtly leading users to collaborate. Our results agree with her experience that 'seemingly trivial design decisions (such as system size, placement and number of tools) had a huge impact on group behaviour, session dynamic and atmosphere' (Hornecker 2004). Moreover, there is a rich repertoire of forms, objects, spatial configurations, and materials to select from in tangible user interface design. These almost limitless possibilities pose conceptual problems, requiring designers to carefully analyse and constrain, so as to make the design harmonize with the ecologies of space, materials, devices, and people and to keep interactions simple and transparent.

In designing for physical interaction, particular attention has to be paid to the fact that the language of form is expanded to three dimensions and to a wider range of physical expressions (movement, gesture). This influences the ways meaning is generated and experienced in the interplay between ideas, physical interactions, and their mixed-reality expressions. Designing for tangible interactions needs to include design experiments as a part of the research.

This example illustrates the need for, and the challenges of, supporting embodied interactions that make use of material objects within physical space. Designing a tangible user interface has the potential for creating a richer interaction experience, incorporating emotional expression in tangible interaction (Ross and Keyson 2007). Larssen et al. (2006) have analysed the *feel dimension* of technology interactions, referring to the work of Merleau-Ponty (1962). They describe tangible interaction 'as a particular kind of dialogue between bodies and things'. Brown and Duguid (1994) have emphasized the role of material features, in their peripheral, evocative, and referential function, as providing border resources for interaction. Jacucci and Wagner (2007) have studied how materiality is part of performative action.

We can also read this example as a story about performing design research while engaging in design. Research was tightly interwoven with design, as observing and analysing users' interactions with the tangible user interface, the mixed-reality scenes they co-constructed and debated, directly fed back into the design process. This exchange between research and design did not only bring novel ideas and pointed to opportunities for design changes; concepts offered by researchers were turned into reflective tools in the hand of designers (Maquil et al. 2008).

Communication Design

Information and Communication Technologies (ICTs) have been widely applied in contexts of technology-enhanced leisure and social interaction, as well as in those centred on learning and work. With respect to digital design practices and related research, however, *communication design* and research into the *design of communication* have received more oblique attention.

As the label communication design suggests, it is communication that is at the core of the practices and study of digitally mediated meaning making. Communication design (Mansell and Silverstone 1996; Frascara 2004; Morrison 2010) acknowledges that what characterizes human communication is its dialogical, situated and dynamic character. This character is realised through the interplay of tools and signs with technical and cultural resources (e.g. Bødker and Andersen 2005; Jenkins 2006). Together these depend on and are constituted by a complex mix of relations (Thackara 2005) between information systems design, media and their joint mediation through our situated actions. This is to reconceptualize some of the earlier relations in 'interaction' design (Poppenpohl 2006). In terms of exploring design research and practices, these relations are ones that are concerned with the socio-cultural, semiotic, aesthetic and participative (see Chapter 3). Communication design is complementary to approaches to interaction design that originate in HCI but that are motivated less by the earlier functionalism of such research and more by user and context rich exploration and development (Ehn and Löwgren 2003; Löwgren and Stolterman 2004; Fallman 2008; Skjulstad 2007a). In communication design, humanistic, social science and informatics, perspectives may be woven together in the design of artefacts and environments for communicative use and engagement. Also central is the acknowledgement that digital technologies are an increasingly crucial part of our daily, mediated communication. Conceptualizing moves between practices of design and analysis involve concepts of metadesign (Giaccardi and Fischer 2008) and of mediated meaning making and the explorative and emergent nature of creativity on digital design (Morrison in press).

Such communication is a dynamic of different modes of expression and articulation that are conducted in a medley of media through our situated practices. The ways digital technologies are taken up in our professional, personal and popular cultural contexts may also help extend repertoires for design. Attention to the interplay of practice and theory in graphic design, for example concerning designers' portfolios on the web (Skjulstad 2007b), is one area that has begun to be developed in digital design. Conceptually, the practices of communication design need to take into account the relationships between human and machinic actors. This extends also to the design of generative elements in digital environments. For example, in art installations and exhibitions of various types, communicative purpose and potential are realized through the design of affordances for enactment and multiple combinations and iterations (e.g. Reas and Fry 2006). Meaning is generated through the emergent and *communicative* interplay between users' and systems' agencies (Ehn 2006; Morrison et al. 2010).

We now turn to two examples of digitally designed artefacts and environments that illustrate these developments relating to Communication design. The first is a collaborative project, *Ballectro*, exploring how digital elements may be a part of a dance performance work and its mediation as research and extension to other related projects. The second example is from a project developing new ways of mediating cultural heritage carried out as participatory process with school children and a museum. Related theoretical and analytical frames are discussed further in Chapter 3 in sections on relations and networks, and on socio-cultural approaches to communication design.

The Digital in Choreography, Performance and Mediation

The 'performative turn' in post-structuralism is perhaps under-articulated in design research. However, it is increasingly present in electronic arts, where design and performance (as professions and disciplines) are themselves being reconfigured *by their being performed*. Mixed reality works, media, digital tools and computational systems may be seen as actors in performative domains (e.g. Sparacino et al. 2000). Mixed reality refers to a flexible, emergent blend of media types and modes of mediation in which movement or oscillation between pixel and place, bit and site are in play. In this context, technology becomes an actor. This is especially so in electronic arts in which the white cube of the gallery and the distanced gaze of the viewer are transformed into spaces and designs for performativity by participants, with design still embedded in aspects of digital works but not necessarily written on their 'outer skins'. There is, then, a move from representation to performance (Sha and Kuzmanovic 2000), and this extends from installation arts to net-art and gaming (Lindley 2005) and onwards, processurally to the role of time in ludic design and enactment (e.g. Lemke 2005).

Developments in electronic arts stress the multi-sitedness of works, lodged between curatorial and artistic practices and viewers' uptake and touch. Viewers engage in the effecting of the performative as processual as much as in attending to the designed result, where results, too, are modified and reshape their perceptions and expectations, often drawing them into meta views of these activities as making, designing and expressing. The viewer as the one who fulfils the artwork may also be extended to a multiplicity of participants, across networks and relations in their unfoldings. A particular challenge here is to locate not only where design takes place but indeed when it occurs, and the status we give it at that time.

A number of terms have been invented to express these new qualities. Manovich (2003), for example, refers to the 'loop' as part of the realization of 'cultural software', pointing at the recombinatorial qualities that digital storage and retrieval enable. Mignonneau and Sommerer (2003) discuss how a digital poetics – Aristotle's fictive construction: that which is fashioned, shaped, and given identity by being given form – is a blend of programming and user's patternings. The terms 'software art' and 'software aesthetics' (Fishwick 2006) have been developed to capture such a jouncing, or movement, between the designed and the emergent and their attendant texturings as a poetics built on uncertainty and the liminal, and not

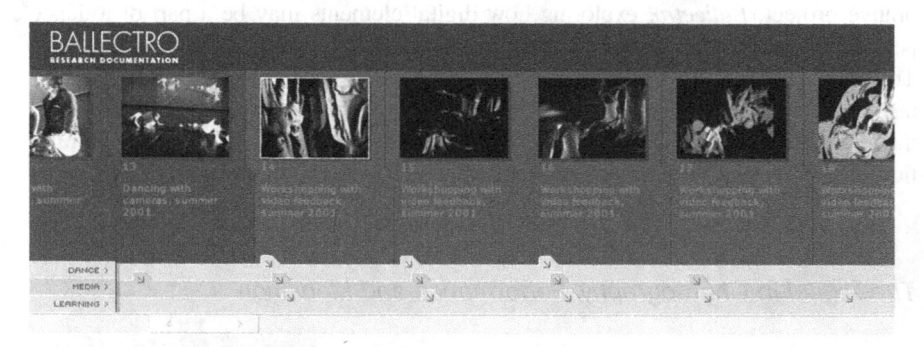

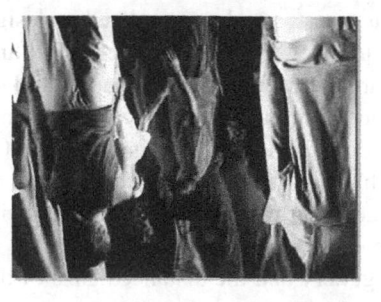

Curiosity improvisation

The set up was not introduced to the students when they arrived to one of the workshop sessions at the stage at the National College of Ballet and Dance. As they passed the camera and discovered their up side down projections, they started to improvise to the media set up. As they all had entered the room, they gathered in front of the camera, figuring out how their movement worked when projected up side down.

Fig. 2.8 Video and text based documentation in the *BallectroWeb*[1]

---

[1] The media track has been selected and a video on media with accompanying text is served. The text has links from this choreography and digital scenography workshop session to a final performance. Available: http://imweb.uio.no/ballectro/

on fixity and immovability (Reiser 2003). The term 'generative art' conceptualizes the very nature of the oscillation between a system with some degree of autonomy and our embodied engagements with it (Galanter 2003). Digital designs are seen as being built of networks of complex meaning making that also depend in part on our prior understandings and ontological interaction (Walker 2003). In electronic arts, we may enter into acts of performance that shift the stage, staging and the role of the performer in varying relations of presence (e.g. Murphie 2003). Increasingly these involve embodied interaction (e.g. Dourish 2003; Larssen et al. 2007) in which mixed reality performative spaces and mediated enactments unfold.

These are some of the challenges that face digital designers and artists in their collaborative explorations. We now address this with reference to a previous project called *Ballectro* (Fig. 2.8). This was a collaborative communication design and performance project that drew together designs for choreography, the shaping of digitally mediated scenography and processes of collaborative learning between higher education dance and media students. Methodologically, *Ballectro* worked towards the exploratory production of a dance performance work through workshopping, improvisation, guided pedagogy in choreography and experimentation with elements of digital scenography. The team included a choreographer-educator, herself a dancer and choreographer, a group of final year degree level choreographers, and three media designer-researchers supported by a small technical team. Attention to media elements as part of the wider performativity of the piece allowed us to see choreography and dance as enacted on an extended 'stage'. The mediated projections were moved by hand to follow the dancers' movements, for example. This focus was taken up in a later project, also with student choreographers and this time with media students, called *Extended*. On the basis of this interplay between dance and digital media, a further installation work *Tapet* (meaning wallpaper in Norwegian) was devised. We have analysed this in terms of multimodality and multi-level activity in the interplay between responsive and generative elements where the performativity of the viewer-participant is central (Morrison et al. 2008).

As part of our design and research inquiry in the domain of Communication Design, we developed an additional element to the *Ballectro* project. In the *BallectroWeb*, we developed a multi-level, multimediational website to convey the variety of activities involved in the process-based project. Here the digital design included video documentation, which we then selected and included as a core feature in the multi-level interface. This interface was designed together with a web designer (a media and informatics student), taking the production and performative component in choreography into the mediation of the project as research. We devised a three-track representation (dance, media, learning) with corresponding broadband video. Internal links in this XML and *Flash* based site also allow users to see jumps between workshops and final performances. We have analysed this site as an example of an experimental digital research rhetoric (Skjulstad and Morrison 2005). In this analysis we developed a set of core concepts for framing 'movement in the interface'. The site has become part of our portfolio of research by design, where practice and analysis are intertwined, constituting material for research conference presentations (e.g. Morrison et al. 2004) that have, themselves, referred to moves from the linguistic and gendered focus on performativity (Butler 1997) to ones of multimodal and multi-activities that involve the digital in design and enactment (Morrison et al. 2010). The focus on kinetic and dynamic aspects of interface and communication design in the *BallectroWeb* has been further investigated in a recent multi-partner project, called *RECORD,* in interface design for dynamic media and social networking. Morrison and Eikenes (2008) have investigated how social semiotics may be drawn upon to devise a set of broad categories for characterizing the relations between moving media and kinetic features of navigation in interfaces; an intersection Eikenes has termed 'navimation'.[2] The longer-term project goal is to connect the performative across the graphic and informational design of kinetic interfaces for laptops and mobile devices to richer inputs from users in building the performative into interaction design: a field that is in need of further humanities research in addition to that from Human Computer Interaction, that often has more functionalist flavour.

Developments and research in electronic art have now built up a considerable body of both theoretical and applied work that applies to digital design in explorations between the technical and the expressive. This body of work offers digital design research additional substance with which to further build transdisciplinary knowledge in which designing for participation may now also include *designing for performativity (*Stuedahl 2004) *and performing design* (Skjulstad et al. 2002). This is taken up in Part 2 of the book in a chapter that explores the design of a social network service and the roles of users' performativity in its iterative design (see Chapter 8).

Engaging Digitally with Cultural Heritage

In the domain of digital cultural heritage communication, numerous digital design projects focus on new and engaging ways to communicate, in particular with young people. On-site, in the museum's exhibits, audiovisual and tangible user interfaces are designed to support visitors' interactions with replicas of objects and exhibition spaces. One example is an interactive chair that supports reflection upon art masterpieces by way of audiovisual communication. The chair is shaped like an egg, big enough for young people to crawl into and providing possibilities for listening and reflecting, together with a voice posing questions related to the exhibit (Gottlieb et al. 2004). Other types of reflection are encouraged by interactive desks supporting collaborative activities related to the exhibit themes (Hall and Bannon 2006). Digital traces of museum visits based on RFID-tags are used in science museums for making dynamically-produced reports on individual museum visits, collecting information about objects visited, and communicating them online (Hsi and Fait 2005).

---

[2] For further details on RECORD, please see: http://www.recordproject.org/index.php/about/

The value of mobile context devices for guiding in museums (Abowd et al. 1997) has been challenged by the unintended side effects of their rather demanding interfaces, which in fact promote a rather individual, isolating experience that directs the visitor's attention towards the device rather than to the exhibit (Proctor and Tellis 2003; vom Lehn and Heath 2005; vom Lehn et al. 2005; Angliss 2006a, b). PDA based electronic guidebooks that promote interaction between museum visitors through content and audio sharing (Luyten et al. 2006) have paved the way for more flexible and mobile interactions between visitors that are meant to support collective reflection.

Mobile cooperative and educational games (Laurillau and Paternò 2004) introduce new genres of interaction between museums visitors and the exhibit by engaging them in, for example, trading games (Luyten et al. 2006). Lately, mobile telephones represent a step further in the development of visitors' interactions with museum objects, where the mobile telephone can be understood as an exhibition tool (Kahr-Højland 2006) that can support visitors' constructions of learning trails (Walker 2007). Earlier studies have shown that the success of exploring a museum exhibition using digital media is highly dependent on the familiarity of the users with the media (Falk and Dierking 2008). One argument for focusing on mobile phones for engaging a group of young visitors is that earlier projects have shown that visitors with limited technical knowledge tend to concentrate on the content-focused hand-held devices (Falk and Dierking 2008).

There is a growing understanding of the development of social media as major challenge for museum communication. A new museum identity is established by museums using podcasting, weblogging (Russo and Watkins 2006), tagging (Chan 2007; Trant 2006), bookmarking, image sharing, RSS syndication and other web 2.0 resources. The use of these media paves the way for new relations between museums and society, as well as for the positioning of museums in relation to the development of popular culture. Opening up for new ways for public participation in museums presents considerable design challenges in relation to types of engagement, types of referential material and ways to include visitors (Salgado 2008).

Here we describe a design-based research project for digital cultural heritage communication related to the reconstruction of a Viking boat. A design experiment was set up inside a museum that had no technical infrastructure and digital content. A solution to the lack of technology was to set up a mobile media centre at a gallery level that did not interfere with the museum exhibition, but still had a spatial relation to the exhibition. The infrastructure for digital communication by mobile telephone and a museum-visit wiki made on-site support for the teenagers' museum visit possible. The design also enabled us to observe how digital communication of a historical reconstruction project of a Viking boat could happen in a museum setting.

The installation was set up to study digital cultural heritage communication with the target group of young people, 10–15 years of age, that has limited knowledge about Viking boats, but has some knowledge about Viking times from history education at school. A major design ambition was to build a relationship with young visitors by way of the media they use in their everyday life, such as mobile phones and social online media. The mobile phone represents personal media that are deeply involved in identity construction and the social life of young people (Prøitz 2007). Norwegian teenagers are quick adopters of new technologies, and the diffusion of mobile phones among this target group is rather high. These studies show that young people are competent users of mobile phones; however, the knowledge differs with age. We arranged a design experiment with a school class of 13 year olds, and learnt that the majority of the class was familiar with technologies for uploading files by way of proximity-based technologies such as Bluetooth. A later design experiment taught us that 10 year olds share knowledge about the use of cameras and sound services on mobile phones, but that they understand less about the relations to other media in space.

The design was based on the idea that using the mobile phone for taking pictures and answering a set of questions during the exhibition visit would be motivating. The phone would be a tool for interaction with the information offered in the exhibit. Also, its character of being personal as well as a social media makes the mobile phone an important tool for engaging young people in the exhibition.

Two design concepts in support of the explorations and interpretative work of young exhibition visitors was implemented: using mobile phones for (a) collecting information (see also Walker 2007) and for (b) exploring the artefact's history. Collecting has been conceptualized as an activity that museum visitors perform collaboratively or individually. In the design, this was realized by introducing the youths to alternative narratives about the Viking ships, asking them to find traces of these in the museum exhibition. The young people used their own mobile phones or they used the phones of the project. All mobile phones had integrated camera and video recording features. The task was to document alternative arguments in the museums exhibit, and to publish these on a visitor wiki in the mobile media centre (Fig. 2.9).

Fig. 2.9 Using mobile phones for collecting and sharing cultural heritage interpretations

The media centre is built with an ICEbox (a mobile device for broadband service using the NTM cellular system). This helped solve the problem of lack of Internet connection in the museum. The youths had to upload their video recordings and pictures by way of Bluetooth features, and comment on these on the wiki-page made for their group. The multiple narratives of the visitors were, in this way, given a voice (Fig. 2.10).

Fig. 2.10 Sharing and collaborating at the temporal media centre

One key observation was that taking pictures and videos can be part of the meaning making activities visitors engage in. By taking pictures and video sequences with their mobile phones, and writing text pieces on the wiki, the interpretative work became more media rich and more active during the museum visit.

The experiment illustrates that the engagement of the visitors in creating their own narratives is encouraged by the possibilities of interaction with museum objects in the museum space. Also, the narratives about alternative content offer an opportunity for interaction. The digital design of the exhibition is performative in that the exhibition space is planned in relation to its visitors' meaning making, drawing on a network between architecture, artefacts, texts, visual material, visitors, curators, researchers and designers. Visitor meaning making can only be enhanced by personal media if they enable visitors to personally customize their visits in ways that build on and make use of their prior experiences, connect to their social group and support their motivations for visiting, and their interests before, during and after the experience

The cultural heritage and the mediated performance examples given above illustrate how the possibilities for interactivity created by digital designs challenge earlier humanist theoretical foundations and open up for new ways of conceptualizing and understanding human communication and cultural processes (e.g. Bolter 2003). They also exemplify a 'constructive approach' from a humanist perspective: they are oriented toward making and experimenting with the digital elements of communication – challenging traditional humanist research values and practices, but also drawing them into processes of digital designing.

The Practices of Digital Design Research

The diversity of digital design research projects has prepared the ground for reflections on design practice and the practices of digital design research. Researchers perform ethnographic studies of design, studying the practices as they unfold, or are initiating and/or participating in design while studying it. In the first case, designers and researchers are different people, and very often researchers observe design practitioners engaged in a result-driven project for a client. In the second case, researchers participate in carrying out design and reflect upon their own practice. In this case, the design practice is also a research practice, constituting a different frame for the design process: less emphasis on producing a design within sometimes narrow budgetary and time constraints and more emphasis on experimenting with innovative materials, forms, and methods where failure is also a (research) result. Some design practitioners deeply engage in experimentations but do so with the aim of producing an innovative design result for a client, while researchers may sometimes go on experimenting, losing the grasp on their aim to create a novel, exciting solution. Design experiments within research projects are therefore different from design experiments in result-driven design projects – but still may provide insights into design. Both types of research are important sources for knowledge about design practice. Studying design practitioners at work helps us understand the everyday skilful activities that go into design work. Doing design experiments focuses on uncertainties, and questions these work practices in specific ways. In the last two cases design is a method for research driven by theoretical positions, what some call design-based research.

In the following, we discuss aspects of design that we see as crucial to understanding the practice: design as a collaborative activity that sometimes involves a large network of actors (client, investor, specialists of all sorts, and more); the multidisciplinarity of design work, which influences the ways designers express, represent, and communicate an evolving design concept; the role of artefacts and materials; the diversity of material practices which shape the design object, their historical-cultural roots and specificity; and the multiplicity of the design object itself, its changing representations in different media, and how it gets translated/ transformed in the process of design.

Design Practice as an Object of Research

At the centre of design is the making of things that will enter into somebody's practices – design is itself a contextual and situated activity. We see design as a situated doing and undergoing, experiencing and expressing of people as they engage in practical action, often together with others. We look at design work as open-ended, exploratory, complex, continuously produced, and intensely collaborative and interactive. Design practice is the activities that designers engage in when doing design.

The design process is a difficult object of research. It does not have a clear starting or ending point (Krystad 1997; Bratteteig 2004a), although we may study design between the formal start and end. Design ideas, inspirational materials, professional and social connections are constantly being attended to, also before any contract has been signed or kick-off meeting has been held. The end of a design process may be when the design description (specification) is handed over to someone implementing the design (Bødker et al. 2004), when the design object becomes a 'thing', or we may include use, maintenance and redesign until the life cycle of the artefact ends (Bjerknes et al. 1991; Bratteteig 2004a). Much of the design process happens in people's heads or in conversations, maybe leaving only inscrutable scribbles on white boards and napkins (Newman 1998; Henderson 1999).

There is a long history in design research of investigating design practice as a basis for understanding design. Most influential has been the work of Schön (1983, 1987), who studied design practices across a range of design disciplines (architecture, engineering etc.) and discussed design as a reflective process, illustrating how design practice differs from the formal models of design popular at that time. He maintains that design is a process of 'naming and framing' the problem, and that the problem setting is as important to design as problem solving. Bucciarelli (1994) carried out detailed ethnographic studies of engineering projects and describes through a series of stories from design work how engineers work with different 'object world' materials and representations. Lawson (1997, 2007) studied architects' thinking and Cross (Cross 1984, 1994, 2007; Cross et al. 1996) investigated product design and use of design methods a basis for discussing 'designerly ways of knowing'.

Studying designers at work has been an important part of information systems (IS) and PD research from their beginnings. Mathiassen (1981) applied Schön's concept of reflective practice for building a theory of information systems design (cf. Andersen et al. 1990). Stolterman (1991) developed a model of design in information systems development based on an empirical study of design work. One of his key observations refers to how systems designers developed 'an operative image' – a vision – very early in the design process. He argues that the 'sketching' activities leading up to the 'specification' should be seen as parallel activities at different levels of abstraction (or concretization, see Mörtberg 2001; Bratteteig 2004a). Winograd (1996) includes stories by software designers and design researchers about (their) design practices and argues for 'bringing design to software'. He looks at design as a conscious, human-oriented, materially-focused, creative, communicative social and political process. The political is put forward in PD, where the focus is to design better tools for users and their work practices by widening the number of people who participate in making design ideas and design evaluations (see Nygaard and Bergo 1975; Bjerknes and Bratteteig 1988b, 1995; Ehn 1989; Greenbaum and Kyng 1991; Bratteteig and Stolterman 1997).

Within CSCW there have been very detailed studies of design work. Among the 'classical' studies are the ethnographies of software developers at work by Button and Sharrock (1994). Grinter (1996, 1997, 1998, 2003) has studied software development teams in a variety of settings. She has, for example, looked into the adoption of a configuration management tool by software developers, into how developers engage in recomposition so that the organization can assemble software systems from parts, or how system architects garner support and commitment from distant departments, always with a focus on the collaborative aspects of design work. Potts and Catledge (1996) describe a detailed field study of a large industrial software project where they observed the development team's conceptual design activities for 3 months, with follow-up observations and discussions. They emphasize the organization of the project, and how patterns of collaboration affected the team's convergence on a common vision. Some research projects offer detailed accounts of parts of the design process, like Bowers and Pycock (1994) who document some of the details in the design of a computer interface, analysing dialogues between a programmer and a user about how to get the details right. Tellioglu and Wagner (2001) discuss the notions of place and boundaries to identify sources of heterogeneity, and to understand how these are oriented to within the practicalities of design work. Mörtberg (1997) analyses the gendered work practices and discusses the negotiations between professional and gendered practices that take place in design work. Robertson (1997) studied design teams working over a distance, analysing how their embodied work knowledges made sense over distance. These analyses of digital design practice deeply challenge notions of design as embedded in formal 'scientific' methods and models of digital design, like those presented in software engineering (see Bratteteig 2008).

The emergence of new digital artefacts, such as 'social software', poses additional challenges to digital design research. These digital artefacts leave more space for users to (continue to) design social environments for communication with other people. The design of the digital artefact enables communication – if the functions and meanings are communicated so that it is clear how the artefact can be enrolled into a practice (Bratteteig 2002), which thereby changes its meaning and function. The roles of designers and users become blurred and encourage a discussion about when design stops and use begins (cf. e.g. Brand 1995). Attention to the 'performative' focuses on the negotiations between actors, and invites us to study purpose, intentions and strategies – those that are visible and articulated, as well as those that are invisible and silent (Star and Strauss 1999; Berg et al. 2005; Stuedahl 2004; Mörtberg and Stuedahl 2005). The narratives created may be displaced by other versions and accounts, and multiple performances may draw together alliances between participants and technologies. Design by users after design contributes to changes in the designer-user relations and roles challenging established work organizations and knowledges. However, producing 'content' in a digital system often does not require skills or knowledges in digital design – and does not necessarily make the user into a designer. Furthermore, design after design most often happens within already designed limits – whether or not the user is aware of them. Designing for 'design after design' aims to lower those limits.

Collaboration in Design

'Design is both individual and social, and involves people with different skills and knowledges … in what can be seen as multidisciplinary, cooperative, constructive negotiation.' (Bratteteig 2004a: 127). Chapter 1 gives a brief overview of the broad range of (inter)disciplinary sources we draw on in this book (Fig. 1.2), and Chapter 3 goes into some of these in more detail: CSCW, socio-technical and socio-cultural approaches pointing to humanistic research, and feminist critical technoscience. Typical of design work are the different types of collaboration it involves – collaboration within the design team and with external specialists, collaboration with users and/or clients. Schmidt and Wagner (2004) describe the work of designers as a 'mixture of concurrent, sequential, and reciprocal action' (p. 350), partly co-located and partly spatially distributed, and communicative. Collaboration, coordination and organization of work form an important part of design and design knowledge in systems design (Andersen et al. 1990).

Practices of collaborating and sharing, if with words or through artefacts, if face-to-face or mediated by technology, vary enormously, depending on the stakeholders involved, on their having a history of collaborating with each other, the constraints a project has to face, and so forth. Design as practised by design practitioners is very often a task given by a client, who to a varying degree specifies the task beforehand – limiting the problem space and/or the resources (people, time, materials, see Andersen et al. 1990; Borum and Enderud 1981; Bjerknes et al. 1991). The client may already have defined a problem to be solved, which may make it very difficult to suggest alternative problem definitions (which is what the first PD projects were all about; see Nygaard 1996).

Large design projects need to engage a variety of external actors. They have to enlist many professional competencies, ranging from basic architecture and infra-structures to interface design. An architectural project typically includes technical consultants for construction, electricity and heating to specialists for façade construction and materials. Mobilizing their support and integrating their perspectives requires careful preparation and ongoing communication. When it comes to digital design small projects may also have to integrate multiple perspectives and skills. Wagner et al. (2002) describe how, in designing the 3D visual archive of 'Wunderkammer', designers combined an architectural approach with the language of film, comics, painting, and stage design and explored the suitability of these visual languages for a digital medium. In multimedia production, strategic partnerships and networking activities are very important – cooperation with specialists in, for example, video processing, journalism, film making, graphic design, comics, and music; contracting out, for instance maintenance or programming activities; mergers, joint ventures, strategic partnerships; cooperation on the Internet by means of newsgroups, mailing lists or free groupware.

In addition to including different competencies, large software design projects may spread out globally, implying a variety of relations between people and teams in the larger project. Outsourcing – the distribution of work tasks – requires unambiguous written communication, which turns out to be near to impossible (Sahay et al. 2003; Imsland et al. 2003). A study of an internationally-distributed software team demonstrated that many of the collaboration difficulties and conflicts between distributed team members had their origin in language problems (Beyene et al. 2009) and cultural differences (Hinds and McGrath 2006; Hinds and Bailey 2003).

Nardi and Whittaker (2002), in studying cross-organizational collaborations in multimedia production, such as between a designer team and consultants, vendors, etc., have introduced the notion of intensional networks, arguing that 'collective subjects are increasingly put together through the assemblage of people found through personal networks rather than being constituted as teams created through organizational planning and structuring' (p. 205). Designer teams need the skill to build, maintain, and extend such networks of people that have the shared experience of joint work and knowledge about each other's work skills, styles of communicating, etc.

Many researchers have adopted the notion of community of practice (Lave and Wenger 1991) to underscore the sometimes long experience of collaboration needed to be able to skilfully perform tasks and produce high quality outcomes. We talk of a community of practice when we observe a shared repertoire of ideas, commitments, and memories, as well as common resources (tools, documents, routines, vocabulary, symbols) that in some way carry the accumulated knowledge of the community. This applies to design teams and can also apply to some forms of user participation in design. Involving users in design ranges from inviting them to evaluate design suggestions (e.g. Nielsen 1994), to participate in designing the user interface (Bowers and Pycock 1994), or even to participate as co-designers, having a voice in setting the design problem as well as developing a solution (Bjerknes and Bratteteig 1987; Kyng 1991). In the last case, the users become members of the community of practice that constitutes the design team – opening up for additional possibilities for design by including a different set of experiences and competencies from which to build design ideas. To have the design team base their design on a broader range of perspectives ('placements' cf. Buchanan 1995) requires a process of mutual learning and the building of trust and respect for all competencies involved – including both design and use contexts (Bjerknes and Bratteteig 1988a; Bratteteig 1997, 2004a).

Diversity of Artefacts and Material Practices

Given the intense collaborative character of design work, we can say that at its heart, therefore, is the need to share materials and to mobilize support. Designers' artefacts have a crucial role in this process. They are created and used for expressing, developing, detailing, communicating, and presenting an evolving design concept. Designers work with materials, translating and transforming them until they converge to a 'thing' (De Michelis 2009). The explorations of the materials that are part of design often have their origin in a larger context, even if they may be carried out in a lab – outside of that context. However, they cannot be fully understood unless brought back to that same context for use in a practice.

An important characteristic of design work is that it is open-ended. With Lave we consider designers' situated doing and knowing as 'inventive' in the sense of that they are 'open-ended processes of improvisation with the social, material, and experiential resources at hand' (Lave 1993: 13). The need to maintain openness in a design project has implications for how designers collaborate. Openness means that decisions about possible design trajectories should not be made too quickly, and requires that the different actors present their work in a form that is open to the possibility of change. Here, designers' artefacts play a large role.

Many studies point to the richness and diversity of design representations and working materials, which include plans, sketches, physical models, samples, flow diagrams, story boards, probes and prototypes, game boards and props, as well as the full range of 'normal' documents; and the diversity of the activities that consti-tute them, which range from the aesthetic, creative and imaginative, to the technical and scientific. Designers' sketches or (3D) visualizations are often conceptual and metaphorical; they are open to extensions, modifications, and novel interpretations, inviting others into a dialogue (Henderson 1995; Bjerknes and Bratteteig 1988b). A design representation may be created primarily for expressing qualities of space, interaction, light, atmosphere, and materials; providing a vision rather than a detailed specification. For this, designers may mobilize a diversity of resources – artwork, concepts and metaphors from other fields (e.g. from biology, mathematics, drama), analogies, video clips, project examples, samples of materials, and technologies. Designers of physical things collect materials that they display, constituting an inspirational design space while maintaining an account of the design team's history

In a study of engineering work, Henderson looked at the role of visualizations as 'network-organising-devices', acting as 'individual and interactive thinking tools, organisers of interdisciplinary communication, either being discussed and worked on cooperatively, or being handed off, enlisting additional work and knowl-edge' (Henderson 1995). Schmidt and Wagner (2004) make a distinction between artefacts that are primarily designed to help manage the complexity of coordinating and integrating cooperative activities (coordinative artefacts) and representational artefacts that make the 'not-yet-existing and in-the-process-of-becoming field of work immediately visible, at-hand, tangible' (p. 363). The role of designers' visu-alizations in the absence of the object of communication has been observed by others (cf. Newman 1998). Henderson (1995) uses the notion of 'conscription devices', which she borrows from Latour (1986), who pointed to the advantage of visual and graphical material in its ability to create 'persuasion' and to invite others into a dialogue. The design of the 3D visual archive 'Wunderkammer' illustrates the diversity of artefacts: sketches, visual examples, and the prototypes themselves, and their crucial role in creating a persuasive way of including different specialists (architect, graphic designer, 3D designer, and computer graphics specialist), into the process of design. Wagner and Lainer (2003) argued:

> The user interface of a prototype is an image, which is open to interpretations and discover-ies. It is resonant with multiple voices, inviting participants to activate their imagination. It is incomplete and preliminary, yet very concrete. It is concrete in the sense of being visible and tangible, offering users as well as designers the possibility of manipulating, exploring, and evaluating what has been achieved. It clearly is something preliminary and unfinished – a *placeholder* of something to be – and as such gives space to ideas of what to change, how to develop further, including alternative or novel ideas, of how to approach the design (Wagner and Lainer 2003: 18).

Observing designers at work, we can see how having the diversity of design repre-sentations available, reading and re-reading them from different points of view, eventually going back to a moment when a particular issue emerged, is crucial to design. Much of individual and cooperative design work is done through creating assemblies of materials for representing and envisioning a problem, task or solution. These assemblies represent design representations 'in context'; one of their central features is their narrativity. Assembling and reading materials such as sketches, drawings, samples of materials, diagrams, storyboards, and so forth, is a fundamentally collaborative process, which helps the designer team to:

> Create a common understanding of a design idea or task; Talk about a design in a rich, metaphorical way, supported by images to be pointed at and referred to; Imagine qualities of space and appearance, which could not easily be communicated in words; Act as reminders of design principles, approach, method, open questions, etc.; Preserve the memory of a design solution and the arguing behind it (Wagner 2000: 387).

The work of detailing a design solution is often referred to as sketching (Henderson 1999; Cross 1995; Arnheim 1995; Buxton 2006) but design practices show that many other different ways of concretizing design ideas are used.

Linde (2007) describes design work 'as an act of metamorphing, to create the metamorphoses of the objects of design and to reflect on the effects of the changes is at the core of design work'. Representations are translations of ideas into new forms, with new 'languages'. Translations are always also interpretations, adding and subtracting meaning and emphasizing particular aspects and silencing others (see Mörtberg 2001; Bowker and Star 1999). Digital design researchers have observed that some representational methods and tools impose very limited languages on the translation, thus constraining both, what the problem and the solution can be (Bjerknes and Bratteteig 1988a). In digital design, these translations can involve many types and layers of translation that make use of very different materials that in the end become part of the design result, seen as a whole.

The final representation – the 'thing' to be handed over – is either the finished design or the specification supposed to instruct someone else to build the design and make the vision real. The specification is mainly a communication device that may function well if the designer knows enough about the production and is able to communicate unambiguously to the builder, which is often not the case and the actual builder has to develop his/her own interpretation and solution. Even if the designers take a final decision, the 'thing' is subject to change through the appropriation of the users and integration with culture and everyday life – but within limits set by the designers' decisions.

Closing Comments

In this chapter we have moved from presenting and analysing a set of digital design stories – our own – to more general reflections on digital design, with a focus on designers' material practices and on the artefacts they create, share, translate and transform. We have looked at design practice as researchers, from a perspective that is nourished by a diversity of traditions and experiences, to address some of the core questions of this book: what are the ways in which we come to know what we know about design and design practice? What relations are there between making and reflecting? What place does knowledge in, through and about practice have for digital design research?

There is knowledge that lives in the design process and is embedded in designed artefacts. There is knowledge we generate as researchers-observers, and knowledge that stems from also being engaged in making digital designs – which sometimes involves making them happen as an occasion for studying them. Our examples cover this range of design and research practices. The story of the *Sisom* project has been written from the perspective of a PD researcher and practitioner, who critically examines the evolving design, looking into how many of the children's ideas and activities have influenced the design. The focus is on PD practice. The story of the tangible user interface in support of collaborative urban planning is the outcome of a close cooperation between design practitioners and researchers and reflects both perspectives. At the core are ethnographic observations of users working with the tool, with a view onto re-design. The *Ballectro* project is also evidence of a multimodal bridging of design and design research, addressing the issue of how to combine and integrate a live dance performance with its digital representations. The cultural heritage example is the first phase of a project on experience design for young people engaging in conventional, non-digital environments – such as in museums where cultural heritage objects play the main role. The digital design here focuses on supporting experiences of the authentic.

We have identified different practices that are genuine to digital design: participation with users in the design, cross-disciplinary cooperations, such as analysis of use and re-design, engaging users to experiment with and explore digital designs, translations between media and modalities, and so forth. We have analysed different design representations and their role in design and use situations.

In the second part of this chapter, we expressed these observations on a more conceptual level, exposing a multi-disciplinary analysis that has proven useful for thinking and doing digital design. The first section discussed the work practices of digital design with the aim of pointing to different bodies of research that analyse these practices in different ways. The second section addressed the collaborative nature of design practices and the many different types of actors and roles involved in design. They all influence the design process as well as the design result. At last, we covered the materiality of design: the object of work as it develops through cycles of intermediate forms and conceptual translations, finally becoming an artefact that can act as a design result. Design practices are these translations and transformations: to understand design we need to see the skills and knowledges at work. Our research adds more disciplinary and interdisciplinary perspectives, more layers and relations in the practices of digital design, enabling a richer understanding of how they evolve.

References

Abowd, G.D., Atkeson, C.G., Hong, J., Long, S., Kooper, R., & Pinkerton, M. (1997). Cyberguide: a mobile context-aware tour guide. *Wireless Networks*, 3(5), 421–433.

Andersen, N.E., Kensing, F., Lassen, M., Lundin, J., Mathiassen, L., Munk-Madsen, A. et al. (1990). *Professional systems development: Experiences, ideas, and action.* Upper Saddle River: Prentice-Hall.

Andersen, R., Ruland, C. M., Røslien, J., & Slaughter, L. (2005). Clustering techniques for organizing cancer-related concepts into meaningful groups for patients. *Annual Symposium of the American Medical Informatics Association*, October 2005, 882.

Angliss, S. (2006a). Talking sense. *Museum Practice Magazine*, 34, 46–47.

Angliss, S. (2006b). Sound and vision. *Museum Practice Magazine*, 34, 51–52.

Arnheim, R. (1995). Sketching and the psychology of design. In V. Margolin & R. Buchanan (Eds.), *The idea of design: A design issues reader* (pp. 70-74). Cambridge, MA: MIT Press.

Bannon, L., Benford, S., Bowers, J., & Heath, C. (Eds. 2005). Hybrid design creates innovative museum experiences. *Communications of the ACM*, 48(3), 62–65.

Baudisch, P. (2006). Interacting with large displays. *IEEE Computer*, 39(3), 96–97.

Benford, S., Crabtree, A., Reeves, S., Sheridan, J., Dix, A., Flintham, M., et al. (2006). Designing for the opportunities and risks of staging digital experiences in public settings. In R. Grinter, T. Rodden, P. Aoki, E. Cutrell, R. Jeffries & G. Olsen (Eds.), *Proceedings of the SIGCHI conference on human factors in computing systems (CHI '06)* (pp. 427–436). New York: ACM.

Berg, E., Mörtberg, C., & Jansson, M. (2005). Emphasizing technology: sociotechnical implications. *Information Technology and People*, 18(4), 343–358.

Beyene, T., Hinds, P. J., & Cramton, C. D. (2009). *Walking through jelly: language proficiency and disrupted meaning making in internationally distributed work*, HBS working papers No. 09-138, Harvard Business School. http://www.hbs.edu/research/pdf/09-138.pdf.

Bjerknes, G., & Bratteteig, T. (1987a). Florence in wonderland. System development with nurses. In G. Bjerknes, P. Ehn & M. Kyng (Eds.), *Computers and democracy. A Scandinavian challenge* (pp. 279–296). Aldershot: Avebury.

Bjerknes, G., & Bratteteig, T. (1988a). The memoirs of two survivors – or evaluation of a computer system for cooperative work. In I. Greif (Ed.), *Proceedings of the 1988 ACM conference on computer-supported cooperative work*, Portland, Oregon, USA (pp. 167–177). New York: ACM.

Bjerknes, G., & Bratteteig, T. (1988b). Computers – utensils or epaulets? The application perspective revisited. *AI & Society*, 2(3), 258–266.

Bjerknes, G., & Bratteteig, T. (1995). User participation and democracy. A discussion of Scandinavian research on system development. *Scandinavian Journal of Information Systems*, 7(1), 73-98.

Bjerknes, G., Bratteteig, T., & Espeseth, T. (1991). Evolution of finished computer systems: the dilemma of enhancement. *Scandinavian Journal of Information Systems*, 3, 25–46.

Bolter, J. (2003), Critical theory and the challenge of new media. In M. Hocks & M. Kendrick (Eds.), *Eloquent images: Word and image in the age of new media* (pp. 19–36). Cambridge, MA: MIT Press.

Borum, F., & Enderud, H. (1981). *Konflikter i organisationer: Belyst ved studier af edb-system-arbejde (Conflicts in organizations: Illuminated through studies of IT systems development, in Danish)*. Copenhagen: Copenhagen Business School.

Bowers, J., & Pycock, J. (1994). Talking through design: requirements and resistance in cooperative prototyping. In B. Adelson, S. Dumais & J. Olson (Eds.), *Proceedings of the SIGCHI conference on human factors in computing systems: Celebrating interdependence*, Boston, Mass, United States (pp. 299–305). New York: ACM.

Bowker, G. C., & Star, S. L. (1999). *Sorting things out: Classification and its consequences.* Cambridge, MA/London/England: MIT Press.

Brand, S. (1995). *How buildings learn: What happens after they're built.* New York: Penguin Books.

Bratteteig, T. (1997). Mutual Learning. Enabling cooperation in systems design. In Braa, K., Monteiro, E. (eds): Proceedings of IRIS'20. (pp. 1-20) Department of Informatics, University of Oslo.

Bratteteig, T. (2002). Bringing gender issues to technology design. In C. Floyd, G. Kelkar, S. Klein-Franke, C. Kramarae & C. Limpangog (Eds.), *Feminist challenges in the information age* (pp. 91-105). Germany: Verlag Leske + Budrich.

Bratteteig, T. (2004a). *Making change. Dealing with relations between design and use.* Diss. Oslo: Department of Informatics, University of Oslo.

Bratteteig, T. (2004b). Participatory design in present society. Invited keynote speech, *Participatory Design Conference 2004*, Toronto, July 27–31.

Bratteteig, T. (2008). Design research in informatics: a comment to Iivari. *Scandinavian Journal of Information Systems*, 20 (1), 65–74.

Bratteteig, T., & Stolterman, E. (1997). Design in groups – and all that jazz. In M. Kyng, & L. Mathiassen (Eds.), *Computers and design in context* (pp. 289–316). Cambridge, MA: MIT Press.

Brown, J. S., & Duguid, P. (1994). Borderline issues social and material aspects of design. *Human-Computer Interaction*, 9(1), 3–36.

Bucciarelli, L.L. (1994). *Designing engineers.* Cambridge, MA: MIT Press.

Buchanan, R. (1995). Wicked problems in design thinking. In R. Buchanan & V. Margolin (Eds.), *The idea of design: A design issues reader* (pp. 3–20). Cambridge, MA: MIT Press.

Butler, J. (1997). *Excitable speech: A politics of the performative.* New York: Routledge.

Button, G., & Sharrock, W., (1994). Occasioned practices in the work of software engineers. In M. Jirotka & J. A. Goguen (Eds.), *Requirements engineering: Social and technical issues* (pp. 217–240). San Diego: Academic.

Buxton, B. (2006). *Sketching user experiences: Getting the design right and the right design.* San Francisco: Morgan Kaufmann.

Bødker, K., Kensing, F., & Simonsen, J. (2004). *Participatory IT design. Designing for business and workplace realities.* Cambridge, MA: MIT Press.

Bødker, S., & Andersen, P.-B. (2005). Complex mediation. *Human-Computer Interaction*, 20(4), 353–402.

Chan, S. (2007). Tagging and searching: Serendipity and museum collection databases. In J. Trant & D. Bearman (Eds.), *Proceedings museums and the Web 2007* April 11-14, San Fransisco, California. http://www.archimuse.com/mw2007/papers/chan/chan.html

Ciolfi, L., & Bannon, L. (2005). Space, place and the design of technologically enhanced physical environments. In P. Turner, E. Davenport (Eds.), *Space, spatiality and technology* (pp. 217–232). London: Springer.

Cooper, A. (1999). *The inmates are running the asylum: [Why high-tech products drive us crazy and how to restore the sanity].* Indianapolis, IN: Sams.

Cross, N. (Ed.). (1984). *Developments in design methodology.* Chichester: Wiley.

Cross, N. (1994). *Engineering design methods: Strategies for product design.* Chichester: Wiley.

Cross, N. (1995). Discovering design ability. In R. Buchanan & V. Margolin (Eds.), *Discovering design* (pp. 105–119). Chicago: University of Chicago Press.

Cross, N. (2007). *Designerly ways of knowing.* London: Springer.

Cross, N., Christiaans, H., & Dorst, K. (1996). *Analysing design activity.* Chichester: Wiley.

De Michelis, G. (2009). The phenomenological stance of the designer. In T. Binder, J. Löwgren & L. Malmborg (Eds.), *(Re)Searching the digital bauhaus.* (pp. 145–162). London: Springer.

Dindler, C., Eriksson, E., Iversen, O. S., Ludvigsen, M., & Lykke-Olesen, A. (2005). Mission from mars: a method for exploring user requirements for children in a narrative space. In M. Eisenberg & A. Eisenberg (Eds.), *Proceedings of the 2005 conference on Interaction design and children (IDC '05)*, Boulder, Colorado (pp. 40–47). New York: ACM press.

Djajadiningrat, J. P., Overbeeke, C. J., & Wensveen, S. A. G. (2000). Augmenting fun and beauty: a pamphlet. In W. E. Mackay (Ed.), *Proceedings of DARE 2000 on designing augmented reality environments*, Elsinore, Denmark (pp. 131–134). New York: ACM press.

Dourish, P. (2001). *Where the action is: The foundations of embodied interaction*. Cambridge: MIT Press.

Dourish, P. (2003). Implications for design. In R. Grinter, T. Rodden, P. Aoki, E. Cutrell, R. Jeffries & G. Olsen (Eds.), *Proceedings of the SIGCHI conference on human factors in computing systems (CHI '06)*, Montréal, Québec, Canada (pp. 541–550). New York: ACM.

Druin, A. (Ed.). (1999a). *The design of children's technology*. San Francisco, CA: Morgan Kaufmann.

Druin, A. (1999b). Cooperative inquiry: developing new technologies for children with children. In M.G. Williams & M. W. Alton (Eds.), *Proceedings of the SIGCHI conference on human factors in computing systems: The CHI is the limit (CH'99)*, Pittsburgh, Pennsylvania, United States (pp. 592–599). New York: ACM press.

Ehn, P. (1989). *Work-oriented design of computer artifacts*. Hillsdale, NJ: Lawrence Erlbaum.

Ehn, P. (2006). Participation in interaction design: actors and artefacts in interaction. In S. Bagnara, & G. Crampton Smith (Eds.), *Theories and practice in interaction design* (pp. 137–154). Mahwah: Lawrence Erlbaum.

Ehn, P., & Löwgren, J. (2003). *Searching voices: Towards a canon for interaction design. Studies in arts and communication 01*. Malmö: The School of Arts and Communication.

Falk, J., & Dierking, L. (2008). Learning with digital technologies. In L. Tallon, & K. Walker (Eds.). *Digital technologies and the museum experience: Handheld guides and other media*. Alta Mira Press.

Fallman, D. (2008). The interaction design research triangle of design practice, design studies, and design exploration. *Design Issues, 24*(3), 4–18.

Farringdon, J., Moore, A. J., Tilbury, N., Church, J., & Biemond, P. D. (1999). Wearable sensor badge and sensor jacket for context awareness. In *Proceedings of the 3rd IEEE international symposium on wearable computers (ISWC '99)* (pp. 107). Washington, DC, USA: IEEE Computer Society.

Fishwick, P. (Ed.). (2006). *Aesthetic computing*. Cambridge: MIT Press.

Frascara, J. (2004). *Communication design: Principles, methods and practice*. New York: Allworth Press.

Gasser, L. (1986). The integration of computing and routine work. *ACM Transactions on Office Information, 4*(3), 205–225.

Giaccardi, E., & Fischer, G. (2008). Creativity and evolution: a metadesign perspective. *Digital Creativity, 19*(1), 19–32.

Galanter, P. (2003). What is generative art? Complexity theory as a context for art theory. In *Proceedings of generative Art 2003*. 9-13 December. Milan, Italy.

Gottlieb, H., Insulander, E., & Simonsson, H. (2004). Access in mind: enhancing the relationship to contemporary art. In *Proceedings from digital culture and heritage* (ICHIM'04), Aug. 31–Sept. 02, Berlin. http://www.archimuse.com/publishing/ichim_04.html

Greenbaum, J., & Kyng, M. (Eds.). (1991). *Design at work: Cooperative design of computer systems*. Hillsdale, N J: Lawrence Erlbaum.

Grinter, R.E. (1996). Supporting articulation work using software configuration management systems. *Computer Supported Cooperative Work, 5*(4), 447–465.

Grinter, R. E. (1997). Doing software development: occasions for automation and formalisation. In J. A. Hughes, W. Prinz, T. Rodden & K. Schmidt (Eds.), *Proceedings of the fifth conference on European conference on computer-supported cooperative work (ECSCW'97)* Lancaster, UK (pp. 173–188). Norwell, MA: Kluwer.

Grinter, R. E. (1998). Recomposition: putting it all back together again. In I. Greif (Ed.), *Proceedings of the 1998 ACM conference on computer supported cooperative work (CSCW '98)* Seattle Washington, USA (pp. 393–403). New York: ACM.

Grinter, R. E. (2003). Recomposition: coordinating a web of software dependencies. *Journal of Computer Supported Cooperative Work (CSCW), 12*(3), 297–327.

Grudin, J. (1988). Why CSCW Applications Fail: problems in the design and evaluation of organizational interfaces. In I. Greif (Ed.), *Proceedings of the 1988 ACM conference on computer-*

supported cooperative work (CSCW'88) Portland, Oregon, United States (pp. 85–93). New York: ACM.

Gutwin, C., & Fedak, C. (2004). Interacting with big interfaces on small screens: a comparison of fisheye, zoom, and panning techniques. In *Proceedings of graphics interface*. London, Ontario, Canada (pp. 145–152). Waterloo, Ontario, Canada: Canadian Human-Computer Communications Society, School of Computer Science, University of Waterloo.

Hall, T., & Bannon, L. (2006). Designing ubiquitous computing to enhance children's learning in museums. *Journal of Computer Assisted Learning*, 22 (4), 231–243.

Hardenborg, N. (2007). *Designing work and IT systems: A participatory process that supports usability and sustainability*. Diss. Uppsala: Department of Information Systems, University of Uppsala.

Henderson, K. (1995). The visual culture of engineers. In S. L. Star (Ed.), *The cultures of computing* (pp. 197–218). Oxford: Blackwell.

Henderson, K. (1999). *On line and on paper: Visual representations, visual culture, and computer graphics in design engineering*. Cambridge: MIT Press.

Hinds, P.J., & Bailey, D. E. (2003). Out of sight, out of synch: understanding conflict in distributed teams. *Organization Science*, 14, 615–632.

Hinds, P.J., & McGrath, C. (2006). Structures that work: social structure, work structure and coordination ease in geographically distributed teams. In P. Hinds & D. Martin (Eds.), *Proceedings of the 2006 20th anniversary conference on computer supported cooperative work (CSCW'06)*, Banff, Alberta, Canada (pp. 343–352). New York: ACM press.

Hornecker, E. (2004). *Tangible user interfaces als kooperationsunterstützendes medium*. Diss. Bremen: Staats und Universitätsbibliothek Bremen.

Hornecker, E. (2005). A design theme for tangible interaction: embodied facilitation. In H. Gellersen, K. Schmidt, M. Beaudouin-Lafon & M. Mackay (Eds.), *Proceedings of the ninth conference on European conference on computer supported cooperative work (ECSCW'05)*, Paris, France (pp. 437–446). New York: ACM press.

Hornecker, E., & J. Buur (2006). Getting a grip on tangible interaction: a framework on physical space and social interaction. In R. Grinter, T. Rodden, P. Aoki, E. Cutrell, R. Jeffries & G. Olsen (Eds.), *Proceedings of the SIGCHI conference on human factors in computing systems (CHI '06)* Montréal, Québec, Canada. (pp. 437–446). New York: ACM press.

Hsi, S., & Fait, H. (2005). RFID enhances visitors' museum experience at the exploratorium. [Special issue]*Communications of the ACM*, 48 (9), 60–5.

Hutchinson, H., Mackay, W., Westerlund, B., Benderson, B. B., Druin, A., Plaisant, C., et al. (2003). Technology probes: inspiring design for and with families. In G. Cockton & P. Korhonen (Eds.), *Proceedings of the SIGCHI conference on human factors in computing systems (CHI '03)*, Ft. Lauderdale, Florida, USA (pp. 17–24). New York: ACM press.

Hämäläinen, P., Höysniemi, J., Ilmonen, T., Lindholm, M., & Nykänen, A. (2005). Martial arts in artificial reality. In G. Van der Veer, C. Gale, W. Kellogg & S. Zhai (Eds.), *Proceedings of the SIGCHI conference on human factors in computing systems (CHI '05)* Portland, Oregon (pp. 781–790). New York: ACM press.

Imsland, V., Sahay, S., & Wartiainen, Y. (2003). Key issues in managing a global software outsourcing relationship between a Norwegian and a Russion firm: some practical implications. *Proceedings of IRIS'26* , Haikko, Finland.

Ishii, H., Mazalek, A., & Lee, J. (2001). Bottles as a minimal interfaces to access digital information. In J. Jacko & A Sears (Eds.), *Proceedings of the SIGCHI conference on human factors in computing systems (CHI '01)*, Seattle, Washington (pp. 187–188). New York: ACM Press.

Ishii, H., & Ullmer, B. (1997). Tangible bits: towards seamless interfaces between people, bits and atoms. In S. Pemberton (Ed.), *Proceedings of the SIGCHI conference on human factors in computing systems (CHI '97)*, Georgia, United States (pp. 234–241). New York: ACM press.

Ito, M. (2003). Mobile phones, Japanese youth, and the re-placement of social contact. In R. Harper, L. Palen, A. Taylor (Eds.), *Inside the text: Social perspectives on SMS*. Dordrecht: Springer.

Iversen, O. S., & Nielsen, C. (2003). Using digital cultural probes in design with children. In S. MacFarlane, T. Nicol, J. Read & L. Snape (Eds.), *Proceedings of the 2003 conference on interaction design and children (IDC '03)*, Preston, UK (pp. 154). Ney York: ACM press.

Jacucci, G., & Wagner, I. (2007). Performative roles of materiality for collective creativity. In B. Schneiderman, G. Fischer, E. Giaccardi & M. Eisenberg (Eds.), *Proceedings of the 6th ACM SIGCHI conference on creativity & cognition (C&C '07)*, Washington, DC, USA (pp. 73–82). New York: ACM press.

Jansson, M. (2007). *Participation, knowledges and experiences: Design of IT-systems in e-home health care*. Diss. Luleå: Luleå University of Technology.

Jenkins, H. (2006). *Convergence culture: Where old and new media collide*. New York: New York University Press.

Jensen, J. F. (1998). Interactivity. Tracking a new concept in media and communication studies. *Nordicom Review*, 19(1), 185–204.

Kahr-Højland, A. (2006). Changing paradigms within museum exhibitions: the use of mobile technologies within semi-formal learning settings. In *NODEM 06*. Oslo 7.-9. December 2006. http://www.tii.se/nodem/06/nw_06/papers/papers.htm.

Kanstrup, A.M., Bertelsen, P., Glasemann, M., & Boye, N. (2008). Design for more: an ambient perspective on diabetes. In *Proceedings of participatory design conference 2008* Indiana Bloomington (pp. 118–127). New York: ACM press.

Krystad, S. (1997). *EDB-støtte for designprosessen: Et eksempel fra klesdesign (IT support for the design process: An example from clothing design, in Norwegian)*. Diss. Oslo: Dept. of Information Technology, University of Oslo.

Kyng, M. (1991). Designing for cooperation – cooperating in design. *Communications of the ACM*, 34(12), 64–73.

Larssen, A., Robertson, T., & Edwads, J. (2007). The feel dimension of technology interaction: exploring tangibles through movement and touch. In B. Ullmer & A. Schmidt (Eds.), *Proceedings of the 1st international conference on tangible and embedded interaction (TEI'07)*, Baton Rouge: Louisiana (pp. 271–278). New York: ACM.

Larssen, A. T. (2004). Physical computing – representations of human movements in human-computer interaction. *Computer Human Interaction*, Springer Lecture Notes in Computer Science, Berlin.

Larssen, A.T. Robertson, T., Loke, L., & Edwards, J. (2006). Introduction to the special issue on movement-based interaction. *Personal and Ubiquitous Computing*, 11(8), 607-608.

Latour, B. (1986). Visualization and cognition: Thinking with eyes and hands. *Knowledge and Society: Studies in Sociology of Culture Past and Present*, 6, 1–40.

Laurillau, Y., & Paternò, F. (2004). Supporting museum co-visits using mobile devices. *Lecture Notes in Computer Science*, 3160/2004, 451–455.

Lave, J. (1993). The practice of learning. In S. Chaiklin & J. Lave (Eds.), *Understanding practice, perspectives on activity and context*. (pp. 3–32) New York: Cambridge University Press.

Lave, J., & Wenger, E. (1991). *Situated learning. legitimate peripheral learning*. New Yersey: Cambridge University Press.

Lawson, B. (1997). *How designers think. The design process demystified*. Oxford: Architectural Press.

Lawson, B. (2007). *What designers know*. Amsterdam: Elsevier.

Lee, Y., & Bichard, J-A. (2008). 'Teen-scape': designing participations for the design excluded. In *Proceedings of participatory design conference 2008* Indiana Bloomington (pp. 128–137). New York: ACM press.

Lemke, J. (2005). Place, pace, and meaning: multimedia chronotopes. In S. Norris & R. Jones (Eds.), *Discourse in action: Introducing mediated discourse analysis* (pp. 110–122). London: Routledge.

Linde, P. (2007). *Metamorphing – The transformative power of digital media and tangible interaction*. Diss. Karlskrona: Blekinge Institute of Technology.

Lindley, C. (2005). The semiotics of time structure in ludic space as a foundation for analysis and design. *Game Studies*, 5(1) http://www.gamestudies.org/0501/lindley/

Loke, L., Larssen, A. T., & Robertson, T. (2005). Labanotation for design of movement-based interaction. In Y. Pisan (Ed.), *Proceedings of the second Australian conference on Interactive entertainment* (pp. 113–120). Sydney, Australia: Creativity & Cognition Studios Press.

Luyten, K., Van Loon, H., Gabriels, K., Teunkens, D., Robert, K., Coninx, K., et al (2006). ARCHIE; Designing for interaction – socially-aware museum handheld guides. In *NODEM'06*, http://www.tii.se/nodem/06/nw_06/papers/loon.htm

Löwgren, J., & Stolterman, E. (2004). *Thoughtful interaction design: A design perspective on information technology*. Cambridge, MA: MIT Press.

Manovich, L. (2003). *The language of new media*. Cambridge, MA: MIT Press.

Mansell, R., & Silverstone, R. (1996). *Communication by design: The politics of communication and information technologies*. Oxford: Oxford University Press.

Maquil, V., Psik, T., Wagner, I., & Wagner, M. (2007). Expressive interactions supporting collaboration in urban design. In T. Gross & K. Inkpen (Eds.), *Proceedings of the 2007 international ACM conference on supporting group work (Group 2007)*, Sanibel Island, Forida, USA (pp. 69–78). New York: ACM press.

Maquil, V., Psik, T., & Wagner, I. (2008). The colortable: a design story. In A. Schmidt, H. Gellersen, E. Van den Hoven, A. Mazalek, P. Hollies & N. Villar (Eds.), *Proceedings of the 2nd international conference on tangible and embedded interaction (TEI'08)* Bonn, Germany (pp. 97–104). New York: ACM press.

Marti, P. (2006). The evolution of the concept of participation in design. keynote lecture at *PDC 2006*, August 1-5 2006, Trento, Italy.

Mathiassen, L. (1981). *Systemudvikling og Systemudviklingsmetode*. Diss. Aarhus: Dept. of Datalogy (DAIMI).

Merleau-Ponty, M. (1962). *Phenomenology of perception*. London: Routledge.

Mignonneau, L., & Sommerer, C. (2003). From the poesy of programming to research as an art form. In G. Stocker & S. Schöpf (Eds.), *CODE- The language of our time* (pp. 242–249). Osterfildern-Ruit: Hatje Cantz Verlag.

Moe, E. Y. (2006). *Evaluation of children's usability criteria*. Masters thesis Oslo: Dept. of Informatics, University of Oslo.

Moggridge, B. (2007). *Designing interactions*. Cambridge: MIT Press.

Morrison, A. (Ed.). (2010). *Inside multimodal composition*. Cresskill, NJ: Hampton Press.

Morrison, A., & Eikenes, J.-O. (2008). *The times are a-changing in the interface*. Paper presented at International Conference on Multimodality and Learning: New Perspectives on Knowledge, Representation and Communication, University of London, 19-20 June 2008, London.

Morrison, A., Skjulstad, S., & Smørdal, O. (2004). Choreographing augmented space. In *Proceedings of futureground international conference 2004 Vol 2*. Mebourne: Monash University.

Morrison, A., Sem, I., & Havnør, M. (2010). Behind the wallpaper: Multimodal performativity in mixed reality arts. In A. Morrison (Ed.), *Inside multimodal composition*. Cresskill, NJ: Hampton Press.

Murphie, A. (2003). Negotiating presence: performance and new technologies. In P. Auslander (Ed.), *Performance: Critical concepts in literary and cultural studies Vol 4*. (pp. 351–364). London: Routledge.

Mörtberg, C. (1997). 'Det beror på att man är kvinna ...' Gränsvandrerskor formas och formar informationsteknologi ["It's because one is a woman..." Transgressors are shaped and shape information technology]. Diss. Luleå: Luleå University of Technology.

Mörtberg, C. (2001). Abstracting, quantifying, classifying, simplyfying, standardising, building hierachies: what are the systems designers sorting out? In *Proceedings of the conference information technology, transnational democracy and gender*, Nov. 17, Ronneby, Sweden.

Mörtberg, C., & Stuedahl, D. (2005). Silences and sensibilities: increasing participation in IT design. In O. W. Bertelsen, N. O. Bouvin, P. G. Krogh & M. Kyng (Eds.), *Proceedings of the*

4th decennial conference on critical computing: Between sense and sensibility, Aarhus, Denmark (pp. 141–144). New York: ACM press.

Naghsh, A.M., Bratteteig, T., Danielsson, K., Blomberg, J., Fischer, G., & Nocera, J.A.. (2008). Distributed-PD: challenges and opportunities. In *Proceedings of participatory design conference 2008* Indiana Bloomington (panel) (pp. 290–291). New York, Ny, USA: ACM.

Nardi, B., & Whittaker, S. (2002). NetWORKers and their activity in intensional networks. *Computer Supported Cooperative Work,* 11(1/2), 205–242.

Newman, S. (1998). Here, there, and nowhere at all: distribution, negotiation, and virtuality in postmodern ethnography and engineering. *Knowledge and Society,* 11, 235–267.

Nielsen, J. (1994). *Usability engineering.* Boston: Morgan Kaufmann.

Nielsen, J. (1999). *Designing web usability.* Berkeley: Peachpit Press.

Nygaard, K. (1996). "Those Were the Days"? Or "Heroic Times Are Here Again"? IRIS Opening speech 10. August 1996. *Scandinavian Journal of Information Systems,* 8(2), 91–108.

Nygaard, K., & Bergo, O.T. (1975). *Planlegging, styring og databehandling (Planning, management and computing).* Oslo: Tiden Norsk Forlag & Arbeidernes opplysningsforbund.

Oritsland, T.A., & Buur, J. (2000). An aesthetic sense of direction in interface design. In *Proceedings of the first nordic conference on human-computer interaction,* Stockholm.

Patten, J., Ishii, H. (2000). A Comparison of Spatial Organization Strategies in Graphical and Tangible User Interfaces. In W. E. Mackay (Ed.), *Proceedings of DARE 2000 on designing augmented reality environments (DARE '00),* Elsinore, Denmark (pp. 41–50). New York: ACM press.

Philipose, M., Fishkin, K.P., Perkowitz, M., Patterson, D.J., Fox, D., Kautz, H. & Hahnel, D. (2004). Inferring Activities from Interactions with Objects. In *IEEE Pervasive Computing,* 3 (4), 50–57.

Poppenpohl, S. (2006). Interaction as an ecology. Building a framework. In S. Bagnara & G. Crampton Smith (Eds.), *Theories and practice in interaction design* (pp. 287–299). Mahwah: Lawrence Erlbaum Associates.

Potts, C., & Catledge, L. (1996). Collaborative conceptual design: a large software project case study. *Computer Supported Cooperative Work* (CSCW), 5(4), 415–445.

Proctor, N., & Tellis, C. (2003). The state of the art in museum handhelds in 2003. http://www.archimuse.com/mw2003/papers/proctor/proctor.html

Prøitz, L. (2007). *The mobile phone turn. A study of gender, sexuality and subjectivity in young people's mobile phone practices.* Diss. Oslo: Faculty of Humanities, University of Oslo.

Reas, C., & Fry, B. (2006). On generative systems? In P. Fishwick (Ed.), *Aesthetic computing* (pp. 197–226). Cambridge, Mass.: The MIT Press.

Reiser, M. (2003). The poetics of interactivity: the uncertaintly principle. In M. Reiser, A. Zapp (Eds.), Rieser, Martin & Zapp, Andrea (Eds.), *New screen media: Cinema/art/narrative.* London: British Film Institute.

Robertson, T. (1997). *Designing over distance: A study of cooperative work, embodied cognition and technology to enable remote collaboration.* Diss. Sydney: Dept. of Information Technology.

Ross, P., & Keyson, D.V. (2007). The case of sculpting atmospheres: towards design principles for expressive tangible interaction in control of ambient systems. *Personal and Ubiquitous Computing,* 11(2), 69–79.

Ruland, C. M. (2008). Personal communication.

Ruland, C. M., Slaughter, L., Starren, J., & Vatne, T. M. (2006). Children as design partners in the development of a support system for children with cancer. *Studies in Health technology & Informatics,* 122, 80–5.

Ruland, C. M., Slaughter, L., Starren, J., Vatne, T. M., & Moe, E. Y. (2007). Children's contributions to designing a communication tool for children with cancer. In *Proceedings of international medical information association (IMIA) medinfo congress* (pp. 977–82), August 2007.

Ruland C. M., Starren, J., Vatne, T. (2008). Participatory design with children in the development of a support system for patient-centered care in pediatric oncology. *Journal of Biomedical Informatics,* Aug 41(4), 624–35.

Russo, A., & Watkins, J. (2006). Social media effect (on) museum communication. *NODEM'06*, Oslo University 7.-9. December. http://www.tii.se/nodem/06/nw_06/papers/papers.htm

Sahay, S., Nicholson, B., & Krishna, S. (2003). *Managing global software alliances*. Cambridge: Cambridge University Press.

Salgado, M. (2008). Breaking apart participation in museums. In J. Trant & D. Bearman (Eds.), *Museums and the web 2008, Proceedings*, Toronto: Archives & Museum Informatics. http://www.archimuse.com/mw2008/papers/salgado/salgado.html

Schmidt, K., & Wagner, I. (2004). Ordering systems. Coordinating practices and artefacts in architectural design and planning. *Computer Supported Cooperative Work*, 13(5–6), 349–408.

Schön, D. (1983). *The reflective practitioner. How professionals think in action*. New York: Basic Books.

Schön, D. (1987). *Educating the reflective practitioner*. San Francisco: Jossey-Bass Publishers.

Sending, V. A. C. (2006). *En kvalitativ undersøkelse av elementer som motiverer barn til å bruke et diagnostiseringssystem*, Masters thesis. Oslo: Dept. of Informatics, University of Oslo.

Sha, X. W., Kuzmanovic, M. (2000). From representation to performance: responsive public space. In *Proceedings of shaping the network society (DIAC 2000)*.

Skjulstad, S. (2007a). Clashing constructs in web design. In A. Melberg (Ed.), *Aesthetics at work* (pp. 81–103), Oslo: UniPub.

Skjulstad, S. (2007b). Communication design and motion graphics on the web. *Journal of Media Practice*, 8(3), 359–378.

Skjulstad, S. & Morrison, A. (2005). Movement in the interface. *Computers and Composition*, 22(4), 413–433. Doi:10.1016/j.compcom.2005.08.006

Skjulstad, S., Morrison, A., & Aaberge, A. (2002). Researching performance, performing research: dance, multimedia and learning. In A. Morrison (Ed.), *Researching ICTs in context* (pp. 211-248). Oslo: Intermedia/UniPub.

Sparacino, F., Davenport, G., Pentland, A. (2000). Media in performance: interactive spaces for dance, theater, circus, and museum exhibits. *IBM Systems Journal*, 39(3 & 4), 479–510. Available online http://www.research.ibm.com/journal/sj39-34.html

Stanton, D., Bayon, V., & Neale, H. (2001). Classroom collaboration in the design of tangible interfaces for story telling. In M. (Mantei) Tremaine (Ed.), *Proceedings of conference on human factors in computing systems (CHI '01)*, Seattle, Washington, United States (pp. 482–489),. New York: ACM press.

Star S. L., & Strauss, A. (1999). Layers of silence, arenas of voice: the ecology of visible and invisible work. *Computer Supported Cooperative Work* 8(1-2), 9–30.

Stolterman, E. (1991). *Designarbetets dolda rationalitet – en studie av metodik och praktik inom systemutveckling*, Diss. Umeå: Department of Informatics, University of Umeå.

Stuedahl, D. (2004). *Forhandlinger og overtalelser. Kunnskapsbygging på tvers av kunnskapstradisjoner i brukermedvirkende design av ny IKT (Negotiations and persuations. Knowledge building crossing knowledge traditions in user participation in design of new ICT, in Norwegian)*. Diss. Oslo: InterMedia, Faculty of Education, University of Oslo.

Tapia, E.M.; Intille, S.S., & Larson, K. (2004). Activity recognition in the home setting using simple and ubiquitous sensors. *Proceedings of PERVASIVE 2004*, vol. LNCS 3001 (pp. 158–175). Berlin Heidelberg: Springer-Verlag.

Tellioglu, H., & Wagner, I. (2001). Work practices surrounding PACS. The Politics of space in Hospitals. *Computer Supported Cooperative Work* 10(2), 163–188.

Thackara, J. (2005). *In the bubble: Designing in a complex world*. Cambridge: The MIT Press.

Thoresen, K. (1997). Simple, but cumbersome. In I. McClelland, G. Olson, G. Van der Veer, A. Henderson & S. Coles (Eds.), *Proceedings of the 2nd conference on designing interactive systems: Processes, practices, methods, and techniques (DIS '97)*, Amsterdam, The Netherlands (pp. 385–394). New York: ACM press.

Trant, J. (2006) Exploring the potential for social tagging and folksonomy in art museums: proof of concept. *The New Review of Hypermedia and Multimedia*, 12(1), 83–105.

Ullmer, B., Ishii, H. (2000). Emerging frameworks for tangible user interfaces. *IBM Systems Journal*, 39(3-4), 915–931.

van der Velden, M., Bratteteig, T., Finken, S., & Mörtberg, C. (2009). Autonomy and automation in an information society for all. In J. Molka-Danielsen (Ed.), *Proceedings of the 32nd information systems research seminar in Scandinavia, IRIS 32*, Inclusive Design, Molde University College, Molde, Norway, August 9-12, 2009. ISBN 978-82-7962-120-1.

vom Lehn, D., & Heath, C. (2005). Accounting for new technology in museum exhibitions. *International Journal of Arts Management*, 7(3), 11–21.

vom Lehn, D., Heath, C., & Hindmarsh, J. (2005). Rethinking interactivity: design for participation in museums and galleries. In Ciolfi, L., Cooke, M., Hall, T., Bannon, L.J. and Oliva, S. (Eds.), *Proceedings of the international workshop on rethinking technology in museums*. Limerick: University of Limerick, Ireland 2005.

Wagner, I. (2000). *Persuasive artefacts in architectural design and planning*. Nottingham: CoDesigning.

Wagner, I., & Lainer, R. (2003). Designing a visual 3D interface – a reflection on methods. *ACM Interactions Magazine*, X/6, Nov/Dec 2003, 12–19.

Wagner, I., Kompast, M., & Lainer, R. (2002). Visualization strategies for the design of interactive navigable 3D worlds. *ACM Interactions Magazine*, IX 5, 25–34.

Walker, J. (2003). Fiction and interaction: how clicking on a mouse can make you part of a digital world. Diss. Bergen: University of Bergen.

Walker, K. (2007). Visitor-constructed personalized learning trails. In *Proceedings of museums and the Web 2007, the international conference for culture and heritage online*, 11-14 April 2007, San Francisco, California.

Winograd, T. (Ed.). (1996). *Bringing design to software*. New York: Addison-Wesley.

Wu, M., Richards, B., & Baecker, R. (2004). Participatory design with individuals who have amnesia. In *Proceedings of the eighth conference on Participatory design: Artful integration: interweaving media, materials and practices* Toronto, Ontario, Canada (pp. 214–223). New York, NY, USA: ACM.

Yang, G-Z. (Ed.). (2006). *Body sensor networks*. London: Springer-Verlag.

3

Analytical Perspectives

Andrew Morrison, Dagny Stuedahl, Christina Mörtberg,
Ina Wagner, Gunnar Liestøl, and Tone Bratteteig

As we draw towards the end of the first decade of the twenty-first century, digital design research faces a complex conceptual and analytical landscape. This is one that concerns relations between multiples of tools, technologies and information systems, their social semiotic, multimodal mediations and cultural practices, and their interpretation. Given the scope of interdisciplinary practices and theories that are to be found in much digital design research, researchers in this field are faced with considerable challenges in identifying, selecting and applying analytical frameworks. This is more pronounced when digital design research entails a multitude of practices and knowledges, as demonstrated in Chapter 2.

In this chapter we have selected some of the major frameworks that we include in our own research into digital design. Some of the main thematics that we take up in the sub-sections below that are related to these perspectives on analysing digital design are: collaboration, complexity, relations, translations, transformation, mediation and positionality. The perspectives we present are not all-inclusive. Nor do we claim their sequence suggests an order of superiority. Given that this is a selection of perspectives and domains in which they have tended to be applied, readers may well find scant mention of their own areas of research into digital design, such as the emerging ones of service design or experience design (e.g. Morello 2000; McCarthy and Wright 2004; Norman 2004).

In taking up these views, a number of key issues arise. To what extent are these perspectives and critiques explicitly articulated as part of already existing research into digital design? How do they influence and impact on its construction? In what ways does previous research on design impact on research into the digital? These are approaches we carry into Chapter 4 on research methodologies as well as into part two of the book and its case-like chapters. Addressing these issues is not simply a review of research literatures in different domains, but a take on the frameworks and approaches that have been adopted and circulated.

Much of research into design has its genesis in studies of engineering and industrial design, where a certain degree of positivism prevailed. Yet this was certainly not all that has transpired since the 1960s and 1970s in face of the expansion of design practices and education, as well as in related research with a focus on action (Schön 1983, 1987) and discursive interpretation (e.g. Krippendorff 2006).

I. Wagner et al. (eds.), *Exploring Digital Design: Multi-Disciplinary Design Practices*,
Computer Supported Cooperative Work, DOI 10.1007/978-1-84996-223-0_3,
© Springer-Verlag London Limited 2010

In terms of explorations into digital design, the domain of Communication Design research offers a multidisciplinary approach for inquiry into interactions and relations between systems, tools and digital articulations where the design for communication, whether, for example, narrative or aesthetic, is central (see for example Chapters 7 and 8). Such a focus, alongside those developed by CSCW researchers on practices, as well as attention to the socio-technical developed by feminist analysts, are a counterweight to the approaches in some of the major, and indeed dominant, fields of inquiry into the digital, such as Human Computer Interaction (HCI) or Computer Mediated Communication (CMC). Where we ourselves hold various analytical approaches, we have a shared concern with the design of contexts, uses and experiences for situated and engaged participants.

Multiple analytical perspectives are critical to building understanding of existing and emerging digital design practice, knowledge and critique. These perspectives and approaches are concerned with investigation into collaborative, cultural, semiotic, technical, and communicative contexts in, for, and by design (Frayling 1993). This is to place weight on the cultural resources, and mediated significations in and through designing, in addition to consideration of tools, systems and use, and on relations to them as well. As mentioned in Chapter 2, practice-based research links analytical frameworks with emerging and established practices of designing and researching (e.g. McCullough 1996; Grillner and Ståhl 2003; Rust et al. 2007).

Our views on digital design research are not simply gathered through academic study; they are informed by skills and insights garnered from working with different designers and in engaging in design. They have also been arrived at by way of connecting design and analysis in practice-based inquiry through which, for example, we have experimented with participation, aesthetics, narrative, and rhetoric in the design of digitally mediated communication (e.g. Liestøl 1999; Morrison 2003). Our collective understanding of digital design is also informed by our disciplinary and multidisciplinary training and experience. On the one hand, we have formal established academic disciplines that provide us with robust theoretical approaches from which to investigate, analyse and critique digital design. On the other hand, we have all worked in various disciplines and also between and across them (e.g. Liestøl 2003; Wagner 2004; Jacucci and Wagner 2007). Taken together these perspectives and practices help to critically and analytically engage with emerging technologies, practices and their material, mediated and participant discourses.

Collaboration and Participation in Digital Design Work

Computer Supported Collaborative Work

Most of CSCW research has been focusing on understanding and developing technologies that can support both the immediate interaction in small groups and collaboration in complex, distributed, work settings. Over the years, ethnographic studies of actual cooperative work in domains such as air traffic control, hospitals, manufacturing, aircraft maintenance, software engineering, and so forth, have contributed a range of more or less elaborate and more or less successful frameworks that address specific types or aspects of cooperative work. CSCW researchers are also investigating technologies in the home and have started looking into social computing.

Typical of CSCW research is its focus on work practices, and its strong connection with ethnography has resulted in highly detailed analyses of such practices that cannot be easily found in related research fields, such as, for example, organization theory or social studies of technology. Also work inspired by Actor Network Theory (ANT) hardly reaches the level of detail to be found in ethnographic studies of practice 'in the wild'. CSCW research also reaches beyond CMC (computer-mediated communication), which mostly looks at communication as an activity abstracted from people's actual practice and investigates use of generic applications, such as email, chat, instant messaging, and so forth. Moreover, CMC research may be seen to be reactive, concentrating on evaluating technologies that already have been deployed, whilst CSCW is strongly committed to informing the design of new applications and systems.

The question then is what CSCW research can contribute to understanding and building new digital designs and digital design research? Based on an ethnographic study of location-based games, Crabtree et al. (2005) make an elaborate argument for including 'ludic pursuits' in CSCW research. In this study they show how 'through map reading and orienteering, sweeping the streets, and managing interruptions, runners concert and orchestrate interaction, methodically so, time and time again' (2005, p. 18). They apply concepts developed within CSCW research, such as routines, distributed coordination, working with constant interruptions, surreptitious monitoring, and distributed awareness in their analysis. We do not want to enter the argument here about how relevant studies of complex work settings (of which there are far too few) are for CSCW research and certainly do not advocate a general move towards studying 'ludic pursuits'. But we feel that a CSCW perspective can contribute to understanding new digital designs, if work-related or not.

First of all, CSCW researchers study design practice and they have done so in fields such as architecture (e.g. Schmidt and Wagner 2004), multimedia design (e.g. Bellotti and Rogers 1997), software development (Grinter 2000; Rönkkö et al. 2005), and so forth. Secondly, they can examine the ways users participate in the co-evolution of some digital designs, such as blogs, Wiki or other social computing applications. 'People engage in cooperative work when they are mutually dependent in their work and therefore are required to cooperate in order to get the work done', Bannon and Schmidt (1992) have argued. This also applies to new digital designs that are articulated collectively. A good example is the account of the making of *Underskog* (Chapter 8), a web-based social calendaring service. Morrison et al. describe the emergence of *Underskog* 'through the expressive activities and interchange of needs and wants between the participants to the service and its designers', in an ongoing process of design refinement. The authors used what they call multimodal ethnography which combines an analysis of a diary one of the co-designers kept, recording all the design decisions (among other things), with textual analysis of screenshots illustrating actual use, as well as users' design contributions. Although rooted in an activity theory framework and multimodal discourse analysis (more than in CSCW research), a notion of collaborative practice emerges from their account, partly co-located, partly distributed, with participants expressing their ideas of use and suggesting new features through the multimodal genre *Underskog* affords.

The authors refer to participants' multimodal articulations. Here the term articulations seems to be used in a rather generic way, in contrast to CSCW research, where articulation work denotes the ongoing adjustment of action in view of the relentless contingencies that are to do with the situatedness of all social action, hence the fact that practice takes place locally, in specific and known contexts of interdependence, uncertainty, particular resources, competing tasks, shared conventions, and so on (Gerson et al. 1986). Collaborative activities require co-actors to articulate – distribute responsibilities, explain, guide, align, clarify misunderstandings, and so forth. Articulation work is an integral part of collaborative work and, at the same time, a sort of 'meta' activity: 'Articulation work is work to make work work'; it comprises all the 'activities undertaken to ensure the articulation of activities within the cooperative arrangement' (Schmidt 2002a: 462). This is an interesting perspective when it comes to analysing social software, such as *Underskog*. How to distinguish articulations that 'make work work' in the sense of communicating events, aligning people's activities, and communicating needs and ideas to designers? How to identify these articulations as being part of a material practice and how to characterize this practice – by shared artifacts (the webpages to read and contribute to), procedures, discursive or representational conventions?

Interaction Through Artefacts

Many researchers have addressed the crucial role of inscription and material artefacts in cooperative work. It is typical of cooperative work in modern work settings that multiple actors so to speak interact 'through' a *collection* of artefacts of various kinds. A number of interesting studies have been published over the years, analysing wallboards for scheduling (Whittaker and Schwarz 1999), flight progress strips (Hughes et al. 1992), patient records (Berg 1999; Fitzpatrick 2004), CAD plans (Henderson 1999), the affordances of paper (Sellen and Harper 2002). These and other studies have demonstrated the role of artefacts – tools, machines, infrastructures, documents, and other physical objects – in making work visible, structuring communication, providing workspace and template, helping manage interdependencies, and so forth. They have studied how artefacts are created and shared as part of collaborative activities. In their analysis of architectural practice, Schmidt and Wagner (2004) talk about the crucial part representational artefacts, such as CAD plans, scale models, samples of building materials, 3D visualizations, have in making the invisible visible, specifying, making public, persuading others (of a design idea), enabling designers to explore, evaluate options, and so forth. They also point at the multiplicity, multimediality, multimodality, and openness of many of these design artefacts. Morrison et al. (2007) examined such multiples in artefacts of coordination and coordinating artefacts with respect to the mediation of new waterfront properties (see also Chapter 7).

What are the artefacts to study when it comes to new digital designs? In their study of multimedia producers Newman and Landay (2000) have described some of these artefacts in detail. High fidelity mock-ups for instance 'contain(ed) images, icons, rich typography, and sophisticated colour schemes, and these details of the visual presentation were meant to be taken literally' (2000: 266). Another example of visual artefacts used in multimedia production are story-boards, which provide a schematic illustration of the interaction sequences in an informal way. Linking and navigation are usually presented as sketches on paper or in the form of 'site maps'. These are designers' artefacts but in many digital designs we have user–participants actively create their own multimedial artefacts or modify and annotate those provided by others and it is this co-created multiplicity through which a design is involving and being transformed. When it comes to mixed-reality applications, we experience and have to consider intriguing new mixes of material and digital.

Going back to the example of mixed-reality technologies and a tangible user interface in support of groups of urban planners, citizens, politicians, etc. in collaboratively envisioning urban change (the *ColorTable* described in Chapter 2), we can distinguish two types of artefacts: the tangible user interface of table, colour tokens, and other physical devices, on the one hand, the mixed-reality scenes users co-construct on the other hand. Observing the evolving material practices around this set-up, we can analyse how users communicate through participating in the construction of mixed-reality scenes, and how this highly visible, expressive enactment of ideas is, in turn, an invitation to others to participate, co-experience, and contribute to this dynamic enactment. We can also understand how interacting with tangible objects is an important part in expressing and experiencing a mixed-reality scene and how their shape and texture contributes to this (Maquil et al. 2007).

Jacucci et al. (2009) describe another tangible user interface, the *CityWall,* a multi-touch screen, which, installed in a public place in Helsinki, invited passers-by to physically manipulate and share images they had sent by mobile phone. The authors show how the particular size and interaction technology of the *CityWall* supports bodily interactions with the display; for example, gestures like photo-moving and scaling turned into games like Pong playing. Content on the wall and features of the interface were used as resources to coordinate activity or to create eventful episodes. Also the presence of strangers – people walking past the installation, sometimes stopping by to observe what went on – had an effect on players' activities at the *CityWall,* which can be perceived as a performance in the city space. This is similar to public art projects that engage audience participants in large scale performative activities that involve a medley of design, programming aesthetics and embodied interaction that results in shared experience and meaning making in a mixed reality setting (e.g. Lozano-Hemmer 2001).

Boundary Objects

CSCW research has examined the role of boundary objects (e.g. Bowker and Star 1999) – objects that are an interface between various communities of practice – in collaboration. Boujut and Blanco (2003), in a paper on cooperation in engineering design, introduce the concept of 'intermediary objects', which they see as central to forming a common understanding of a design situation:

> More precisely we think that co-operation can be considered as a process of "disambiguation" if it is properly framed. Negotiation and compromise setting are particular ways for creating specific shared knowledge. The concept of intermediary objects can provide a tool that allows the production of a conceptual frame that formalizes and represent this shared knowledge through objects and various representations. (Boujut and Blanco 2003: 216)

We can think of the set of technologies, such as the mixed-reality tools described above, as supporting the creation of 'intermediary objects' that help make the transformation process of an urban site more collective or, in the case of the *CityWall*, augment the local urban experience with remote experiences represented by shared images.

In a recent paper, Lee (2007) introduced the notion of 'boundary negotiation artefacts', arguing that negotiating boundaries may be considered a special form of cooperative work, where actors discover, test and push boundaries. In relation to *Underskog*, the *ColorTable* and the *CityWall*, this notion suggests we may look at the emerging new digital designs as challenging boundaries and notions of artefacts, and as inviting participants to negotiate and redefine those boundaries: between private and public, material–physical and projected, design and use, professional competence and the perspective of informed citizens, and so forth.

Awareness

Another powerful concept connected to CSCW research is awareness. First thematized as peripheral awareness, as an aspect of professional practice in co-located environments (Heath and Luff 1992), awareness as a concept emerged in CSCW 'as a placeholder for those elusive practices of taking heed of what is going on in the setting which seem to play a key role in cooperative work' (Schmidt 2002b: 285). Schmidt argued that 'awareness' is not the product of passively acquired 'information' but is a characterization of some highly active and highly skilled practices: 'Competent practitioners are able to align and integrate their activities because they know the setting, they are not acting in abstract space but in a material environment which is infinitely rich in cues' (Schmidt 2002b: 292). Awareness also became a design feature for distributed workspaces, where it can be supported through, for example, sharing materials, representations of people active in the space or notification mechanisms. A lot of interface mechanisms in support of presence have been invented, from embodiment solutions to the use of colours and characteristic sounds.

Awareness cues form a useful concept in many digital designs. Licoppe and Inada (2005) in their analysis of the use of a geo-localized game in Japan, show how gamers may become aware that their unknown co-gamers are on the same commuter train and perceive this as a legitimate pretext to initiate a physical encounter. They describe this situation as: 'Equipped players are hybrid beings; they perceive the world from their own bodies but also perceive themselves as icons on the map of the radar interface. ... The "onscreen encounter" in which the protagonists are able to perceive their respective icons on the screen map and to share that perception configures a form of encounter peculiar to context-aware cooperative devices' (Licoppe and Inada 2005: 11 and 14). Similarly, Jacucci et al. (2007) describe their observations with *CoMedia*, a mobile application supporting distributed spectators of a large scale event to share and co experience, in terms of awareness. *CoMedia* features several awareness cues. The application provides users with cues about the context of other members (their physical location and time of being there), nearby members, usage of the phone. In addition, several other cues about the activity of the member inside the system, like the presence of a member in a story, are conveyed.

Gaver (2002) has explored additional aspects of awareness which he calls 'provocative awareness', concentrating on forms of interaction that are more sensuous, less explicit and symbolic. Particularly interesting in this approach is the use of ambiguity to increase people's engagement. We can also see from his work that we can approach awareness as not 'merely' a cognitive phenomenon but one that allows the addressing of a wider range of emotional relationships. The 'Bench Object', for example, provides peripheral awareness of other people, but in a form that is unfamiliar and disturbing. Its effects rely on two features: first, in using warmth to indicate the presence of another person, the bench conveying a direct sense of their corporeality; second, its situation in a public space implies intimacy with strangers, challenging assumptions of public inaccessibility to which urban dwellers are accustomed. Gaver stresses that work like this 'reflects a stress on the evocative potential of design concepts, their ability to provoke understanding and imagination, and implies a form of evaluation centred on the richness of insights and inspiration they may offer' (Gaver 2002: 478).

Classification Systems and Archives

Finally, CSCW researchers have also embarked on studying classification systems and archives. Schmidt and Wagner (2004), in their study of architectural practice, have identified highly specialized artefacts and material practices that help architects manage the complexity of coordinating and integrating collaborative activities.

They call such combinations of coordinative artefacts and practices ordering systems and argue that, in many areas of work, developing, modifying and maintaining such ordering systems is a part of collaborative work. Ordering, indexing, classifying, and searching are important activities in museums. As the study on sustainability (Chapter 9) shows, new digital media and the widening opportunities of representing artefacts, their history, their reconstruction, as well as the perspectives of different disciplines, pose considerable challenges to established classification systems.

In some digital designs the issue is how to capture complex personal and cultural associations rather than establishing a scientific systematic. The physical world offers different types of archives and ordering systems – boxes for keeping items together, books for creating sequence, narrative, and links between image and text, walls for hanging, etc. The digital world, with its possibilities of linking multimedia materials (including sound and video), and its openness to the participation of many people of mixed and unknown competencies and perspectives, may make established ways of ordering and classifying obsolete. Asked to transit the borders between factual and fictitious, original and imitation, and to look for strange combinations and weird neighbourhoods, users have to develop new practices of ordering and searching. Stafford (1996) sees nothing totally new in this. She compares today's Internet searches with pre-scientific practices: 'Much as today's students select an icon by touching a keyboard or manipulating a mouse, eighteenth century-beholders of polymathic diversity mentally clicked on a theatrical roster of automata, watch-works, and decorative arts in a fantastic case' (Stafford 1996: 75). This perspective reaches beyond work but it challenges CSCW research into identifying collaboration patterns and sustainable practices.

CSCW research mainly focuses on work practice, although this view is subject to a heated debate. With regards to digital designs that are not necessarily part of work, it offers a methodological challenge that is to do with its high standards in producing detailed ethnographic accounts of practices, and it proposes a set of powerful concepts for analysing such practices that reach beyond the textual and ground meaning making in material practices of producing, engaging, evaluating, performing, and so forth.

Networks and Relations

Making Relations in Digital Design

Actor Network Theory (ANT) deals with the complexities of knowledge production in a very specific way. Originating in studies of scientific knowledge production which saw science as socially constructed, ANT opened up for the analysis of social relations inscribed in science as well as technology. More recently this approach has also been used in studying design processes. A key perspective within ANT is the 'network' of actors, human and non-human. This network mediates the emergence of an object of inquiry or design. In design knowledge production this happens on several related levels. It involves not only collectives of designers but is shaped by infrastructures, policies, ideologies, and relates to the cultural and historical roots of a society.

What makes ANT especially attractive for design research is its focus on the diversity of 'actants' (or actors as Latour more recently prefers), on design negotiations, and on the divergent understandings of the 'what' and the 'how' involved in collaborative design processes. ANT draws attention to the 'politics' in design, through its understanding of designing as inscribing the object, the medium or the materials with competences, motives, and political 'prejudices'. Akrich (1992: 208) phrases this as follows:

> Designers thus define actors with specific tastes, competences, motives, aspirations, political prejudices, and the rest, and they assume that morality, technology, science, and the economy will evolve in particulars ways. A large part of the work of innovators is that of inscribing this vision (or prediction about) the world in the technical content of the new object.

This perspective goes beyond the notion of a co-operative ensemble used within CSCW research, or the focus on activity systems, as it is more dynamic, focusing on the changing configurations of actors. CSCW research focuses on material practices and the artefacts that are created, shared, and read as part of these practices, analysing their format, content, and structure and their material–social realizations; ANT focuses on their role as 'actants' that drive processes of negotiations and translation.

As a framework for studying design, ANT offers several experimental ways of following relevant actors in their contextual networks and networks of translation, with an emphasis on heterogeneity and multiplicity. These have import for digital design research. The approach has been criticized for its 'Machiavellian' departure point that tells the story from the point of view of the strong actors. Rendered invisible are those that are left out of the world-building activities (Cockburn 1992) and the marginalised, that do not fit the pattern of configured networks (Star 1991). ANT-based studies do not necessarily focus on the weak relations, the actants with less capability or potential for a network and the actants that do not pass the obligatory points or align to the network. What relevance do they have for the building of relation between the actors inside a network? The critique has been successful in that is has drawn attention to ways of thinking of difference. Strathern (1996) points out that relations can be based on difference and discontinuity. This critique draws attention to our conception of what a relation is (Hetherington and Law 2000) and asks that digital design research pay attention to 'difference' and disjuncture as part of understanding relations and their emergence in digital artefacts and the cultural expressions voiced through and in them.

In the 10 years or so of ANT-related writings and discussions, the focus of the framework and its uses has developed. From being used as a theoretical framework for analysing relational structures in development of technology as successful stories, ANT is now increasingly understood as a methodological framework for describing complex processes in heterogeneous networks (Law and Mol 2002). ANT addresses complexity by taking multiple points of departure, with humans and non-humans not just relating directly but also as part of the cultural, historical, institutional, and political context of a project.

'Post-ANT' places greater weight on heterogeneity, on political negotiations in democracy, and on multiple ontologies (Spinuzzi 2003). In this way, ANT provides a semiotic framework for making available descriptions 'which differ in important ways from many traditional social science approaches' by providing 'an attitude and method emphasising sensitivity to the multiplicity of world-making activities' (Gad and Bruun Jensen 2005). The post-ANT approach focuses on multiple voices as 'it is not possible to draw everything together to offer a single account' (Hetherington and Law 2000: 129). These multiple voices are captured by the notion of 'actant-rhizomes'. 'Rhizome' is a term used in several recent studies related to design to describe the relation between material and non-material processes. This metaphor, drawn from biology, illustrates the underground, horizontal stem of a plant, especially related to ferns, that sends out roots and shoots from its nodes, has been used by Deleuze and Guattari (1989). In their work 'rhizomes' also stands for how invisible connections can be part of world-making.

Symmetry, Agency and Translations

An important perspective in ANT, as compared to general network perspectives in sociology and theories of politics of knowledge production, is the symmetrical positioning of humans and non-humans, of human and material (machine) agency. It is because of this thinking of humans and non-humans that ANT is increasingly used in studies of the relation between technology and the social. Further, ANT's perspective on network-building is not reduced to the networks per se but to what makes participants capable of negotiating their own goals within other actors' building activities. In this way, ANT focuses on agencies instead of actors, taking capabilities and potential as its departure point. The more refined concept would, therefore, be to speak about 'actors' as the role that allows them to move in networks. The actant may be an individual or collective, it may be human or machine; actants are the driving force of the network building activities.

Networks also inscribe actors with values, programmes or facts; actors denote networks by their linkages and relations. But actants also negotiate the programmes of a network; actants persuade other actants to become allied so to make their programmes strong. They align or do not align with existing networks, and they accept or do not accept obligatory points of passage set up by powerful actants. In this way the ANT approach provides a set of concepts that are useful as methodological tools for describing and bringing to the forefront issues that are relevant for understanding the outcome of transformation processes. Translation is one of the key concepts of ANT. It is used to describe processes through which actors relate to each other (Latour 1987, 2005). As a result, actor-networks are understood as networks of translations (Callon 1986), where translations are the result of compromises and mutual adjustments.

Translations are an important part of building alliances and relations. For Callon (1991: 143), they are the elementary operations that move the process of science or design. For Callon, '... the elementary operation of translation is triangular: it involves a translator, something that is translated, and a medium in which that translation is inscribed.' The term 'translation' can be understood as describing a drift or mediation in our intentionality while using technology. The strength of the notion of translation is that it resonates with observations of how an emerging design is expressed in different media and materials, representational formats and scales (Shiga 2007).

Circulating References

For studies of knowledge-building and communication (that may also entail design), the notion of 'circulating reference' is of special interest. It points to elements of continuity in processes that cross time and space: 'It seems that reference is not simply the act of pointing or a way of keeping, on the outside, some material guarantee for the truth of a statement; rather it is our way of keeping something constant through a series of transformations' (Latour 1999: 58). This aspect of continuity in changing processes also captures the historical aspect of the actor network processes, in the way that historical trajectories influence the negotiations involved in design processes (Stuedahl 2004). Continuity also characterizes some of the knowledge traditions that are involved in design processes. Even if design processes involve new knowledge and understandings, the departure point is knowledge traditions where knowledge and ways of understanding are related to specific practices put to work. Circulating references here explains the historical background of the different translations that actors provide in the networks, in that former understandings are referred to and circulated in a new setting. Circulating references provide continuity in the network, and the possibility of building trust in the quality of a 'statement', such as a scientific result or a design argument. Circulating references describes how traditions and ontologies are part of knowledge building processes, pointing to how former knowledge actually works as frameworks for the interpretative translations that circulate in design processes (Stuedahl 2004).

Linde (2007) uses the concept of circulating references differently. He points to how 'circulating references' describe ways in which ideas and expressions are transformed throughout the design process:

> Design ideas gain material significance as they are expressed by the designer in the form of different design representations. They are subject to metamorphoses and conceptual change and they are subject to further materialization in new representations. This is done in relation to the previous expressions, and those expressions circulate like Latour's references, not only until the designers take a final decision, but they are also subject to change through the appropriation of the users and integration with culture and everyday life. (Linde 2007: 89)

Analysing a diversity of digital design practices (architecture, installation art, interaction design), Linde describes how designers develop a multiplicity of design representations in parallel (e.g. in the case of architects sketches showing forms of for example façade, detailed plans, drawings showing atmospheres and situations, 3D models, and collage of visual and tactile material) and that these heterogeneous representations are often manipulated simultaneously. He argues that in design work, in particular in artistic work, 'the experience of the transformations is equally important as the experience of the object' (2007: 16).

Furthermore, ANT draws attention to the relational and non-singular aspects of objects and of materialization processes. Objects are performed and they are emerging. Storni explicates this view with respect to design, arguing: 'In fact, rather than talking about ontological multiplicity (according to which the object becomes a completely different one in different places), I would rather prefer to talk of a metonymic plurality where the object is not a different object per se but it is rendered as such according to different relational circumstances which activate different elements, features and characters of the same, never simple and single, object' (Storni 2007: 378).

Using a richly documented case of jewellery design (and a second case of interaction design), Storni analyses the translations and alignments that happen in a network of human and non-human actors, including all the different materials and techniques that are used for shaping the jewellery and making it machine-producible. He also offers a reading of the object-in-design as undergoing a 'passage from thing to object'. This passage, he argues, may be viewed as a move towards ordering and assembling rather than diffused. Here the thing may refer to gathering of the human – from designers right through to customers – and the non-human. Through association the thing becomes object. What applies to jewellery design is the more relevant for understanding digital designs where there is no 'final' object but an ongoing chain of associations and translations.

The process from thing to object is a negotiation process between not only the 'beast' of the material in the forefront, but also the material history of this beast: the circulating references and the former and tacit knowledge that is bound to the material, and that has to be negotiated and transformed into new knowledge. This makes for an understanding of 'relations' in actor networks as including a relation to the material (the physical negotiation with the material), as well as a negotiation with former practices and knowledge traditions that are culturally, as well as socially, established and embedded in the same material (Stuedahl 2004; Clausen and Yoshinaka 2007). This is what we take up in Part 2 of the book.

Performing Relations

Law and Singleton (2000) point to the subject of technological use and talk about a performative turn in Science Technology Studies (STS) research and in studies of social construction of reality. What is significant in this approach is the bonding of ontological and epistemological in the act of performance. They write that:

> The differences between realism and pragmatism are important, but neither share the performative assumption that reality is brought into being in the process of knowing. Or, to put it more precisely, neither would assume that the object that is known and the subject that does the knowing are co-produced in the same performance, that the epistemological problem (what is true) and the ontological question (what is) are both resolved (or not) in the same moment. (Law and Singleton 2000: online)

This attention to the performative offers us some means of attending to the emergent in digital designing. It also allows us to attend to the enactment of digital designs in our own uses and shapings of them. These too are co-present in that they cannot come into being without one another. Actor Network Theory and STS have applied the performance perspective to their own stories, 'following the actors' (Latour 1987). In her study of the construction of health programmes to investigate and support work into aetherosclerosis, Mol (1998, 1999, 2001) has argued that in order to examine performance in settings such as these, one needs to see how such co-ordination is realized and the implications and effects this has on the very shaping and performance of that network. Here, as Law has also argued, the narratives that parties to such networks build, exchange and perform are central because the building of a network is also a performance' (Law and Singleton 2003)

In this view, performativity focuses on the negotiations between actors, and invites us to study purpose, intentions and strategies, those that are visible and articulated as well as those that are invisible and silent (Stuedahl 2004; Mörtberg and Stuedahl 2005), that build the constituting forces. This focus is valuable for design research. It may enrich research related to the design process, the collaborations between participants, and understanding of users' relation to designed products.

With respect to exploring digital design, there are many strengths in analysing relations, performance and networks. Concepts such as translations, negotiations and circulating references undoubtedly offer us powerful means for addressing the complex formations and shapings of socio-technical spaces in and via digital design. However, these approaches do not fully take into account the multiple intersecting activities and mediations that characterize much of the emerging nature of the digital in which relations are also made between the socio-technical and the humanities. We take this up later (see Chapter 9) with respect to sustainability and design.

In the next subsection we further examine the importance of the social and cultural in exploring digital design analytically, with reference to Activity Theory, semiotics, 'new media' studies, rhetoric and genre theory. Discussions between ANT and Activity Theory are in the process of being expanded from a somewhat earlier binarism about their ontological differences (Latour 1996; Miettinen 1999) to points of limited complementarity (e.g. Morrison 2010b).

Socio-Cultural Perspectives

On Communication Design

Digital design processes, products and services come into being by virtue of the interplay of technological affordances and mediational potential. The interplay is realized as mediated discourse and communicative articulations. These technologies and mediations are ones that are situated in socio-cultural contexts and practices. Such contexts and practices concern the emergence and exploration of the new as well as ways in which we access and inscribe earlier conventions and knowledge. A socio-cultural perspective on digital design is composed through the medley of inter-related theoretical concerns and their relations to praxis. Central to these concerns is the principle that meaning making is situated in shared and intersecting communicative and cultural activities. These activities include the technical and the textual, the social and the symbolic in designing the digital.

In this subsection we link and situate the psychological, the semiotic, genre, rhetoric and communicative in researching digital design. From psychology we draw on cultural–historical approaches that have collaborative and reflexive meaning making at their core. Concerning semiotics, our focus is on social semiotics and shared design, culturally situated enactment and participative meaning making. Typologically, rhetoric and genre are important in digital design when user and participants' views and enactments increasingly percolate the many and flexible layers of designing in digital systems and with digital tools. Designing and realising cultural artefacts also place digital design discourses, both as processes and products, as part of digital communication design. In making explicit these links to the communicative – as representational, mediated and performative – we build on views on interaction design (Löwgren 2002; Löwgren and Stolterman 2004) that move away from earlier functionalist stances on human computer interaction to instead link interaction with culturally mediated communication. Different aspects of socio-cultural perspectives on digital design are taken up in four of the case-based chapters in Part 2 of the book.

From a socio-cultural perspective, digital design research builds and analyzes design for, and communication through, digitally mediated interfaces. Compositionally, curatorially and choreographically, these are socio-cultural interfaces. They come into being via our rhetorical and articulatory moves between database and digital document (e.g. Manovich 2003) as well as our situated practices through which they are materially constituted. As mediated discourses of design and as design, these moves entail shifts between input and output devices which themselves are not simply neutral 'participants'. Importantly, this involves the multimodal mixing of retrieved, found and inserted cultural, symbolic and mediated material that entails a complex blending of design practices and user knowledge and experience. This too leads to matters of digital materiality that concern text production, media types and multimodal constructions. There is a need to examine the design for the potential 'texturings' and types of media, for example the style, texture and role of photos in blogging (Cohen 2005), or emergent genre features and their related social practices (Miller and Shepherd 2004), as well as the communicative contexts of textual production, mediation and affordances for use (Morrison and Skjulstad 2010; Skjulstad 2007b).

The importance of communication to digital design and of digital designing for communication has not been fully developed in research into 'interaction design', including that with a semiotic take on 'engineering' in HCI (de Souza 2005). A Communication Design perspective places media types, meditational means and communicative and cultural aspects as its design material, whether designing a mobile narrative for and in use (Morrison 2009), or a museum exhibit that is linked to social media practices to enable user participation (Pierroux 2009). What is new in our view is the attention to media and communication and especially the ways in which digital design processes, practices, products and use need to attend to the ways in which narrative, aesthetics, social semiotics and poetics are of part of interaction. Important here is the overall focus on communication that involves links between representation, mediation and participation. This is to place emphasis on the design of cultural, symbolic resources and affordances for engagement and enactment that are digitally mediated and mixed with other materials. This is distinct from structuralist and determinist models of communication (see e.g. Crilly et al. 2008a), and also ones proposed in informatics (e.g. Winograd 1996). A media and communication informed view allows us to access research and practice from domains such as aesthetics, semiotics and rhetoric and to connect them to aspects of interaction design that are not merely procedural and functionalist in their human–machine relations. It is also important that such a view acknowledges the value of designers' intentions (Crilly et al. 2008b) in communication, not simply that these are embedded in a product or product semantic perspective. Developing and analysing tangible interfaces (see Chapter 2) may then be placed in contexts of practice and use, but also located in wider cultural, historical and meditational view that gives weight to what is being said or articulated and how this is being achieved and conveyed via different modes of communication and media types that are themselves mediating artifacts. A cultural historical view on semiosis may thus be distinguished from one in which phenomenological views are given more emphasis (e.g. O'Neill 2008). As mentioned in Chapter 2, meaning is made in and through practice.

Developmental and Transformative Views

Through a socio-cultural approach to the communicative and cultural significations in digital design, we may approach design products and processes in relation to activity, development and transformation. Our particular focus is on developing a communication design orientation to digital design from within a socio-cultural perspective. This places more emphasis on the design relation between tools, signs and mediation in relation to design. This matters for designing culturally framed resources for communicative use. With strong roots in psychology (Vygotsky 1962, 1978), a socio-cultural approach emphasizes that our designed and mediated worlds are constructed through design activity, where action is realized in inter-relations between tools, signs and their significations. Here relations between tools and signs are especially important (Wartofsky 1979) in shaping relations between design resources through which mediated meaning making may be materialized. Cultural Historical Activity Theory (CHAT) places activities of mediation and meaning making within both cultural and developmental contexts and constituent activities.

Meaning making occurs in what are called activity systems through which these components are realized. Activity is a core unit of analysis; meaning is made collaboratively, via activity and in activity that Vygotsky reminds us is to do with mediation, and mediated meaning making (Wertsch 1991). Such an approach has been conceptualized in Activity Theory and applied and extended in design-related studies of work (e.g. Engeström 1987), learning (e.g. Ludvigsen and Mørch 2005) and informatics (e.g. Kuutti 1995; Kaptelinin and Nardi 2006). However, understanding and analysing digital design process and products where the tools and signs are culturally and communicatively constituted (e.g. Bazerman 1997) has not received similar attention. This, for example, was the focus of a large multidisciplinary project called MULTIMO that placed communication design and 'composition' at the centre of explorations of digital discourse and multimodality from a socio-cultural frame (Morrison 2010a). Practice and analysis were interwoven in research that investigated the changing dynamic of digitally mediated communication and its design in different environments, ranging from web interfaces to installation arts.

As technologies, symbolic means and our mediated expressions become more closely entangled in complex communicative activities, it becomes even more important to focus on the motivations or object of our activity (Leont'ev 1978, 1981). Utterances refer to the speech acts of saying; articulation refers to the means, ways and modes of enactment in and as digitally mediated communication (as opposed to grammar, or function). The design of symbolic and meditational resources or communication, such as style of animation in an interface, may be accentuated. This attention to the culturally communicative also then needs to be seen in relation to the growth of multiple activity systems that intersect and produce new objects of activity. The strongly developmental and transformational character of the socio-cultural approach allows us to take part in processes of emergence and change, both in terms of special intervention and as participants to a longer path of alteration and reflection. In communication that is enhanced by technology, a socio-cultural approach helps untangle a complex of intersections between digital artefacts and their meditational materialities, modes of their collaborative construction and distribution, and our unfolding and mediated meaning making. Such an approach provides a useful and flexible frame for approaching emerging areas in which digital design is deeply embedded – such as Game Studies (e.g. McGonigal 2007; Bogost 2007) or production-based media education (Burn and Durran 2006) – but is not necessarily made plain analytically in terms of design practices and design studies.

Engeström (2007), one of the leading proponents of Activity Theory, has recently observed, for example, that while we have paid considerable attention to learning environments in technology-enhanced education, we have not given adequate attention to the granulated media and communicative qualities of those environments, or designs for learning. This observation also applies to the culture and creative industries (Lash and Lury 2007), including digital design, where attention is needed on the multilayered activities of creative arts and their digitally mediated cultural production. Here digital design research may be informed directly and abductively by studies in new media. In addition to studies in interaction design with an informatics bent, humanities views such as those in new media studies place weight on (analysing) interpretation (Strain and van Hoosier-Carey 2003; Hayles 2002; Bertelsen and Pold 2004) by participants in digitally mediated texts, events, discourses and practices. This is also carried out in analyses of iterative and participatory design that comes not only from inside influential studies in informatics and collaboration in work (see Chapter 8) but is located in cultural, historical and social semiotic analyses of mediated communication that are a part of their reflexive design and enactment. Importantly, this communication is realized in action via the mediated affordances and cultural resources that are provided and suggested to participants in digital discourse events and environments. These are events and environments that are themselves in flux, in and through development, in their emergence. They too need to be related to their antecedents and distinguished from them. Communication Design offers us some means to study the links between production and reflection that may be understood as distinct from earlier transmission and transfer based models of mediation.

In approaching digital design research and its changing character, the influential work of Engeström in conceptualizing development and learning as expansion may be applied. In a recent publication addressing co-configuration in work environments, Engeström (2007: 38) identified, among others, two tentative features that are pertinent for digital design and that are related to activities that cross boundaries and forge links. He refers to 'Learning by experiencing' as an activity, whereby participants engage in imagined or simulated situations '... that require personal engagement in actions with material objects and artifacts (including other human beings) that follow the logic of an anticipated or designed future model of the activity.' (see Chapter 7). Hakkarainen et al. (2004) see collaborative meaning making as complex configurations and co-ordinations of multiple participants, views and media types. This entails the activities and practices of enacting digital designs: constructively, expressively and critically. Moreover, there is a need to account for how a complex of design, designed and designing (e.g. Thackara 2005) may be understood more relationally. ANT suggests ways in which we may approach this as sets of relations and negotiations and build outwards from what Latour (2005) refers to as the assembly of assemblages. Yet such assemblies have material discursive characters and characteristics, enfolded in how we articulate our views and versions in digitally mediated communication (such as in feminist perspectives on the socio-technical as in the last subsection of this chapter).

71

Affordances and Mediating Artefacts

What has been not so fully explored with respect to the analyses of digital design concerning the symbolic and the communicative, as opposed to the functional and instrumental, has been a focus on the qualities and affordances of different media and their mixings in the array of multimodal expressions that are now being designed. It is through designs for use and their performative enactments in mediated discourse that we may explore such affordances as utterances of cultural design. The notion of affordances was originally advanced by Gibson (1966) to refer to a relational quality between organism and environment; he pointed out that opportunities or limitations for action are also perceptual and based on users' abilities to act in their context. Affordances were later taken up in HCI by Norman (1988) with specific reference to end users and little on the socio-cultural activities in which they were situated. This weight on action and activity has been further connected to an Activity Theory view (Bærentsen and Trettvik 2002). Connections between activity and affordance have been applied within the exploration in the collaborative design of RFID technologies and the design of affordances for Near Field Interaction (NFI) in a project called TOUCH, based at the Oslo School of Architecture and Design. The term 'material affordances' (Nordby and Morrison under review) has been developed to describe digital materialities and RFID technology that are available to designers and teams involved in explorations that are geared towards providing resources for digitally mediated communication and interaction.

The invisibility of RFID fields may also be made explicit through the design of 'visual affordances' that move technical and symbolic mark-up and physical placement of RFID tags to representations of the magnetic 'auras' of near field zones into visual mediations of their scope and reach. These are visualisations that reveal what is otherwise invisible in the form of radio fields (Arnall and Martinussen 2010) and cannot thus be 'accessed' by designers who are motivated to move beyond function driven ticketing or payment applications. Giving visible body to unseen material form of RFID makes it possible to envisage the design for other types of communication with the technology, including ones that may involve richer tangible interactions between RFID embedded data and physical products, such as toys (Johanssen 2009). This is a communication design geared towards also helping designers better access properties of the material with which they experiment, such as in the development of communicative prototypes (Knutsen and Morrison 2010), and may then review and apply for wider use.

A key concept is that of 'mediating artefact' (see also Chapter 7). In contrast to CSCW research, in an Activity Theory view the notion of artefact (and tool) subsumes mental as well as material phenomena. The artefact encompasses techniques, practices, skills, signs, notations, along with their material counterparts such as diagrams, maps, and blueprints, and so forth. Wartofsky (1979), from within psychology, proposed the concept of the tertiary artefact to move from levels of representation to mediated imagination and formulation (as opposed to primary and secondary artefacts as tools and representations respectively). This may then also be framed in terms of Communication Design where tools and signs are located in designs for mediated meaning making and as Cole (1998) argues as culturally medatied activity. Morrison and Skjulstad (in press) argue that this is a matter of complex mediation (Bødker and Andersen 2005) between system, structure and semiosis, in which the projection of design concepts and innovation are articulated through digital aesthetics that access popular and technological metaphors and discourses. In an example taken from digital advertising on the web, Morrison (2009) analyse how a leading global car maker uses metaphors and visualizations of design innovation of hybrid luxury vehicles as part of the persuasive character of branding online. In this digitally mediated advert, it is a website that has been designed to persuade; it is an example of mediated digital semiosis where use and interpretation by publics are to a large degree framed via a sophisticated cultural and symbolic imaginary. Digital imagery rendered in Flash and the web-based cross linking of references and allusions to a variety of media types and genres (from handbooks to science fiction film) are used to project arguments in favour sustainable design geared to consumers. This is pictured as partly technological but also through the mediation of the artefact of a hybrid-engine passenger vehicle that is then result of innovative design and manufacturing that surpasses that of other automakers. Better design is conveyed through the promotion of sophisticated web media as part of a multi-level communication design strategy that also has a culturally located view on materials and expression.

Such multimodal online marketing discourse uses artistic visualizations and metaphors of neurological processes in a communication design campaign to promote the advanced technologies of the hybrid vehicle. As is taken up in Chapter 7, the mediating artefact refers not only to text and media types but, importantly, to what is signified and communicated symbolically and culturally. Digital design also entails such communicative intent and, importantly, engagement. A growing trend in the design and enactment of digital branding, for example concerning mobile phones, is to include consumers as producers of digital adverts and their collaborative distribution and exchange (Morrison and Skjulstad in press). The design for collaboration and for engagement in community has become a major growth area in digital design (see Chapter 8).

The concept of the mediating artefact allows us some means to moving further inside the interface (Bertelsen 2006) as a site of complex mediation, as well as to extend earlier notions and practices of multimodality based in social semiotics. Through this concept, we may engage with design-in-the-making and the realizations and grapplings with materiality, now digital, now a mix of materials and materialities, that we employ in our shared meaning making. For example, the *Gesturetek* phone accentuates the kinetic in mobile gaming where the mobile phone camera operates as a movement recognition device for the handset that, like the *Wii* from Nintendo, has an accelerometer that allows users to enact a set of gestures that produce movements in the screen. This is most important for digital design research as it allows us to analyse the dynamics of interaction *and* communication design. Concerning the portfolios of web designers, this focus on interaction and communication has been applied through the extension of notions of montage in the linear medium of film to the dynamic and multiple activity levels of dynamic mediation within and across media types in the design and textualization of motion graphics (Skjulstad 2007b). Such portfolios are textual products, but their symbolic and expressive qualities and affordances for engagement need to be unpacked as meditational artefacts in which cultural expressions and practices of web design are embedded. These sites are examples of exploratory, leading web design professionals and they offer us meditational resources with which to design. Their realization as innovative communicative resources for designers, and as designed artefacts, entails the intersection of information and communication structures and designs at a textual level. In turn, their textual aplomb makes it possible for users to engage with multimodal representations and expressions. It is important that interaction design approaches be extended to also explore how such environments for use are composed, on the one hand, and how their meditational affordances are made 'material' by users, one the other. In this view, digital design research could usefully extend approaches of Activity Theory to also investigate what Diaz-Kommonen (2003) calls the vibration between 'artefacts of expression' and 'expressive artefacts'. An approach to digital design as exploring and incorporating mediating artefacts makes it possible to further study the activity between humans and machines in complex relations of design dynamics as well as in their contexts of professional and popular use.

In the next subsection we turn to polyvocality and address as concepts that may be applied in understanding designing for mediated articulation and participation and their contextual analyses.

Polyvocality and Addressivity

Concerning the articulation of mediated communication and its complex designing and collaborative genesis, it is fruitful to look at the work of Bakhtin (1981, 1984, 1986) and some of his core concepts. Bakhtin's work covered both literary and language domains and thus offers a substantial resource for design researchers. Bakhtin developed the concept of what has come to be labelled the *dialogical*. This refers to his assertion that all communication is enacted, it occurs in dialogue but enunciated in contexts and tempered by conventions. This 'social language' of conventions he labelled *speech genres*, accentuating the socio-cultural construction of all communication as mediated through language but also other modes of expression and exchange. Bakhtin argued that we also consider communication as only ever partial and always unfinished. This notion of the dialogical resonates with some current concerns in digital design research, such as in electronic installation works and online discourse, where dialogue is realized only online and in the time of its telling. In Chapter 2 we related the dialogical to current concerns with digitally designed and mediated communication, such as in blogs. Here we suggest how explorations in the 'dialogical' may be extended into interaction and communication design as part of seeing design as multiply made, that is with a variety of media types and discourse modes. It is the interplay of unfolding digital textual materialities and artefactual mediations that challenge our interpretative and explanatory frames, such as in the shared constructions and interpersonal activities of online gaming that are only possible because of their underlying digitally conceived and afforded communication design. The unfolding of these digital designs has major implications for how we also, today, relate to Bakhtin's concept of addressivity; he saw all communication, whether in fictional narrative or sociolinguistic encounters, as being addressed to a potential hearer and respondent, and by extension, to the wider body of related and antecedent discourse. Seen as communication, digital designs within and via digitally mediated environments are thus also social and cultural discursive constructs and exchanges; they are interpersonal, culturally rooted, and collaborative, but also in flux.

Taken together, these concepts may also be related to Bakhtin's notion of polyvocality. This concept provided a central shift from notions of primary and overbearing authorship – here the romantic lone designer – to meaning that is collectively created through a medley of speaking positions. Referring to applied discourse theory and communication as dialogically framed, attention to the level of the utterance is essential. Utterance refers to socially situated 'speech' and not to language rules. It places weight on how the dialogical may be realized at the level of articulation, i.e. what is said. This is a level of articulation is still very much under-theorized in design research that may still move further from artefacts and their co-ordination to digital artefacts and their symbolic and cultural communication. Yet around us we see that polyvocality is in the process of being realized through a range of media types, co-occurring in websites and increasingly present on mobile devices and in public spaces. By placing communication at the centre of a socio-cultural perspective, digital design research is able to connect information systems and application design and their affordances with the shaping and multimediational character of digital utterances in, as and through, design artefacts and discourses.

Bakhtin further developed the concept of the *chronotope* to account for relations between space and time in written narrative communication. This concept is useful even today in the shaping and study of digital genres, such as blogs (Miller and Shepherd 2004), design portfolios with their mix of online mediation and media types, and the features and functionalities of simulated online environments such as *Second Life*. The chronotope is the activity of the knotting together and untying of a 'narrative' (Bakhtin 1981: 250). It allows us to move analytically within emerging practices of digital communication design and their enactment. Morrison and Thorsnes (2010) extend the chronotope from the original literary written narrative to the conceptual design and actual multimodal expression of a blog and its unfoldings in a creative, performing arts context. They also connect this to recent work on social semiotics into space and time; for example on the *Sims* (Lemke 2005), and has been discussed concerning space-time relations and interfaces influenced by film (e.g. Wood 2007). As a result, a multi-accented, process-driven blog, one that draws together choreography as design with experimental reporting online in the form of creative and research mediation, highlights the need for working through practice with theory to generate reflections on design. Reflections on practice and its analysis are thus themselves cast in a digital communication design mode.

Current views of Activity Theory take up Bakhtin's notion of polyvocality and extend these to the mapping of intersecting activity systems (Wells 1999), in which the object or motivated focus (actor, participant, process, product) is itself part of a synthetic reframing in relation to other systems. This is one of the theoretical and methodological challenges of understanding digital design, as reflected in recent developments in social and network software (*flickr, technorati, MySpace*) and wikis in particular. Here we need to account for the design of digital tools and means for articulation that are in several respects under-determined. They gather and gain their identity and discursive capacities and communicative strength by way of their being articulated collectively (See Morrison et al. Chapter 8). This bottom-up and emergent character means that digital design research is at once contextualized and also in the process of being made. It is this quality of information, and earlier separations between information systems design and the graphic, that is now challenged. The design of dynamic, visual elements, along with kinetic ones in various tangible interfaces, whether in mixed reality installations or on mobile devices, needs to be carried out in tandem with programming. In relation to the spread of 'social media' especially, what we need to heed analytically is how to simultaneously attend to designing for, and researching affordances for, participation, along with means to investigate participants' experience and the dynamic relations of their articulations. To do this is to centre on both the anticipation of involvement and its prefiguring in digital design objects and environments. Participants to such digital discourses may become engaged in the designed and, thereby, further contribute to its refinements and extensions through their own mediated meaning making, by way of co-construction of digital 'compositions' (Morrison 2010a).

Social Semiosis and Digital Design

Social semiotics examines the relations between textual and interpersonal representations and exchanges. In many digital texts and environments different modes of communication and media are intertwined. From a social semiotic point of view, analysts approach such 'texts' – artefact and events – as situated in contexts of culture and historical trajectories of genesis and use. This is to move onwards from the concern of earlier semiotics with structures and systems (van Leeuwen 2005: xi) towards investigations of multimodal constructions and analyses. In terms of digital design, these constructions and analyses are an interplay of finding and communicating resources for mediated meaning making and the active, adaptive and emergent uses of them (Morrison 2010a). While reference, importantly, may still be made to theories and analyses of representation (e.g. Hall 1997) and mediation (e.g. Fornäs 2000), these need to be transposed to the settings and activities of digital designing and its multidisciplinary analysis and practices (Andersen 2001; Bolter 2003; Bolter and Gromala 2003; Julier 2005). This has provenance in fields such as visual digital culture (Darley 2000). Further, it concerns how we continue to conceptualize and analyse matters of textual materiality in 'new media' (e.g. Munster 2006) and how we critically unpack notions of convergence and hybridity, multimediation and intersemiotic complementarity or the mixing and selection of semiotic resources in new communicative ensembles (Couchot 2002; Friedberg 2006; Royce 2007) in relation to an emergent understanding and exploration of digital design.

This emergence may be theorized in terms of sociogenesis: it is developmental and located in cultural historical contexts of articulation. Emergent digital communication accesses historical resources and patternings at the same time as it is part of an emergent ecosocial system (Lemke 1995, 1998). Mediation and the textual, communicative and participative and overall communicative materiality are simultaneously central in digital design's evolution as a field They also impact on the ongoing experimental and innovative unfolding that are typical to designing affordances and multimodal mediated communication.

The construction and analysis of texts, environments and events has been framed in terms of language as social semiotic, principally following the linguistics of Halliday (1985/1994). Kress and van Leeuwen (1996, 2001) have taken this approach beyond logocentric notions of communication to one that is conceptualized as multimodal, that is crossing modes and media. However, this approach often maintains a structuralist search for 'grammar', even when it approaches 'new media' (e.g. Martinec and van Leeuwen 2009). Recently, as part of a social semiotic approach to digital multimodality and the design of multimodal affordances we have taken up challenges to text production and critique by way of exploratory experiments and situated multidisciplinary investigations into digital design and its mediated communication (see Morrison 2010a, b). The concept of multimodality has considerable import for the analysis of digital design research, such as has been applied in visual analysis (van Leeuwen and Jewitt 2001). It provides designers and researchers with a framework from which to extend understanding of mediated meaning making within and across discourse modes as has already been addressed in studies of multiliteracies and learning (e.g. Jewitt 2006). Kress and van Leeuwen see that modes and media are now central to the design and production of digital discourses. They argue that '... meaning is made in many different ways, always, in the many different modes and media which are co-present in a communicational ensemble.' (Kress and van Leeuwen 2001: 111). Such ensembles, however, need considerable investigation concerning the digital, such as in electronic/software art, or in terms of multimodal web texts (see Chapter 7). In analysing digital designs and their fabrication and collaborative uses, social semiotic perspectives need to remember that composition of multimodal discourses is more than a combination of modes. It concerns relations of modes as well as elements within them. Kress and van Leeuwen (2001) argue that the notion and enactment of semiotic resources is central to multimodality. For digital design research it is important to stress that this is a matter of taking into account cultural schema and 'scripts' and their manifestation in digital contexts of mediation.

In terms of analysing digital design processes and products, this also entails reference to developments in emerging and expanding domains of digital expression, articulation and participative performance, such as gaming, social networking and electronic narrative and generative art. Digital design research is beginning to more closely address the ongoing development of such mediated communication, both in its construction and mediated use.

The role of creativity, that is in design and in collaboration that enables it, is important in this emergence (e.g. Shotter 2003). This too has been placed in a developmental and Vygotskian perspective (Moran and John-Steiner 2003) in which collaboration and improvisation are an important part of the shaping and emergence of creativity (Sawyer 2006). This is not to assert the creativity of the gifted designer in a Romantic notion of the artist (Coyne 1999), but acknowledge that creativity is also collectively shaped and articulated in design processes, in the many levels of product design and especially in interaction and experience design. Creativity is also possible via the links between the personal and the collective. Studies of collaboration, creativity and digital design in the humanities are in need of exploration.

The *NarraHand* project into GPS-based collaborative fiction on mobile phones by African immigrants to the capital city of Norway connects collaborative technical and narrative design in a wider communication design framework. In terms of digital design research, what is also studied is the creative co-design that extends to the articulations of the storymakers at the level of multimodal mobile fiction to their own reflections on their artistic, narrative expressions with emerging technologies. GPS-located story entries (written and visual) are linked with entries in an online wiki so that different modes and mediations online make be connected, communicatively and creatively (Morrison 2009). Taken together, in *NarraHand*, creativity may be seen at multiples levels of emerging practice in designing for digitally mediated communication (see Chapter 2). This practice is also positioned within a critical view on emergence and the intersections of designs for communicative use and expressivity, along with reflexive accounts by participants to both the creative (artistic) composition and readers mediated meaning making via comments and personal contributions. This project thus attempts to link personal and collective communication in the design of shared cultural resources via emerging technologies in which attention to meditational affordances and their situated practices of use are seen as part of the design for the potential of shared creative and critical expression. The generating of resources for mediated communication is a design task. Here the technical, cultural, and expressive may be linked in an overall design for communication.

Notions of creativity that originate in and are informed by both psychology and the arts need to be more closely examined. Our critical understandings of design knowledge and of creative practices may also benefit from further study that also does not essentialize creativity. Much knowledge in the practices of designers and their work processes and resulting products needs to be accessed as part of understanding the digital as well as 'mixed reality' (the physical and virtual) in emerging expressions and cultural articulations. Current approaches to social semiotics, claims van Leeuwen (2005), are concerned with finding new ways of generating resources in the production of digital texts and contexts and how they are taken up.

This is not only an issue of designing new information systems or software applications but creating and investigating artistic, mediated and cultural digital design. Research into design and the culture industries that related practice and theory is in need of further attention especially as it is not lodged in the specifics of work practices or the boundedness of formal contexts of learning. Morrison (2010b) argues that in devising digitally mediated communication and its multidisciplinary analysis we may draw on aspects of Activity Theory and Actor Network Theory to conceptualize what may be called 'multimodal assemblages'. Such assemblages are distillations of cultural, technical and communicative resources that await mediated meaning making. This meaning making may also be framed in a wider socio-cultural model of discourse in action (e.g. Norris and Jones 2005). However, this model of discourse in action and its empirical applications have not greatly addressed the challenges and potential of digitally mediated communication, nor the need to focus on design-related issues and processes within it. These are matters we take up in Part 2 of this book and in a related publication that have contributed to the perspectives we present and suggest (Morrison 2010a).

The role of media in digital design research is in need of further emphasis at an analytical level, something few graduate programmes have yet developed greatly. This is a conceptual and analytical challenge for digital design researchers. To strengthen analysis, there is a need to more fully tie into research from new media studies that is not widely included in many international design journals with a focus on information systems design in relation to work or learning, or general design studies research with attention to industrial design or engineering. The role of media, especially visual media and graphic design, have often been relegated to publications on mediated products or housed in practical handbooks developed out of the work of a designer or bureau. Here too rich knowledge may be accessed for selecting, connecting and extending the study of digital tools and applications and their uses in specialist and emerging areas of digital design, such as that of generative morphologies (Sevaldson 2005) and biomometics in Architecture (e.g. Hensel and Menges 2005) and animation in navigation (Eikenes and Morrison 2010). How such developments in emerging areas of digital design impact on design professions and the analysis of designing may also be researched from within a socio-cultural perspective that increasingly needs to engage with the emergence of socio-technical, and aesthetic ecologies of communication (Fuller 2005). These ecologies may be supported by drawing on research into rhetoric and genre that is not merely structuralist; the 'invention' (*inventio*) and analysis of digital genres may also be taken up as a way of understanding the specifically compositional innovations in designing digital texts and environments in a socio-cultural frame.

Rhetoric, Genre, and Digital Design

Chatman (1990: 185) distinguishes between two kinds of rhetoric: prescriptive and descriptive. The goal of the rehabilitators of rhetoric in the twentieth century, following its earlier demise as a persuasive art, has been to make it descriptive rather than prescriptive, from the philosophic ambition of Burke (1969) and the semiotic approach of Barthes (1957/1972) to the critical application in the 'Rhetoric of Inquiry' tradition (Nelson et al. 1987; Simons 1989, 1990). With reference to digital media, in *Heuretics* Ulmer (1994) argues theoretically, and later demonstrates (Ulmer 2003), that the *Inventio* phase of classical rhetoric is particularly relevant to the development of hypermedia communication as it has emerged. Having worked in this domain since the late 1980s, our approach has been to combine these two kinds of rhetorical activities in order to form a synthetic–analytic approach to digital design both in its interpretative and constructive modes (Liestøl 2003). This is in keeping, in part, with the use of rhetoric in the Renaissance as a 'complete and integrated communication system' capable of treating any of the classic Arts, thus also moving from the domain of language as a textual type, spoken or written, to other representational forms: pictures, music and objects/environments in 3D space (sculpture/architecture). This is the approach currently advanced by scholars of digital media, electronic rhetoric (Welch 1999; Ulmer 2003; Morrison 2005; Liestøl 2003, 2006) and related communication design, whose design work ranges from the design and enactment of electronic narrative (Morrison 2003) to the design of the electronic mediation of research as digital designed rhetoric that involves the interactional interplay of different media types, modes of address and spatial articulation in online environments (e.g. Miles 2003).

Faced with the current and expeditiously changing digital communication technologies, providing a complexity of functionality and expressions previously unseen, we may then ask: what are the available means of effective communication in the digital media systems? How are we to find and/or invent them? The method for finding the available resources and applying them for communicational purposes in the digital age is rhetorical in its very essence, despite the fact that it transcends the original verbal dominance. Digital design research has at its disposal an advanced framework for the construction and analysis of digitally mediated texts and their communicative and participative uses. As Chapter 6 shows, rhetoric may be applied as a framework in the 'invention' of digital genres; we show by way of a rhetorical experiment – one that is grounded in computational and communicational development work – how textual analysis may coexist and interact with productive, textual synthesis in a process of research. Within the tradition of the human sciences, rhetoric offers an elaborate means for making sense of these activities. However, as digital designers and digital design researchers, multiple media types and modes of expression and communication present us with both theoretical and methodological challenges at a level of the design of mediation and communication: that is in conceptualizing, constructing and articulating multimodal, multimediational discourse. Here both the unfolding conversation and the context need to be highlighted, again with reference to digital material discursive practices.

The design of digital media – as text, events and environments – is central to the immense output of the culture industries (e.g. Lash and Lury 2007). One of the great challenges in digital media design has been the integration of static and dynamic text types. This has been the case from early CD-ROM design right through to current mobile media (Morrison and Eikenes 2008). Writing and still images as static text types have developed over thousands of years, and the combination of the two is seamless, complex and efficient. Yet, audio and video are dynamic text types and have a much shorter history than the static text types. Within the institutions and traditions of film and television we have also seen intimate and inventive combinations of the dynamic text types. For instance, if one intends to create multi-linear narratives using branching video, as was carried out by Liestøl (1994), it is necessary to link the various video nodes. Linking implies active reference between nodes, out of one video clip into another. Link anchors in the hypertext tradition have basically been restricted to text and graphics (still imagery) that is static text types, and build on the general adaptation of the footnote convention. The literary footnote, the verbal hypertext link and the micon (moving icon) convention, are all drawn upon for *Inventio* of the video footnote (Liestøl 1994). Such an approach is not often taken up in the domain of interaction design centred on the web; the burgeoning presence of video on sites such as *YouTube,* although innovative and widely accessed, in its design and enactment does not include features of video-linking or hypermediated communication. Analytically speaking there is still relatively little study of video as part of a wider expansion of communication design that includes the reflexive deconstruction of motion graphics and 'movement in the interface' itself as part of mediated discourse (see Chapter 2; Skjulstad and Morrison 2005; Skjulstad 2007b).

In his survey of classical rhetoric, Barthes (1988: 65–69) distinguished between three uses of the topics, or sources and places/sites of generating rhetoric (topos). Within a socio-cultural perspective, these topics may be seen as semiotic resources. First, as method the topics make it possible, by means of standardized procedures, to find the substance of discourse even without knowing the subject matter. Second, as a grid the topics provides a network of empty forms. When the speaker passes a given subject over this network, various places are filled, for example, as answers to a set of questions. Third, as a storehouse the topics serve as an assembly of filled forms; they are established commonplaces which can be used by the orator as ready-mades. In a socio-cultural perspective on mediated design and communication, the topics are then reified and stereotyped by common uses of language, establishing truisms and clichés for reuse.

In the context of digital media design, the effort is to find (technical) solutions – conventions or devices – that may help us exploit and indeed create (or invent) the potential functionality of a new medium. Ancient rhetoric works with and within language only but in its more general form the rhetorical techniques and procedures are indeed compatible with the multimodal material of digital media. The object of rhetoric as digital design is primarily the compounds of text types. A relevant approach to conceive of the design potential of digital textuality is the understanding of its form as genre. Genre has always been a fundamental concern of rhetorics. However, genre has also been theorized in terms of socio-cultural contexts of emergence and production where Miller (1984) has framed genre in terms of social action, wherein scripts and schema are realized and moulded via the enactment of situated discourses.

We focus on a genre approach to innovative development in digital environments. This approach includes a double perspective: it is both directed towards *Inventio* of digital genres (often conducted in environments of learning) while at the same time it is concerned with developing a methodology to direct and improve such a process of innovation. How do we locate or position the genre aspect of digital media? Although the modern word genre is French (from Latin gener, genus = kind or class), the related conceptual category for classification of artistic compositions characterized by style, structure or topic is as old as rhetoric's and poetics' (for a critical discussions of genre, see Genette 1992; Devitt et al. 2004).

In recent years, interest in genre has expanded beyond the humanities and traditional subject areas such as literature and film studies (Genette 1997) and academic communication and composition studies (Berkenkotter and Huckin 1995). The notion of genre has also been taken up in the computer science sub-discipline, Information Systems, and so far resulted in promising research (Yates and Orlikowski 2002; Yoshioka et al. 2001). In these projects, the genre perspective is used to analyse, categorize and improve ICT-based communication within organisations. Here too genres evolve and change constantly.

We have seen this with online news sites and services (Boczkowski 2004). Within a certain genre, practical and theoretical knowledge about that specific genre is used to encode and decode, construct and interpret individual genre messages. There is also communication and exchange between genres, and messages may be identified as belonging to several genres at the same time (e.g. Lemke 2005). In this process of continued interplay between genres, there is an ongoing exchange of qualities mediated by the production and consumption of (new) individual messages. This exchange of traits and features is an important requisite for genre innovation. In our context we are not content with reproducing individual messages within existing genres. The problem with digital media is that little attention given to the innovative potential of genre and design (e.g. van Leeuwen 2005). It is here in the interaction that a socio-cultural perspective can contribute to processes of innovation.

In digital design the purpose often is to intentionally research and experiment with the expressive potential of digital means in order to create prototypes capable of becoming future digital genres – that is to conduct genre design (e.g. Askehave and Ellerup Nielsen 2005). Developing genres involves a multitude of knowledge domains relating to technology, theory, subject matter and pedagogy. The formation of such a method must thus include multidisciplinary combinations of both analytical (interpretative) and synthetical (constructive) approaches. This calls for intimate interaction between methodologies of both the human sciences and informatics, including information systems design. Double (or multiple) perspectives are needed that can simultaneously handle approaches of both critical analysis and critical construction. There is also a need for the negotiation of research strategies, concepts, and models. This is one of the analytical challenges facing digital design. References to communication design and concepts and constructs from rhetoric, (including attention to genre theory and construction) offer digital design research considerable means to unpack relations between 'composition' and critique. We return to genre design and the digital in Chapter 6.

Towards Communication Design

In exploring what digital design composition and analysis means for the human sciences, it is necessary to distinguish between communication and interaction. In our view, to focus on designing for communication and inscribing communicative media and mediation in designing allows us to centre on the cultural, social and aesthetic in digital design. This is important because interaction design itself is widely acknowledged as a broad and slippery term (Aarseth 2003; Poppenpohl 2006). Much of the research literature on interaction design is formally lodged in both the practices and theories of Human Computer Interaction. Wider, mediated practices of interaction design, for example, that focus on graphic design, tend not to be taken up very formally in research publications (Crampron-Smith and Tabor 1996; Engholm 2002). Moving on from earlier functionalist origins of HCI, researchers in informatics working with interaction design have indeed concentrated on building knowledge of interaction through studies of use and through user-based design (Ehn and Löwgren 2004; Löwgren and Stolterman 2004; Kolko 2007). Research through design and practice has been advocated as a method for HCI (Zimmerman et al. 2007). Human science related views on the design of digital media have tended to be overshadowed by attention to for example narrative or performance and not the connections at levels of communication between representation, mediation and enactment.

Humanist digital design researchers thus meet versions of HCI that may be rich, but there they do not find the humanities in the analytical foreground, compositionally or analytically. This has implications for what is meant by practice and critique, and for our understanding of use and users in a world that now is not only about ubiquitous computing but also 'social media'. Fallman (2008), for example, argues that interaction design in an HCI view may be usefully approached through a model that has three 'interfaces': with industry, academia and society. These correspond respectively with design practice, design studies and design exploration. He argues that it is the movement between these areas that gives interaction design its dynamic character (Fallman 2008: 10). Through such movement, he claims on the basis of his own work practice, we may begin to develop an emergent 'language' for interaction design that distinguishes it from other interactive systems design (Fallman 2008: 18). This model, however, places aesthetic, artistic and communicative aspects of interaction design in the domain of the explorative. It unnecessarily shears them off from both design practice and design studies.

In contrast, focus on communication design places cultural, social and aesthetic aspects of designing at the centre of digital design where the object of activity is communication. It acknowledges contextual and interpersonal aspects of information systems and HCI views on interaction design rather than setting them up as a 'clash of cultures' (Cloninger 2000; Skjulstad 2007a). In a communication design view, links exist to particular approaches to interaction design where the study of artefacts and contexts of use are central (e.g. Ehn and Löwgren 2004; Linde 2007; Löwgren 2007a, b). When communication is the focus, however, mediation may be culturally and symbolically framed. Its design for use is key to the emergence, exploration and study of practices of digitally enacted communication. This is the case for researchers who analyse text, contexts and uses of the digitally designed and mediated. These enactments are where designers and researchers, and researchers and participants are joined in shared processes and enactments of digitally mediated meaning making. Communication design depends on, and is informed by, such dynamics.

Matters of identity, both of self and community, come to be important where our experience and engagement with the changing materialities of digitally mediated communication cross back over in the physical world of the 'here-and-now'. This is especially the case in the rapid and enormous growth of social networking and multimodal mediation through sites and services such as *MySpace* and *Facebook*. Kirschenbaum (2008: 25) writes that '... new media cannot be studied apart from individual instances of inscription, object, and code as they propagate on, across, and through specific storage devices, operating systems, software environments, and network protocols ...'. The practices and analyses of Communication Design draw on changing notions and approaches to 'interaction design' in HCI that offer new inscriptions of participation but need to recall earlier ones, too (Bødker 2006; Löwgren 2008). They also are taking up emerging and developing understandings of 'new media' that are increasingly participative and generative when it comes to users' mediated practices (e.g Jenkins 2006; see also Chapter 8) in, and as, media, mediated utterances and digital articulations.

These notions of communication design also relate to material discursive practices (see also Chapter 2). The next subsection extends this with a specific focus on gender and the construction and study of material discursive practices and digital design.

Feminist Perspectives

Feminist theorizing is present in the theoretical discourses relevant to digital design. It represents particular voices. This is why we tell stories of how to understand design, designing and digital designing from this perspective of feminist research. We do this by first looking at design projects and women designers from a gender perspective to then take up key concepts for analyzing gender in design.

Voice and Gender

Design takes place in a variety of practices and settings with involvement of designers, users and other stakeholders. Does it make a difference for the design process and the object of design, whether the designers are men or women, how s/he is defined, how s/he is defined in relation to the users and other stakeholders, and where 'use' is situated? As a starting point for looking into this question we take Bratteteig and Verne's (1997) suggestion to see the process of designing as not independent or neutral but subjective, that is, deeply dependent upon the persons involved in the process and upon whose voices are given space or who is heard or has the preferential right of interpretation. Related to this view is the debate about design in use and whether users can be designers.

This question has been explored by Karasti (2003) in a study on digital radiology. Karasti and her co-researchers focused on a particular occupational group, all of them women, called film developers, a term that dates back to the time when the film was developed in dark rooms. Their task was to mount the film on a light panel – 'hanging the films' – for the radiologist's examinations; a task that seemed to be simple and routine but also demanded qualifications that were not obvious. The film developers had to find the most relevant images by reading the patients' records, comparing current images with previous ones, and arranging them in an order that was optimal for the radiologists. Coordinating activities related to the films and patient records were other important tasks – supportive work that took place in the background. As film developers' work had been considered trivial and of no interest and their work was invisible, they were not involved in the project from the start. However, the research team involved the film developers, giving space also to their stories and embodied experiences.

Were they, or did they become, designers? Karasti argues that in the course of the project film developers became designers of their work situation and of how their work supported other professional groups, and that their involvement challenged the existing hierarchies and power relations – medical and technological. She stresses the importance of not only paying attention to the front stage but also to what takes place in the background – to make supportive work visible and to focus on design as a gendered process. She discusses the film developers' situated and embodied knowledge as women's knowledge. Certainly, the occupation was female dominated but the question is if the fact that these women possess the knowledge depends on their gender or is due to what they are doing in their everyday work in radiology.

Pluralistic Understandings of Gender and Digital Design

Another way of analysing gender in design is to look at symbols or gender symbolism. Bratteteig (2002) characterizes artefacts and systems by their functionality and meaning, and their ability to communicate those. She emphasizes that designers want to find ways to communicate the functionality of the artefact to prospective users and do so by means of cultural symbols. These symbols have various meaning in different societies and contexts. That is, cultural and social factors as well as asymmetrical power relations such as gender, ethnicity, class, sexuality, etc., are embedded in norms, values and symbols in a society. While words dominate in IT design, a variety of images, symbols or graphic notations are used in addition. But, as Bratteteig stresses, symbols are also used by designers in order to communicate an artefact's functionality, thus in that way, the meaning of symbols intervene in design of artefacts and IT-systems (Bratteteig 2002).

Gender symbolism is also what Lie (2003) uses in her analysis of design artefacts and computer games. Based on Geertz' (1973) approach to the interpretation of cultures, she argues that neither artefacts nor people have gender (a fe/male nature or fe/male essence) but that both are ascribed gender on a symbolic level. Gender is like 'vehicles of meanings', that is, gender is transported from one artefact to another because the models designers think with are gendered. Lie observes gender symbolism in computer games to be something 'internal' that differs from the gender of the players. Game designers create gendered characters, ascribed with gendered attributes, that is, with signs on their bodies. An example is Lara Croft in *Tomb Raider*, a female figure with both feminine and masculine attributes (http://www.laracroftonline.com). A different genre is represented by games such as the SIMS, where players select to act as a particular person with specific characteristics, and perform everyday activities, such as going to work or furnishing the house. Lie suggests that computer games like the SIMS support and maintain a model of 'gender as an empty shell', which can be filled with desirable attributes and qualities based on personal preferences' (Lie 2003: 277).

Flanagan (2002) takes a similar but also a different standpoint compared with Lie when she explores gender, knowledge, and subjectivity in games and cyberpunk. She underscores how 3-D products such as games are designed within an epistemological model built on objectivity, rationality and universalism: 'Virtual environments are entirely mathematically based constructions that create the sense of a cohesive, seamless, scientific system, and a unified order of knowledge' (Flanagan 2002: 427). Hyperbodies like Lara Croft are virtual subjects/objects designed by humans where gendered norms and values are (re)produced or questioned (Butler 1993, 2004). Flanagan (2002:430) writes about Lara Croft '"She" exists for us as a site of becoming–winning or losing the game, adventuring, controlling, pleasuring, moving, fighting'. Flanagan highlights also how the dominant discourse, 'design from nowhere' (Suchman 2002), replaces multiplicity with omniscience and also how an indiscernible responsibility for the digital design or virtual environment is built in the view from nowhere.

Regardless of the designer's perspective it is not, predictably, how users use digital artefacts/media or how they interact with the characters in a game. Flanagan refers to five subject positions whereby players interact with 3-D action games: the player controls the characters actions and movement, actions are performed irrespective of the player, the player positions herself/himself beside the character, a third person position, and s/he acts through/within the character. The player cannot escape from her/his physical body though s/he chooses one of these ways to interact with the game. Flanagan argues, therefore, for a double consciousness because the performance between the physical body and the virtual body is a 'combination of gender, self and other' (Flanagan 2002: 439). Flanagan emphasizes, though, that we cannot ignore that digital designs are also made up of negative gender performance, limited stories and games, and not all citizens have online access. Simultaneously with this, the online world is opening up for multiple subject positions for male players but also for female players.

In her analysis of the world designed within the game *World of Warcraft*, Corneliussen (2008: 80) confirms Flanagan's arguments that games are possible sites for subject positions other than dominant gender stereotypes. Corneliussen shows that gender is not constructed in a uniform way in the game world but with 'diversity, multitude, and plurality'. Corneliussen concludes: '*World of Warcraft* is not – from a feminist perspective – perfect, but it does point toward a gender-inclusive design, proving game universes to be an interesting playground for challenging cultural perceptions of gender.' (Corneliussen 2008: 82). Flanagan's and Corneliussen's findings are important in order to contest dominant discourses with gender stereo-typical images of female and male players and also about the game design and its characters. Designers also act inside this world howsoever they design virtual worlds and 'They are subjects to, subjects in, and accountable for *this* world.' (Haraway 1997: 97).

Design of technologies has also been interpreted as texts or textualities (Woolgar 1991; Vehviläinen 1997, 2005). A writer's end product is a text. S/he has an intention as well as an aim with the writing, that is, meaning is created by the writing. The text is the mediator between the writer and the reader as well as with time and place. The reader has a more or less obvious understanding of the writer, her/his intention, and how s/he has produced the text. When the end product – a book or an essay – is read, the reader interprets the text from a subject position s/he positions herself/himself in or is placed in; positions which give her/him rights and obligations (Laclau and Mouffe 1985). Translations, situatedness and giving life to the text are practices related to the reading. Designing can be compared with writing, that is, a practice where persons design artefacts and IT systems, exhibitions and services, based on ideas and suggestions, using particular methodologies, modelling and programming languages. Use of these IT systems can then be compared with the reading. Vehviläinen (1997, 2005) focuses on information technology as textuality when she explores both the material and social organisation of construction and use of IT. These 'take place as the socially-organised and materially-based activities and practices of actual and particular people' (Vehviläinen 2005). IT systems and artefacts get their meaning in the design process and in the use of the final products. Gender, identity and subjectivity are constructed and constituted, that is, in the textual orders of the relations and practices or in the interplay between people and systems, a position that has similar arguments as those of Flanagan and Corneliussen.

Designers, Users and Boundary Crossings

Oudshoorn et al. (2004) have studied how designers configure 'the user' in two projects with the aim of designing 'virtual cities for all'. In one of the projects, which used the I-methodology, the designers regarded themselves as representatives of 'all' future users. Hence, the designers' qualifications, competences, ideas and conceptions became the foundations for the design. User tests were conducted but in ways that invited confirmation or legitimation rather than being open to divergent or unexpected views. In the second case, the designer team used a variety of techniques (prototyping, consulting, interviews, surveys) in order to create a more diverse view of future users and their needs. But this was done at a point when it was too late in relation to the stabilization of the prototype. The rather closed methodology as well as the male-dominated design team converged in producing a gender script.

Akrich (1992) uses scripts and inscriptions to explain how designers are inscribing various values or visions in the technology. The inscription builds on designers' definition of the actors' skills, competences, motives and so forth, and also their assumptions of how the society will evolve. Designers' definitions and their inscribing of their visions in technology illustrate exactly the two cases that Oudshoorn et al. (2004) analyse. Related to this is the debate of to what extent users can find their own ways of using a technology; rewriting or modifying the script. Researchers have reported many examples of how technology disciplines people and limits their agency, but other stories are also told (see for example Zuboff 1988). The text message service, SMS in the mobile system GSM, is an example of a service that has been used in many unexpected ways (Prøitz 2005; Mörtberg 2003).

Participatory design (PD) has, in contrast to the I-methodology, always included users and other stakeholders in the design process (see Chapters 1, 2, and 4 for more detailed descriptions of PD). PD was one frame of reference in the research project *From government to e-government: gender, skills, learning and technology*. 11 civil servants in four municipalities in the county of Blekinge, in the south east of Sweden, participated in the project conducted between 2005 and 2007 (see Chapters 4 and 9 for a more detailed description of the project). A range of methods were used in order to involve the civil servants to make visible their qualifications, voices and to design their work situation in transformation of the Swedish public sector with the use of e-services and IT (see also Chapter 4). Digital Story-Telling was one method used in a workshop (see http://www.storycenter.org/memvoice/pages/cookbook.html). The idea was to use mixed media to design a story based on the civil servants' experience in their work practices and if possible, related to technology. The civil servants prepared a story in advance; it was written on paper and audio recorded in the workshop. Further, they browsed images and music on a public website to be included in their narratives. The participants used particular software to record the story, and to integrate the pictures and the music with the audio recorded story. A storyline was about one civil servant's experience of a training course she had been in charge of related to the municipalities' accounting system. She had everything in place and the training room equipped with computers was reserved. The civil servant welcomed the participants, all women. They had received their user names, they logged on, and they had started with the first example (see also Mörtberg and Elovaara 2010). The training was stopped abruptly when two carpenters entered the room and told they were there to reconstruct the room. The training course was cancelled. The participants logged off the computers, collected their things and left the room once they had ascertained that the carpenters had the right information.

Gender was performed in various layers: the woman's lived experience, in her design of the digital story, and also when she presented it for the workshop's participants. The participatory approach helped to make visible how the civil servant and her female colleagues reproduced gendered norms and values when they gave no resistance to the cancellation of the training course. The participatory approach made visible issues such as whose job has a higher value, who has the preferential right to interpret the situation, who is informed and not informed in an organization, and how genders intersect with these. In a follow-up interview, the civil servant said that today she would not have accepted such a thing, that she is now more experienced and self-confident (see also Thoresen 1999; Bjerknes and Bratteteig 1995; Jansson 2007; Jansson et al. 2007, for gender analysis in PD projects).

Technologies for the home are good for studying issues of gender in design. One is the development of the microwave oven – from design, manufacture, marketing, distribution, and service to use – which has been analysed by Cockburn and Ormrod (1993) using ANT. Their study shows how gender and technology were negotiated and performed in ongoing processes; that is, 'the meaning of each has varied over time and in accordance with where the actors stand in the networks' (Ormrod 1994: 57). One storyline is about home economists testing the microwave oven in the test kitchen and designing programmes for cooking and control. Their work was seen as non-technical in contrast to the work of the design engineers responsible for the design of electrical and electronic components. Two discourses – 'a discourse of equality and a more traditional gender dichotomy' (Ormrod 1994: 50) – competed in representing 'reality'. Based on home economics and technology, domestic science casts light on discipline boundaries as well as transgressions of these boundaries. Even if some actors admitted and understood the need for transgressions, the actor-network was dominated by the technical discourse. Cockburn and Ormrod also looked into how 'the user' was configured, with women responsible for activities related to food and cooking, men as buyers of, or payers for, microwave ovens as well as experimenters.

These are familiar stories by now, one would believe, but the canonized versions of social construction of technology and ANT do not problematize gender and, often, the ways in which the stabilization of actor-networks are described make gender, as well as other asymmetrical power relations, invisible (Cockburn 1992; Wajcman 2000). Star explores how those who do not fit the 'standards' find themselves located at the margins or in the centre of different social worlds (networks) (see also Mörtberg 2003). Star emphasizes that power is 'about whose metaphor brings the worlds together, and holds them there' (Star 1991: 52). She shows how the borders of personal belonging or not belonging to a particular category or community may be put into question by one's gender, race, ethnicity. Boundary crossings are often experienced as what Star describes as a 'high tension zone between dichotomies'; the negotiation of identities, within and across groups, domains, and disciplines is an extraordinarily complex and delicate task.

Material Discursive Practices: A Different Epistemology

Feminist researchers have argued for a different epistemological approach, one which is more apt at dealing with multiplicity, multiple personalities, and marginality. Although much of this work has a critique of the dominant ways of practising science as its starting point, it can also be used to think of alternative ways of practising design. Wagner (1994) has argued for epistemological pluralism and polyvalence – to develop a working culture which supports the participation of different communities and partial translations between their 'situated' knowledges. This requires:

Self-reflection – thinking about one's individual and professional one-sidedness ("Befangenheit"), including the implicit cultural norms inherent in the practice of science and technology (notions of efficiency, internalized hierarchies of knowledge, practices of coding reality, images of work, communication, social relations, and nature); intersubjective communication with others that exposes different ways of being concerned, contradictory interpretations and interests; getting involved in a wider political discourse which looks beyond the perspective e.g. of a specific scientific community, or a specific group of affected people or organization, or a selected aspect of the environment'. (Wagner 1994: 262–63)

A different epistemological and ontological approach is Barad's (2007) agential realism. One of her starting points is Butler's (1990: 112) notion of performativity and how gender is 'a kind of becoming or activity'; a becoming that takes place through repeated activities or iterative actions. Butler underlines that 'if gender is performative, then it follows that the reality of gender is itself produced as an effect of the performance' (Butler 2004: 218). The subject, but also the materiality of the body, is produced in the performance. Barad takes a step further than Butler (and also Foucault) in her view of performativity by focusing on both discursive and material practices, arguing that not only 'the surface or contours of the body but also of the body in the fullness of its physicality, including the very 'atoms' of its being' (Barad 2003: 823) has to be taken into account. This is an interesting position when it comes to digital design, where the body is often treated as 'external' to articulating and performing a design.

In Barad's agential realism 'reality is sedimented out of the process of making the world intelligible through certain practices and not others' (Barad 1999: 7). Taking up Bohr's epistemological framework as a source of inspiration that emphasizes a non dualistic whole where the observer and the observed object are inseparable, Barad argues that subjects and objects are not pre-given, but constituted in performances, thus, in a world of becoming. The becoming takes place in intra-actions where apparatuses encounter, or are entangled until a cut is created. Hence the cut creates the specific moment where subject and objects emerge or are constituted (Barad 2007; Suchman 2007). A genealogical analysis is a way to identify the included and excluded apparatuses after a cut has been performed.

We can see that the re-configurations of the world, for example in design, in what is made to 'exist' and which realities are sedimented out, is dependent on the apparatuses included in the intra-action of the material and the discursive. Apparatuses consist of an integrated group of materials or devices, but Barad does not limit the boundary to instruments or machines but also includes techniques, the gendered division of labour, global and local conditions that make an experiment possible; thus expands a range of practices to get the instrument to work or a material-discursive practice to work (Barad 2007). Many different apparatuses or assemblages can be identified in stories of design – playful methods, provocation, cultural and technology probes, prototyping, games, theatre, scenarios, specifications, designers, design models, operating systems, programming languages, computers, protocols, managers, time, money, workplace culture, division of labour, gender, and so on.

The relationship between humans and machines has been explored in various communities, with the use of various perspectives. Although humans and nonhumans are underscored as actors in interaction, for example in ANT, the actors pre-exist the enrolment – that is, they meet as separate entities in the network, where they do things together. In intra-action, on the other hand, the subjects and the objects emerge in the enactment – that is, they are constituted in material-discursive practices (Barad 2003, 2007; Suchman 2007). The agential realism approach makes it possible to explore understandings of knowing and doing, but also how boundaries are in the making in design practices or research of design practices. Hence Barad invites us to discuss design as performances of material-discursive practices where specific apparatus are involved or excluded in boundary-making practices (see also Mörtberg and Elovaara 2010; Sefyrin 2010).

Particular choices of apparatuses or assemblages are involved in every practice. In participatory design projects the apparatuses reach from technical specifications, models, methods and techniques to, for example, first-hand experiences (Bødker et al. 2004), notions of use (Bratteteig 2004), a particular division of labour, demo-cratic principles (Bjerknes and Bratteteig 1995); hence they introduce multiple and various logics into a project (Gregory et al. 2005). In contrast, a design project may entirely build on the designer's own assumptions of presumptive uses, expectations and needs. The enactments of these two practices differ in terms of what is excluded and included, the boundaries drawn between experts and non-experts, but also the final product. The inclusion of gender issues is not something that can be taken for granted, neither in participatory design nor in projects that use the I-methodology. Nevertheless, gender is performed in the reconfigurations of the work practices, in the design or the application domain, and it may take various forms.

The design practices discussed in this section are examples of material-discur-sive practices where designers, users, gender, knowledge, understandings, and imaginations are constituted in the reconfigurings of the practices (worlds). Due to the apparatuses at work in the specific cases, different realities are material-ized or emerging. The performances or practices/doing/actions depend on the chosen apparatuses, that is, what is included or excluded in the enactments or in the intra-actions (see also Chapters 4, 5 and 9).

Closing Comments

Digital design continues to extend into technology-related aspects of our learning, work, organizations, leisure and commerce. As it becomes more widely embedded in, and consitutive of, our political, communicative and cultural production, it is important that we distinguish between what, where and how our understandings of the roles, potentials and constraints of the digital in design are framed analytically. This matters as we continue to meet emerging technologies and their combinations. It also matters how we engage with them analytically in designing and research. This is a most important distinction where focus on the next gizmo or the latest slider is not necessarily linked with the situated, communicative and cultural uses of digital design. At an analytical level, we believe that this is all the more important in terms of research where what conceivably may be published under the rubric 'digital design' does not sit within one discipline or practice. This immediately raises for us a key issue that distinguishes digital design research from previous research into design that was very much concerned with establishing design as a science (Simon 1969) and also design as a discipline (Cross 2006). Identifying analytical frameworks and perspectives from which to explore digital design – that is *in, as, and through designing* – demands a fair degree of multidisciplinary configuring.

Design research now includes the digtal in many incarnations, ranging, for example, from ubiquitous and pervasive computing (e.g. Bell and Dourish 2006) to exhibition design and public spaces (e.g. Dernie 2006; Skolnick et al. 2007). A general design literature still prevails, not all of its explicitly engaged with the digital. Exploring digital design analytically requires a considerable degree of negotiation of this general literature, its legacies and its ongoing application in researching the digital. Our research distinguishes itself from that which is cognitivist and positivist. We place digital designing and researching firmly within socio-cultural and socio-technical approaches that are motivated by situating human action and interpretation in regard to culture, communiction and context.

In parallel to such publications, there is now an immense body of media material – across magazines, manuals, blogs and even *YouTube*. This provides invaluable information about developments in digital design and especially technical and cultural uses. Designer-researchers refer to this literature as part of keeping apace with the rapid changes in digital technologies and media (Stolterman 2008). Many designers also contribute to such 'sites' of knowledge and circulation. For digital design researchers, however rich as such sources of knowledge may be, it is necessary to incorporate formal frameworks and methods in their refereed research publications. This requires shifting between different design and digital design practices, discourses and their sites and processes of mediation and exchange. These also include methods, the theme of the next chapter.

References

Aarseth, E. (2003). We all want to change the world: The ideology of innovation in digital media'. In G. Liestøl, A. Morrison & T. Rasmusen (Eds.), *Digital media revisited: Theoretical and conceptual innovation in digital domains* (pp. 418–425). Cambridge, MA: MIT Press.

Akrich, M. (1992). The de-scription of technical objects. In W.E. Bijker & J. Law (Eds.), *Shaping technology/building society: Studies in sociotechnical change* (pp. 205–224). Cambridge, MA: MIT Press.

Andersen, P. (2001). What semiotics can and cannot do for HCI. *Knowledge-Based Systems*, 14(8), 419–424.

Arnall, T. & Martinussen, E. (2010). 'Depth of field: discursive design research through film.' Special Issue on *Research by Design. FORM Akademisk*

Arnall, T., & Morrison, A. (in progress). Revealing the invisible. Available: http://www.nearfield.org/

Askehave, I., & Ellerup Nielsen, A. (2005). What are the characteristics of digital genres? Genre theory from a multi-modal perspective. In *the Proceedings of the 38th annual Hawaii international conference on system sciences (HICSS'05)* (pp. 98.1). Washington, DC, USA IEEE Computer Society. Available: http://csdl2.computer.org/comp/proceedings/hicss/2005/2268/04/22680098a.pdf

Bærentsen, K., & Trettvik, J. (2002). An activity theory approach to affordance. In O. W. Bertelsen (Ed.), *Proceedings of the second Nordic conference on human-computer interaction (NordiCHI '02)*, Aarhus, Denmark (pp. 51–60) New York: ACM press.

Bakhtin, M. (1981). *The dialogic imagination: Four essays by M.M Bakhtin*. In M. Holquist (Ed.), Emerson, C. & Holquist, M. (transl.). University of Texas Press: Austin.

Bakhtin, M. (1984). *Problems of Dostoevsky's poetics*. [C. Emerson, C. (Ed. & transl.).]. University of Minnestota Press: Minneapolis.

Bakhtin, M. (1986). *Speech genres and other late essays*. [C. Emerson & Holquist, M. (Eds.) V. McGee (Transl.)]. University of Texas Press: Austin.

Bannon, L., & Schmidt K. (1992). Taking CSCW seriously. Supporting articulation work. *Computer Supported Cooperative Work*, 1(2), 7–40.

Barad, K. (1999). Agential realism: Feminist interventions in understanding scientific pratices. In M. Biagiolo (Ed.), *The science studies reader* (pp. 1–11). New York and London: Routledge.

Barad, K. (2003). Posthumanist performativity. Toward an understanding of how matter comes to matter. *Signs: Journal of Women in Culture and Society*, 28(2), 801–831.

Barad, K. (2007). *Meeting the universe halfway: Quantum physics and the entanglement of matter and meaning*. Durhamn & London: Duke University Press.

Barthes, R. (1957/1973). *Mythologies*. [New ed.] London: Paladin.

Barthes, R. (1988) The old rhetoric: An aidé-mémoire. [translated by Richard Howard]. In *The semiotic challenge* (pp. 11–94). Oxford: Basil Blackwell.

Bazerman, C. 1997. Discursively structured activities. *Mind Culture & Activity*, 4(4), 296–308.

Bell, G., & Dourish, P. 2006. Yesterday's tomorrows: notes on ubiquitous computing's dominant vision. *Pers Ubiquit Comput*, 11 (2), 133–143.

Bellotti, V. & Rogers, Y. (1997). From web press to web pressure: multimedia representations and multimedia publishing. In S. Pemberton (Ed.), *Proceedings of the SIGCHI conference on human factors in computing systems (CHI '97)*, Atlanta, GA USA (pp. 279–286). New York: ACM press.

Berg, M. (1999). Accumulating and coordinating: occasions for information technologies in medical work. *Computer Supported Cooperative Work*, 8(4), 373–401.

Berkenkotter, C., & Huckin, T. (1995). *Genre knowledge in disciplinary communication.* Northvale: Lawrence Erlbaum Associates.

Bertelsen O. (2006). Tertiary artefactness at the interface. In Fishwick, P. A. (Ed.), *Aesthetic computing* (pp. 357–368). Cambridge, MA: The MIT Press.

Bertelsen, O., & Pold, S. (2004). Criticism as an approach to interface aesthetics. In R. Raisamo (Ed.), *Proceedings of the third Nordic conference on human-computer interaction (NordiCHI '04)*, Tampere, Finland (pp. 23–32). New York: ACM press.

Bjerknes, G., & Bratteteig, T. (1995). User participation and democracy: a discussion of Scandinavian research on system development. *Scandinavian Journal of Information Systems*, 7(1), 73–98.

Boczkowski, P. J. (2004). *Digitizing the news: Innovation in online newspapers.* Cambridge, MA: The MIT Press.

Bogost, I. (2007). *Persuasive games: The expressive power of videogames.* Cambridge, MA: MIT Press

Bolter, J. (2003). Theory and practice in New Media Studies. In G. Liestøl, A. Morrison, & T. Rasmussen (Eds.), *Digital media revisited: Theoretical and conceptual innovation in digital domains* (pp. 15–33). Cambridge, MA: The MIT Press.

Bolter, J., & Gromala, D. (2003). *Windows and mirrors: Interaction design, digital art, and the myth of transparency.* Cambridge, The MIT Press.

Boujut, J-F., & Blanco E. (2003) Intermediary objects as a means to foster co-operation in engineering design. *Computer Supported Cooperative Work*, 12(2), 205–219.

Bowker, G., & Star, S. L. (1999). *Sorting things out: Classification and its consequences.* Cambridge, MA: The MIT Press.

Bratteteig, T. (2002). Bringing Gender Issues to Technology Design. In Floyd, C., Kelkar, G., Kramarae, C., Limpangog, C. & Klein-Franke, S. (Eds.), *Feminist challenges in the information age.* International Womens' University 2000. Oplade: Leske and Budrich. 91–105.

Bratteteig, T. (2004). *Making change. Dealing with relations between design and use.* Diss. Oslo: Department of Informatics, Faculty of Mathematics and Natural Sciences, University of Oslo.

Bratteteig, T., & Verne, G. (1997). Feminist or merely critical? In search of a Gender Perspective in Informatics'. In I. Moser & G Aas (Eds.), *Technology and democracy: comparative perspectives, workshop on gender, technology and politics in transition?* (pp. 59–74), 17–19 January, Oslo: TMV.

Burke, K. (1969). *The rhetoric of motives.* Berkeley: University of California Press.

Burn, A., & Durran, J. (2006). Digital anatomies: Analysis as production in media education. In D. Buckingham & R. Willett (Eds.), *Digital generations: Children, young people, and new media* (pp. 273–293). London: Lawrence Erlbaum.

Butler, J. (1990). *Gender trouble: Feminism and the subversion of identity.* New York, London: Routledge.

Butler, J. (1993). *Bodies that matter: On the discursive limits of "sex".* New York: Routledge.

Butler, J. (2004). *Undoing gender.* New York: Routledge.

Bødker, S. (2006). When second wave HCI meets third wave challenges. Keynote address. *NordiCHI '06.* 14–18 October. Oslo.

Bødker, K., Kensing, F., & Simonsen, J. (2004). *Participatory IT design. Designing for business and workplace Realities.* Cambridge, MA: The MIT Press.

Bødker, S., & Andersen, P. (2005). Complex mediations. *Human Computer Interaction*, 20(4), 353–402.

Callon, M. (1986). Some elements of a sociology of translation: domestication of the scallops and the fishermen of St. Brieuc Bay. In J. Law (Ed.), *Power, Action and Belief: A New Sociology of Knowledge* (pp. 196–233). London: Routledge & Kegan Paul.

Callon, M. (1991). Techno-economicnNetworks and irreversibility. In J. Law (Ed.), *A Sociology of Monsters? Essays on power, technology and domination, Sociological Review Monograph* (pp. 132–161). London: Routledge.

Chatman, S. (1990). *Coming to terms: The rhetoric of narrative in fiction and film.* Ithaca: Cornell University Press.

Clausen, C., & Yoshinaka, Y. (2007). Staging socio-technical spaces: translating across boundaries in design. *Journal of Design Research*, 6(1–2), 61–78.

Cloninger, C. (2000). Usability experts are from Mars, graphic designers are from Venus. Available: http://www.alistapart.com/articles/marsvenus/

Cockburn, C. (1992). The circuit of technology. Gender, identity and power. In R. Silverstone & E. Hirsch (Eds.), *Consuming technologies* (pp. 32–47). London: Routledge.

Cockburn, C., & Ormrod, S. (1993). *Gender and technology in the making*. Newbury Park, Ca and London: Sage.

Cohen, K. (2005). What does the photoblog want? *Media, Culture & Society*, 27(6), 883–901.

Cole, M. (1998). *Cultural psychology: A once and future discipline*. Cambridge: The Belknap Press of Harvard University Press.

Corneliussen, H. G. (2008). World of warcraft as a playground for feminism. In H. G. Corneliussen & J. Walker Rettberg (Eds.), *Digital culture, play, and identity: A world of warcraft® reader* (pp. 63-86). Cambridge: The MIT Press.

Couchot, E. (2002). Digital hybridisation: a technique, an aesthetic. *Convergence*, 8(19), 19–28.

Coyne, R. (1999). *Technoromanticism: Digital narrative, holism, and the romance of the real*. Cambridge, MA: The MIT Press.

Crabtree, A., Rodden, T., & Benford S. (2005). Moving with the times: IT research and the boundaries of CSCW. *Computer Supported Cooperative Work*, 14(3), 217–251.

Crampron-Smith, J., & Tabor, P. (1996). The role of the artist-designer. In Winograd, T. (Ed.), *Bringing Design to Software* (pp. 37–57). New York: ACM Press/Addison-Wesley Press.

Crilly, N., Good, D. Matravers, D., & Clarkson, P. (2008). Design as communication: exploring the validity and utility of relating intention to interpretation. *Design Issues*, 29(5), 425–457.

Crilly, N., Maier, A., & Clarkson, P. (2008). Representing artefacts as media: modelling the relationship between designer intent and consumer experience. *International Journal of Design*, 2(3), 15–27.

Cross, N. (2006). *Designerly ways of knowing*. London: Springer.

Darley. A. (2000). *Visual digital culture: Surface play and spectacle in new media genres*. London: Routledge.

Deleuze, G., & Guattari , F. (1989). *A thousand plateaus*. London: Athleone Press.

Dernie, D. (2006). *Exhibition design*. New York: W.W. Norton & Co.

de Souza, C. (2005). *The semiotic engineering of human computer interaction*. Cambridge, MA: The MIT Press.

Devitt, A., Reiff, M., & Bawwarshi, A. (2004). *Scenes of writing: Strategies for composing with genres*. Longman: New York.

Diaz-Kommonen, L. (2003). Expressive artifacts and artifacts of expression. *Working Papers in Arts and Design*. Vol. 3. Available at: http://www.herts.ac.uk/artdes1/research/papers/wpades/vol3/ldkfull.html.

Ehn, P., & Löwgren, J. (2004). (Eds.), *Design [X] research. Essays on interaction design as knowledge construction*. School of Arts and Communication. Malmö: Malmö University.

Eikenes, J.O. (2009). Social navimation: engaging interfaces in social media. In *Proceedings of third Nordic design research conference* (NORDES). Oslo School of Architecture and Design (AHO), Oslo, 31 August-2 September. At: www.nordes.org

Eikenes, J.O., & Morrison, A. (2010). *Navimation*: exploring time, space & motion in the design of screen-based interfaces. *International Journal of Design*. 4(1). Available: http://www.ijdesign.org/ojs/index.php/IJDesign/article/view/622/284

Engeström, Y. (1987). *Learning by expanding: An activity-theoretical approach to developmental research*. Helsinki: Orienta-konsultit.

Engeström, Y. (2007). Enriching the theory of expansive learning: lessons from journeys toward coconfiguration. *Mind, Culture & Activity*, 14(1–2), 23–39.

Engholm. I. (2002). Digital style history: The development of graphic design on the Internet. *Digital Creativity*, 13(4), 193–211.

Fallman, D. (2008). The interaction design research triangle of design practice, design studies, and design exploration. *Design Issues*, 24(3), 4–18

Fishwick, P. (2006). (Ed.), *Aesthetic computing*. Cambridge, MA: The MIT Press.
Fitzpatrick, G. (2004). Integrated care and the working record. *Health Informatics Journal,* 10(4), 291–302.
Flanagan, M. (2002). Hyperbodies, hyperknowledge: Women in games, women in cyberpunk, and strategies of resistance (criticism). In M. Flanagan & A. Booth (Eds.), *Reload: Rethinking women and cyberculture* (pp. 425–454). Cambridge: The MIT Press.
Fornäs, J. (2000). The crucial in between: the centrality of mediation in cultural studies. *European Journal of Cultural Studies*, 3(1), 45–65.
Frayling, C. (1993). *Research in art and design*. Royal College of Art, Research Papers. 1, 1. 4, pp.
Friedberg, A. (2006). *The virtual window: From Alberti to Microsoft*. Cambridge, MA: The MIT Press.
Fuller, M. (2005). *Media ecologies: Materialist energies in art and technoculture*. Cambridge: The MIT Press.
Gad, C., & Bruun Jensen, C. (2005). *On the consequences of post-ANT*. Centre for STS Studies, Department of Information and Media Studies. Århus: University of Århus.
Gaver, B. (2002). Provocative awareness. *Computer Supported Cooperative Work,* 11(3/4), 475–493.
Geertz, Cl. (1973). *The interpretation of cultures*. New York: Basic Books.
Genette, G. (1992). *The architext: An Introduction*. [Transl. Jane E. Lewin]. Berkely: University of California Press.
Genette, G. (1997). *Paratexts: Thresholds of interpretation*. [Transl. Jane E. Lewin]. New York: Cambridge University Press.
Gerson, E., Elihu, M. and Star, S.L. (1986). Analyzing due process in the workplace. *ACM Transactions on Office Information Systems,* 4(3), 257–270.
Gibson, J. (1966). *The Senses Considered as Perceptual Systems*. Boston: Houghton Mifflin.
Grinter, R. (2000). Workflow systems: Occasions for success and failure. *Computer Supported Cooperative Work,* 9(2), 189–214.
Gregory, J., Hyysalo, S., & Kangasoja, J. (2005). Imaginaries at work: conceptualizing technology design beyond individual projects. Working Paper, January 2006. Originally presented at *4S Annual Meeting, Society for Social Studies of Science, Technology & Medicine*, Atlanta, GA, 16–18 October, 2003.
Grillner, K., & Ståhl, L-H. (2003). Developing practice-based research in architecture and design. *Nordisk Arkitekturforskning* (Nordic Journal of Architectural Design). No, 1, 15–22.
Hakkarainen, K., Palonen, T., Paavola, S., & Letninen, E. (2004). *Communities of networked expertise: Professional and educational perspectives*. Amsterdam: Elsevier.
Hall, S. (Ed.). (1997). *Representation: Cultural representations and signifying practices*. London: The Open University Press.
Halliday, M. (1985/1994). *Functional grammar*. 2nd edition. London: Edward Arnold.
Haraway, D. J. (1997). *Modest_witness@second_millenium. Female man©_meets_ oncomouse™: Feminism and technoscience*. New York and London: Routledge.
Hayles, C. (2002). Print is flat, code is deep: the importance of media specific analysis. *Poetics Today*, 25(1), 67–90.
Heath, C., & Luff, P. (1992). Collaboration and control: crisis management and multimedia technology in London underground line control rooms. *Computer Supported Cooperative Work*, 1(1–2), 69–94.
Hetherington, K., & Law, J (2000). After Networks. *Society and Space*, 18 (3), 127–132.
Henderson, K. (1999). *On line and on paper. Visual representations, visual culture, and computer graphics in design engineering*. Cambridge, MA: The MIT Press.
Hensel, M., & Menges, A. (2005). Morpho-ecologies: Towards and inclusive discourse on heterogeneous architecture. In M. Hensel & A. Menges (Eds.), *Morpho-Ecologies* (pp. 16–60). London: Architectural Association.
Hughes, J., Randall, D., & Shapiro, D. (1992). Faltering from ethnography to design. In M. Mantel & R. Baecker (Eds.), *Proceedings of the 1992 ACM conference on computer-supported cooperative work (CSCW '92)*, Toronto, Ontario, Canada (pp. 115–122). New York: ACM press.

Jacucci, G., Oulasvirta, A., Ilmonen, T., Evans, J., and Salovaara, A. (2007). Comedia: mobile group media for active spectatorship, *Proceedings of the SIGCHI Conference on Human Factors in Computing Systems (CHI '07)*, San Jose, California, USA (pp. 1273–1282). New York: ACM Press.

Jacucci, G. & Wagner, I. (2007). Performative roles of materiality for collective creativity. *Proceedings of the 6th ACM SIGCHI Conference on Creativity & Cognition (C&C '07)*, Washington, DC, USA (pp. 73–82). New York: ACM Press.

Jacucci, G., Peltonen, P., Morrison, A., Salovaara, A., Kurvinen, E. & Oulasvirta, A. (2009). Ubiquitous Media for Collocated Interaction. In K.S.Willis, G. Roussos, K. Chorianopoulos & Struppek, M. (Eds.): Shared Encounters. New York: Springer, 23–45.

Jacob, R., Girouard, A., Hirshfield, L., Horn, M., Shaer, O., Solovey, E., & Zigelbaum, J. (2008). Reality-based interaction: a framework for post-WIMP interfaces. In M. Czerwinski, A. Lund & D. Tan (Eds.), *Proceeding of the twenty-sixth annual SIGCHI conference on human factors in computing systems (CHI '08)*. Florence, Italy (pp. 201–210). New York: ACM press.

Jansson, M. (2007). *Participation, knowledges and experiences: Design of IT-systems in e-home health care*. Diss. Luleå: Luleå University of Technology.

Jansson, M., Mörtberg, C., & Berg, E. (2007). Old dreams, new means- An exploration of visions and situated knowledge in information technology. *Gender, Work and Organization*, 14(4), 371–387.

Jenkins, H. (2006). *Convergence culture: Where old and new media collide*. New York: New York University Press.

Jewitt, C. (2006). *Technology, literacy and learning: A multimodal approach*. London: Routledge.

Johanssen, S. (2009). 'Sniff: designing characterful interaction in a tangible toy'. In P. Paolini & F. Gartotto (Eds.), *Proceedings of the 8th international conference on interaction design and children (IDC '09)*, Como, Italy (pp. 186–189) New York: ACM press.

Julier, G. (2005). From visual culture to design culture. *Design Issues*, 22(1), 64–76.

Kaptelinin, V., & Nardi, B. (2006). *Acting with technology. Activity, theory and interaction Design*. Cambridge: The MIT Press.

Karasti, H. (2003). Can film developers be(come) technology developers? Reflections on gendered expertise and participation in system design. In C. Mörtberg, P. Elovaara & A. Lundgren (Eds.), *How do we make a difference: Information technology, transnational democracy and gender* (pp 1–24). Luleå: Printing Office Luleå University of Technology.

Kirschenbaum, M. (2008). *Mechanisms: New media and the forensic imagination*. Cambridge: The MIT Press.

Knutsen, J., & Morrison, A (2010). Have you heard this? Designing mobile social software for discovery of independent music. Commissioned for Special Issue on Practice Based Research. *Form Akademisk*.

Kress, G., & van Leeuwen, T. (1996). *Reading images*. London: Routledge.

Kress, G., & van Leeuwen, T. (2001). *Multimodal discourse*. London: Arnold.

Krippendorff, K. (2006). *The semantic turn*, Boca Raton, FA: CRC Press, Taylor & Francis Group.

Kolko, J. (2007). *Thoughts on interaction design*. Brown Bear: Savannah.

Kuutti, K. (1995). Activity theory as a potential framework for human computer interaction research. In B. Nardi (Ed.), *Context and consciousness: Activity theory and human Computer Interaction* (pp. 17–44). Cambridge, MA: The MIT Press.

Laclau, E., & Mouffe, C. (1985). *Hegemony and socialist strategy*. London: Verso.

Lash, S., & Lury, C. (2007). *Global culture industry. The mediation of things*. Cambridge: Polity Press.

Latour, B. (1987). *Science in action: How to follow scientists and engineers through society*. Cambridge, MA: Harvard University Press.

Latour, B. (1996). On interobjectivity. *Mind, Culture & Activity*, 3(4), 228–245 & 246–269.

Latour, B. (1999). *Pandora's hope: Essays on the reality of science studies*. Cambridge: Harvard University Press.

Latour, B. (2005). *Reassembling the social: An introduction to actor-network-theory*. Oxford: Oxford University Press.

Law, J., & Mol, A. (2002). (Eds.), *Complexities: Social studies of knowledge practices.* Durham: Duke University Press.

Law. J., & Singleton, V. (2000). This is not an object. Centre for Science Studies, Lancaster University: Lancaster. Available: at http://www.comp.lancs.ac.uk/sociology/papers/Law-Singleton-This-is-Not-an-Object.pdf

Law, J., & Singleton, V. (2003). Allegory and its others. In D. Nicolini, S. Gherardi & D. Yanow (Eds.), *Knowing in organizations: A practice-based approach* (pp.225–254). Armonk, N.Y.: M.E. Sharpe.

Lee, C. (2007). Boundary negotiating artifacts: unbinding the routine of boundary objects and embracing chaos in collaborative work. *Computer Supported Cooperative Work*, 16(3), 307–339.

Lemke, J. (1995). *Textual politics: Discourse and social dynamics.* London: Taylor & Francis.

Lemke, J. (1998). Metamedia literacy: Transforming meanings and media. In D. Reinking, M. McKenna, L. Labbo & R. Kieffer (Eds.), *Handbook of literacy and technology: Transformations in a post-typographic world* (pp. 283–301). Mahwah: Lawrence Erlbaum.

Lemke, J. (2005). Place, pace, and meaning: Multimedia chronotopes. In S. Norris & R. Jones. (Eds.), *Discourse in action: Introducing mediated discourse analysis* (pp. 110–112). London: Routledge.

Leont'ev, A. (1978). *Activity, consciousness, and personality.* Englewood Cliffs: Prentice Hall.

Leont'ev, A. (1981). *Problems of the development of the mind.* Moscow: Progress Publishers.

Licoppe, C., & Inada, Y. (2005). 'Seeing' one another onscreen and the construction of social order in a mobile-based augmented public space. The uses of geo-localized mobile game in Japan. In *Proceedings of the 2005 learning in the mobile age conference*, Hungarian Academy of Sciences, April 28–30. Available: http://www.socialscience.t-mobile.hu/2005/index.htm#pr

Lie, M (2003). The new amazons. Gender symbolism on the Net. In M. Lie et al. (Eds.), *He, she and IT revisited new perspectives on gender in the information society.* (pp. 251–277, 300–303). Oslo: Gyldendal.

Liestøl, G. (1994). Aesthetic and rhetorical aspects of linking video in hypermedia. In I. Ritchie & N. Guimarães (Eds.), *Proceedings of the 1994 ACM European conference on hypermedia technology (ECHT '94)*, Edinburgh, Scotland (pp. 217–223). New York: ACM press.

Liestøl, G. (1999). *Essays in rhetorics of hypermedia design.* Diss. Oslo: Department of Media & Communication, Faculty of Humanities, University of Oslo.

Liestøl, G. (2003). 'Gameplay' – from synthesis to analysis (and vice versa). Topics of construction and interpretation in digital media. In G. Liestøl, A. Morrison & T. Rasmussen (Eds.), *Digital media revisited: Theoretical and conceptual innovations in digital domains* (pp. 389–413). Cambridge, MA: The MIT Press.

Liestøl, G. (2006). Conducting genre convergence for learning. *International Journal of Continued Engeneering Education and Lifelong Learning,* 16(3–4), 255–270.

Linde, P. (2007). *Metamorphing - The transformative power of digital media and tangible interaction.* Diss. Karlskrona: Blekinge Institute of Technology.

Löwgren, J. (2002). How far beyond human-computer interaction is interaction design? *Digital Creativity*, 13(3), 186–189.

Löwgren, J. (2007a). Fluency as an experiential quality in augmented spaces. *International Journal of Design*, 1(3), 1–10. Available: www.ijdesign.org

Löwgren, J. (2007b). Pliability as an experiential quality: Exploring the aesthetics of interaction design. *Artifact*, 1(2), 85–95.

Löwgren, J. (2008). Interaction design considered as a craft. In T. Erickson & D. McDonald (Eds.), *HCI remixed: Reflections on works that have influenced the HCI community* (pp. 199–203). Cambridge, MA: The MIT Press.

Löwgren, J., & Stolterman, E. (2004). *Thoughtful interaction design: A design perspective on information technology.* Cambridge, MA: The MIT Press.

Lozano-Hemmer, R. (2001). *Body movies.* Austria: Ars Electronica. Linz.

Ludvigsen S., & Mørch A. (2005). Situating collaborative learning: educational technology in the wild. *Educational Technology*, 45(5), 39–43.

Manovich, L. (2003). The poetics of augmented space. In A. Everett & J. Caldwell (Eds.), *New media: Theories and practices of digital textuality* (pp. 75–92). New York: Routledge.

Maquil, V., Psik, T., Wagner, I., & Wagner, M. (2007). Expressive Interactions Supporting Collaboration in Urban Design. In T. Gross & K. Inkpen (Eds.), *Proceedings of the 2007 international ACM conference on supporting group work (Group 2007)*, Sanibel Island, Forida, USA (pp. 69–78). New York, NY, USA: ACM.

Marshall, T., & Newton, S. (2000). Scholarly design as a paradigm for practice-based research. *Working Papers in Art and Design*. 1. Available: http://www.herts.ac.uk/artdes/research/papers/wpades/vol1/marshall2.html

Martinec, R., & van Leeuwen, T. (2009). *The language of new media design: Theory and practice*. London: Routledge.

McCarthy, J., & Wright, P. (2004). *Technology as experience*. Cambridge: The MIT Press.

McCullough, M. (1996). *Abstracting Craft: The practiced digital hand*. Cambridge, MA: The MIT Press.

McGonigal, J. (2007). The puppet master problem: Design for real-world, mission-based gaming. In P. Harrigan & N. Wardrip-Fruin (Eds.), *Second person* (pp. 51–64). Cambridge :The MIT Press.

McKeon, R. (1987). *Rhetoric. Essays in invention and discovery*. Woodbridge: Ox Bow Press.

Miettinen, R. (1999). The riddle of things. Activity theory and actor network theory as approaches of studying innovations. *Mind, Culture, and Activity*, 6(3), 170–195.

Miles, A. (2003). The violence of text. *Kairos*, 8.1(1 Spring). At: http://english.ttu.edu/kairos/8.1/binder2.html?coverweb/vot/index.html

Miller, C. (1984). C. Genre as social action. *Quarterly Journal of Speech*, 70(2), 151–167.

Miller, C., & Shepherd, D. (2004). Blogging as social action: A genre analysis of the weblog. In L. Gurak, S. Antonijevic, L. Johnson, C. Ratliff, C. & J. Reyman, J. (Eds.), *Into the blogosphere: Rhetoric, community and culture of Weblogs*. At: http://blog.lib.umn.edu/blogosphere/blogging_as_social_action.html

Mol, A. (1998). Missing links, making links: The performance of some artheroscleroses. In A. Mol & M. Berg (Eds.), *Differences in medicine: Unravelling practices, techniques and bodies* (pp. 141–163). Durham: Duke University Press.

Mol, A. (1999). Ontological politics: A word and some questions. In J. Law & J. Hassard (Eds.), *Actor network and after* (pp. 74–89). Oxford: Blackwell.

Mol, A. (2001). *The body multiple: Artherosclerosis in practice*. Durham and London: Duke University Press.

Moran, S., & John-Steiner, V. (2003). Creativity in the making: Vygotsky's contemporary contribution to the dialectic of development and creativity. In K. Sawyer, V. John-Steiner, S. Moran, R. Sternberg, D. Feldman, Nakamura, D., et al. (Eds.), *Creativity and development* (pp. 61–90). Oxford Oxford University Press.

Morello, A. (2000). Design predicts the future when it anticipates experience. *Design Issues*, 16(3), 35–44.

Morrison, A. (2003). From oracy to electracies: Hypernarrative, place and multimodal discourses in learning. In G. Liestøl, A. Morrison, & T. Rasmussen (Eds.), *Digital media revisited: Theoretical and conceptual innovation in digital domains* (pp. 115–154). Cambridge, MA: The MIT Press.

Morrison, A. (2005). Inside the Rings of Saturn. Commissioned article for Special Issue on Gunther Kress. *Computers & Composition*, 22(1), 87–100.

Morrison, A. (2009). Collaborative mobile fiction and mediated creativity. *3rd International Roundtable on Discourse Analysis: Discourse and Creativity*. 7–9 May. City University of Hong Kong.

Morrison, A. (Ed.). (2010a). *Inside multimodal composition*. Cresskill N.J.: Hampton Press.

Morrison, A. (2010b). Scrabble in a conceptual toolbox. In A. Morrison (Ed.), *Inside multimodal composition*. Cresshill N.J.: Hampton Press.

Morrison, A., & Eikenes, J.O. (2008). The times are a-changing in the interface. Paper presented at *International Conference on Multimodality and Learning*. Institute of Education: University of London. London, 19–20 June 2008.

Morrison, A., & Skjulstad, S. (2010). Mediating hybrid design: Imaginative renderings of automotive innovation on the Web. In A. Morrison (Ed.), *Inside multimodal composition*. Cresskill N.J.: Hampton Press.

Morrison, A., & Skjulstad, S. (forthcoming). Laying eggs in other people's pockets: Marketing multiliteracies via mobile technologies. In B. Gentikow, E. Skogseth & S. Østerud (Eds.), *Literacy and mediated Cultures*. Creskill: Hampton Press.

Morrison, A. Skjulstad., S., & Sevaldson, B. (2007). Waterfront development with Web mediation. *Proceedings of design inquiries*. 2nd Nordic design research conference. Konstfack, Stockholm, 27–30 May 2007. Available: http://www.nordes.org/upload/papers/109.pdf

Morrison, A. & Thorsnes, P. (2010). Blogging the emphemeral. In A. Morrison (Ed.), *Inside multimodal composition*. Cresshill N.J.: Hampton Press.

Mörtberg, C. (2003). Heterogenous images of (mobile)technologies and services: A feminist contribution. *Nora: Nordic Journal of Women's Studies*, 11(3), 158–169.

Mörtberg, C., & Stuedahl, D. (2005). Silences and sensibilities: increasing participation in IT design. In O. W. Bertelsen, N. O. Bouvin, P. G. Krogh & M. Kyng (Eds.), *Proceedings of the 4th decennial conference on critical computing: Between sense and sensibility*, Aarhus, Denmark (pp. 141–144). New York, NY, USA: ACM.

Mörtberg, C., & Elovaara, P. (2010). Attaching people and technology: Between e and government. In S. Booth, S. Goodman S & G. Kirkup (Eds.), *Gender issues in learning and working with information technology: Social constructs and cultural context* (pp. 83–98). Hershey, USA: IG Global.

Munster, A. (2006). *Materializing new media: Embodiment in information aesthetics*. Hanover, NH: Dartmouth College Press.

Nelson, J., Megill, A., & McCloskey, D. (1987). (Eds.). *The rhetoric of the human sciences. language and argument in scholarship and public affairs*. Madison: University of Wisconsin Press.

Newman, M., & Landay, J. (2000). Sitemaps, storyboards, and specifications: a sketch of Web site design practice. In D. Boyarski & W. A. Kellogg (Eds.), *Proceedings of the 3rd conference on designing interactive systems: Processes, practices, methods, and techniques (DIS'00)*, New York City, New York, United States (pp. 263–274) New York: ACM press.

Nordby, K., & Morrison, A. (under review). Conceptual design and technology: Short range RFID as design material.

Norris, S., & Jones, R. (2005). (Eds.), *Discourse in action: Introducing mediated discourse analysis*. London Routledge.

Norman, D. (1988). *The psychology of everyday things*. New York: Basic Books.

Norman, D. (2004). *Emotional design: Why we love (or hate) everyday things*. New York: Basic Books.

O'Neill, S. (2008). *Interactive media: The semiotics of embodied interaction*. Vienna: Springer.

Ormrod, S. (1994). 'Let's Nuke the Dinner': Discursive practices of gender in the creation of a new cooking process. In C. Cockburn & R. Fürst-Dilić (Eds.), *Bringing technology home: Gender and technology in a changing Europe* (pp. 42–58). Buckinghamn Philadelphia: Open University Press.

Oudshoorn, N., Rommes, E., & Stienstra, M. (2004). Configuring the user as everybody: gender and design cultures in information and communication technologies. *Science, Technology & Human Values,* 29(1), 30–63.

Pierroux. P. (2009) Newbies and design research: Approaches to designing a learning environment using mobile and social technologies. In G. Vavoula, A. Kukulska-Hulme & N. Pachler (Eds.), *Researching mobile learning: Frameworks, methods and research designs*. Bern: Peter Lang.

Poppenpohl, S. (2006). Interaction as an ecology. Building a framework. In S. Bagnara & G. Crampton Smith (Eds.), *Theories and practice in interaction design* (pp. 287–299). Mahwah: Lawrence Erlbaum Associates.

Prøitz, L. (2005). Cute boys or game Boys? The embodiment of femininity and masculinity in young norwegians' text message love-Pfojects, *Fibreculture Journal 2005 Issue 6 - Mobility, New Social Intensities and the Coordinates of Digital Networks*. Available: http://journal.fibreculture.org/issue6/issue6_proitz.html#top

Rönkkö, K., Dittrich, Y., & Randall, D. (2005). When plans do not work out: How plans are used in software development projects. *Computer Supported Cooperative Work* , 14(5), 433–468.

Royce, T. (2007). Intersemiotic complementarity: A framework for multimodal discourse analysis'. In T. Royce & W. Bowcher (Eds.), *New directions in the analysis of multimodal discourse* (pp. 63–109). London: Routledge.

Rust, C., Mottram, J., & Till, J. (2007). *Review report. AHRC reserch review. Practice-led eesearch in art, design & achitecture.* Arts & Humanities Research Council, UK. Available: http://www.ahrc.ac.uk/images/Practice-Led_Review_Nov07.pdf

Sawyer, K. (2006). *Explaining creativity: The science of human innovation.* New York: Oxford University Press.

Schmidt, K. (2002a). Remarks on the complexity of cooperative work. *Revue des sciences et technologies de l'information.* Série Revue d'intelligence artificielle (RSTI-RAI), 16(4-5), Hermes/Lavoisier: Paris. 443–483.

Schmidt, K. (2002b). The Problem with 'Awareness': Introductory Remarks on Awareness in CSCW'. *Computer Supported Cooperative Work,* 11(3/4), 285–298.

Schmidt, K., & Wagner, I. (2004). Ordering Systems: Coordinative Practices and Artifacts in Architectural Design and Planning. *Computer Supported Cooperative Work,* 13(5–6), 349–408.

Schön, D. (1983). *The reflective practitioner: How professionals think in action.* London: Temple Smith.

Schön, D. (1987). *Educating the reflective practitioner.* San Francisco: Jossey-Bass.

Sefyrin, J. (2010) 'For me it doesn't matter where I put my information': Enactments of agency, mutual learning, and gender in information systems development. In S. Booth, S. Goodman S & G. Kirkup (Eds.), *Gender issues in learning and working with Information Technology: Social constructs and cultural context* (pp. 65–97). Hershey, USA: IG Global.

Sellen, A., & Harper, R. (2002). *The myth of the paperless office.* Cambridge, MA: The MIT Press.

Sevaldson, B. (2005). *Developing digital design techniques: Investigations on creative design computing.* Diss. Oslo: Oslo School of Architecture and Design.

Shiga, J. (2007). Translations: artifacts from an Actor-Network perspective. *Artifact,* 1(1), 40–55.

Shotter, J. (2003). Cartesian change, chiasmic change: the power of living expression. *Janus Head,* 6(1), 6–29.

Simon, H. (1969). *The sciences of the artificial.* Cambridge, MA: The MIT Press.

Simons, H. (1989). *The rhetoric of the human sciences.* London: Sage.

Simons, H. (Ed.). (1990). *The rhetorical turn. Invention and persuasion in the conduct of inquiry.* Chicago: University of Chicago Press.

Skjulstad, S. (2007a) Clashing constructs in web design. In A. Melberg (Ed.), *Aesthetics at work* (pp. 81-103). Oslo: UniPub.

Skjulstad, S. (2007b). Communication design and motion graphics on the web. *Journal of Media Practice,* 8(3), 359–378. doi: 10.1386/jmpr.8.3.359_1

Skjulstad, S. & Morrison, A. (2005). Movement in the Interface. *Computers & Composition,* 22(4), 413–433.

Skolnick, L., Lorenc, J., & Berger, C. (2007). *What is exhibition design?* Rotovision: Mies.

Spinuzzi , C. (2003). *Tracing genres through organizations: A sociocultural approach to information design (acting with technology).* Cambridge Mass.: The MIT Press.

Stafford, B. (1996). *Good looking: Essays on the virtue of images.* Cambridge, MA: MIT Press.

Star, S. (1991). Power, technology and the phenomenology of conventions: On being allergic to onions. In Law, J. (Ed) *A sociology of monsters: Essays on power, technology, and domination* (pp. 26–56). London: Routledge.

Stolterman, E. (2008). The nature of design practice and implications for interaction design research. *The International Journal of Design,* 2(1), 55–65. Available: http://www.ijdesign. org/ojs/index.php/IJDesign/article/view/240

Storni, C. (2007). *Design in Practice: On the construction of objects.* Diss. Trento: Faculty of Sociology, University of Trento.

Strain, E., & van Hoosier-Carey, G. (2003). Eloquent interfaces: Humanities-based analysis in the age of hypermedia. In M. Hocks & M. Kendrick (Eds.), *Eloquent images* (pp. 257–281). Cambirdge: The MIT Press.

Strathern, A. J. (1996). *Body thoughts*. Ann Arbor: University of Michigan Press.

Stuedahl, D. (2003). Stillheter i fortellingen – Hvordan bruke fortellinger for å lage ny IKT. [Silences in narratives: How to use narratives to make new technology]. In K. Lundby (Ed.), *Flyt og forførelse [Flow and seduction]* (pp. 106–131). Oslo: Gyldendal Akademisk.

Stuedahl, D. (2004). *Forhandlinger og overtalelser. Kunnskapsbygging på tvers av kunnskapstradisjoner i brukermedvirkende design av ny IKT (Negotiations and persuations. Knowledge building crossing knowledge traditions in user participation in design of new ICT, in Norwegian)*. Diss. Oslo: InterMedia, Faculty of Education, University of Oslo.

Suchman, L. (2002). Located accountabilities. In technology production. *Scandinavian Journal of Information Systems*, 14(2), 91–105.

Suchman, L. (2007). *Human-machine reconfigurations: Plans and situated Actions, 2nd Edition*. Cambridge: Cambridge University Press.

Thoresen, K. (1999). *Computer use*. Diss. Oslo: Department of Informatics, Faculty of Mathematics and Natural Sciences, University of Oslo.

Thackara, J. (2005). *In the Bubble: Designing in a complex world*. Cambridge: The MIT Press.

Ulmer, G. (1994). *Heuretics. The logic of innovation*. Baltimore: Johns Hopkins University Press.

Ulmer, G. (2003). *Internet invention: From literacy to electracy*. Longman: New York.

van Leeuwen, T. (2005). Multimedia, genre and design. In S. Norris & R. Jones (Eds.), *Discourse in action: Introducing mediated discourse analysis* (pp. 73–94). London: Routledge.

van Leeuwen, T., & Jewitt, C. (2001). (Eds.). *Handbook of visual analysis*. London: Sage.

Vehviläinen, M. (1997). *Gender, expertise and information technology*. Diss. Tampere: Department of Computer Science, University of Tampere.

Vehviläinen, M. (2005). The numbers of women in ICT and cyborg narratives: On the approaches of researching gender in information and communication technology. H. Isomäki & A. Pohjola (Eds.), *Lost and found in virtual reality: Women and information technology* (pp. 23–46). Rovaniemi: University of Lapland Press.

Vygotsky, L. (1962). *Thought and language*. Cambridge: The MIT Press.

Vygotsky, L. (1978). *Mind in society: The development of higher psychological processes*. Cambridge: Harvard University Press.

Wagner, I. (1994). Connecting communities of practice: Feminism, science and technology. *Women Studies International Forum*, 17 (2/3), 257–265.

Wagner, I. (2004) Open planning: A reflection on methods. In R. Boland & F. Collopy (Eds.), *Managing as designing* (pp. 153–163). Palo Alto, CA: Stanford University Press.

Wartofsky, M. 1979. *Models: Representation in scientific understanding*. Dordrecht: D. Reidel Publishing Co.

Wajcman, J. (2000). Reflections on gender and technology Studies. In what state is the art? *Social Studies of Science* 30(3), 447–64.

Welch, K. (1999). *Electric rhetoric: Classical rhetoric, oralism, and a new literacy*. Cambridge: The MIT Press

Wells, G. (1999). *Dialogic inquiry: Toward a sociocultural practice and theory of education*. Cambridge: Cambridge University Press.

Wertsch, J. (1991). *Voices of the mind. A sociocultural approach to mediated action*. Cambridge, MA: Harvard University Press.

Whittaker, S., & Schwarz, H. (1999). Meetings of the board: The impact of scheduling Medium on long term group coordination in software development. *Computer Supported Cooperative Work*, 8(3), 175–205.

Winograd, T. (Ed.). (1996). *Bringing design to software*. New York: ACM Press/Addison-Wesley.

Wood, A. (2007). *Digital encounters*. London: Routledge.

Woolgar, S. (1991) *Knowledge and reflexivity: New frontiers in the sociology of knowledge.* London: Sage Publications.

Yates. J & Orlikowski, W. (2002). Genre systems: Structuring interaction through communicative norms. *Journal of Business Communication,* 39(1), 13–35.

Yoshioka, T., Herman, G., Yates, J., & Orlikowski, W. (2001). Genre taxonomy: A knowledge repository of communicative actions. *ACM Transactions on Information Systems,* 19(4), 431–456.

Zimmerman, J., Forlizzi, J., & Evenseon, S. (2007). Research through design as a method for interaction design researchin HCI'. In M. B. Rosson & D: Gillmore (Eds.), *Proceedings of the SIGCHI conference on human factors in computing systems (CHI '07),* San Jose CA, USA (pp. 493–502). New York: ACM press.

Zuboff, S. (1988). *In the age of the smart machine: The future of work and power.* New York: Basic Books.

4

Methods That Matter
in Digital Design Research

Christina Mörtberg, Tone Bratteteig,
Ina Wagner, Dagny Stuedahl, and Andrew Morrison

Theories and analytical perspectives are linked to methods. The discussion of the methods used to capture the complexities of practices with a focus on social, cultural and economic layers (Jordan and Henderson 1994; Wagner 1994; Sjöberg 1996; Newman 1998) represents an important resource for a discussion of designers' interpretative work with both traditional and new experimental methods. In previous chapters we have described our collaborative and multidisciplinary perspectives that are also mirrored in the methods we use in the exploration of practices. These practices are technical, organizational, knowledge-based and socio-cultural. Our aim is to explore and maintain the complexity in design as a mix of all of these.

The chapter is structured in two parts; the first is processual and the second experimental. The first part starts with a discussion of what social science and humanities can contribute, followed by thoughts on reflexivity and methodological sensibility in digital design research. Then we move to a brief introduction of ethnographic analysis and its use in design research. Ethnography in participatory design (PD) and some aspects of participatory design are described, followed by concrete examples. New social media raise methodological challenges and also consideration of ethical aspects that appear in virtual or digital encounters. Further, technology or the digital becomes a more obvious actor as the site of the research or, rather, where to do the research is more ambiguous or unstable than in offline settings. Guiding principles for virtual or digital ethnography are presented and also discussed with practical examples in mobile communications and design experiments for digital engagement in museums.

Methods employed in digital design research do not differ from design research in general, but in addition to this there is a need to develop new experimental methods. In the second part of the chapter we describe a set of experiments concerned with the design of physical and tangible digital systems, emphasizing the development of new practices. These experiments illustrate the use of creative and experimental methods that are playful and engaging: among them cultural probes and technology probes, as well as performative techniques for designing interactive installations. Finally, the importance of creating a rich design space and of 'having a sense of somewhere to go' (Heape 2007: 5) is addressed.

I. Wagner et al. (eds.), *Exploring Digital Design: Multi-Disciplinary Design Practices*, 105
Computer Supported Cooperative Work, DOI 10.1007/978-1-84996-223-0_4,
© Springer-Verlag London Limited 2010

Reflexive Approaches to Digital Design

How can knowledge, theories and methods from social sciences and humanities be integrated and made to support digital design research? What ontological and epistemological frames from these disciplines can be involved in design discussions and design work? What role does a researcher of informatics and humanities take when s/he is designing the object s/he is studying? These questions touch upon issues that are reminiscent of current problems discussed in conventionalist directions of social science and humanities concerning analysis of social groups, social practices and the researchers' role in their research (Bauman 1993; Foucault 1973; Rorty 1994).

In design research literature, reflexivity is discussed in relation to interpretative skills and its important influences on design. Harold Nelson and Erik Stolterman state that, even in the most objective and truth-focused approaches in design, there is still a need for interpretation:

> Interpretation, as a part of the design process, serves the same purpose as evidence and proof does in science. Interpretation is part of our attempt to grasp the conditions and context that exist and will set the stage for our ideas and new design. (Nelson and Stolterman 2003: 154)

Nelson and Stolterman continue their argument where they also underscore a difference between interpretation in research – and interpretation in design. Research has developed tools for studying and describing an existing reality – while in design these tools do not fully support the work of creating new realities. They write:

> Design is intentional; therefore design interpretations are also intentional. It is intention that predisposes us towards certain data and values. This means that interpretation cannot be done without an understanding of a direction – without desiderata. (Nelson and Stolterman 2003: 156)

The concept of interpretation with a direction lends a special character to the interpretations, translations and communications in a design process (Stuedahl 2004) and research process as well. Implementing a reflexive methodology in digital design means, therefore, to be aware of the intentionality that lies behind interpretations and translations in addition to the theoretical and methodological aspects that legitimate the design. In relation to establishing a reflexive methodology in design, the intentionality, stated by Nelson and Stolterman, makes it clear that to be reflexive in design research, we need a strong theoretical framework that captures the object, the process, and the use of the object.

We would like to add another aspect of interpretation that is of crucial importance for the researchers' judgement and creativity during both their fieldwork and their design work. That is, to be able to use intuition, judgement, and to be able to communicate with the research subjects and objects requires a certain sensibility in order to perceive and to be open to the unexpected and to contradictions. Following Law (2004), we call this 'methodological sensibility' (see also Stuedahl 2004; Mörtberg and Stuedahl 2005). Methodological sensibility directs the attention towards what researchers are hearing, listening, seeing, and understanding during their fieldwork or design work, as well as what they are defining as relevant empirical material when they are doing their research in the field. Sensibility may for example result in that the invisible work becomes visible (Star and Strauss 1999) and one pays attention to the not articulated work (Stuedahl 2004). Methodological sensibility therefore introduces a specific focus on the communication or interaction that researchers establish with the research subjects and objects. In combination with Alvesson and Sköldberg's (2000) concepts of reflexive interpretation, this focus can be a good theoretical and methodological grounding for digital design research (see also the discussion of reflexivity in Chapter 1 in this volume).

It is necessary for researchers and designers to integrate diverse theoretical aspects in their creative work, to be able to reflect upon not only activities in the design process, but also upon the multiple intentions and interpretations that build the analytical lens of the research or design project. In addition, the communication processes between designers and users involved in the multidisciplinary team calls for methodological reflections on a general level. The need for a methodology that addresses reflexivity as reflections upon reflection, integration of theoretical backgrounds, methods in use, and issues of multidisciplinary collaboration, is clear. In the following subsection we discuss ethnographic analysis in design research, in PD and in virtual or digital encounters.

From Ethnography in PD to Digital Ethnography

Ethnography's origin was in the travels of anthropologists to study ethnic cultures and claimed to produce 'true' descriptions of cultures and communities – in particular remote native ethnic tribes (Malinowski 1961 [1922]); Mead 1973 [1928]). Today ethnography includes studies of organizational lives and contemporary cultures, and aims to stimulate conversation and broaden multidisciplinary communities (Jordan 1997). A definition of ethnography that includes most ethnographic studies is that of Hammersley and Atkinson:

> In its most characteristic form it involves the ethnographer participating, overtly or covertly in people's daily lives for an extended period of time, watching what happens, listening to what is said, asking questions – in fact, collecting whatever data are available to throw light on the issues that are the focus of the research. (Hammersley and Atkinsons 1995: 1).

Ethnography has a long tradition in design as a method for understanding work practices and technological artefacts in use (Suchman and Wynn 1984; Suchman 1987; Orr 1996; Luff and Heath 1998), or it is used in technology design in order to include user perspectives (Ehn 1989; Blomberg et al. 1993; Beyer and Holtzblatt 1998; Greenbaum and Kyng 1991). Ethnographic methods have also been used in analysis of organizations, with the intention of immersing the participant observer in the naturally occurring activities that are explored (Ruhleder and Jordan 1997).

When the aim of the ethnographic study is to inform designers, the ethnographers do the observations, the analysis, write the ethnographic account and inform designers about their analysis. In more collaborative projects the ethnographers facilitate conversations with users rather than collecting data (Blomberg et al. 1993), or work together with the designers (Bjerknes et al. 1985). Being part of a design project has implications for the role of the ethnographer, and also for the goal of ethnography-based research. Ethnographic methods become both a means to facilitate communication and a vehicle for producing information relevant for the design of new products. Users, designers, and ethnographers explore a practice together, contribute from their knowledge and perspective, and try to create a common ground in order to enable the design. In this case, ethnography has the potential of providing a context in which mutual understanding can evolve. This makes ethnography a tool for making relations in participatory design projects and raising the dialogical dimension.

Work practice includes work-arounds (Gasser 1986) and a lot of 'non-work' necessary for doing the primary work. Articulation work (Strauss 1985, see also Chapter 3) is normally not talked about, and it is not considered 'real work'. Nurses for example often complain that they have no time for 'real nursing', that is, spending time at the bedside. If, however, you consider articulation work as work, the administration and coordination necessary for giving care to each and all patients is very much a nursing skill – and should be considered 'real nursing' (Bjerknes and Bratteteig 1987a, c). Theoretical concepts can help in making sense of what is observed and also to provide a critical distance – and outsider perspective – to the practice (Gregory 2000). Analytical sensibility is also needed to obtain understandings of invisible knowledge and experiences in order to find ways to integrate and articulate this in technology design (Karasti 2001, 2003; Elovaara et al. 2006). Whether it is possible or not for outsiders to capture embodied and situated knowledge or more tacit aspects of knowing and learning is a demanding methodological question in studies of practices.

Ethnography has been taken up in a range of studies and disciplines and it is used not only for studies of the social or professional life of a community as a whole, but, also for more limited aspects. The ethnographic approach has been integrated in technology and digital communication design in a number of ways. This has resulted in discussions of what ethnography is or how the approach is used (e.g. Shapiro 1994; Plowman et al. 1995). The evolution of CSCW moved the focus from design of technologies for individual support to design of technologies that support teamwork and cooperation. The shift to cooperation also had consequences for how to conduct fieldwork and the necessity of understanding group work (Blomberg et al. 1993). Ethnographic analysis focuses, then, on interactions, artefacts, and how they unfold in day-to-day activities in work practices in their implications in design. The examination also results in broader understandings of how well or badly technologies fit with people's everyday lives (Brown et al. 2007).

Hughes et al. (1994) discuss four ways in which ethnographic studies may inform design: concurrent, quick and dirty, evaluative, and re-assessment of previous studies. Concurrent ethnography is a reiteration of field work, discussion with the designers, construction of prototype, and additional field work. The iterations end when saturation appears in terms of what one gains by more fieldwork. The second category, quick and dirty, already implies that the analysis is fast and limited in time, taking risks in quality, for example, for gaining a proper understanding of the practice. The quality can be achieved in short time periods of field work, however, if the research is well organized and limited (Harper 2000). Evaluative ethnography involves an evaluation of design that has already been completed. There are similarities between the quick and dirty way and this way of using ethnography. The latter is more focused because the target is given. Ethnographic analysis focuses on the details of activities and is very valuable in evaluation. Re-assessment of previous studies is the fourth way to use ethnographic analysis (Hughes et al. 1994). In this process, the researcher re-uses previous studies of the work practice in question. The studies are not necessarily conducted by designers but by researchers, for example working life researchers; sociologists or anthropologists. These studies are valuable in life-cycle perspectives and give possibilities of reassessment of the impact of technologies that are already in use.

The extensive use of ethnography use also has resulted in a critique of how it is used. For example, Forsythe (1999) criticizes the software designers' common sense use of ethnography. There are risks that researchers with an epistemological background in natural sciences treat ethnographic methods in the same way as the positivist techniques they normally use. Although the approach is used for data collection, they may not pay attention to the philosophical foundation of the conceptual structures that are deeply intertwined with ethnographic techniques. Forsythe (1999: 138) writes: 'The resultant "insider ethnography" takes local meanings at face value, overlooking tacit assumptions rather than questioning them'. Interdisciplinary collaboration between ethnographers, designers and users are possible ways to build bridges between disciplines and to cross boundaries between disciplines and various foundational starting-points.

Within CSCW research there is an ongoing debate on the relationship between ethnography and design. At its core is what Grudin and Grinter (1995) have coined 'the ethnographer's dilemma' and points at the potentially problematic nature of a design endeavor grounded in work practices that may not be all that solid and may even be merely transitory. In the following, we describe some aspects of participatory design, their implications for methods, and some concrete examples.

Ethnographic Studies in Participatory Design

Ethnographic studies and analyses have a long tradition in Scandinavian information systems research communities, in particular within participatory design research. Ethnography has been used as a means to study work practices, i.e. the studies have constituted the foundation for the design. The first participatory design projects all had multidisciplinary research teams – the Florence project (1983–1987) for example employed a full time anthropologist researcher. Scandinavian research included ethnographic studies of work and use of computers in work, in the work place (Thoresen 1981, 1999; Bermann 1983; Bjerknes and Bratteteig 1984, 1987a; Bermann and Thoresen 1988) have made connections to North American research of use practice studies (Wynn 1979; Suchman and Wynn 1984; Suchman 1987). A range of collaborative and discussion methods are employed in PD, together with observations, interviews and document analyses (e.g., Bjerknes and Bratteteig 1987c; Greenbaum and Kyng 1991; Bødker et al. 2004).

Mutual learning is important when different categories of people participate in the design process, and the learning typically deals with knowledge about the application area and the work that the future digital artefact or system is supposed to support, as well as technology itself and possible applications of new technology. Understanding a practice builds the body for recognizing people's skills, their logics, and their rationale in design projects. The more collaborative approaches of ethnography (Blomberg et al. 1993) have contributed to the mutual learning i.e. in developing an environment where both users and designers learn from each other.

Mutual learning involves learning in two ways, and the most widespread approach is to have designers do ethnographic fieldwork; basically observations and interviews, in the use setting. Normally, fieldwork involves studies of artefacts, and documents, organizational routines and structures and a lot of other elements in the use setting. The designers' ability to empathize with the users and recognize their expertise as well as their logic comes from experiencing the use practice as it unfolds when users do what they normally do. Knowledge about the use practice enables you to see and listen, but does not guarantee that you are willing to take the users' views seriously. There are still negotiations about whose knowledge counts; who has the preferential right to talk and interpret the situation.

Observation of practices is one method for starting the process of mutual learning. In the beginning, observations always give a very chaotic first impression (Bjerknes et al. 1985; Bjerknes and Bratteteig 1987a). It is difficult to 'see what you see': it is actually very difficult to notice actions and operations that you do not understand (Bratteteig 2004). Here is Tone Bratteteig's story from the Florence project that still has relevance:

> I was observing nurses at the Cardiology ward disguised as a trainee in a white coat, with a notebook and pen. After the morning meeting, the nurses and doctors go for a morning round to see all the patients. The first time I was part of the morning round it made a strong impression on me, and I noticed how the professional communication varied when the doctors and nurses talked with the different patients and with each other. They sat down at each bed and showed that they cared and were open to talking with each of the patients – even if the round was quite quickly over. Later that day, one of the nurses explained about heart diseases and mentioned that an indicator of the heart not functioning well is that your ankles get swollen. On my next morning round I suddenly became aware of how the nurse lifted the blanket by the feet of a patient, and patted the feet when greeting him and asking him how he was doing that day. I could see that she observed his ankles and that what she saw affected how she talked with him. What I had considered to be a warm and personal greeting on my first round turned out to be a professional activity intended to add information to the evaluation of the patient. It was obvious to me that you need time to get enough knowledge about the use practices to appreciate it.

Doing observations may seem like an impossible task: what should you observe? Where should you start? A good way to start is by following a person around for some time (e.g. a work shift), trying to get her/his perspective on the practices. Adding observations from following other people around – similar and different – will give you a richer picture of the work practices that make up the use setting. Other perspectives can also be used, e.g. being in a particular place (a particular room) or following a particular object (paper, medical journal, lab test, equipment, see Bratteteig 1997), or trying to get a sense of the social culture by mingling in the lunch room (Jordan 1997). Applying a particular perspective on the observations, e.g., information flow or cooperation, also represents a way of focusing your observations while being aware of what is not in focus (Bjerknes and Bratteteig 1987b). Interviews are necessary to get closer to the tacit knowledge involved in the professional practice.

Observations and interviews with nurses in work revealed that there are interesting differences between the formal routines and what the nurses actually do in order to get the work done (Bjerknes and Bratteteig 1987a) – a finding that can be confirmed by many other researchers (e.g. Suchman and Wynn 1984; Suchman 1987; Gregory 2000). Some routines are just very cumbersome, and everyday work practices include short cuts. A good example is that of rigid security procedures aimed at securing client data, but end up not being used because they take too much time and energy and mean that the terminals remain logged on and less secure than before (Kaasbøll et al. 1992). Social rules, like hierarchy, influence how people communicate and can create problems in situations where the more powerful have less knowledge than their subordinates (Bratteteig 2004).

The second – and most characteristic – part of mutual learning is the ambition to teach the users enough about the technological possibilities to enable them to imagine future design results. The challenge is a pedagogical one: to teach the users about technology while maintaining their professional basis for assessing that same technology (Bratteteig 2004). To teach someone something new and still want them to think for him/herself is difficult, but possible. However, it takes time. The process of teaching users about technology should not involve making them technologists – rather, the aim is to provide knowledge about technological possibilities and limitations. User's increased technological skills together with ethnographic analyses may contribute to extended understandings that have implications for the design and also in finding out how poorly or well the suggested system goes with people's day-to-day activities.

Prototyping as a Method to Involve Users

Prototypes or presentations of possible design solutions are methods used in PD together with ethnographic studies. These methods may help to evaluate design suggestions and hopefully improve them. System presentations (Bjerg and Nielsen 1978) are presentations of systems and system models (e.g. prototypes Floyd 1984; Budde et al. 1992). We include excursions and demonstrations of systems in this method category. Excursions, typically, are visits to other similar organizations that

Fig. 4.1 Mutual learning in the Florence project: system presentation (*left, middle*) and system description: wallgraphs (*right*) (Bratteteig 2004: 28)

use relevant information systems. The excursions aim at giving the users concrete knowledge about a variety of systems, and of a variety of use practices.

Specific system demonstrations – prototypes – are useful for getting ideas about concrete system solutions as well as for discussing technical possibilities. System presentations can be used to:

- Demonstrate alternative designs of the same application. We particularly recommend versions with errors and an unfinished appearance in order to demonstrate to the users that their knowledge is needed for designing a usable system, see Fig. 4.1.
- Give hands-on practice: to lend out new types of ICTs in the work place for a couple of weeks for the users to get hands-on experience with simple applications. Be aware that the users' imagination will be heavily influenced by their technology experiences.
- Create discussions about computers in work: prototypes and pilot systems should be used as bases for discussions about how users would be using computers in work. Users' critical evaluation of prototypes is valuable, especially for how their assessments are explained (Bjerknes and Bratteteig 1987a, b).

System description is a basic method in design of software when analysing and specifying a system. However, they can also be used for discussing computers in work at different organizational levels, engaging users and designers in discussing which aspect of work could use computer support (Bjerknes and Bratteteig 1987c; Munk-Madsen 1978). Systems design typically involves descriptions and drawings. Formal system descriptions encourage a particular perspective on the world (like information processing), which can also be used to juggle insider and outsider views on work and thus enabling professional and organizational views to be discussed. Figure 4.1 shows examples of 'Wall graphs' made by nurses, doctors and computer scientists depicting information processes in a hospital. With very simple means: slightly miniaturized copies of actual forms and different colour pens, information flows are drawn and discussed – the simplicity of the method also allows for 'home-made' symbols, like running feet (Bjerknes et al. 1985). Lively discussions about information, work and work organization add to the concrete discussions about the work toll from the prototyping sessions.

These discussions complete the mutual learning phase – the participants should have learnt enough to create visions for the future and negotiate which one to realize.

There are obvious problems concerned with determining when there is 'enough knowledge' – and sometimes you cannot tell that you do not know enough until you fail (Bratteteig 2004). This fact should be considered when planning the mutual learning process.

Ending the mutual learning process is the design decision – the problem setting and solving. This process can be carried out in many ways: like informal discussions with all involved or, more formally, as two parties making suggestions and negotiating the final result (Bjerknes and Bratteteig 1988a). The most difficult part of this process is to give the logic of the users the same power as the design logic, when deciding on the design. Normally designers have the power to decide – and the responsibility for their design result. Sharing the power to decide is therefore also sharing responsibility: neither giving away nor accepting power is not easy (Bratteteig 1997).

Design is the responsibility of the designers, as they have the technical know-how: they are responsible for the technical quality of the artefact – and without technical quality there is no use quality (Bjerknes et al. 1991). Technical quality of an information system, for example, is concerned with things like stability, reliability, durability, and maintainability; characteristics that are of limited interest to users in the moment of design. Giving away parts of the power to design means giving priority to aspects other than the technical, or even giving lower priority to technical aspects. The choice is professionally difficult, even if several of the technical issues mentioned depend on users' commitment and knowledge: durability increases if the system is based on the stability afforded by professional knowledge; reliability depends on the users' ability to operate and trust the system, as well as to maintain and use the information in the system. The decision to have the users decide on the design is not easy, but possible in a research project like the Florence project (Bjerknes and Bratteteig 1988a, b).

Ethnography in PD combines interviews, observations, document analysis, prototypes and other collaborative techniques in order to extend the views and to create rich pictures of the practices, people and artefacts, in and of the design process.

'I, My Workplace and My Work' – Carthographies

Visions or intentions to give the users the right to participate in design decisions or the vision of participation on equal terms have also resulted in the development of collaborative methods and techniques (Bødker et al. 2004). We describe other examples in the following, with a particular focus on what we termed 'the cartographic exercise' (see also Fig. 4.1 where another kind of 'cartography' was used). The Swedish public sector is in transformation; something not unique to Sweden as similar changes are taking place in many other countries. Information technology is a means to transform the sector to an e-service society. The overall notion for the transformation process is e-government. Terms such as rationalization, efficiency, effectiveness, and e-services are entangled in dominating discourse. This discourse is, however, silent about the employees' participation in the design of the e-service society. One purpose in the research project *From Government to e-Government: gender, skills, learning and technology*[1] has been to explore how the skills and experiences of the employees can be integrated in, and provide valuable knowledge for, the design of the e-service society. Civil servants in four local authorities in the county of Blekinge in the south east of Sweden participated in the project. In the autumn of 2005, working groups of 2–3 people were established in each authority. The methods employed have been inspired by the use of ethnography in PD projects and its methods and techniques (see e.g. Bødker et al. 2004). We have, however, elaborated and adapted them to the particular context, setting and participants. Feminist technoscience (Haraway 1997) influenced our methodological considerations, and feminist pedagogy as well (hook 2000). A guiding principle has been not only to explore 'what is' but also 'what could be' (Madison 2005: 5). Three workshops were held between 2005 and 2007, with informal interviews in between.

Methods used were a cartographic exercise, scenarios, walking through with disposable cameras, in situ interviews, informal interviews (individual and group), and Digital Story telling. The aim was to create understandings of civil servants' day-to-day work in order to give space to the employees, their agency, and participation in the design of Swedish e-service society (see also Chapter 9, Mörtberg and Elovaara 2010). The participants were not expected to do any preparation in advance. The researcher however made preparations: pleasurable work browsing magazines and catalogues, cutting a range of images representing persons and artefacts to be used in the mapping, going to the supermarket to buy pens, tape, post-it notes, scissors, woollen yarn, pens, crayons, white sheets, and other craft material – just simple and cheap materials. All the material was packed into two paper bags. A number of scenarios were also created in advance; illustrated in form of cartoons.

The cartographic exercise was used in the first workshop. We were welcomed with coffee and cakes, which created a positive atmosphere when we introduced ourselves to each other. Then the research project, its aim and the method were presented. 'I, my workplace, and my work' were the guidelines for the participant's cartographic exercise. The exercise was a way for the participants to talk about their work at the same time as they created the maps. In-situ interviews were also conducted, depending on how the mapping unfolded; sometimes in order to clarify things, other times to complement their maps. The participants also included the most important relationship with their closest colleagues, other employees at the local authority, politicians, citizens, IT-systems, phones, faxes, wastebaskets, web pages and so forth. How the mapping unfolded is illustrated in Fig. 4.2: to the left we can see the blank white sheet without any images, in the next some subjects and objects are pasted on the sheet, and to the right, subjects, objects, and the relations (lines) between subjects and objects are included.

The scenarios were enacted as role-plays, where the researchers acted as citizens who made personal visits, phone calls, used e-mail, or web inquiries etc., in order to

---

[1] Pirjo Elovaara and Christina Mörtberg conducted the research.

Fig. 4.2 Stages of the cartographic exercise

get in touch with the local authority. In addition to the map exercise, the participants walked through their offices with disposable cameras with the aim of being able to include additional illustrations, details and activities in their descriptions of their day.

The method worked well; it was collective and involved many hands (Haraway 1994). The maps consisted of, and were filled with, diffractive stories or cartographies with many layers. It also became apparent how the civil servants communicated with many people, both inside and outside the local authority, and how various technologies were used in that communication, such as telephone, sms, e-mails, fax, ordinary mail, and so forth. The maps also showed how the civil-servants intra-acted in material-discursive practices. Turnball (2007: 143) writes that '[t]elling a story and following a path are cognate activities, telling a story is ordering events and actions in space and time – it is a form of knowledge making'. Hence mapping is a way to produce knowledge where subjects, objects and connections emerge out of the enactment.

One resulting experience was that the make-up of the group mattered. The storytelling with the creation of maps was carried out together with the participants and the researchers. The interplay in the groups differed: some worked very well together and in other groups it went rather slowly because the people were more shy. The workshops, however, were full of joy and laughter when the participants conducted the mapping. Another experience was that it is only possible to capture partial or diffractive stories of a complex and varying business. Using a variety of methods and techniques, however, allows researchers to pay attention to various aspects of the day-to-day activities. The method was simple and the participants were familiar with the material, thus it was very easy to spark off their accounts. Topographic maps consist of elevations in order to visualize the landscape. The cartographies in combination with the recordings, the photos, scenarios and stories told in interviews and during the digital story-telling workshop, made the elevations figuratively visible. The cartographic workshop was only recorded audially. In retrospect this seems strange, since the method of visualization was used but it was perhaps a consequence of an over dominant focus on simplicity.

Ethnography together with methods and techniques for participatory design have been used many times, in many other participatory-oriented projects. The *Sisom* project (see Chapter 2) also applied several of the participatory techniques in order to engage children in discussions about the design in question. Ethnographic studies and participatory techniques have also been used as part of a large health information systems development project in developing countries (Puri et al. 2000; Elovaara et al. 2006).

Digital Ethnography

Explorations of mobile communication and online communication, networking and community building are new application areas where digital or virtual ethnography is used. New social media and virtual ethnography 'provide an opportunity for interrogating and understanding our methodological commitments' (Hine 2005: 9). But how to interact with the subject in virtual settings and how do you conduct digital or virtual ethnography? Hine (2005) argues that new forms of communication also have methodological implications, but that it is important not to exaggerate the differences between the virtual and other settings. Further, virtual ethnography asks for adaptations that raises specific methodological issues. (Hine 2000). Hine uses the notion of 'virtual' in her discussion of ethnographic challenges of digital communication, above all related to the Internet. We use 'digital' to capture mixed reality and new ways of communication, social networking, and community building.

In virtual or digital ethnography, the Internet or new social media are explored in their use and (re)interpretation. New social media and their uses are not considered as potentially problematic, but as cultural artefacts and expressions that are integrated in people's everyday lives. Another question relevant for virtual or digital ethnography is where to go to conduct the research. Hence, an obvious difference between online and face-to-face ethnography is where the researcher is located when s/he collects data. In offline sites s/he mostly collects data in the field, outside the office, but online ethnographers mostly collect their data in their offices, or in combination with both on- and offline data-gatherings (Rutter and Smith 2005). Even if the field site is taken account of, the virtual or digital is not separated from face-to-face or physical interactions but is interwoven with people's day-to-day activities and how they unfold. While the body is always located somewhere, the site where the interaction takes place may be mobile rather than located in a particular place. This implies that neither culture nor community have to be located in one place – they are multi-locational. Consequently, location and boundary can be replaced with flow and connectivity as organizing principles for the field site. Nevertheless, virtual ethnography has to examine boundary-making and connectivity, particularly between the physical and the digital because they also are in the making, through and in the interaction and the exploration.

Both spatiality and temporality are dislocated in virtual settings or when social media are used. Digital interactions or social networking with the use of digital media are interspersed with other kinds of interactions. The research encounters take place in between other activities, whereby the immersion is irregularly achieved. Rutter and Smith (2005) argue, based on their experiences of online ethnography, that immersion is also indispensable in an online setting. The ethnographer and the research subject/object 'have to find ways of immersing themselves in life as it is lived online, and as it connects through into offline social spheres' (Hine 2005: 18). Further, Hine (2000: 65) explains that a virtual ethnography can only be partial, and she argues that '[t]he notion of pre-existing, isolable and describable, locales and cultures are set aside'. It is true that the sites one explores do not always pre-exist, but the question is whether or not all ethnographic accounts are partial due to the fact that knowledge is not comprehensive but partial, local and situated (Haraway 1997).

Presence and absence are also methodological issues that one has to deal with in explorations of online communications or social media. Both the informant and the ethnographer are occasionally present in the virtual setting. An unstable setting is another issue, in that neither the researcher nor the informant can see when the other is online. In addition, new people enrol and some leave the community. On the other hand, this also happens in offline explorations, for example, in work places, some people leave and others begin. Communication and community building is enabled through digital media in the way ethnographers have to interact with the technology, and it is through the technology that the ethnographer and the research subjects meet, Hines (2000: 65) writes: 'The shaping of the ethnographic object as it is made possible by the available technologies *is* the ethnography. This is ethnography *in, of* and *through* the virtual.' This too, we argue, is part of the discursive material practices of performance of digital ethnography.

Trust and how to create trust between researchers and the research subjects is an issue that becomes obvious in virtual settings and digital media. Although it is important in all settings, the conditions differ when the encounters are online and not always face-to-face. When on- and offline encounters are combined, researchers may use similar techniques as in face-to-face interactions in order to create informed consent and trust. However, how researchers create trust in face-to-face interactions or offline settings does not always work in online settings (Sanders 2005). Hence it is still a challenge and something researchers have to deal with and to explain to those involved in the research. Sometimes the informants help the researchers in the process. Rutter and Smith (2005) examined sociability in newsgroups through both online and offline data collection. In their research, the face-to-face interaction resulted in some participants posting messages to tell other newsgroup members that the researchers were also trustworthy. Further methodological challenges will be elaborated in the later sections.

Mobile Communication, Methodological Implications and Ethical Aspects

The mobile phone has become the possession of almost all, independently of where one is located. Mobiles are also used in areas without the electricity to charge the phones batteries. The extensive use of mobile phones has changed people's way of communication. Research has reported how the mobile phone enabled and facilitated the coordination of day-to-day activities in families (Berg et al. 2005, Ling 2008). The coordination has mostly dealt with the immediate surroundings (sometimes on longer distances). Horst's (2006) ethnographic study focuses, however, on transnational settings and on long-term absence from parents or partners. Mobile phones have enabled Jamaican children and adults to facilitate and maintain their contact with parents, partners, and relatives outside Jamaica. In 2004, the number of mobile subscribers exceeded 2 million, out of a population of 2.6 million in Jamaica: an extensive improved access compared to the limited access to landlines (7.2% of the households) (Horst 2006). Horst describes the new situation as the blessings and burdens of communication. She also points to cultured practices; for example, to how the address book reflects practices of naming, sharing, hiding contacts a partner should not be aware of, and so forth.

Research has also reported how existing norms have been contested by the creation of new social practices among young people's use of mobiles in Japan (Ito and Okabe 2005); of young people's performances of gender and sexuality in mobile practices in Norway (Prøitz 2007); or how the mobile phone has become a social prosthetic (Berg et al. 2005). The last was an outcome of a research project on mobile services. The researchers[2] used participant observations, interviews and a web-based questionnaire. Interviews were carried out both in working lives (care assistants and middle managers in a social services department, property maintenance workers, and with designers of mobile services in Sweden) and private lives (people aged 25–70 years). The observations in the project actually followed the practice of lurking (listening to a person's mobile calls without the person's consent), because the informants were people in the researchers' immediate surroundings – located in public spaces, such as on buses, in shops, in restaurants, in the lounge at airports, and so forth. Most of the conversations were short private calls but some also dealt with business matters e.g. one person who, during approximately 15 min, made four calls to various people and, in the last one, stated that everything was in place so a contract should be faxed. The most common calls were, for instance, to inform relatives that the plane had just landed and s/he will be home within a certain time; to make appointments; or to get information about meetings.

The new communication practices and mobile technology also raise questions on how to study them. A re-reading of this project with Hine's principles for virtual ethnography shows that the boundaries between the public and the private were in the making, on one hand by the fact that people making telephone calls in public space involve others in their private lives, whether they want to be or not; they are not asked. The boundaries were, on the other hand, also created through the researcher's lurking, her listening and documentation of a person's calls. The physical body is entangled with the mobile phone, software and hardware, and the person s/he calls. If the actors do not make phone calls or do not answer the calls, the lurking

---

[2] Elisabeth Berg, Maria Jansson and Christina Mörtberg.

or observations do not result in any data; the researcher has to find a new setting. Thus, the field site can be both temporary and unstable, despite the fact that mobile calls are conducted almost everywhere and in no particular room or space. Further, the partial became apparent because it was only part of the conversation the researcher was able to listen to.

Three researchers were involved in the research, but it was only one who was successful in the lurking. Two failed because they felt that to listen to others' calls created an awkward situation that offended the person, although the calls were conducted in public spaces and were impossible not to overhear. In any case, lurking raises a range of ethical questions (see also Rutter and Smith 2005; Sanders 2005): how public is talk that takes place in public spaces? How do you create trust in explorations of new social media? How do you create informed consent? Ethnography is emerging in virtual or digital settings with a range of methodological challenges. In the following we describe the use of blogs for design of digital engagement.

Using Blogs for Digital Engagement

Digital media represents new spaces and virtual environments that invite us to study users' virtual activities with ethnographic observations. Virtual environments, such as blogs and wikis, can be used as tools in virtual ethnographies, but it poses several questions related to the information that is gathered and the type of empirical material that blog transcripts represent (Stuedahl and Smørdal 2010). This will be illustrated with an experiment conducted within the RENAME project.[3] Two different design settings were set up in order to explore youth's engagement in relation to cultural heritage (see also Chapters 2 and 9 in this volume). Mobile telephones were used in one setting and weblogs in the other. The experiment was set up in a real museum context, the Viking Ship museum in Oslo, in collaboration with a school class of 25 13-year-old pupils from a nearby school, familiar with the museum content. Nine mobile phones were given to the pupils so that they had to collaborate in groups of two and three during the visit. They were asked to take pictures and then to upload their pictures to a museum visitors' blog, accessible in an experimental mobile media centre in the museum. (see Fig. 4.3). The blog was set up on the project's website with a new blog entry for each group. In this way the group was made visible as a collective and could report and share their experiences from their visit.

The visitor's blog was temporary and accessible in a mobile media centre in a gallery; a quieter part of the museum. This, in a museum with no infrastructure for digital technologies, became a real design challenge. The aim of establishing design spaces in which inquiry could happen was based on the overall purpose of focusing

---

[3] Dagny Stuedahl, Ine Fahle, Live Roaldset and Morten Vøyvik.

on engagement as activity in digital spaces (Heape 2007). The experiment had a particular focus on how the visitors created their own narratives in the activities through taking pictures and sharing the experience with others. Hence engagement was understood as activity in relation to the content and the artefacts presented in the museum. Museum research and interaction research related to museum design have so far paid little attention to engagement in terms of activity.

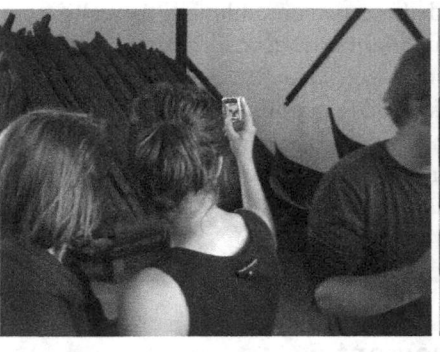

Fig. 4.3 The school class of 13-year olds used mobile phones to collect interesting photos in the exhibition. In the media centre these photos was shared on a visitor blog

The design experiment was planned as a museum visit. An ethnologist opened it with a talk about his research into the reconstruction of Viking boats. The pupils were asked to use both the camera and the video on the mobile phones to collect clues and arguments related to one of the ships during their visit. They were also given two tasks to choose between. The latter gave them an opportunity to explore different levels of the existing exhibition in the museum. The pupils had 30 min to explore the museum's permanent exhibitions, and collect clues, photos and video recordings related to the tasks. Then they went to the media centre and uploaded their recordings by making a blog entry and writing some comments related to the visual material.

The pupils had a day off from school, although their teacher joined them. The experiment was defined as leisure time by the teacher because it was not connected to planned learning activities in the class, but being with school mates instead of with friends might have had a bearing on the activities the pupils were asked to do in the museum.

The material the pupils collected consisted of mainly video recordings made up of small video documentaries of the museum exhibition. Video recordings were uploaded to the blog in the media centre with the use of Bluetooth – which in fact represented a major technical hindrance, since, with Bluetooth, this took a very long time.

One of the major methodical findings of the experiment was that too many activities in a design setup can make the empirical outcome chaotic and fragmented. The museum visit was planned to last for 2 hours and it included a talk, introduction of new mobile telephones, collection of pictures and recordings, uploading of the collected material, and blogging. It seemed to be too tight. Also, the fact that the pupils had not made any preparations about reconstructions of Viking times in advance was a challenge for the outcome of their museum visit and their understanding of the message of cultural heritage built on interpretative work. The major outcome of the experiment was, therefore, not related to the technical limits of Bluetooth-uploading time, but to the limits of building a design set-up based on blog entries and camera photos without having enough time to conduct more than one iteration. The group was familiar with *Facebook* communication, as well as MSN communication, but blogging was a challenge, also to find out how to make blog entries on the visitor blog, as well as to find ways to publish the documentation they had made with the mobile telephones. Apart from these challenges, it seemed that the use of the mobile telephones as tools for exploring the museum exhibits was successful. This supports findings from other studies of museum communication with mobile telephones (Walker 2007) (Fig. 4.4).

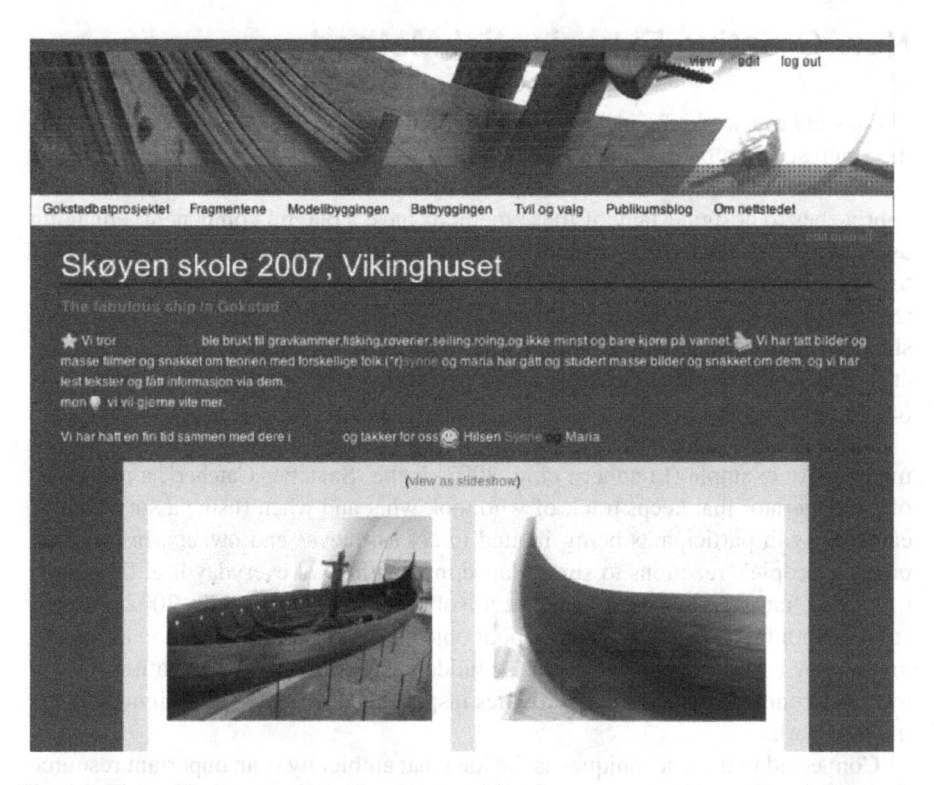

Fig. 4.4 The weblog communicates the museum visitors' engagement with specific artefacts and information exhibited

Limitations in terms of time had implications for how the weblogs were used as a source for the collection of virtual ethnographies. The pupils did not have enough time to concentrate on the articulation of their visits with the blog entries. They probably communicated in a similar way with the blog entries to how they do with MSN, hence, with many visual tags, smiley's and use of colours but with little focus on the photos they had uploaded and with even less effort on the written text.

The design experiment with blog entries mirrored the digital competencies that the 13-year-old group possessed. It also gave an impression of the youth's engagement and motivation to explore the museum exhibits with the use of mobile telephones and social media. However, the experiment gave less information about the experience gained from the museum exhibit and the understanding of cultural heritage reconstruction and research. The example brought up questions related to the design set-up, the number of activities, and technologies or new social media. Along with methodological challenges in digital design, new experiential methods are also needed to envision the direction of digital design research.

New Creative Experiential Methods

PD has always worked with users in imaginative ways. We can also observe how the interest in embodied interactions, tangible, personal and gestural interfaces, ambient media and the like, has spurred the use of creative and experimental approaches to design. Many of these methods have a playful component; engaging users and designers in joint explorations of the design space, and helping designers to better understand user needs. Techniques range from open-ended interventions in real life to envisioning change in a simulated environment. While some of the envisioning methods use high-tech representations of a design/context (e.g. Bardram et al. 2002), others work with simple mock-ups, with 'props' or miniature environments (e.g. a dolls house).

Some creative and experimental design projects make use of provocation as a method. An example (Lundberg et al. 2002) is the 'Snatcher-Catcher', a prototype of a refrigerator that keeps track of who took what and when (using a surveillance camera), with participants being invited to act as thieves and owners, in this way probing people's reactions to surveillance in situations of everyday life. Designers have used 'un-useless objects' or 'Placebo objects' (Dunne and Raby 2002) to elicit stories, both factual and imagined, about objects and places. Provocation as a technique, they argue, brings the otherwise hidden aspects of peoples' relationships to their environment to the fore; it provides inspirational material for designers to use in their work.

Connected to these techniques is the idea that ambiguity is an important resource for design, as it 'allows the designer's point of view to be expressed while enabling users of different sociocultural backgrounds to find their own interpretation' (Gaver et al. 2003: 233). Ambiguous situations may provoke participation in meaning-making. Ambiguity may reside in the object – a famous example is Marcel Duchamp's 'Fountain' (1917) which is a piece of art but also mass manufactured, ready-made, and an urinal; in the information – which may be blurred or fragmented; or in the personal relationship of the viewer with the piece – as in Van Lieshout's 'Love Carvan', where a simple container has been furnished with a functionally decadent, elegant interior, provoking reflection about conditions and standards of living, aesthetic values, etc. (Gaver et al. 2003).

Working with 'cultural probes' – carefully designed packages of postcards (with images and questions), maps (for identifying relevant places), disposable cameras with listed requests for pictures, photo albums (for a story in pictures), media diaries, and other material (Gaver et al. 1999) – is a method for provoking inspirational responses from large numbers of people. They make sense where the aim is to understand local cultures, bridge distance, identify diversity and differences. This method is inspired by the Situationists and the Fluxus movement who worked with the concept of psycho-geographical maps of cities as representations of the topology of people's longings, fears, isolation, sociality, etc.

Another group of creative design methods makes use of games, theatre, and performance as a means for stimulating participation and creating and performing 'scenarios of use'. The spectrum reaches from scripted plays/games to ad-hoc improvisation. Design games are widely used in urban planning, with miniature environments helping participants to understand the design of a place, identify problems, and talk about future developments. While some of these environments are pre-designed and 'realistic', others are more abstract, encouraging people to envision and act out their own ideas.

'Props' have an important role in these playful explorations. They not only represent design ideas, but also help evoke futures and serve as 'dream tools'. While abstract objects give space to imagination, expanding the solution space for a design, more concrete objects help focus and narrow down. 'Pivots' (Urnes et al. 2002), for example, are partly abstract, partly concrete material-symbolic representations of devices or contexts that allow participants to move between imagined and real worlds. Participants may have to imagine 'a day in their life', solving a particular problem with the help of a 'pivot' which may stand for a particular technical solution. In general, props stand for places, objects, themes (e.g. mobility), and roles; they may be used as part of a scripted play or of ad-hoc improvisations in users' environment, with users creating realistic and authentic scenarios (Jacucci and Kuutti 2002). Often, videos are produced as part of these explorations, with users enacting their ideas. This video material can in turn be used by participants to engage in different forms of interactive story-telling.

'Drama' and 'theatre' as design methods open up a wide range of possibilities of engaging participation in a context of digital design. They allow people to learn in an experiential way, involving all their senses and emotions. Alternative actions can be explored in a safe environment. Designers have a chance to develop empathy for situations, people, and cultural differences; and they benefit from people's expertise concerning their own environment. Design often involves strong narrative elements. Participants may use multimedia material – diagrammatic sketches, video clips, sound, etc. – for expressing their stories.

In the following, we describe some practical examples of using creative-experiential design methods as part of developing digital designs, discussing their potential.

123

Working with Cultural Probes

Cultural probes are a widespread technique, but there are few discussions of the problems related to developing evocative probes on the one hand and analysing and translating them into meaningful interventions or design ideas on the other. Here are some examples of probes that students at Vienna University of Technology designed as part of their year project, in which they collaborate in small groups with the aim to research a topic and develop a design. The project involves a series of activities: setting up a design space and elaborating the theme; research – video observation and expert interviews; the use of creative design methods (e.g. cultural probes, drama and props, design games) with the aim of generating 2–3 design ideas; selection of a design idea and development and presentation of an interactive prototype with a tangible user interface. This is a complex learning situation. The students' background is purely technical and this project is the first (and only) time when they are confronted with a participatory and creative design approach, which here is about 'living with disabilities'.

This was the first time these students were confronted with this technique and the probes they designed were of varying quality and not all of them successful. What is interesting to see is that students quickly learned what was working and what was not. Through the probes that they returned (or failed to return), participants provided immediate feedback on what they thought of as being evocative.

One of the student groups[4] that had chosen people in wheelchairs for their design project produced a series of pictures of places that may be difficult to access, letting different people identify spots they thought of being hard to reach, and provide an explanation. For example the phone box in Fig. 4.5 (left) has been marked with six arrows. The yellow arrows point to the slot for inserting coins (too high),

Fig. 4.5 Marking accessibility problems for people in wheelchairs

---

[4] Patrick Kastner, Helmut Chlebecek, Clemens Czermak, Andreas Regner, Wolfgang Spreicer.

the position of the receiver (also too high); one the green arrows highlights a threshold (an obstacle for people in wheelchairs). In the picture to the right, showing a place in a supermarket for checking in film rolls, respondents have marked the table and computer screen, as well as the upper shelves, as too high and the whole construction with its pink drawers as difficult to access.

With these probes, students used people (mostly their friends) for increasing their own awareness of barriers in different urban places for people in wheelchairs. The probes proved very useful as they documented a series of concrete situations to pay attention to when creating design ideas.

Another group[5] had decided to work with non-hearing people. As, in their first naïve approach, the students thought of communication between non-hearing and the hearing as being 'impeded', they designed probes that required written input, such as a diary and a story,. The students were disturbed to experience that non-hearing people may have considerable difficulty in expressing themselves in writing (see the returned probe Fig. 4.6). They learned that, up to very recently, BSL (the sign language) was not properly taught in Austrian schools to non-hearing people, and this made it very difficult to learn read and write in German (which from the point of view of non-hearing could be considered a second language).

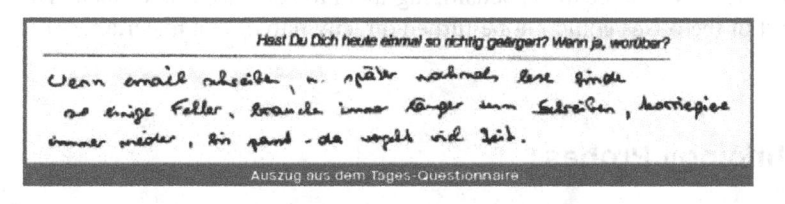

Fig. 4.6 Probe with question: 'Do you remember having been really angry? Why was it so?' – 'When I write an email and read it later I usually find mistakes, writing always takes time, I correct until it fits, and this takes a lot of time'

The students also designed a small box that participants were supposed to fill with small relevant objects that told of events of their day (Fig. 4.7). The students cleverly introduced the constraints of box size and small opening so as to limit the input to 'small, ideally foldable objects such as old theatre tickets or notes but also newspaper clippings or wrappings from sweets'. Also important was the impossibility of opening the box, having placed something in it. What they found in the boxes were, for example, an uncooked noodle (for what the person had been cooking), a used pen (reminding of the difficulties of non-hearing students to follow a university course), a turquoise ribbon (standing for the official recognition of BSL, but also for 'deaf power'), and a print-out of an email informing the recipient that a particular course was being translated into sign language. The messages embedded in these boxes were very personal and did not necessarily lend themselves to a

---

[5] Florian Grashäftl, Bernhard Holzer, Albert Kavelar, Peter Smejkal, Criselda Tasico.

Fig. 4.7 Small box with carefully designed constraints

straightforward analysis. They rather helped students establish a relationship with the people they worked with, sensitizing them to some aspects of their lives. The content of the boxes could not be turned directly into design materials.

Technology Probes

The notion of 'probes' can be extended to simple objects or prototypes of a design, which are placed in person's environment to find out about their habits, patterns of communication, and so forth: 'A probe is an instrument that is deployed to find out about the unknown – to hopefully return with useful or interesting data' (Hutchinson et al. 2003:18). The technology probes that were installed in people's homes as part of the *Interliving Project* were supposed to be open-ended and co-adaptive, encouraging people to use them in unexpected ways. The technologies were also used to collect data about their own use. They were simple but functioning: a writable LCD tablet and pen placed in a high traffic area of the family home; a video probe and customized remote control for sharing impromptu images among family members.

Looking at first, rough implementations of a design idea as 'probes' is intriguing, as it helps developers focus on the concept rather than on a specific technical implementation. We (see Chapter 2) worked with this approach while developing mixed reality tools in support of participation in urban renewal (Maquil et al. 2007, 2008). Very early on in the project, we brought what we termed 'technology probes' to a psychiatric hospital in Paris to engage in first conversations with users – architects engaged in designing interventions, some hospital staff including two senior professors of psychiatry at the Sorbonne, as well as some additional urban planners – about our idea of collaborative envisioning.

We considered these 'technology probes' as design concepts rather than early prototypes, and our interest was in a conceptual discussion of issues around collaborative envisioning. We had at this stage developed a rough notion of a tangible user interface, consisting of a tabletop, on which colour objects could be placed, representing different kinds of content. We used a simple colour tracking mechanism and a barcode interface.

Fig. 4.8 A probe of a tangible user interface and mixed-reality scene

Workshop participants quickly learned to create visual scenes, with a background image and virtual objects that can be manipulated (turned, sized up and down) by moving the colour objects with which they are associated. The functionalities we had provided were very limited and the resulting visual scenes crude (as compared with architects' representational techniques, see Fig. 4.8) but they spurred participants, imagination and a lively debate about which way to go.

A major topic of this discussion was how to change perspective. Participants wanted to be able to see an object from different points of view, or to have the impression of moving around, to be able to turn the head and get another perspective. This discussion sparked the idea of building a rotating table and to experiment with a static and/or a video panorama. The positioning of objects was experienced as difficult. There was a lack of depth, and exact sizing and placement were near to impossible. The idea took shape to project the map of the area onto the table to facilitate the positioning of objects in the scene relative to each other. Controlling the size of virtual objects by combining several shapes also produced some problems. As the tracking system was not sufficiently precise, the virtual objects seemed to 'jump' because the 'noise' of tracking made them change their size.

Another issue connected to tracking was that users partly overlapped the shapes when touching them with their hands. This pointed to the need for a different design of the colour objects that would invite users to grasp them from the side instead of touching them from above. Another problem was that users were not able to recognize immediately which content the objects they were manipulating represented and they sometimes disagreed about which colour was linked to what content (see Maquil et al. 2008).

These and other observations sparked a hectic phase of re-design. Our intuition had worked. Participants immediately captured the conceptual issues we were interested in and contributed to them. 'Technology probes' are sketchy implementations of concepts and it requires some imagination on the users' part to understand the concept and how a fully developed mixed reality tool could help them in their work. Still, as others have also argued, the 'hands-on' experience within a real context supports this imagining and extending the possibilities of the probes.

Setting Up a Design Space

Observations of design practice point to the importance, in particular at the beginning of a project, of mobilizing a wide array of resources that help designers to expand their problem and solution space. An essential part of creative-experimental design, therefore, consists in what we call 'setting up a design space' (Fig. 4.9). We have seen that the material-physical presence of these resources is supportive of designers 'seeing things differently'.

When we enter an architectural studio, we will see that it is used as a design space. Most of the desks are covered with various artefacts: plans, sketches, notes, photographs, faxes, books, samples. On shelves are large collections of binders for each of the current projects; in the entrance area a collection of scale models is on display, and on the walls are 3D visualizations, sketches, photographs, and newspaper clippings from previous and current work. The walls close to the architects' workspaces, too, are used as an exhibition space and decorated with materials from current work. These materials do not only make work visible: they are reminders of ideas, design principles, ways of working, and so forth. Visitors are implicitly invited to

Fig. 4.9 Design spaces: an architectural office (*left, middle*), experimental design course in Oslo (*right*)

look, ask and comment. Some of the material can be termed, 'inspirational'. We know that designers take inspiration from many different aesthetic and scientific discourses – from the fine arts and the theatre to biology and mathematics. Some designers use pictorial material for generating and expressing their ideas, others prefer poetry, metaphorical text, music, 'data'.

This can be illustrated using the example of an experimental design course at the University of Oslo, where the task was to create a tangible user interface in relation to skiing. The small group started with the creation of a design space in the studio. Low-tech prototype materials, like coloured sheets of paper, modelling clay, pencils, scissors, tapes etc., were provided. The participants were asked to bring an object (a probe) associated with skiing and a second one with no association to skiing. Furthermore, the participants collected images, created a story, and filled the design space with visual associations and texts in relation to skiing. The design material was pasted onto the wall in order to inspire the creation of ideas and suggestions. The material illustrated the participants' experiences of skiing through the images of equipment needed for skiing, feeling for snow, what one carries along (food, chocolate to drink, sweets), pleasure and fun. The illustrations helped bringing small-talk and laughter about cross-country skiing as a Norwegian phenomenon to the multi-cultural group. The aim with the visual representations was also to stimulate ideas related to the theme instead of moving directly to solutions (see also Mörtberg and Stuedahl 2005).

A richly populated design space serves several purposes: it helps designers to break away from premature problem definitions and ready-made, conventional approaches – because design problems are not 'given', design work is about defining and framing problems rather than working with predefined solutions; it supports 'openness' – that decisions about possible design trajectories are not made too quickly and it requires that the different actors present their work in a form that is open to the possibility of change.

Performative Development

The renewed interest in the body in design has introduced opportunities to include performance in design – and design as performance. The performative spans the spatial, the temporal and the enactive, and engages people's bodies in the creation of the new. The performative aspects are found in both, process and result.

A number of methods for envisioning make use of performance as a means for multi-sensory and processual understanding and experience. Playing out a scenario for a new work situation, a new organization of work, or a new action gives both, designers and users, a 'feeling for' the envisioned result. In many experience design projects performance as a method is used to enact user experiences thereby making them better understandable to designers (e.g. Buchenau and Suri 2000). Drawing on knowledge about performance and theatre adds to the design of the design process with concepts of dramaturgy, choreography, and narration, in particular exploring the non-textual sides of the design.

Performance as part of the design result draws on knowledge about performativity to a much larger extent. As a design result, the performance is locally situated, it is ephemeral, unique, and personal as well as cultural, historical and social. A simple form of performance is a computer system where performance of bodily movements is the input (e.g. games like Wii Sports). The system can make for improved performance (Larssen, forthcoming). Staged performances engage the spectator bodily, allowing her/him to turn into a co-player (Sunderburg 2000). Interactive installations used to objectify, present, and discuss design projects are inherently different from the performance.

Performative events have an important role for the collective creativity of designers. We had the opportunity to observe this in another research project where we observed architectural students in their work and provided them at the start with rather simple technologies for animating their designs (barcode and sensors). One of the students – she participated in a semester project studying stadiums – presented her design ideas for an 'extreme stadium' (one of the design tasks), which she imagined in the heart of Vienna, occupying the area between Vienna's Fine Arts and Natural History Museums (Jacucci et al. 2005). The student had prepared a football field and two slide shows, with one screen displaying cultural aspects of football (images, sound, video) and the second screen displaying her design ideas in the making. The slide show was operated through a sensor that had been fixed underneath the football field (Fig. 4.10). The presentation itself was designed as a football game, with the building sites being the teams – stadium versus museums – and the design ideas being the team-tactics, and herself as the referee, with a yellow card and a whistle signalling a 'bad idea' and a goal as a 'good idea'. In the words of the performer, 'it was the idea to have soccer-games or soccer tools like the ball, yellow card as sensor tools. Also the architectural project used soccer terminology instead of common architecture words'.

The performative arts engage the full bodily spectrum to create user experiences that involve all senses and – in particular – emotions in the user as spectator or co-

Fig. 4.10 A miniature football field as an interface to guide the presentation

actor (e.g. Morrison et al. 2010). Games are designed to be used by co-actors, while theatre normally leaves the user as a spectator. Digital design has the option to design for a larger range of user roles, with a more complex mix of arts and utilities to create user experiences. The performative is a central strand in understanding and creating emerging aspects of digital design.

Manipulate Media: A Workshop on Performative Development

One of the contexts that experimented with techniques from improvisation theatre for designing interactive installations was the CONVIVIO Workshop 'Manipulate Media', which was held in July 2005 at the Centre of Contemporary Art in Glasgow. (www.convivionetwork.net).[6] The aims of this workshop, which attracted participants from systems design, web design, performative arts, and digital arts, were to:

- Experiment with applications of tangible interfaces to media production (e.g. participative media), media literacy and learning.
- Discover how selected practices and approaches from performance art may inspire interaction design.
- Explore a combination of (tangible) interaction design and media design (genres, formats, etc.).
- Observe and try out interactions with a mixed media installation in a public exhibition as a common base for discussion and reflection.
- Participate in the emergence of a new area: performative development of ubiquitous multimedia.

The workshop started with a demonstration of techniques from improvisation theatre. The idea was to show participants how to exploit the role of constraints that can be imposed (designed) within collective activities. Two actors (under the direction of Carlo Jacucci) improvised scenes working with different types of constraints:

- *Imposing Verbal Constraints* – e.g. limiting the number of words actors are allowed to utter.
- *Composing with Different (Conflicting) Wills or Tasks* – e.g. embodying a character in a scene and playing the 'tale game' at the same time.
- *De-Composing the Actor* – e.g. decomposing hands and body; decomposing bodies and voices.
- *Playing with Time* – e.g. repeating a scene within different timeframes.

The researchers prepared three installations, all set up within one large room. Each installation was used by two different groups during the practical sessions. In the first practical session, the task was to construct a narrative using one of the three

---

[6] Carlo Jacucci, Giulio Jacucci, Thomas Psik, Ina Wagner, and Mira Wagner.

installations and working with two self-defined constraints (to physical action and time) and to present the narrative collaboratively. The task for the second practical session was to perform without speaking, and to find interesting new constraints.

Cubes on Glass Surface: This installation had been designed to support the editing and montage of digital material (Fig. 4.11). It allowed the composition of video clips using small cubes, the faces of which were covered with visual markers, which were detected by a camera placed underneath a glass table. Stills from video clips or drawings represented the content. The audio files were covered with white cardboard, because we were interested in the annotations the users would create to represent and remember a certain sound. This approach was not successful, because they found other ways of ordering the cubes without marking them.

The glass surface was relatively small so that only three cubes could be aligned joining each other. The space was divided into two areas: the upper rectangle was dedicated to recognizing video files, and the lower one for audio files. A separate marker was used to activate the reading of the installation. When playing the installation, the last image played always stayed as a projection, until a new arrangement was activated. The size of the gaps between the cubes represented time and could also be used as a compositional element. We decided to use segments of very different video clips and audio material for content.

Fig. 4.11 The cube installation

Participants soon realized that there were random time-space gaps between the activated images. The rhythm of their performance came from the engagement with the interface. Participants picked up cubes, positioned them telling a piece of a story, which was picked up by someone else. It turned out that the initial technical instability of the system enriched the story-telling process.

What we learned in particular from users' performances with this installation was how to come to terms with the physical limitations of the interface and what determines the rhythm of a performance – the role of physical action (picking up cubes) and of a technology-based time lag.

Staging Experience: The concept of the second installation was to experiment with the relationships between actor, space and action, using tagged figurative objects (Fig. 4.12). Participants could associate the props with video clips, stills, and sound.

One group selected a person who orchestrated the story-telling through words, images and sound, thereby setting a time constraint, giving structure and rhythm to the group. Participants took turns in picking up a prop for creating their part of the story. The second group (which was not allowed to use words) used the props as puppets. They introduced them as shadow actors into the setting of the projected clips, skilfully merging the shadows with the images to transform the scene, or using the image as background in which smaller events could take place. In this way they could re-contextualize the content and create a space around the projections, making a stage in which the images became three-dimensional. The puppets represented the element of control, with which they tried to structure the randomly appearing images and sounds.

Fig. 4.12 Story-telling using tagged objects

We found that the constraints forced participants to generate a grammar similar to that of improvisation theatre. The props had several functions – their digital content was used to trigger the installation and their physical form served to widen the space for interpretation.

Space and Bodies: The initial version of this installation was created for two users, and the space was associated with the metaphor of an elevator. Our scenario was that two people meet in a confined space, wearing/picking up optical markers, each of which is associated with a still image. The unfolding conversation is between these two people facing the wall, and cross-projected sets of images. The images (all but four taken from an advertisement) focused on facial expressions, small gestures, the light situation, props, and the space, the idea being that different combinations of images would lend themselves to differing interpretations.

The constraints in this example were the physical space (a square representing the elevator and the necessity to face the wall – the camera) as well as time and rhythm. The instability of images and difficulties in controlling their creation posed an additional, technology-based constraint.

This installation was used in completely unexpected ways (Fig. 4.13). Participants did not have the patience to relate to the images, so they found other ways of using the tools to expand the possibilities of interaction. For example, one single performer plastered himself with markers and tried to create a specific rhythm by repeating a sequence of motions that would reveal the various markers to the camera. Two performers, each holding 2 or 3 markers, performed rhythmic movements in front of the camera, creating repetitions, delays, and intervals.

Fig. 4.13 Unexpected uses

In this case we decided to re-design the installation (Fig. 4.14). We split the images into thirds so that three markers are required to recreate a complete image. We also made size and format of the image parts dependent on the distance between camera and marker so that users' positions and their distance from each other directly influence the projected collages they create. Furthermore, we played with the time lag between the reading of the image and its projection so that it became possible to overlay two images in the same place. Playing with the time lag also resulted in a rhythmical use of image making along with the possibility of holding onto an image.

In this workshop we used performance as an approach to development, with the performative events generating new insights for participants. The steps are as follows: set up a (public) installation, invite people to perform with it; set constraints, change them, play with them; evaluate and re-design.

The performative uses of installations, such as the simple examples we prepared for the Manipulate Media workshop, reveal aspects of a design that would otherwise not become so evident. For example, we could observe:

- Actors collaboratively composing (in some cases using an 'orchestrator' or 'conductor').
- The use of props – e.g. for triggering action, playing media.
- The use of bodies – expressive gesturing, mimicking, dancing, synchronizing movement.
- The use of media – e.g. as background, as narrative element.

We also learned how to distribute and coordinate tasks, action and gestures and how people move in space collectively, in a compositional way.

An important element of this method is the borrowing of practical wisdom from improvisation theatre. Traditions of work in the performing arts are powerful means to learn about all aspects of life. But we cannot rely solely upon theories and conceptual accounts of those traditions. We need to learn from artists who have found their own personal ways of carrying forward an approach through practical attempts. This is why a special interest is in the personal style and wisdom which directors and actors have in their work. For example, we can devise collective authoring practices through editing, montage and assemblage in mixed media relying on the ways in which collective creation is carried out in the performing arts. Here we can look at this in particular from five specific angles: *creativity and constraints, contiguity, sensitivity, masks,* and *narratives.* By these consideration we found sources for *inspiration,* other than methods to train and devise practical designing work (Jacucci et al. 2005).

Fig. 4.14 The re-designed installation

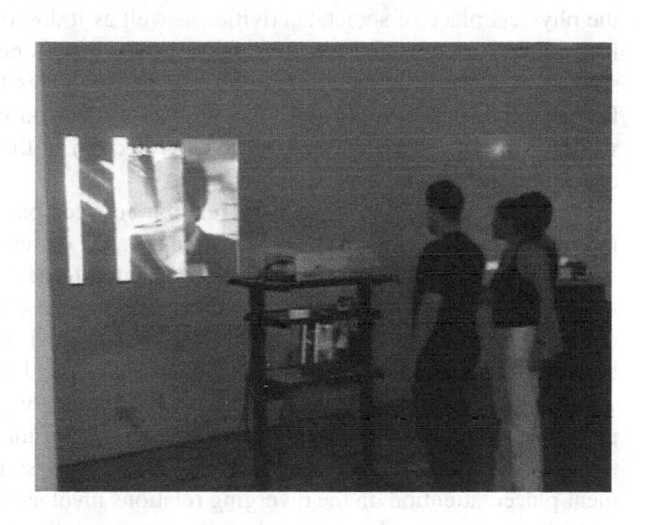

Oikos as Concept for Digital Environments

Designing experiments for communicative digital environments may focus on the relations between several media, tangible or intangible interfaces, movements of the actors as well as narratives that, in a composition, accumulate in the communication with the user – and which, in the end, are part of the engagement and experience of the user. From a media point of view, the concept of a communicative environment involves several different types of media, all communicating with the user in different modalities that all give diverging experiences to the isolated user – but that give an additional experience to users in an assembly. The concept of mixed media only partly describes the experience and the role of the user in these digital environments, as it focuses on the media and less on the relation between mediating artefacts and the narratives involved. Further, important issues for the building of narratives and of the experience of narrative, such as a narrator perspective and the narrator's identity, can quickly be translated into valuable issues of a complex design concept for the digital environment. This forms a challenge for a media-related perspective on communication design for digital environments.

In the search for a design concept that can integrate the assembly of influences in digital environments, as well as with a focus on the users' activities to communicate with this assembly, the Greek concept *oikos* is suitable. Aristotle used *oikos* to describe the state of being content with the things you build yourself, as the process is the goal. The political life in Aristotle's meaning was the dynamic in itself, between collections of parts that cannot exist without the other. *Oikos* has several translations and meanings, related to the belonging and familiarities that humans are born with. In this sense, it conceptualizes complex issues of relations, such as between a place and its social frameworks, between shared values, norms, goals and the experiences of these. Being the seed of the polis, *oikos* both describes the physical place of societal activities as well as it describes strategies and meanings related to this place. In this sense, *oikos* represents the opposite of public spaces, as it involves the community and the identities that are part of place. In feminist discourses, the concept has implied a focus on good functions combined with good care, as *oikos* also worked as protection of the Greek societal structure and family relations.

With this focus on place and the relation between parts, *oikos* seemed to be an interesting concept for a design experiment based on an ecological understanding of digital environments. In a design case related to designing narrative spaces in mixed media environments, the goal was to engage users in communication with diverging media and narrative forms. The design goal was to establish a concert between digital material, digital media, narratives and the activities of actors in exhibits. The leading concept of a digital environment was the notion of *oikos* as a place with both a specific ecology, with a diversity of materials and with a certain topography that is related to this. Using *oikos* as a design concept for the experiment placed attention on the diverging relations involved in communication, where both the spatial and the temporal were of major influence, as well as the actors' procedural activities.

The *oikos* helped realize a design space for the designers involved in the project, as well as it represented a narrative space and a place for engaging in activities related to the narratives. The concept opened up for possibilities of focusing on the relation between the different elements of the environment; the media, the content, the visual effects, the embodiments of the narratives, the types of activities invited for, as well as the visitors activities in the space.

In this installation, a large design studio was fitted with several exhibition boards, replicas, objects and other physical things well-known from exhibition contexts. The exhibition-prototype was organized in relation to the concept of *oikos,* where the digital media and the digital content were understood as a relationship between the visitor's engagement, activities and exploration of the exhibition space. The tangible media were supported by digital media communicating digital recordings of the project that were to be communicated in the exhibition.

The project was about the reconstruction of a Norwegian Viking boat, from the translations of archaeological fragments to building a model, and then to the building of the wooden boat in a full scale version. It was a goal in the design project to prevent the communication of the reconstruction process as a linear narrative, and to take as a starting point the stages of the reconstruction that were visible and tangible. The aim was to provide a link between the digital documentation of the reconstruction process, and the tangible outcome of the reconstruction – with the interactions of the visitor. The exhibition was structured with the use of four stands: (a) an introduction; (b) a station for telling the story about the fragments and the work of interpretation; (c) translation of archaeological fragments to building a model as an understanding of a boat, and; (d) building the wooden boat and sailing the reconstructed interpretation (Fig. 4.15).

Fig. 4.15 Children exploring the digital environment of an exhibition

A class of 10-year-old pupils was invited to explore the exhibition in groups of two and three. Each group was given a mobile phone and had 1 hour to explore the exhibition. The had to register their mobile phones as users in the Bluetooth system in order to get access to the digital video clips and audio files that were uploaded on their mobile phones as they moved close to the stations. In addition, the children were encouraged to build their own version of the cardboard model, in that they could puzzle out part of the boat as a paper puzzle and attach it to an interactive model. They were asked to document each station of activities and information, and send it to the social space– where their material was projected on a wall in the exhibition.[7]

Understanding the digital environment as a relational ecology between diverse digital media, diverse media as well as diverse narratives from audio and video to photo, as well as tangible replicas in cardboard and wood, is a design challenge. The challenges as may focus on these relations without any understandings of the variety of relations experienced by the user. This is especially the case where the relations that were built by ubiquitous technologies, in the Bluetooth-based system for nearfield downloads and uploads, offering a system for making relations between visitors, their mobile phones and a visitor WIKI on the project website – as well as a social space projected on a wall in the exhibition. The complexity challenged the concept of relation in the planning of the environment, and one tool for this was the concept of relevance drawn from the *oikos*. *Oikos,* understood as an environment, where function and care of the inhabitant's activities, did, to a certain degree, guide the set up of the design space to make it ready for the users to explore. Still, it needs to be further explored in relation to the understanding of the narrative relations that are also essential for the experience and meaning making of participants in digital environments.

Closing Comments

We have described a range of methods; some are familiar and have been used many times; others new, creative and experimental methods that open up for new opportunities but pose new challenges. We addressed ethnography and its relationship with design, as well as ethnography as part of PD pointing at new challenges posed by digital or virtual settings. New social media opens up for new ways of communication that also have methodological implications. We have discussed implications with Hine and her arguments that new technologies allow for de- and re-construction of commitments made in non-digital practices. Some of these examples of de- and re-constructions are, e.g. where to do the research, how to create trust in online interactions, how to create informed consent, ethical issues related to 'lurking' as a method, and also new demands related to the design set up. Digital design research will also benefit from the development of creative and experimental methods. We have provided examples of how to use cultural and technology probes, and the use of narrativity and performances as methods that

---

[7] The exhibition experiment was based on a collaboration between the two research projects RENAME at Department of Media and Communication and ENCODE 01, InterMedia University of Oslo December 2007 and February 2008. An important part of the practical development of the exhibition space was offered by the staff at InterMedia Lab; Ole Smørdal, Live Roaldset, Idunn Sem, Jeremy Toussaint, Thomas Drevon, Per Christian Larsen, Knut Quale, Marcus Marsilius Gjems Theie as well as the master students Morten Vøyvik and Ine Fahle.

enable the creation of new design ideas and application areas but also produce new problems to be considered.

We started with a discussion about reflexivity, pointing out that reflexivity goes beyond understandings of how assumptions intersect in research. The extension from reflections to reflexivity was made to move away from the risk that almost the same story is told again depending on that the individual researcher turns back to her/his interpretation. Also with reflexivity there is a risk that it (a similar understanding) 'only displaces the same elsewhere' (Haraway 1997: 16). However, our analytical perspectives are multidisciplinary and most of the methods described in this chapter are collaborative and use multidisciplinary perspectives whereby it is possible first to juxtapose the different perspectives and then to compare. Multiple approaches may contribute to multiple understandings and views. The individual chapters in Part II may serve as additional discussions on this issue.

References

Alvesson M., & Sköldberg K. (2000). *Reflexive methodology: New vistas for qualitative research.* London: Sage.
Bardram, J., Bossen, C., Lykke-Olesen, A., Nielsen, R., & Halskov-Madsen, K. (2002).Virtual video prototyping of pervasive healthcare systems. In B. Verplank, A. Sutcliffe, W. Mackay, J. Amowitz & W. Gaver (Eds.), *Proceedings of the 4th conference on Designing interactive systems: processes, practices, methods, and techniques (DIS '02)*, London, England (pp. 167–177). New York: ACM press.
Bauman Z. (1993). *Postmodern ethics.* Oxford: Blackwell
Berg, E., Mörtberg, C., & Jansson, M. (2005) Emphasizing technology: Sociotechnical implications. *Information Technology and People*, 18(4), 343–358.
Bermann, T. (1983): *Ansattes kunnskap og læring under innføring av EDB, med bibliotek som eksempel* (In Norwegian: Employees' knowledge and learning when introducing EDP, exemplified with libraries). LOFIB Læringsorienterte forsøk i bibliotek Report series. Oslo: Work Research Institute.
Bermann, T., & Thoresen, K. (1988). Can networks make an organization? In I. Greif (Ed.), *Proceedings of the 1988 ACM conference on Computer-supported cooperative work (CSCW '88)*, Portland, Oregon, United States (pp. 152–166). New York: ACM press.
Beyer, H., & Holtzblatt, K. (1998). *Contextual design: Defining customer-centered designs.* San Francisco, Calif.: Morgan Kaufmann.
Bjerg, L., & Nielsen, L. Verner (1978). *Edb-systemer inden for avisproduktion.* Master's thesis. Århus: DAIMI, University of Århus.
Bjerknes, G., & Bratteteig, T. (1984). The application perspective: An other way of con-ceiving edp-based systems and systems development. In M. Sääksjärvi (Ed), *Report of the seventh Scandinavian research seminar on systemeering* Helsinki School of Economics, Studies B-75 (pp. 204–225). Helsinki: Helsinki School of Economics.
Bjerknes, G., & Bratteteig, T. (1987a). Florence in wonderland. System development with Nurses. In G. Bjerknes, P. Ehn, M. Kyng (Eds.), *Computers and democracy. A Scandinavian challenge* (pp. 279–296). Aldershot: Avebury.
Bjerknes, G., & Bratteteig, T. (1987b). Perspectives on description tools and techniques in system development. In P Docherty, K. Fuchs-Kittowski, P. Kolm & L. Mathiassen (Eds.), *System design for human development and productivity: Participation and beyond* (pp. 319–330). Amsterdam: North-Holland.
Bjerknes, G., & Bratteteig, T. (1987c). *Å implementere en idé. Samarbeid og konstruksjon i Florence-prosjektet* (Florence report no 3). (In Norwegian: To implement an idea. Collaboration

and construction in the Florence project). Oslo: Department of Informatics, University of Oslo.

Bjerknes, G., & Bratteteig, T. (1988a). The memoirs of two survivors— or evaluation of a computer system for cooperative work. In I. Greif (Ed.), *Proceedings of the 1988 ACM conference on Computer-supported cooperative work (CSCW '88)*, Portland, Oregon, USA (pp. 167–177). New York: ACM press.

Bjerknes, G., & Bratteteig, T. (1988b). Computers—utensils or epaulets? The application perspective revisited. *AI & Society*, 2(3), 258–266.

Bjerknes, G., Bratteteig, T., & Espeseth, T. (1991). Evolution of finished computer systems: the dilemma of enhancement. *Scandinavian Journal of Information Systems* 3(1), 25–46.

Bjerknes, G., Bratteteig, T., Kaasbøll, J., Sannes, I., & Sinding-Larsen, H. (1985). *Gjensidig læring* (Florence report no 1). Oslo: Department of Informatics, University of Oslo.

Blomberg, J., Giacomi, J., Mosher, A., & Swenton-Wall, P. (1993). Ethnographic field methods and their relation to design. In D. Schuler and A. Namioka (Eds.), *Participatory design: Principles and practices* (pp.123–156). Hillsdale, NJ: Lawrence Erlbaum Assoc.

Bratteteig, T. (1997). Mutual learning. Enabling cooperation in systems design. In K. Braa & E. Monteiro (Eds.), *Proceedings of IRIS'20*, Oslo: Department of Informatics, University of Oslo.

Bratteteig, T. (2004). *Making change. Dealing with relations between design and use.* Diss. Oslo: Department of Informatics, Faculty of Mathematics and Natural Sciences, University of Oslo.

Brown, B, Lundin, J., Rost, M., Lymer, G., & Holmquist, L-E. (2007). Seeing ethnographically: Teaching ethnography as part of CSCW. In L. Bannon, I. Wagner, C. Gutwin, R. Harper, and K. Schmidt (Eds.), *Proceedings of the 10th European Conference on Computer-Supported Cooperative Work (ECSCW'07)*, Limerick, Ireland (pp. 411–430). London: Springer.

Buchenau, M., & Suri, J.F. (2000). Experience prototyping. In D. Boyarski & W. A. Kellogg (Eds.), *Proceedings of the 3rd conference on Designing interactive systems: processes, practices, methods, and techniques (DIS'00)*, New York City, New York, United States (pp. 424–433). New York: ACM press.

Budde, R., Kautz, K., Kuhlenkamp, K., & Züllighoven, H. (1992). *Prototyping: An approach to evolutionary systems development.* Berlin: Springer.

Bødker, K., Kensing, F., & Simonsen, J. (2004). *Participatory IT Design. Designing for Business and Workplace Realities.* Cambridge, Massachusetts, London, England: MIT Press.

Dunne, A., & Raby, F. (2002). The placebo project. In B. Verplank, A. Sutcliffe, W. Mackay, J. Amowitz & W. Gaver (Eds.), *Proceedings of the 4th conference on Designing interactive systems: processes, practices, methods, and techniques (DIS '02)*, London, England (pp. 9–12). New York: ACM press.

Ehn, P. (1989). *Work-oriented design of computer artifacts.* Hillsdale, N. J.: Lawrence Erlbaum Associates.

Elovaara, P., Igira, F., & Mörtberg, C. (2006). Whose Participation? Whose Knowledge? – Exploring PD in Tanzania-Zanzibar and Sweden. In I. Wagner, J. Blomberg, G. Jacucci & F. Kensing (Eds.), *Proceedings of the ninth conference on Participatory design: Expanding boundaries in design - Volume 1*, Trento, Italy (pp. 105–114). New York: ACM Press.

Floyd, C. (1984). A systematic look at prototyping. In R. Budde, K. Kuhlenkamp, L. Mathiassen & H. Züllighoven (Eds.), *Approaches to prototyping* (pp. 1–18). Berlin: Springer.

Forsythe, D. E. (1999). 'It's just a matter of common sense': Ethnography as invisible work. *Computer Supported Collaborative Work*, 8(1–2), 127–145.

Foucault M. (1973). *The birth of the clinic: An archaeology of medical perception.* [Original 1963]. London: Tavistock Publications, Ltd.

Gasser, L. (1986). The integration of computing and routine work. *ACM Transactions on Office Information*, 4(3), 205–225.

Gaver, B., Dunne, T., & Pacenti, E. (1999). Design: cultural probes. *Interactions*, 6(1), 21–29.

Gaver, W. W., Beaver, J., & Benford, S. (2003). Ambiguity as a resource for design. In G. Cockton & P. Korhonen (Eds.), *Proceedings of the SIGCHI conference on Human factors in computing systems (CHI '03)*, Ft. Lauderdale, Florida, USA (pp. 233–240). New York: ACM press.

Greenbaum, J., & Kyng, M. (Eds.). (1991). *Design at work: Cooperative design of computer systems.* Hillsdale, N.J.: Lawrence Erlbaum Associates.

Gregory, J. (2000). *Sorcerer's Apprentice: Creating the Electronic Health Record, Re-inventing Medical Records and Patient Care.* Diss. San Diego: Department of Communication, University of California-San Diego.

Grudin, J., & Grinter, R. E. (1995). Ethnography and design, *Computer Supported Cooperative Work,* 3(1), 55–59.

Hammersley, M., & Atkinsons, P. (1995). *Ethnography: Principles in practice.* London: Routledge.

Haraway, D. J. (1994). A game of cat's cradle: science studies, feminist theory, cultural studies. *Configurations,* 2(1), 59–71.

Haraway, D. J. (1997). *Modest_witness@second_millenium. Female man©_meets_ oncomouse™: Feminism and technoscience.* New York and London: Routledge.

Harper, R. H. R. (2000). The organisation in ethnography: a discussion of ethnographic fieldwork programs in CSCW. *Computer Supported Cooperative Work,* 9(2), 239–264.

Heape, C. R. A. (2007) *The Design Space: the design process as the construction, exploration and expansion of a conceptual space.* Diss. Sønderborg: Mads Clausen Institute Syddansk Universitet.

Hine, C. (2000). *Virtual ethnography.* London, Thousand Oaks, New Delhi: SAGE Publications.

Hine, C. (Ed.). (2005). *Virtual methods issues in social research on the Internet.* Oxford, New York: BERG.

hook, b. (2000). *Feminism is for everybody: Passionate politics.* Cambridge MA: South End Press.

Horst, H. (2006). The blessing and burdens of communication: cell phones in Jamacian transnational social fields. *Global Networks* 6(2), 143–159.

Hughes, J., King, V., Rodden, T., & Andersen, H. (1994). Moving out of the control Room: ethnography in system design. In J. B. Smith, F. D. Smith & T. W. Malone (Eds.), *Proceedings of the 1994 ACM conference on Computer supported cooperative work (CSCW '94),* Chapel Hill, North Carolina, United States. (pp. 429–439). New York: ACM press.

Hutchinson, H., Mackay, W., Westerlund, B., Benderson, B. B., Druin, A., Plaisant, C., et al. (2003). Technology probes: inspiring design for and with families. In G. Cockton & P. Korhonen (Eds.), *Proceedings of the SIGCHI conference on Human factors in computing systems (CHI '03),* Ft. Lauderdale, Florida, USA (pp. 17–24). New York: ACM press.

Ito, Mizuko and Okabe, D Daisuke (2005). Technosocial situations: Emergent structuring of mobile e-mail use. In M. Ito, D. Okabe & M. Matsude (Eds.), *Personal, Portable, Pedestrian: Mobile Phones in Japanese Life* (pp. 257–273). Cambridge, MA: MIT Press.

Jacucci, C., Jacucci, G., Wagner, I., & Psik, T. (2005). A manifesto for the performative development of ubiquitous media. In O. W. Bertelsen, N. O. Bouvin, P. G. Krogh & M. Kyng (Eds.), *Proceedings of the 4th decennial conference on Critical computing: between sense and sensibility,* Aarhus, Denmark (pp. 19–28). New York: ACM Press.

Jacucci G., & Kuutti, K. (2002). Everyday life as a stage in creating and performing scenarios for wireless devices. *Personal and Ubiquitous Computing,* 6(4), 299–306.

Jacucci, G., & Wagner, I. (2005). Performative uses of space in mixed media environments. In Davenport, E., & Turner P. (Eds.), *Spaces, spatiality and technologies* (pp. 191–216). London: Springer.

Jordan, B. (1997). Transforming ethnography: reinventing research. *CAM, Cultural Anthropology Methods Journal,* 9(3), 12–17.

Jordan, B., & Henderson, K. (1994). Interaction analysis: foundations and practice. *The Journal of the Learning Sciences* 4(1), 39–103.

Karasti H. (2001). *Increasing sensitivity towards everyday work practice in systems design.* Diss. Oulu: The Faculty of Science.

Karasti H. (2003). Can film developers be(come) technology developers? Reflections on gendered expertise and participation in system design. In C. Mörtberg, P. Elovaara, & A. Lundgren

(Eds.), *How do we make a difference: information technology, transnational democracy and gender* (pp. 29–49). Lueå: Printing Office Luleå University of Technology.

Kaasbøll, J., Braa, K., & Bratteteig, T. (1992). User problems concerning functional integration in thirteen organizations. In Avison, Kendall & DeGross (Eds.), *Human, Organizational, and Social Dimensions of Information Systems Development, Proceedings of the IFIP WG 8.2 Working Conference*, Noordwijkerhout (pp 61–81). Amsterdam: North-Holland.

Larssen, A.T. (forthcoming). *'How it feels, not just how it looks': Kinaesthetic experience as an experiential quality for technology design and the study of technology use.* Diss. Sydney, Australia: Department of Computer Systems, Faculty of Information Technology.

Law, J. (2004). *After method: Mess in social science research.* London, New York: Routledge.

Ling, R. (2008). *New tech, new ties: how mobile communication is reshaping social cohesion.* Cambridge, Mass.: MIT Press.

Luff, P., & Heath, C. (1998). Mobility in collaboration. In S. Poltrock & J. Grudin (Eds.), *Proceedings of the Conference on Computer-Supported Cooperative Work (CSCW '98)*, Seattle, WA (pp. 305–314). New York: ACM Press.

Lundberg, J., Ibrahim, A., Jönsson, D., Lindquist, S., & Qvarfordt, P. (2002). 'The snatcher catcher': an interactive refrigerator. In O. W. Bertelsen (Ed.), *Proceedings of the second Nordic conference on Human-computer interaction (NordiCHI '02)*, Aarhus, Denmark (pp. 209–212). New York: ACM Press.

Malinowski, B. (1961[1922]). *Argonauts of the Western Pacific: an account of native enterprise and adventure in the archipelagoes of Melanesian New Guinea.* New York: E.P.Dutton & Co, Inc.

Madison, D. Soyini (2005). *Critical ethnography. Thousand Oaks: methods, ethics, and* performance. London; New Delhi: Sage Publications.

Maquil, V., Psik, T., Wagner, I., & Wagner, M. (2007). Expressive Interactions Supporting Collaboration in Urban Design. In T. Gross & K. Inkpen (Eds.), *Proceedings of the 2007 international ACM conference on Supporting group work (Group 2007)*, Sanibel Island, Forida, USA (pp. 69–78). New York: ACM press.

Maquil, V., Psik, T., & Wagner, I. (2008). The colortable: a design story. In A. Schmidt, H. Gellersen, E. Van den Hoven, A. Mazalek, P. Hollies & N. Villar (Eds.), *Proceedings of the 2nd international conference on Tangible and Embedded Interaction (TEI'08)* Bonn, Germany (pp. 97–104). New York: ACM Press.

Mead, M. (1973[1928]). *Coming of age in Samoa: A psychological study of primitive youth for western civilisation.* Magnolia: Peter Smith.

Morrison, A., Sem, I. & Havnør, M. (2010). Behind the wallpaper: performativity in mixed reality arts. In A. Morrison (Ed.), *Inside multimodal composition* . Cresskill, NJ: Hampton Press.

Munk-Madsen, A. (1978). *Systembeskrivelse med brugere* (In Danish: System description with users). Masters thesis, Århus: DAIMI, University of Aarhus.

Mörtberg, C., & Stuedahl, D. (2005). Silences and Sensibilities - increasing participation in IT design. In O. W. Bertelsen, N. O. Bouvin, P. G. Krogh & M. Kyng (Eds.), *Critical Computing-Between Sense and Sensibility Proceedings of The Fourth Decennial Aarhus Conference* (pp. 141–144). Aarhus, Denmark: ACM Press.

Mörtberg, C., & Elovaara, P. (2010). Attaching People and Technology – between e and government. In S. Booth, S. Goodman S & G. Kirkup (Eds.), *Gender Issues in Learning and Working with Information Technology: Social Constructs and Cultural Context* (pp. 83–98). Hershey, USA: IG Global.

Nelson, H. G., & Stolterman, E. (2003). *The design way: Intentional change in an unpredictable world foundations and fundamentals of design competence.* Englewood Cliffs, N.J.: Educational technology publ.

Newman, S. (1998). Here, There, and Nowhere at All: Distribution, Negotiation, and Virtuality in Postmodern Ethnography and Engineering. *Knowledge and Society*, 11, 235–267.

Orr, J. E. (1996) *Talking about machines: An ethnography of a modern job.* Ithaca, NY: ILR Press.

Plowman, L., Rogers, Y., & Ramage, M. (1995). What are workplace studies for?, In H. Marmolin, Y. Sundblad & K. Schmidt (Eds.), *Proceedings of the fourth conference on European*

Conference on Computer-Supported Cooperative Work (ECSCW '95) (309-324). Dordrecht: Kluwer Academic Publishers.

Puri, S., Byrne, E., Nhampossa, J.L., & Quraishi Z.B. (2000). Contextuality of participation in IS design: a developing country perspective. In A. Clement & P. van den Besselar (Eds.), *Proceedings of the eighth conference on participatory design: Artful integration: interweaving media, materials and practices* – Volume 1, Toronto, Ontario, Canada (pp. 42–52). New York: ACM Press.

Prøitz, L. (2007). *The mobile phone turn. A study of gender, sexuality and subjectivity in young people's mobile phone practices*. Diss. Oslo: Department of Media & Communication, Faculty of Humanities, University of Oslo.

Rorty R (1994). Method, social science and social hope. In S. Seidman (Ed.), *The postmodern turn: New perspectives in social theory* (pp. 46–64). New York: Cambridge University Press.

Ruhleder, K., & Jordan, B. (1997). Capturing complex distributed activities: Video-based interaction analysis as a component of workplace ethnography. In A. S. Lee, J. Liebenauer & J. I. DeGross (Eds.), *Proceedings of the IFIP TC8 WG 8.2 International Conference on Information Systems and Qualitative Research* (pp. 246–275). London UK: Chapman & Hall, Ltd.

Rutter, J., & Smith G. W. H. (2005). Ethnographic presence in a nebulous setting. In C. Hine (Ed.), *Virtual methods issues in social research on the Internet* (pp. 81–92). Oxford, New York: BERG.

Sander, T. (2005). Researching the online sex work community. In C. Hine (Ed), *Virtual methods issues in social research on the Internet* (pp. 51–66). Oxford, New York: BERG.

Shapiro, D. (1994). The limits of ethnography. In J. B. Smith, F. D. Smith & T. W. Malone (Eds.), *Proceedings of the 1994 ACM conference on Computer supported cooperative work (CSCW '94)*, Chapel Hill, North Carolina, United States. (pp. 417–428). New York: ACM Press.

Sjöberg, C. (1996). *Activities, voices and arenas: Participatory design in practice*. Diss. Linköping: University of Linköping.

Star, S. L., & Strauss, A. (1999). Layers of silence, arenas of voice: the ecology of visible and invisible work. *Computer Supported Cooperative Work*, 8(1–2), 9–30.

Strauss, A. (1985). Work and the division of labor. *The Sociological Quarterly*, 26(1), 1–19.

Stuedahl, D. (2004). *Forhandlinger og overtalelser. Kunnskapsbygging på tvers av kunnskapstradisjoner i brukermedvirkende design av ny IKT (Negotiations and persuasions. Knowledge building crossing knowledge traditions in user participation in design of new ICT, in Norwegian)*. Diss. Oslo: InterMedia, Faculty of Education, University of Oslo.

Stuedahl, D. & Smørdal, O. (2010) Design alignment of modalities. In A. Morrsion (Ed.), *Inside mulitimodal composition*. Creshill N.J.: Hampton Press.

Stuedahl, D., Smørdal, O., Dindler, Petersen, C. P. D. (2007). Use of blogs for studying users engagement with mobile telephones in museum environments. Short paper for the *10th European Conference on Computer Supported Cooperative Work (ESCW '07)* Workshop Techniques and Methodologies for Studying Technology Use 'In the Wild', Limerick, 24–28 September 2007.

Suchman, L. A. (1987). *Plans and situated actions. The problem of human-machine communication*. Cambridge: Cambridge University Press.

Suchman, L., & Wynn, E. (1984). Procedures and problems in the office. *Office Technology and People*, 2(2), 133–154.

Sunderburg, E. (Ed.). (2000). *Space, site, intervention: Situating installation art*. Minneapolis: University of Minnesota Press.

Thoresen, K. (1981). *Terminalarbeidsplasser* [Computer Screen Work Places]. Oslo: Tanum-Norli.

Thoresen, K. (1999). *Computer use*. Diss. Oslo: Department of Informatics, Faculty of Mathematics and Natural Sciences, University of Oslo.

Turnball, D. (2007). Maps narratives and trails: performativity, hodology and distributed knowledges in complex adaptive systems: an approach to emergent mapping, *Geographical Research*, June 2007, 45(2), 140–149.

Urnes, T., Weltzien, Å., Zanussi, A., Engbakk, S., & Kleppen Rafn, J. (2002). Pivots and Structured Play: stimulating creative user input in concept development. In O. W. Bertelsen (Ed.), *Proceedings of the second Nordic conference on Human-computer interaction (NordiCHI '02)*, Aarhus, Denmark (pp. 187–196). New York: ACM Press.

Wagner, I. (1994). Connecting communities of practice: feminism, science and technology. *Women Studies International Forum*, 17 (2/3), 257–265.

Walker, K. (2007). Visitor-constructed personalized learning trails. In *proceedings from Museums and the web 2007, the international conference for culture and heritage online*, 11–14 April 2007, San Francisco, Carlifonia.

Wynn, E. (1979). *Office conversation as an information medium*. Diss. Berkeley: University of California, Berkeley.

Part 2

Multiple Perspectives on Design Research

5

A Matter of Digital Materiality

Tone Bratteteig

Design is about imagining future possibilities and making things that enable us to live some of these possibilities. 'Maybe the most fascinating thing about design is that it is a process that starts with a thought and ends with the world looking different' says Stolterman (2007: 13). Design starts with the making of ideas – of possibilities and of problems and solutions (Schön 1983; Lanzara 1983). The ideas get clearer as they are formulated and communicated, concretized and tried out in detail (Bjerknes and Bratteteig 1987; Henderson 1999). The imagining of the design result drives the process forward.

An essential part of design is giving form to some material so that it embodies the idea(s). Designers thus think both abstractly and very concretely about materials, making an effort to choose the right one. Design is 'thinking with materials', and designers need deep knowledge about their materials (Stolterman 2007: 16). The future possibilities – the ideas – are grounded upon how well the designer understands the materials: the material opens possibilities but also creates limits and conditions for the design. Some even say that the material 'tells' the craftsperson what it 'wants to be' – a particular piece of wood 'wants to be' a particular form in a chair. Similarly, the craftsperson must have a feeling for how a particular idea 'wants to be' manifest in a material or be expressed in different materials. Design thinking is thus very closely connected with the physical world, with the material and with the complex reality – with the hand (Stolterman 2007: 18).

What about digital design? Löwgren and Stolterman (1998) claim that the computer is a 'material without qualities', referring to Robert Musil's (1996) novel '*The man without qualities*'. Computers are extremely malleable, and everything that can be described can be represented on a computer. Vallgårda and Redström (2007) criticize Löwgren and Stolterman's view by commenting that a material without qualities or properties can 'hardly qualify as a material' (p. 514). The fact that the material is 'so flexible it almost can take on any form we want' misleads us to see it as 'immaterial'.

This chapter sets out to discuss whether it makes sense to talk about computers as material in digital design. After a brief introduction to computers and the digital, I move on to talk more generally about materials in design, and discuss how the vocabulary for describing materials can be used to talk about digital material.

I. Wagner et al. (eds.), *Exploring Digital Design: Multi-Disciplinary Design Practices*, Computer Supported Cooperative Work, DOI 10.1007/978-1-84996-223-0_5, © Springer-Verlag London Limited 2010

Because of the 'immaterial' nature of digital material, I also consider other ephemeral and less physical ('immaterial') creative processes, and how they might help us understand digital design and digital materials. The last section looks at relations between materials and the design process, and points to the work and the knowledges concerned with materials needed in design. The conclusion summarizes my view on whether it makes sense to talk about digital material and whether it matters that it is digital.

Characteristics of the Digital

It is well known that the term digital comes from 'digit', which means number – originally 'finger' referring to counting on the fingers. 'Digital' means represented as digit(s), using calculation by numerical methods that involve the Arabic numbers 1–9 and the symbol 0, or by discrete units. According to this definition, anything represented by numbers is digital: my old thermometer is digital because I measure the temperature according to a scale and read it as a digit.

However, we normally use the term 'digital' about digital representations implemented on, or by means of, a computer: the digital is also electronic. In an electronic digital system – a computer – the digital representation is binary, as zeroes and ones. Everything represented – the system's 'content' or information – is converted to binary form. Moreover, an electronic digital system (a 'digital system' for short) is a system that uses discrete values represented as binary numbers or non-numerical symbols like letters, signs, icons for input, processing, transmission, storage, or display of information, rather than a continuous spectrum of values as in an analogue system.

Abstractions

The basis for digitization is differences in voltages in electric current defined binary as 0 or 1. The data signals in a digital system carry one of two electronic (or optical) pulses: logical 1 when there is a pulse, logical 0 when the pulse is lacking. The binary representation is an abstraction from the fact that current is continuous; the abstraction is a construct, a choice, like all abstractions. The computer is built up by digital logic, by combinations of zeroes and ones into logical gates: AND if both inputs are high or 1, output is 1; OR if one input is 1, output is 1. The gates are further combined into increasingly complex logical units (see Fig. 5.1).

A digital electronic system is one of abstractions, all the way from the voltages to the surfaces that meet the user (Dourish 2001). When we click on the printer icon on our computer screen, the computer performs a number of operations at many levels of abstraction in order to connect to the physical device and make it print the signs we want it to print. The services offered at the user interface (such as printing, copying, searching) are abstractions that represent programs that are sets of abstractions themselves (like instruction sets, database architectures, communication protocols) materialized in transistors and electrical pulses. Remember: even the binary signals are abstractions imposed on continuous voltages.

The abstraction levels concern types of machine behaviour, and in computing it is common to refer to the physical machine (wires, disks, and integrated circuits); the logical machine (the collection of logical elements made from physical components like and/or gates); and the abstract machine ('a collection of abstract symbolic processors designed to resemble aspects of the world modelled' (Winograd and Flores 1986)). The abstract machine is described in modelling languages constructed to communicate to the programmer as well as to support the translations from the abstract logic into a physical machine (Winograd 1979). It is the idea of an 'abstract machine' that makes us think that the computer is immaterial.

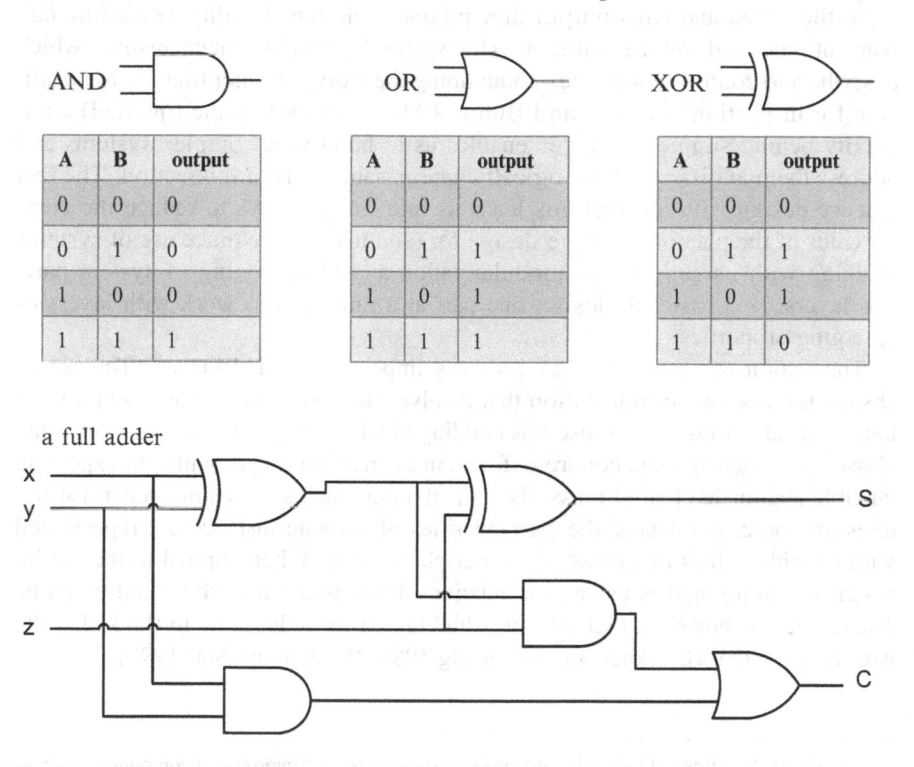

Fig. 5.1 AND, OR and XOR gates and a full adder made up of binary logic (Glette 2009)

Abstraction is the most fundamental characteristic of digital system design. The term abstract originates from Latin *abstrahere*: to pull away. Abstraction means to omit details and represent selected qualities of a phenomenon. Kramer (2007) emphasizes two aspects of abstraction: (1) 'the act of withdrawing or removing something' (p. 38) which means to leave out selected properties of the object in question, and (2) 'the process of formulating general concepts by ... extracting common features from specific examples' (p. 38). Abstraction in this sense is used in other disciplines: in art, where details are omitted in Munch's painting 'The Scream' for example, or in music, with Bach's use of counterpoint. A famous design example is the map of the London Underground, in which the directions and distances do not match the physical, geographical underground tracks – and in this way makes the map easier to navigate from.

In digital design, abstraction allows systems to be considered at different levels of detail, to be broken down into individual components, and to be reassembled. Thus, the activity of systems design is to create and manipulate abstractions. Abstractions help us manage the complexity of a system by allowing us to hide it selectively in logical 'black boxes'[1] that we relate to through the characteristics of their interface. The 'we' above can be human users or pieces of code (i.e. other black boxes), and all we need to know about the black-boxed abstraction is what input they need and what output they produce (the functionality, procedure call conventions, and return values). The system's internal mechanisms, which describe and control how it goes about doing the work, are intentionally not available for inspection (Dourish and Button 1998: 414). Hiding the (internal) complexity behind simple interfaces enables us to build very complex systems and address them at different and logically appropriate levels of interaction. The fact that we design with abstractions leads us into finding ways to reduce the complexities of the phenomenon we design for (and to), and we make use of systems thinking with its support for modularization and black-boxing of system parts and layers. It is easier to design one part at a time, and to work with layers of emerging properties.

The notion of 'abstract' also connotes impersonal and detached. The act of abstraction is an act of translation that involves the creation of generalized logical units and categories that are used as building blocks in a system. Abstractions span classes of objects that are concrete: found in the real world, particular and specific, tangible and made of solid mass. Systems thinking[2] helps in making general structures and processes where the particularities of a single instance are represented with variable values in a class of similar phenomena. When applied to the world, systems thinking makes us see the relationships between the whole and its parts. The danger is, however, that systems thinking easily seduces us to think that the world *is* a system (Bjerknes and Bratteteig 1987; Bowker and Star 1999).

---

[1] Nygaard (2002) defines object-oriented systems as composed of interrelated components, where each component has some properties and some action connected to it. The objects are instances of object classes. Classes can be divided into subclasses that inherit the properties of their superclass. The modularization in object-oriented programming is a method of simplification. The black-boxing achieved with modularization is also discussed by Latour (1999).

[2] Systems thinking applies a systems perspective on the world (for some time and for a purpose, see (Nygaard 2002, 1986)), seeing a part of the world as a whole, built up of interdependent components, where the properties of the system are more than the sum of the properties of its parts; emergent properties appear at different hierarchical levels of the system (Checkland 1981): A bike as a whole has different properties than the sum of each of its parts.

Representations

Abstractions represent concrete objects, structures, and processes that exist in the real world and, as the abstractions are concretized come to exist in the real world themselves. The representations aim to model actual, physical phenomena happening in a real-world context, and represent what are considered to be the important properties of the phenomenon (which means that they embody choices and trade-offs). However, the modeller may over-simplify or mis-represent the phenomenon if that serves the purpose of the modelling.

Representations are not uniquely related to digital systems; they are an integrated aspect of how human beings deal with complex phenomena (e.g. medical diagnosis systems, see Bowker and Star 1999). In the hospital I am represented as a patient and I 'become' my blood test results or heartbeat or dysfunctional body part. Laboratory tests of the enzymes in a blood sample are interpreted as a representation of the size and seriousness of a heart attack.[3] Measurements of the heartbeat on a scope screen need to be interpreted because different monitors display the same rhythm differently (Bjerknes and Bratteteig 1987, 1988). Fortunately, such measurements are interpreted, taking into account the particularities of the individual real patient: the body, the sickness history, the medication, and the physical observations of the phenomena represented. Making and interpreting such representations are part of the professional work that health workers do. The representation is about their work object: the patient, and is a work object itself (Berg 1997).

The making of representations is a basic craft in system design – at many abstraction levels. Literature on system design indicates many different ways to go about representing the system-in-the-making; focusing on objects, data structures, functions etc. Software engineering methods describe how to plan and build a robust system, where the aims and requirements of the system are given. System development methodologies are often built upon a set of methods and tools for making system representations, supporting a particular view on systems and solutions (Andersen et al. 1990; Bjerknes and Bratteteig 1987). At lower levels, the representations detail the system parts, and the representations can be unambiguous, as the context of use is a fully specified computer system rather than a more or less unpredictable human use setting.

Another essential characteristic of the computer as an abstract machine is that it is 'symbolic' (Winograd and Flores 1986). It is made up of symbols taken to be tokens or signs that stand in for something else: they represent something else. A focus on symbols suggests that interpretation and meaning-making is necessary for design and use of the symbolic machine, in fact the machine must be given meaning

---

[3] The enzymes ALT (*alanine transaminase*) and AST (*aspartate transaminase*) leak out of damaged muscles into the blood and can be found after a heart infarct, but can be caused by other muscles as well. The same holds for the enzyme CK (*creatine kinase*). The combination of these should identify the source of the muscle damage. Blood tests for enzyme values are taken until the level is decreasing, signalling that the damage on the muscle has stopped (Bratteteig 2004).

by its users. The users in this sense co-construct the symbolic machine by relating to it in accordance with the meaning s/he gives to it by using it. The challenging ambition for designers is thus to communicate their (intentional) interpretation well enough for the users to share their interpretation and utilize the intended potential of the machinery in question. Symbolic machines therefore depend on successful communication between designer and user (Andersen 1986), and, hence, on how the symbols are materialized and given form in the artefact. This adds to the general challenge in design to communicate functionality of an artefact (Bratteteig 2002). The communication of the functionality of a symbolic machine can make use of both symbolic and physical forms, but need to speak the language of the contemporary culture.

Symbols are culturally and socially defined. Context and genre constitute conventions that shape our interpretations of symbols[4]: the symbol '@' reads differently after you have opened your first email account. Symbols require interpretation and meaning-making: linguists would say that the 'reader' needs to understand the meaning (the signified) that is communicated through the symbol/sign (the signifier). Symbols are concrete forms – matter – that signify meaning.

> [The] representation is in the mind of the beholder. There is nothing in the design of the machine or the operation of the program that depends in any way on the fact that the symbol structures are viewed as representing anything at all (Winograd and Flores 1986: 86).

Representation is an act of signification, which includes creating a concrete expression that can be made sense of by the people in its context. All representations influence the way we act and understand the world, and get embedded in our way of living; a classic example is the clock representing time – deeply embedded in Western society, culture and organizations, even our identity (Weizenbaum 1976).

Process

A basic characteristic of digital electronic systems is that they are program executions: they do things. A program execution is a process characterized by aspects like input (start condition), output (end result), and properties such as speed, duration, rhythm etc. A machine that performs processes automatically is an automaton; the automaton processes input and transforms it to output, it produces responses to stimulus, and it changes its state(s). Simple automatons, like the thermostat, are set to turn the heat on and off for you. More complex automatons, such as the calculator or the bank's account system, do the mathematical calculation for you.

---

[4] cf. Andersen 1986; Andersen & Bratteteig 1989. In this sense, language is a system of symbols, but the meaning-making in our culture also includes iconic symbols and symbols that speak to other senses: hearing the Nokia phone signal three short, one long, three short beeps is easily interpreted as 'sms' in Morse code ▪▪▪ – ▪▪▪ by telegraphers.

'A washer is a washer, whatever clothes you put inside, but when you put a new program in a computer, it becomes a new machine' (Gelernter 1998: 24). A program is a description of a 'virtual machine' that becomes real when activated in a computer. The concept of the virtual machine is 'a way of understanding software that frees us to think of software design as machine design' (Gelernter 1998: 24).

The virtual machine combines two aspects of the digital (and electronic) that makes it into a general machine: (1) the fact that the representation is an abstraction and can refer to anything: a number could be a temperature, an amount of money, a time (hour or date), a measurement of length or weight – it depends on the context in which we set the number; and (2) the fact that the representation is an abstraction of a process in a machine that can change its state based on input, and that contains a specification of operations to produce output.[5] It is the second aspect that I shall discuss in this section.

The abstract machine includes structures for action, both automatic action and responses on input from internal as well as external sources (like humans). The structure for action is called a procedure: a series of operations in a particular order that, when performed, will transform a particular input to a specified output. A procedure specifies the preconditions and frames for action. A simple thermostat measures the temperature and when a certain condition occurs, a certain action is taken; the temperature is below a preset value and so a heater is turned on. The washing machine washes by moving its interior at a certain speed (presented by labels as 'careful' or 'normal' washing), at certain temperatures and for a certain time (not independent of the temperature).[6] The ATM does not give me any money if I input a number greater than the number that the bank computer has registered as the deposit in my bank account.

In an electronic system, the procedure is called an algorithm; a concept traditionally used to denote the solving of mathematical problems. 'Algorithms are abstract descriptions of the solution to a problem, which may be solved by a machine' (Knuth 1973). Algorithms express structures for processes, and can be characterized by properties that refer to the way they are structured – finiteness, definiteness, input, output, effectiveness (Knuth 1973).

Algorithms work with symbols that refer to classes of concrete instances and thus represent abstractions from the specific values of the instances. 'The concept of "a variable" represents an abstraction from its current value' (Dijkstra 1976: 11). The concept of a variable captures the 'the quintessence of programming'.

A well-known example of an algorithm is Quicksort, invented in 1960 by C.A.R. Hoare. Quicksort sorts a set of cards (or whatever needs to be sorted) in an elegant way. It makes use of some basic abstraction mechanisms: recursion (referring to itself), and calling a procedure (a repeated set of operations). It partitions an array into small and big elements, and continues to do the same in each of the two new arrays

---

[5] All digital electronic systems are Turing machines: universal devices that manipulate abstract symbols and can simulate the logic of any computer (Minsky 1967; Knuth 1973).

[6] A curious fact is that the temperature scale on the machine fits the categories of the washing instructions attached to the clothes: the making of wool-washing programs is intertwined with developing ways of preparing wool so that it can stand this kind of machine washing.

(recursively) until there are no arrays left to be sorted. Here follows a short way of specifying this algorithm, below is a program that does the same:

```
pick one element of the array (the "pivot").
partition the other elements into two groups:
    "little ones" that are less than the pivot value, and
    "big ones" that are greater than the pivot value.
recursively sort each group. (Kernighan and Pike 1999: 32)
```

The representation of the Quicksort algorithm – and the algorithm itself – illustrates the way that real phenomena can be translated and represented in an electronic system. The skills and knowledges about forming digital (electronic) materials are just like this: forming abstract structures and algorithms into representations that can be read by humans (like the program below) and translated to electronic signals visible in machine behaviour.

```
/* quicksort: sort v[0] .. v[n-1] into increasing order */
void quicksort(int v[], int n)
{
    int i, last;
    if (n <= 1)                         /* nothing to do */
    return;
    swap(v, 0, rand() % n);             /* move pivotlem to v[0] */
    last = 0;
    for (i = 1; i < n; i++)             /* partition */
    if (v[i] < v[0])
    swap(v, ++last, i);
        swap(v, 0, last);               /* restore pivot */
        quicksort(v, last);             /* recursive sort */
        quicksort(v+last+1, n-last-1);  /* each part */
}
```
The swap operation, which interchanges two elements, appears three times in quicksort, so it is best made into a separate function:
```
/* swap: interchange v[i] and v[j] */
void swap(int v[], int i, int j)
{
    int temp;
    temp = v[i]
    v[i] = v[j]
    v[j] = temp
} (Kernighan and Pike 1999: 32-33)
```

Processes controlled by a machine need to be correct, predictable, controllable, reliable etc.; they must behave according to a set of engineering qualities. We need to trust that the calculation is correct or else the calculator is useless. In particular, processes that are non-transparent and incomprehensible processes must be correct. We accept that we cannot make a call if we have no connection to a provider, or if the battery is flat, but if the telephone cannot be used under normal conditions, we throw it away. Predictability and human control of automatons is crucial.

As the automaton is always right, a certain level of knowledge is required to question its output. This also holds for the automation and digitization of manual processes:

it makes us question the value of the knowledge involved in the manual processes. In the 1970s, Norwegian dairies were automated and knowledge concerned with tasting, smelling, feeling, looking at the milk as it travelled through the factory became obsolete – and eventually disappeared. Instead came knowledges concerned with the representation of temperature and chemical composition, which constitutes a different set of skills and knowledges (cf. Zuboff 1989). The delegation of knowledge work to machinery made it uninteresting to maintain the knowledge about the physical processes.

Automatons are machines that process things and perform operations by themselves. An automaton has been delegated a symbolic process, e.g. calculation (Säljö 2000) and its calculations may be part of a larger human activity system. We can see the automaton as a 'prosthesis' that enhances human capacities (Weizenbaum 1976). As a lever enhances the human capacity to lift, a calculator enhances human capacities concerned with calculations. We can say that the calculator is delegated some calculation work – or even intelligence and memory – and that calculation is performed by an assemblage of humans and machinery.[7]

The level of abstraction of knowledge in society increases when many physical processes get transformed and translated to representations and measurements. The ubiquity of representations influences how we relate to both signifiers and the signified.

Chapters 1 and 2 describe aspects of contemporary ICTs that deeply influence our experiences with computers, both as users and designers: the developments in size-power-price relations, the miniaturization and the distribution of computing on ubiquitously present digital networks (be it gsm, gps, or the Internet). Nano technologies and extremely small computing devices that act as sensors and actuators can be distributed in the environment and embedded in physical materials (even woven into textiles). Wireless and mobile computing enable us to let go of the desk top as the place where we work or gather information. Ubiquitous computing (Weiser and Brown 1997) and 'everyware' (Greenfield 2006) open up possibilities for processing power in virtually all everyday artefacts. Digital design can range from global communication systems to digital dust. Many digital electronic systems are distributed over several devices and parts, and with increasing convergence to other systems. These developments give new possibilities for the digital material to be mixed with other materials, or take different shapes from previous generations of ICTs.

Materials in Design

A material is 'a physical substance that shows specific properties for its kind' (Vallgårda and Redström 2007: 514). Material is the stuff of which things are made. Material – referring to matter – is physical; it has a mass and occupies space, but it does not normally have a specific form and can be shaped. Matter can exist in

---

[7] Like distributed cognition. See Hutchins 1995, Säljö 2000, Latour 1999, and Suchman 2007 for different accounts of distribution of cognition over humans and artefacts.

different phases: solid, liquid, gas or plasma. Material sciences operate with categories of materials referring to their properties or their origin (artificial, natural). We can perceive materials by one or more of our senses.

While contemporary architecture and product design use digital tools to construct their expressive forms (see e.g. Sevaldson 2005; McCullough 1998), the material used is still mainly non-digital: wood, stone, brick, glass, metal, plastic, concrete etc.

The close relation to the material is easy to see in the crafts, for example in traditional boat building (like the Viking ships, see Fig. 5.2 left) where the builder tries to find pieces for the arched ribs by looking for trees with 'knees', as such naturally grown crooks are more rigid and flexible than wood with fabricated bends (Juul-Nielsen 1984).

Fig. 5.2 From *left to right*: Ribs of Viking boat, and Gramazio and Kohler's computer-designed brick wall and corridor, see www.gramaziokohler.com

Architects are also close to their materials, and spend much time getting to know, explore and experiment with materials as part of the inspirational phases of their design processes (Jacucci and Wagner 2007). Contemporary architects' works include experimental use of materials; for example, the architects Gramazio and Kohler (2007) digitally construct and automatically build brick walls that express their design idea – and challenge our conception of a brick wall (see Fig. 5.2 right and middle). The composition of bricks so that they express shapes (grapes) and allow light into the room while avoiding direct sunlight, is impossible to construct without a computer. The automatic production of the brick walls required the bricks to be glued – which gave the wall elements different properties than bricks put together with mortar; the wall elements, for example, can be lifted and moved (Gramazio and Kohler 2007).

The material properties can be characterized on many levels, from the chemical basis to the use value of (compositions of) materials (e.g. timber shifts its properties when glued in layers (laminate)). Vallgårda and Redström (2007) characterize materials according to their:

- *Substance* The substance is the physical stuff that the material is made of. Definitions of materials refer to the atoms and the chemical and physical properties of the stuff.
- *Structure* Materials have structures – we can even say that materials at a molecular level are structures. Some material properties have their origin in chemical properties at the molecular scale.

- *Surface* All materials have surfaces, acting as the interface to the surroundings. Surfaces can be characterized by their texture and colour, but the surface often depends on other characteristics of the material, e.g. temperature, special treatment etc.
- *Properties* The chemistry of materials is important for understanding their properties at higher levels. However, characterizing the properties of a material depends on the perspective, what the material is evaluated in relation to; wood is, for example, seen differently by a chemist or an architect.

Vallgårda and Redström (2007) introduce the term 'composite materials' that are made in order to create a new property or change the properties of a material by combining it with another. They particularly mention the alloy aluminium, made from naturally-occurring bauxite refined into pig-aluminium – which is light-weight but weak – and then combined with other materials to make it strong and flexible – what we normally refer to as aluminium (p. 516).

This leads Vallgårda and Redström to point to the difficulties of distinguishing between materials and products: timber, the product of the sawmill, is a material for the carpenter. The blurring is even more present in composite materials, especially when the composition is fabricated to allow new forms. It comes down to the perspective or purpose of the activity in which the material becomes a part. We can say that it is a material if it is used to create something new that expresses a new idea. A 'bricoleur', who uses products and product parts as materials, can illustrate this point (Harper 1987).

Computers as Material

When discussing computers as material in design we can use the same categories as for characterizing other design materials: substance, structure, surface and properties.

> Perceiving computers as a material is … more than a metaphorical maneuver. It is a question of accepting their similar characteristics as significant enough to hereafter work with the computer in the same manner we work with materials like aluminium or glass (Vallgårda and Redström 2007: 516).

Substance Computers can be characterized at many abstraction levels, ranging from the 'immaterial' information, signs and meaning to the very concrete level of how the electronic mechanisms work: the voltages that 'do' the processing of input to output. At this level there is no difference between software and hardware; all levels we make up to handle the complexities of a computer are, in the end, voltages and manipulations of voltages. The size of the computer refers to the number of instructions processed per clock cycle – which also points to the fact that the computer needs to be whole in order to work, and that a smaller computer is not a big computer cut in two. The substance of a computer is thus the physical workings of an electronic artefact.

Structure the structural aspects of computers can also be discussed at several abstraction levels. At the level of voltages we deal with binary logic, whereas we deal with components as cpu,[8] memory and input/output devices at the physical composition of machinery for the desk top. Like other materials, the abstraction levels refer to particular levels of granularity that at lower abstraction levels are detailed even more. The structure prescribes particular processes in the computers. It is these processes that characterize the computer as material. 'This is analogous to how energy in other materials holds the molecules together as a structure and thereby constitutes them as materials.' (Vallgårda and Redström 2007: p. 517).

Properties We again need to distinguish between levels of abstraction since the lower levels consist of the processes that handle sequences of voltages that are translated into binary logic, while properties of the higher levels are concerned with the quality of the higher order processes. The many layers with emergent properties make it useful to apply a systems perspective on the computer – just as a bicycle as an assembly has different properties than each of its parts. At some level the computer as material is combined with other materials (silicon, metal, plastic, glass) but the 'raw' material of a computer is the processes; the computations. Vallgårda and Redström (2007) therefore compare the computer with aluminium: the raw aluminium is useless unless prepared and combined (in an alloy) with other materials. Raw aluminium is interesting because its properties are potentially useful, but it needs to be treated and prepared in particular ways in order to make use of its potential. They conclude with characterizing the computer as a composite material.

A view on computers as composite materials emphasises that the properties of the 'raw' computing is maintained or realized through its combination with other materials, and that additional or changed properties can develop in such combinations. The combination involves other materials that have particular properties, and it involves the preparing of the composite as one composite material.

Vallgårda and Redström (2007) use the concept of the computational composite to discuss computational textiles, computational concrete and computational 'tensegrity' (tensegrity referring to 'a skeleton structure that consists of members in continuous tension and members in discontinuous compression.' (p. 519). They maintain that the properties of computational composites are concerned with the computational processes, and connect the composite properties to the states that the composite goes through, the transitions between these states, and the control of this process. They therefore connect the properties to the algorithms and data sets in the computation and to whether the control of the process is distributed (an all predetermined, dynamically controlled data set or a set of dynamically changing computing conditions depending on dynamically collected data sets (p. 517)).

Concrete Abstractions

From my walkthrough of digital electronic systems above, it seems that the two properties characterizing digital design results are processes and abstractions. It is

---

[8] CPU central processing unit.

a basic property of computers that computational processes play out in time and also enable the computer to present time-consuming information (e.g., film, music). It is also a basic property that the computer is constructed by means of abstraction: abstraction of processes as well as of the structure and content of the processes. The computer, however, is very concrete.

> At first glance, the title of this book [Concrete Abstractions] is an oxymoron. After all, the term *abstraction* refers to an idea or general description, divorced from physical objects. On the other hand, something is concrete when it is a particular object, perhaps something that you can manipulate with your hands and look at with your eyes. Yet you often deal with concrete abstractions. Consider, for example, a word processor. When you use a word processor, you probably think that you have really entered a document into the computer and that the computer is a machine which physically manipulates the words in the document. But in actuality, when you "enter" the document, there is nothing new inside the computer – there are just different patterns of activity of electrical charges bouncing back and forth. Moreover, when the word processor "manipulates" the words in the document, those manipulations are really just more patterns of electrical activity. Even the program that you call "word processor" is an abstraction – it's the way we humans choose to talk about what is, in reality, yet more electrical charges. Still, although these abstractions such as "word processors" and "documents" are merely convenient ways of describing patterns of electrical activity, they are also *things* that we can buy, sell, copy, and use. (Hailperin et al. 1999: ix)

Hailperin et al. (1999) distinguish between three basic types of (concrete) abstractions: procedural abstraction, data abstractions, and abstractions of state. Procedural abstractions are abstractions of processes, seen as a 'dynamic succession of events' (p. ix) – which leads us to abstraction of states: the changes made by the program that affect the further execution of the program (or other programs). Abstractions of data concern how information is represented and structured so as to fit the computational processes. Their description of computing is a more specific account of the two characteristics addressed above: processes and abstractions. Procedures are structures for processes to go through a sequence of states, and the abstraction of data is the structures limiting the processes – here it makes sense to just talk about abstractions and processes.

Designing with processual material means to create or change processes – to look for processes and how general, repeating, quantifiable processes can be delegated to machines. We look for processes to automate – and create both generalised routines and exceptions to them. However, general categories and routines are creations rather than expressions of real life facts (Star 1991; Suchman 1994; Bowker and Star 1999).

Material for Process Design

Vallgårda and Redström (2007) characterize computational technology as temporal due to its computational processes, and as spatial due to the 'spatial form given to these processes by other materials with strong spatial elements' (p. 514). The secondary property is what Vallgårda and Redström calls spatial: the space made for the process to become concrete – be it physical or virtual. As pointed out above, Vallgårda and Redström are most concerned with the physical (e.g., pillows that combine textiles and computations), and claim that the computational 'immaterial' material is dependent upon other concrete materials to present itself – digital materials are therefore best understood as elements of new, composite materials.

Mazé and Redström (2005) suggest studying the computational object from the inside: from material to form, and from the outside: from interaction to form. They claim that the form of a computational object does not communicate the fundamental characteristics of that object, unlike, for example, how the size of a mechanical object tells us something about its power. 'There is no longer any correspondence between the complexity of the surface and the complexity of the inner workings of an object.' (p. 9). Maeda (2000) claims that this has consequences for both the designer and the user: the user cannot evaluate the object by its exterior; the designer gets less space for expressing his/her ideas – but can instead use the time dimension (when there is not enough space to present all necessary information, you need to present pieces of information over time). Mazé and Redström (2005) discuss the computational form as a combination of spatial and temporal form, claiming that this makes it impossible to separate form from interaction. Temporal form 'is manifested through spatial form elements in use' (p. 10). We therefore need to understand use as the concrete process of the temporal form rather than referring to users' experiences and needs concerned with their practices: use simply means the concretization of temporal form. Through experiments with spatial and temporal form combinations, they suggest considering the interplay of spatial and temporal properties (space may change over time) to recognize how temporal form develops through mobility (users moving), and that form is not entirely determined by the designers if temporal influence on spatial form is allowed – and vice versa. The form is thus dependent upon the interaction with the environment (the users).

Processual Material

Material – or matter – refers to a substance that occupies space. What if the space occupied by digital materials is a symbolic space spanned by the activities in which the process takes attention and time? As a starting point to explore the possibility of talking about processual material, I will use other kinds of processual design results. Candidates for such analogies are design results that exist as an experiential process; music, theatre, dance or other performances. Design of such processes results in descriptions of activities at a very detailed level that are used as prescriptions for the concrete realization of the performance (see e.g. Larssen et al. 2004; Loke et al. 2007). For all performances there exist notations that can be read and interpreted as structure for the process – bearing in mind that the process is a concrete instance of the envisioned process and will be different every time and with every new performer (which may make a new artist's performance enjoyable even if you have heard the piece many times before).

Based on these analogies, it makes sense to characterize processual material as structural representations framing processes, emphasizing that it requires knowledge to 'see' the process when reading the representation. Composers and musicians hear the music when reading the scores; dancers and choreographers feel the dance when they read the choreography; actors and directors experience the story and the characters when reading the manuscript or storyboard; programmers see the computational process when reading program code and systems designers see the system behaviour when reading the system description. Working with processual material thus implies working with representations of process abstractions, recognizing that the concretization of the process will be formed by the situational circumstances (see e.g. Harper 1987; Goodwin 1997). A good abstraction works for all relevant types of concrete circumstances.

It is interesting to bring improvisation into the debate, as seemingly unruly behaviour. However, Becker (2000) has observed that most improvising is 'not quite so inventive as the language we use' and jam sessions have a 'very strict etiquette' that says that, for example, the 'number of choruses the first player played set the standard others should follow. To play more would be rude, pushy, self-aggrandizing; to play less hinted that the first player had gone too far and, worse, that the following players who played less had less to say' (Becker 2000: 171). Theatre sport (a group of actors who gets some of their role-play specifics from the audience in the moment of acting) also follows certain rules of improvisation. Improvisation is thus just another set of rules, opening up for a limited set of variations – just like some computer applications open up for a larger set of user input or include a greater variety of responses to user input – both creating more variation but within frames.

Processual design is to arrange for processes to unfold in particular ways. It seems to make sense to talk about digital design as the composition of processual structures to larger processual structures that can be realized with different symbolic values materializing different process experiences for (and with) users.

Digital Material

Digital design deals with both the electrical processes allowing you to use you phone and the processes you engage in when using your phone. 'When we call a process a *computational* process, we mean that we are ignoring the physical nature of the process and instead focusing on the information content.' (Hailperin et al. 1999: x). If you worry about 'the current carrying capacity of the copper wire' (p. x) when you use your phone, your focus is on the electrical rather than the computational process. Digital design deals with concrete abstractions of processes and their conditions (the data). Some abstractions seem to require knowledge about the concretizations of the abstraction in digitized form, e.g., in order to create an adequate sound or good musical presentation process you need to know about digital representation of sounds.

Stolterman argues that the basic material for building digital systems is bits (Stolterman 2006; Blevis et al. 2006), Vallgårda and Redström (2007) that it is the composite of electrical voltages and other materials (e.g. textiles) that constitutes the digital material. Acknowledging their physical focus, I still maintain that it is the abstractions composed into a general machine that characterises computers as products and thus constitutes the building materials in digital design. I suggest seeing the digital material as concrete abstractions of processes, addressed at different levels of concretization. This view refers back to the view represented in Hailperin et al. (1999) – and many, many other computer science books – that abstracting processes is the basic skill of the digital designer. We need, however, to maintain that digital design can be carried out addressing different levels of concretization though digital design surprisingly often requires us to traverse several levels. One example is the design of a door-opening device: key cards that use magnetic strips as the key and add sound as a feedback to the user to signal correct or faulty card use. To make the sound easy to hear, the wavelength most easily detected by the human ear is chosen (3,000 Hz), also enabling the use of the smallest loudspeaker[9]. Similar need for detailed material knowledge can be found at all levels of digital design, from interface design that chooses a particular blue background colour for ease of reading for dyslexic users (Fjuk et al. 2006), to the design of the capacity of an electronic circuit to match the battery's capacity so that the device does not get over heated when activated.

In line with this, among the challenges of designing the iPod is making the very thin battery which, while providing enough power without overheating, also solves the legal, power-related and technical (storage, interface etc) issues necessary for realising the iTunes web site (Moggridge 2007). The iPod and its properties is a re-formation and re-configuration of (some of) the actors in music practices, providing a form that gives the iPod its identity and meaning – illustrating the complexity and range of a digital design by including the service infrastructure provided by iTunes and the aesthetically pleasing entry point to that service: the iPod. The content and meaning of the iPod crosses any layered model of the digital artefact.

The meaning of the iPod includes all concretization levels; it makes no sense to distinguish between software and hardware when they both cross the iPod artefact and the iTunes service – and the combination of them. With reference to music as a practice, it also makes no sense to single out the 'content' or 'meaningware' as separate from the apparatus in which it has its existence.

Whalley and Barley (1997) confirm that 'technicians work at the empirical interface between a world of physical objects and a world of symbolic representations' (p. 47). They claim that technicians act as 'the link between a larger system of work and the materials on which the system depends' and that 'the materials of relevance may be hardware, software, micro organisms, the human body, a manufacturing process, or a variety of other physical systems' depending on the context.

---

[9] A 3.000 Hertz tone of 0 dB is the softest sound that a normal human ear can hear.

The properties of the iPod are a result of design practices, where the fascination for the pieces, the materials, the small parts and their solutions can drive development of the overall design result: the iPod. Design includes the practices of tedious processes of getting the technical solution right, insisting that the idea will work,[10] and processes of bricolage, utilizing existing materials to achieve what you want.[11] Gelernter (1998) reflects such practices in his emphasis on the joy of programming.

Levels of Digital Design

The concrete abstractions with which we work in digital design can be seen as belonging to different levels of concretization (Mörtberg 2001; Bratteteig 2004), or as packages of 'processed bits' made into higher level logical pieces of hardware–software. Think, for example, of the carpenter who works with boards made of wood, or the tailor, who works with yarn and cloth of wool or cotton. Carpenters and tailors know about the processes of making cloth or boards from wool and cotton – or birch and teak – and about conventions for using particular types of cloth or boards (like 2×4 for building scaffolding or tweed for a suit) even if they do not do this preparation themselves. The building up of 'packages' of digital logic into larger logical units – or abstract processes composed into higher level abstract processes – enable us to apply digital logic at the design process by black-boxing system pieces so that we do not always need to worry about their internal composition, and can focus on the whole design as well as the details. The layering also makes it more difficult to distinguish between the materials and objects.

Earlier, I referred to timber as an example of being both a product of the sawmill and a material for the carpenter, illustrating the difficulty of distinguishing between materials and products. The blurring is even more present in composite materials, especially when the composition is fabricated to allow new forms. Levels of design encourages the packaging of increasingly larger pieces of digital logic to be outsourced during design, as well as sold as pieces to be easily tailored to the use context through integration and modification of variables (Grinter 1995, 1998). It is tempting to compare the levels of concretization to the layers of a building construction suggested by Brand (1994), where he distinguishes between the layers by reference to the rate of changing the layer, ranging from the site where the building stands to the stuff that the people living in the building buy, change, rearrange and throw away.[12] Also, different types of professional expertise are involved in building and changing the different layers: carpenters, electricians, plumbers etc.

---

[10] Hård (1994) documents how engineers try hundreds of times to make their idea work.

[11] Harper (1987) documents the knowledges and skills of a 'bricoleur', cf. also Ciborra (2002).

[12] Brand distinguishes between site, structure, skin, services, space plan, and stuff.

The distinction between tools and materials is particularly ambiguous in digital design. In his discussion of the construction of human–computer interfaces considered as a craft, Wroblewski (1991) says that '[a]ll partially finished work acts both as a tool and material' (p. 6) and also that '[t]he software craftsman works in a virtual toolsmith's shop, where all materials can become tools, and all tools are raw materials' (p. 11).

Close to the Material

McCullough (1998) introduces the term 'digital craft' in exploring how computer-aided design can be seen as a development of craft skills. He emphasises the dematerialized and symbolic nature of computers and thus how interpretational skills become more important. 'Common sense becomes visual sense' (McCullough 1998: 46): we read images rather than feel the artefact; the hand becomes less important as the kinaesthetic and tactile sensitivity of hand skills is replaced with interpretations of representations; where the formal properties are partly in the representation and partly in the phenomenon represented. Form in the representation can be seen directly; in the same way as graphical language elements often present structure in a distinct way (graphic symbols, 'boxes and lines', indentation in texts). McCullough suggests that the activity of seeing the form in the phenomenon represented is analytical, and emphasizes representational aspects of the language (system architecture, logical structures such as class structures and hierarchies of subclasses, interface properties).

Designing with digital (electronic) abstractions makes us focus on the quantifiable aspects of a phenomenon, and makes representations that can be subject to calculations and processing. Representations stand in for something else – but after some time, the original reference may be forgotten and the representation itself gains the status as the real thing (e.g. money). Working with representations is the work of interpretation and meaning-making.

Digital representations can also, however, be processed, presenting a model of the design result (Bjerknes and Bratteteig 1987). Laumann (2005) describes a process of creating a recording of a song. He documents the states that the song goes through, including the manipulation of sounds on his pc by means of the recording studio software. He reads the visual representations of the sound and manipulates the visual representations, cutting and pasting different recordings into one in order to get the sound he wants on the final version to be printed as the record. The skill to read the sound visualisation can be compared to reading musical scores: he hears the sound from seeing the visualisation (Fig. 5.3).

The design processes result in material forms that cross the contexts of design and use – and cross the concretization and abstraction layers of a digital system. Barad (2003) discusses the relation between materiality and signification:

> materiality is discursive (i.e., material phenomena are inseparable from the apparatuses of bodily production: matter emerges out of and includes as part of its being the ongoing

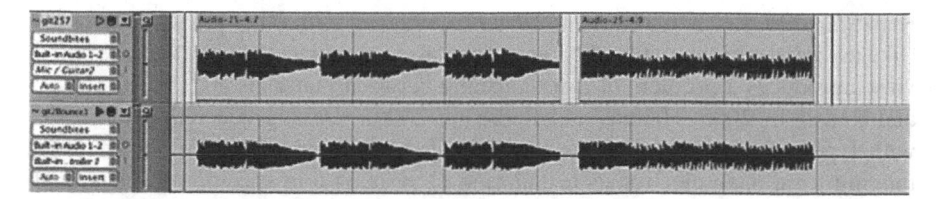

Fig. 5.3 Sound image of guitar recording: bounced recording on top, processed with Freeze Selected Tracks on bottom (Laumann 2005: 89, Fig. 10.21)

reconfiguring of boundaries), just as discursive practices are always already material (i.e., they are ongoing material (re)configurings of the world) (Barad 2003: 822).

Barad argues against the representationalism present in software engineering and other representational crafts. She bases her argumentation on Butler's concept of 'becoming' and insists that action and speaking are inseparable, that language is an act, and that we cannot *not* communicate (see also Winograd and Flores 1986). The meaning of an artefact includes both the conceptual and the material – what Barad (2007) calls material-discursive. Fujimura (1996) similarly discusses how scientific knowledge is translated into methods and tools in scientific practices. Digital material is discursive-material composites, and new digital materials expand the boundaries of symbolic, representations and processes – we can dress in digital textiles, take digital medication, make 3D prints (Capjon 2004), get weather reports from opening a bottle or see the traffic density displayed as a shift in colour on our desk lamp (e.g. Ishii et al. 2001; Ishii and Ullmer 1997), and earn money in digital (virtual) worlds. The symbolic representations become more haptic and the haptic more symbolic.

Digital Matters in Design

The concept 'material' comes from Latin *materia*: matter, and refers to the 'elements, constituents, or substances of which something is composed or can be made' (Webster 2008). 'Matter' means physical substance: 'material substance that occupies space, has mass, and is composed predominantly of atoms consisting of protons, neutrons, and electrons, that constitutes the observable universe, and that is interconvertible with energy'. Matter, however, has a double meaning and refers also to facts. 'Materiality' refers to 'the quality or state of being material' (Webster 2008).

As a design material, the digital characterizes digital design. I have argued that digital material can be seen as concrete abstractions of processes, addressed at different levels of concretization. This view builds on seeing abstraction of processes as the basis in digital design (Hailperin et al. 1999). A levelled view also addresses the view that digital materials at the lowest level are electric voltages (Vallgårda and

Redström 2007), which at this level can be combined with other physical materials (like textiles) as computational composites. I also appreciate the view that a levelled view introduces a problem of distinguishing between materials and objects (Mazé and Redström 2005; Hallnäs and Redström 2006). Linking concretization levels with types of design enables us to acknowledge different kinds of design work ranging from nano-electronics to tailoring of systems to a specific organizational context (cf. Brand 1994).

However, we also should recognize that digital design often addresses different levels of concretization, and that a good design requires that we combine innovation at several levels (cf. the iPod/iTunes). The work of digital design is concerned with the building of working systems by imagining its use – not to be confused with the use perspective of the user in the use experience (see Mazé and Redström 2005). Digital design utilizes the properties of digital materials – building concrete abstractions of processes that fit use activities at the physical as well as on the symbolic level. The discursive-material nature of digital design changes the world in a material as well as a discursive sense. 'Computer programs are unlike any other material, and the form of craftsmanship in software will surely be unique' says Wroblewski (1991: 17). I agree with him that '[f]undamentally, the materials shape the craft' (p. 17): digital design is profoundly shaped by the characteristics of the digital (Bratteteig 2004).

Digital design opens up for new possibilities and for things that embody these possibilities. The materials and tools we use in design influence which possibilities we see and choose to realize. Design is thinking with materials, and the discursive-material digital material brings the head and hand even closer to each other. Seeing digital design as thinking with concrete abstractions of processes, at different levels of concretizations as well as across them, suggests that digital designers should understand their material in a way that enable them to move between levels of concretization and choose the right abstraction for the actual design process as it evolves in time. The many levels of digital design open up for many different competencies being involved in imagining and building possible futures.

Acknowledgments
Thanks to Christina Mörtberg and Erik Stolterman for long-lasting discussions about the material side of computing. Thanks also to Gisle Hannemyr for pointing out the distinction between digital and electronic.

References

Andersen, N.E., Kensing, F., Lassen, M., Lundin, J., Mathiassen, L., Munk-Madsen, A., & Sørgaard, P. (1990). *Professional systems development – Experiences, ideas, and action.* Upper Saddle River: Prentice-Hall.

Andersen, P.B. (1986). Semiotics and informatics: computers as media. In P. Ingwersen et al (Eds.), *Information technology and information use. Towards a unified view of information and information technology* (pp. 64–97). London: Taylor Graham.

Andersen, P.B., & Bratteteig, T. (Eds.). (1989). *Computers and language at work. The relevance of language and language use in development and use of computer systems.* The SYDPOL Programme, Department of Informatics, University of Oslo.

Barad, K. (2003). Posthumanist performativity. Toward an understanding of how matter comes to matter. *Signs: Journal of Women in Culture and Society*, 28(2), 801–831.

Barad, K. (2007). *Meeting the universe halfway: Quantum physics and the entanglement of matter and meaning.* Durhamn & London: Duke University Press.

Becker, H. (2000). The etiquette of improvisation. *Mind, Culture, and Activity*, 7(3), 171–176.

Berg, M. (1997). On distribution, drift and the electronic medical record: some tools for a sociology of the formal. In J. A. Hughes, W. Prinz, T. Rodden & K. Schmidt (Eds.), *Proceedings of the fifth conference on European Conference on Computer-Supported Cooperative Work (ECSCW'97)* Lancaster, UK (pp. 141–156). Dordrecht: Kluwer Academic.

Bjerknes, G., & Bratteteig, T. (1987b). Perspectives on description tools and techniques in system development. In P. Docherty, K. Fuchs-Kittowski, P. Kolm & L. Mathiassen (Eds.), *System design for human development and productivity: Participation and beyond* (pp. 319–330). Amsterdam: North-Holland.

Bjerknes, G., & Bratteteig, T. (1988a). The memoirs of two survivors – or evaluation of a computer system for cooperative work. In I. Greif (Ed.), *Proceedings of the 1988 ACM conference on Computer-supported cooperative work*, Portland, Oregon, USA (pp. 167–177). New York: ACM.

Blevis, E., Lim, Y. K., & Stolterman, E. (2006.). Regarding software as a material of design. Design research society In *Proceedings of Wonderground – the 2006 Design Research Society International Conference*, Lisbon, Portugal.

Bowker, G., & Star, S.L. (1999). *Sorting things out: Classification and its consequences.* Cambridge: MIT Press.

Brand, S. (1994). *How buildings learn: What happens after they're built.* New York: Penguin.

Bratteteig, T. (2002). Bringing Gender Issues to Technology Design. In Floyd, C., Kelkar, G., Kramarae, C., Limpangog, C. & Klein-Franke, S. (Eds.), *Feminist challenges in the information age.* Opladen: Verlag Leske + Budrich.

Bratteteig, T. (2004). *Making change. Dealing with relations between design and use.* Diss. Oslo: Department of Informatics, Faculty of Mathematics and Natural Sciences, University of Oslo.

Capjon, J. (2004). *Trial-and-error-based innovation: Catalysing shared engagement in design,* Diss.Oslo: Oslo School of Architecture and Design.

Checkland, P. (1981). *Systems thinking, systems practice.* Chichester: John Wiley & Sons.

Ciborra, C. (2002). *The labyrinths of information: Challenging the wisdom of systems.* Oxford: Oxford University Press.

Dijkstra, E.W. (1976). *A discipline of programming.* Englewood Cliffs: Prentice Hall.

Dourish, P. (2001). *Where the action is: The foundations of embodied interaction.* Cambridge: MIT Press.

Dourish, P., & Button, G. (1998). Technomethodology: Paradoxes and Possibilities. In M. J. Tauber (Ed.), *Proceedings of the SIGCHI conference on Human factors in computing systems: common ground (CHI '96)*, Vancouver, British Columbia, Canada (pp. 19–26). New York: ACM press.

Fjuk, A., Kaasbøll, J., & Groven, A.-K. (2006). Improvements of teaching and tools for learning object-orientation. In A. Fjuk, A. Karahasanovic, & J. J. Kaasbøll (Eds.), *Comprehensive object-oriented learning: The learner's perspective* (pp. 205–220). Santa Rosa: Informing Science Press.

Fujimura, J. (1996). *Crafting science. A sociohistory of the quest for the genetics of cancer.* Cambridge: Harvard University Press.

Glette, K. (2009): personal communication, Dept. of Informatics, University of Oslo.

Gelernter, D. (1998). *Machine beauty. Elegance and the heart of technology.* New York: Basic Books.

Goodwin, C. (1997). The blackness of black: Color categories as situated practice, resnick. In L. B. Resnick, R. Säljö, C. Pontecorvo & B. Burge (Eds.), *Discourse, tools and reasoning; essays on situated cognition* (pp. 111–140). Berlin: Springer.

Gramazio, F., & Kohler, M. (2007). *Digital materiality*, talk at Oslo Arkitektforening. October 18. 2007.

Greenfield, A. (2006). *Everyware: The dawning age of ubiquitous computing*. Berkeley: New Riders Publ.

Grinter, R.E. (1995). Using a configuration management tool to coordinate software development. In N. Comstock & C. Ellis (Eds.), *Proceedings of conference on organizational computing systems (COCS '95)* (pp. 168–177). New York: ACM press.

Grinter, R. E. (1998). Recomposition: putting it all back together again. In I. Greif (Ed.), *Proceedings of the 1998 ACM conference on computer supported cooperative work (CSCW '98)* Seattle Washington, USA (pp. 393–403). New York: ACM.

Hailperin, M., Kaiser, B., & Knight, K. (1999). *Concrete abstractions*. Pacific Grove, CA: Brooks/ Cole Publ. Co.

Hallnäs, L., & Redström, J. (2006). *Interaction design: foundations, experiments*. Borås: The Interactive Institute.

Harper, D. (1987). *Working knowledge: Skill and community in a small shop*. Berkeley: University of California Press.

Henderson, K. (1999). *On line and on paper.* Cambridge: MIT Press.

Hutchins, E. (1995). *Cognition in the wild.* Cambridge, MA: MIT Press.

Hård, M. (1994). Technology as practice: local and global closure processes in diesel-engine design. *Social Studies of Science*, 24(2), 549–85.

Ishii, H., Mazalek, A., & Lee, J. (2001). Bottles as a minimal interface to access digital information. In J. Jacko & A Sears (Eds.), *Proceedings of the SIGCHI conference on Human factors in computing systems (CHI '01)*, Seattle, Washington (pp. 187–188). New York: ACM pres.

Ishii, H., & Ullmer, B. (1997). Tangible bits: towards seamless interfaces between people, bits and atoms. In S. Pemberton (Ed.), *Proceedings of the SIGCHI conference on Human factors in computing systems (CHI '97)*, Georgia, United States (pp. 234–241). New York: ACM press.

Jacucci, G., & Wagner, I. (2007). Performative roles of materiality for collective creativity. In B. Schneiderman, G. Fischer, E. Giaccardi & M. Eisenberg (Eds.), *Proceedings of the 6th ACM SIGCHI conference on Creativity & Cognition (C&C '07)*, Washington, DC, USA (pp. 73–82). New York: ACM press.

Juul-Nielsen, J. (1984). Personal communication at Risør Trebåtbyggeri Wooden Boat Building, Norway.

Kernighan, B. W. & Pike, R. (1999). *The practice of programming. Simplicity, clarity, generality*, Reading. Massachuesetts: Addison-Wesley.

Knuth, D. (1973). *The art of computer programming vol. 3: Sorting and searching*, Reading. Massachusetts: Addison-Wesley.

Kramer, J. (2007). Is abstraction the key to computing? *Communications of ACM, 50*(4), 37–42.

Lanzara, G.F. (1983). The design process: Frames, metaphors and games. In U. Briefs, C. Ciborra & L. Schneider (Eds.), *Systems design for, with and by the user* (pp. 29–40) Amsterdam: North-Holland.

Larssen, A.T., Loke, L., Robertson, T., & Edwards, J. (2004). Understanding movement as input for interaction – A study of two Eyetoy™ games. In *Proeedings of OZCHI 2004* (1–10). Available at: http://www.ozchi.org/proceedings/2004/index.html.

Latour, B. (1999). *Pandora's hope: Essays on the reality of science studies*. Cambridge, MA: Harvard University Press.

Laumann, K. (2005). *Men er det kreativt? Digitale verktøy i kreative prosesser* (In Norwegian: But is it creative? Digital tools in creative processes) MA thesis. Oslo:Department of Informatics, University of Oslo.

Loke, L., Larssen, A. T., Robertson, T., & Edwards, J. (2007). Understanding movement for interaction design: Frameworks and approaches. *Personal and Ubiquitous Computing*, 11(8), 691–701.

Löwgren, J., & Stolterman, E. (1998). *Design av informationsteknik – materialet utan egenskaper* [In Swedish]. Lund: Studentlitteratur.

Maeda, J. (2000). *Maeda@media*. London: Thomas & Hudson.

Mazé, R., & Redström, J. (2005). Form and the computational object. *Digital Creativity*, 16(1), 7–18.

McCullough, M. (1998). *Abstracting craft. The practiced digital hand.* Cambridge: MIT Press.

Minsky, M. (1967). *Computation: Finite and infinite machines.* Englewood Cliffs: Prentice-Hall.

Moggridge, B. (2007). *Designing interactions.* Cambridge: MIT Press.

Musil, R. (1996). *The man without qualities.* New York: Vintage books.

Mörtberg, C. (2001). Abstracting, quantifying, classifying, simplyfying, standardising, building hierachies: What are the systems designers sorting out? The conference *Information Technology, Transnational Democracy and Gender.* Ronneby, Sweden.

Nygaard, K. (1986). Program Development as a Social Activity. In *Information processing 86: Proceedings of the IFIP 10th World Computer Congress*, Dublin, Ireland (pp. 189–198). Amsterdam: North-Holland.

Nygaard, K. (2002). Foreword. In C. Ciborra, *The labyrinths of information: Challenging the wisdom of systems.* Oxford: Oxford University Press.

Schön, D. (1983): *The reflective practitioner. How professionals think in action.* New York: Basic Books

Sevaldson, B. (2005). *Developing digital design techniques: Investigations on creative design computing.* Diss. Oslo: Oslo School of Architecture and Design.

Star, S.L. (1991). Invisible work and silenced dialogues in representing knowledge. In I. Eriksson, B.A. Kitchenham, & K. Tijdens (Eds.), *Women, work and computerization: understanding and overcoming bias in work and education* (pp. 81–92). Amsterdam: North Holland.

Stolterman, E. (2006). Personal communication.

Stolterman, E. (2007). Designtänkande (In Swedish: Design Thinking). In Harvard, Åsa & Ilstedt, Sara. (Eds.), *Under ytan: en antologi om designforskning [In Swedish: Under the surface: An anthology on design research]* (pp. 12–19). Stockholm: Raster Förlag.

Suchman, L.A. (1994). Do categories have politics? The language/action perspective reconsidered. *Computer Supported Cooperative Work: The Journal of Collaborative Computing*, 2(3), 177–190.

Suchman, L. A. (2007). *Human-machine reconfigurations. Plans and situated actions.* Cambridge: Cambridge University Press.

Säljö, R. (2000). *Lärande i praktiken. Ett sociokulturellt perspektiv* [In Swedish: Learning in practice. A socio-cultural perspective]. Stockholm: Prisma Studentlitteratur.

Vallgårda, A., & Redström, J. (2007). Computational composites. In M. B. Rosson & D: Gillmore (Eds.), *Proceedings of the SIGCHI conference on human factors in computing systems (CHI '07)*, San Jose CA, USA (pp. 513–522). New York: ACM press

Webster (2008). *Webster dictionary and thesaurus online*: www.webster.com. Accessed June 2008.

Weiser, M., & Brown, J. S. (1997). The coming age of calm technology, In P.J. Denning, & R. M. Metcalfe (Eds.), *Beyond calculation: The next fifty years of computing* (pp. 75–86). New York: Springer-Verlag.

Weizenbaum, J. (1976). *Computer power and human reason. From judgement to calculation.* San Francisco, CA: W. H. Freeman.

Whalley, P., & Barley, S. R. (1997). Technical work in the division of labor: Stalking the Wily anomaly. In S. R. Barley, & J. Orr (Eds.), *Between craft and science: Technical work in the U.S. settings* (pp. 23–52). Ithaca: Cornell University Press.

Winograd, T. (1979). Beyond programming languages. *Communications of the ACM*, 22(7), 391–401.

Winograd, T., & Flores, F. (1986). *Understanding computers and cognition.* Norwood: Ablex.

Wroblewski, D.A. (1991). The construction of human–computer interfaces considered as a craft. In J. Karat (Ed.), *Taking software design seriously* (pp. 1–17). Boston: Academic Press.

Zuboff, S. (1989). *In the age of the smart machine: The future of work and power.* New York: Basic Books.

6

On Mobility, Localization
and the Possibility of Digital Genre Design

Gunnar Liestøl

Designing for Current and Future Conjunction

Classical rhetoric can be conceived of as a kind of design theory and method working with verbal material. Historically, rhetoric, as a general system of communicational construction and production, has informed other design practices beyond the linguistic. Earlier in this volume we suggested the possibility of genre design (Chapter 3), that is, a heuristic method (Ulmer 1994), based on rhetorical invention as an architectonic productive art (McKeon 1987), which applies genre theory as a topic for innovation in digital textuality.

In this chapter, from within this context, I will discuss and exemplify the strategy and tactics of how to work practically with realizing or exploiting the potential of current and future media, particularly when it comes to the ongoing conjunction of *multimodality, mobility* and *localization*.[1] This is a means for both doing digital design and generating understanding about the potential features of digital genres at a conceptual level. It links back to aspects of creative methods in designing and in carrying out digital design research, especially at the level of textual and communicative innovation.

There is no question that commercial hardware and software players will be aggressive and inventive in this field of converging features and functionalities. However, hardware and software vendors may not always move in the direction that we, or many of, the users (particularly as educators and learners) would want them to. This is also why a more distributed conception and practice of design is so important.

---

[1] The text in this chapter was basically written in 2007 (final revisions were made in May 2008). In the fall of 2008 we started the real implementation of the designs mentioned in the closing of the chapter. Since then several prototypes of the suggested genre 'situated simulations' have been presented at various conferences, and an article has been published in the *International Journal of Interactive Mobile Technologies* (open access). The article can be found at <http://online-journals. org/i-jim/article/view/963>.

I. Wagner et al. (eds.), *Exploring Digital Design: Multi-Disciplinary Design Practices*,   171
Computer Supported Cooperative Work, DOI 10.1007/978-1-84996-223-0_6,
© Springer-Verlag London Limited 2010

The Pluralistic Character of Designing

Before we move onto this problem in more detail, we need to step back for a moment and reflect upon our current context and topic: the exploration of digital design. As has been demonstrated in a variety of ways in the discussions above, the concept of design is many-faceted, multi-traditional, complex and often (intrinsically) contradictory. The overall conception of *design* is neither systematic nor consistent.

In his pluralistic (and normative) definition of design, Bürdek (2005: 16) suggests that design should: visualize technological progress; make transparent the connections between production, consumption and recycling; promote and communicate services and help prevent products that are meaningless; and finally, simplify the use and operation of products – both hardware and software. This is a pluralistic perspective on design as seen from the product designers' point of view.

But what are the limits of 'product design', and what is actually a *product* of design? According to Bürdek's overview, what we are primarily concerned with here are physical objects in everyday use: door knobs, cars, chairs, electronic devices, computers and, to a certain extent, software systems. Although hermeneutics and semantics are treated as contextual approaches in this design understanding, the textual level of messages and meanings in digital discourse is excluded from this notion of design product. One may ask oneself: is not a literary text, a piece of music, a film, a computer game also subject to design, and thus a candidate to the label of 'design product' and member of the design product family?

Bridging a Gap Between Design and Aesthetics

From a humanistic point of view, the affinity between design products and aesthetic objects is obvious. It is the post-romantic understanding of general aesthetics which has excluded the outcomes of *beaux arts* from the craft-oriented products of design. In the humanistic approach to digital design in this volume, we aim to bridge this traditional gap between design and aesthetics. This is to move our attention from known domains towards those where identifiable markers are of a relational character: somewhat fuzzy in formation and emergent in character.

While the theorist of product design is focused on physical objects in everyday use and how they come into existence, the humanist's position is constituted by other and supplementary perspectives and traditions. In mainstream humanities interpretation, the practices and enactment of conceptualization, critique and theory emerge after the process of textual construction or event in time. The subject matter of their interests is not primarily constituted by physical objects and qualities, but by significations. These include textual types in the media of written words, images, sounds (speech, singing, music etc.), and video, including navigable dynamic 3D representations (the dominant form of representation in current computer games).

'Double Descriptions'

Given the etymology of the term design (from the Latin *designare,* to mark) it is a paradox that the various textual sign types have been excluded from general design theory and practice. We read that this is part of an historical schism between analysis and interpretation, craft and artistic practice. Seldom do we encounter versions of digital design research in which humanists account for their design activity in a mode of research by design; seldom, too, do we find analyses of textual and communicative forms and expressions in the throes of their genesis and modulation. Apprehension on the part of the traditional humanist to digital design processes and products – towards swirling, messy texts that involve technological agents and even generative algorithms let alone a collaborative design group – limits and prevents interdisciplinary approaches to the understanding of design in general, and digital design in particular.

No other type of design material includes more complex relationships and levels of signification than digital textuality. In our understanding of the relationships between humanities and design, we intend to move beyond the one-dimensional, after-the-event relationship to the textual product and combine the double descriptions and perspectives of interpretation and construction. It is in this prospect that rhetoric can be characterized as design with verbal material, that is, as *verbal design,* at least in its prescriptive mode (Chatman 1990).

The Importance of 'Meaningware'

Bürdek limits his history and theory of design to the levels of hardware and software. In our interdisciplinary and humanistically-informed perspective on digital design, digital media is conceived of as a three-level dependent hierarchy of hardware, software and meaningware (Liestøl in press). Meaningware is the primary design domain of the humanities approach to digital design and digital media; it is the domain of individual messages and texts and the genre systems they belong to; it is distinguished from the software level, but still constrained by and dependent upon it.

In the context of media history, digital media are (currently very much so) in the process of becoming. They still constitute an immature and unstable infrastructure and system of communication. While other, older, media, such as books, film, radio and television have proved to be relatively permanent media – at least in their analogue forms, in such mature and stable media, innovation, complexity and diversity tend to continue to emerge at the meaningware level of textuality, rather than at the hardware level. While books, cinema technology and TV-sets have, for a long time, been constant (without radical innovation), creativity and change have taken place at the textual levels.

With digital media, like any medium in its initial stages of development, this relationship is inverted. In digital communication the hardware and software infrastructure have, so far, continually improved in performance and expanded when it comes to features and functionality, while the meaningware level in many contexts is constituted by remediation and recycling of existing genres and textual goods. A good example of this is the *iPod*. The *iPod* is a digital hardware/software device which serves primarily as a vehicle for textual (meaningware) objects developed within traditional and existing genres, which have evolved in other (analogue) media: music, music videos, TV-series and featured films. Some innovations occur, such as the *podcast*. However, even the originality of this 'genre' is disputable. While seemingly new and widely marketed, podcasts often consist of existing broadcast genres such as news and documentaries. Our view on innovation at the level of digital genres is, perhaps, often seduced by the innovation in interface and elegant consumer product.

Projection, Prediction and Production

Hand-in-Hand

In digital media, hardware and software development goes hand-in-hand. In this partnering, the duo-disciplinarity of electrical engineering and informatics is intimately interrelated. The meaningware level, however, tends to fall behind. The reason for this is complex, but in general we are talking about a cultural lag and not a technological one.

The purpose of genre design, informed by rhetoric as an architectonic productive art, is to eliminate this postponement, and place design of digital textuality in the driving seat of media innovation and development. In this strategic project – and one we reiterate as central to an aspect of digital design and potential digital design research – design is a tactical means. Design is what takes us from the present to the future. It has reach. Yet we need to develop a tactic of reaching itself. We also need to project our meaningware designs into the future in order to meet the challenging changes brought forward by hardware and software inventions and innovations. In the following sections I will suggest some possible approaches to making this kind of projection, prediction and production a reality.

The Future Within Grasp

What can we say about the future? To a certain extent, at least, the future is known. There are elements that are likely to continue and others we can fairly safely say will occur. This allows us to remain relatively stable and engaged, even as users of digital products and services.

This is also the case concerning the future of development and change in digital domains. We know beyond reasonable doubt that within the next few years – say a

5 year period – that the mobile sector in developed countries will see the convergence and 'full' dissemination of some key hardware and software features. That is: wireless broadband (3G and beyond) in all populated areas; CPU and graphics power for handling complex multimodal communication (high resolution images, video and dynamic 3D); and, finally, precise positioning/localization systems (GPS, Wi-Fi- and GSM-triangulation).

There is little reason to doubt that the fundamental improvements in *bandwith*, *performance* and *positioning* will create new services and solutions in digital communication and use. Developers, start-ups, venture capitalists and other vendors breathe in this world. But to what extent can these future changes be predicted? How may we describe them? Several of the hardware elements are possible to foresee within such a short period of time, but just how they will converge and interact is more uncertain. This again depends on the software situation. Software innovation and related advances are less susceptible to prediction and pre-vision than their underlying hardware components. Further, beyond hardware and software, at the level of meaningware, how can we even attempt at conceiving of the kinds of digital discourses and textuality that will emerge? We only need to remind ourselves about the case of mobile phones and short text messaging (sms). Nobody had the imagination to foresee the popularity of that service, despite its simplicity and the fact that today it is experienced as an obvious, almost natural communicative feature.

The issue facing digital designers and digital design researchers, especially those who conduct research in and through design, is that it is precisely this 'projection', not just into a design space designing potentially new communicative spaces, texts and interactions, but engagement with the genesis of new communicative forms that is the challenge, and a tantalizing one at that.

'The best way to predict the future is to invent it' Alan Kay once wrote (Kay 1989). In our humanistically-informed take on digital design we have argued that the invention of meaningware is a matter of rhetoric as an architectonic productive art (McKeon 1987). Innovation happens somewhere between accidence (serendipity) and design (heuresis). Or, to put it in a more temporal context, it is realized by combining the past, present and future for the purpose of *finding* the available means of innovation. In rhetoric this is the domain of the topics (*inventio*).

On Aristotelian Rhetoric

For Aristotle, rhetoric is the ability 'in each particular case, to see the available means of persuasion' (2.1). In general, rhetoric is the performance of a faculty, a technique, for finding the best available means for persuasive and efficient communication. This finding could be a discovery of something already existent or an invention of something new. Ancient rhetoric is described as a *'technè'* and as such, in its Aristotelian version, it is focused more on the structuration of discourse, in the form of active operations, rather than its structure: discourse as product. Rhetoric in general evolved in antiquity, from Aristotle via Cicero and Quintilian, to the Middle Ages.

The *'technè rhétorikè'* (the rhetorical technique) is made up of five well-known core operations dominating various steps in the process. Only the first three operations will be discussed here. These operations are not structural elements of the final product but actions executed in the process of making the presentation.

Inventio is the procedure of finding what to say. The focus of this finding is the proofs, or convincing reasons for persuasion. The proofs (*pisteis*) of *Inventio* are not logical proofs, but are based in common sense and known uses of language for support of argument. The proofs, or arguments, are empty forms and need to be filled with content, that is, with individual meaning relevant to the particular context. To discover or invent the content, a certain technique is applied, which consists of consulting the topics, that is, the commonplaces, from where the relevant content is extracted.

Dispositio is the arrangement of the major parts at the level of discourse and is based on the argumentative themes found during the *Inventio* operation. As a process of finding the main organization of discourse – a dramaturgy – the *Dispositio* consists of four sequential elements. These are: *exordium*, the opening introduction of the speech; *narratio*, the description of the bare facts of the events; confirmation, the direct application of the proofs found in *Inventio* and used relevant to the facts of *narratio*; and *epilog* or *peroratio*, the summary or conclusion of the talk.

Elocutio brings ornamentation to the language in use for the purpose of persuasion. When the speaker has found what to say and provided an order of appearance, it is necessary to give the speech an expedient form by providing eloquence. In the history of rhetoric, *elocutio* has produced a tremendous body of classification. Basically, there are two opposing kinds of metaphoric transformation and substitution: tropes and figures. The distinction between tropes and figures are not explicit in Aristotle's work. Later rhetoricians have defined a trope as the conversion of meaning by a single word, while the figure requires several words.

Discovery and Invention in Digital Design

Aristotle's definition of rhetoric as a faculty of finding the available means of persuasion is in fact present and operative at all three levels in the making of a presentation. During *Inventio* this is a question of finding the available means as argumentative content; during *Dispositio* one must find the available means as structure, as dramaturgy; and during *Elocutio*, one must find the available means for optimizing the persuasive power of the language in use. (We could also add *memoria* as the procedure for finding the memorizing means, and *actio* as finding the performative means in the final presentation). Consequently, the act of finding, as both discovery and *Invention*, traditionally located to *Inventio*, is a central performance at all levels in the overall rhetorical operation, not just in its initial stage.

Discovery and *Invention* are the core features of production and creation, and in, classic oratory, the making of a speech always involves transformation and convergence:

the meeting and merger of old and new, of familiar and strange, of used and fresh. Latent in oratory is the need to renew itself in order to be efficient. The well-composed, eloquent and effective speech, as well as rhetoric itself, demonstrates throughout its history that renewal and re*Invention* as a 'reasoned habit of mind in making something' are necessary conditions.

Aristotelian and Ciceronian topics can be reduced to the 'questioning known as W5H1 (Where, What, Who, When, Why and How?) in order to create a grid that point out (finds or discovers) features of purpose, theme, participants/users, timing, location and material/medium. These categories are also defining features in genre theory. They are used by many genre theorists to decide how individual texts and documents belong to certain genres (Yates and Orlikowski 2001). However, they are also projections into the unknown (the not-yet-existing), by means of the known. It is this prescriptive mode we would like to pursue in the following.

An Example of Digital Inventio and Genre Design in Education

In his important investigation of the logic of discovery, Ulmer (1994) proposed a theory of genre invention and its relation to hypermedia. This method and approach he calls heuretics (after the Greek term *euresis*, a synonym of the Latin *inventio*). In his practice of genre invention, however, Ulmer does not venture into the digital. His examples remain literary and suggestive. Still our attempts at genre design are strongly influenced by Ulmer's theoretical reflections. Before we move on to prepare the exploration of the potential genres of mobile and locative media, I would like to briefly describe how we have applied the W5H1 procedure to prototype a possible genre designed for use in educational project work (for a more detailed account, see Liestøl 2006).

The Intro Prototype

In order to establish a digital genre for use within web-based learning, it was obvious that a practicable approach would be to focus attention on the introductory part of project process. Particularly interesting was the area where the linearity of the initial introduction became less constrained and opened out to include options and choice for the user to select where to go next, and which resource to acquire and apply as a means for further knowledge building. In this context, it became obvious that one needed to look for existing genres that played a similar role in related settings and situations. A group of candidates were identified: the lecture, the encyclopaedia article, the documentary film and the computer game introductory movie sequence; other candidates were the movie trailer, the hypertext overview node and portals or entrances to buildings (particularly if the intro should include dynamic 3D environments). These genres where then analysed and examined in order to decide whether they could serve as *suppliers of features and qualities* relevant to the construction and conjoining of a digital genre for the purpose of serving the introductory phase in project work. This process then took on a form, which basically followed the question procedure of classical rhetoric (the most relevant qualities discovered are placed at the top of each list).

The Lecture

Why (purpose): introduce topic, inform, engage, motivate and direct. *What* (theme): any knowledge topic directed towards a learner. *Who* (participants): teachers and students, supervisors and learners. *When* (timing): beginning of topic presentation and early in the student's workflow. *How* (material, medium): speech with support from pictures, graphics etc. *Where* (location): physically face to face.

The Encyclopaedia Article

Why: introduce, inform, direct, point to relevant references (link). *What*: any topic subject to general interest. *Who*: the reading public in need of short overviews and modulated information. *When*: any informal setting for information retrieval. *Where*: Encyclopaedia books etc. *How*: written verbal text (with support form pictures and graphics).

The Documentary Film

How: primarily video and audio, but also text and graphics. *Where*: in front of a screen television or film. *What*: interpretation and representation of topics of factual material. *Why*: Inform, entertain and educate. *Who*: general public. *When*: anytime or when in front of a TV-screen.

The Computer Game Introductory Video Sequence

Why: Introduce task and problem, engage, entertain and motivate user to act and play. *How*: audio, video and rudimentary elements of interaction in 3D environments. *What*: game quest and gameplay. *Who*: gamers, users of this particular game. *Where*: Beginning of computer games, mobile or stable. *When*: Starting to play the game.

We should also add the *Hypertext* format. The link-node paradigm is inherited from hypertext and the small network of linked Intros constitutes a limited hypermedia web.

The structure of this web is, according to Bernstein, categorized as a sieve where users are guided '...through one or more layers of choice in order to direct them to sections or episodes' (Bernstein 1998: 24).

Based on these patterns of features, it is also possible to describe the prototyped genre: *The Intro*: *Why*: Introduce a topic for the purpose of learning; engage and motivate the user towards the learning activity and further independent (or collaborative) work with/on the subject matter. *How*: By means of audio, video, text, images and combined with hypertext linking functionality, this creates a smooth transition from the linear sequence to multilinearity and interaction. *What*: Any particular topic the learner wants to acquire and generate knowledge about and which is positioned within an educational framework. *Who*: Learners and students at different levels in the educational institutions. *Where*: In educational contexts and in front of a computer screen, including 3G mobile phones. *When*: Anytime, but particularly within the time frame of a specific course or assignment.

We see that the prototyped Intro-genre is constituted by a *conducted converging* of a set of characteristics that already existed in the feature-supplying genres. The Intro is not a radically new potential genre: it does not consist of any qualities that did not exist prior to its composition, but it is new to the extent that the *combination and constellation* of qualities cannot be found elsewhere. This innovation was conceived and constructed by means of a predefined conduct: the process of identifying relevant genres that could serve as feature-suppliers for a genre design in the context of educational project work (Liestøl 2006).

Work in Progress: Multimodality, Mobility and Localization

How do we proceed when we intend or aim to invent digital genres based on multimodality (the combination of multiple text types), mobility (unconstrained movement with a wireless terminal) and localization (continued identification of the terminal and the users' where abouts)? To suggest answer(s) to this question I shall first orient ourselves in, and visit, some of the places or topics we tentatively find relevant to the situation, and where corresponding or related features/phenomena are active in our existing and immediate surroundings: (1) a visionary, futuristic example from sci-fi literature; (2) the structural affinity between basic web structures (hypertext) and current positioning/localization technology; (3) the historical convergence of the two important traditions of information technology emerging in the early eighteenth century: cartography and the encyclopaedia; (4) the traditional conventions from tourism, guiding and travel guides; and finally (5) the interaction and navigation in online virtual worlds such as *World of WarCraft* and *Second Life*. These places (*topoi*) and practices might be instrumental in a possible genre design or they may not. That we do not know, and this is the fate of all *inventio* and all design. There is no guarantee that the predictions and projections you are about to embrace will turn out to be good choices. This is, by necessity, always the nature of serendipity. With these suggested contexts in mind I will then preflect on a strategy and tactics for how to proceed in order to conduct digital genre design. To exemplify this process further, I will also draw on two concrete but tentative examples that are being considered as possible candidates for further design efforts.

In all innovative design there are precedents. However, these can only be seen as precedents in hindsight. To identify the precedents is thus crucial. A precedent shares some features with the innovation, but we do not know which until after the event. In the following reconnaissance, I am describing a series of places or possible precedents.

Reconnaissance: Visiting Possible Precedents

Topic 1: The Reality in Fictional Visions

When it comes to invention and innovation in digital domains, many an academic researcher might learn from, or at least be inspired by, fictional writers, particularly those practicing the genre generally known as science fiction – thereby imagining the possible convergence of science and technology in our near or distant future. Science-fiction literature occupies a special place in the art of innovation and future prediction, particularly when it comes to technology. It is also special since it does not only share a resemblance with real solutions but also presents complete examples of fictional designs, for example, potential designs of future information technologies. When these descriptions become particularly relevant, they may serve as guiding examples, or regulative ideas, for how we may proceed in real, digital design. The following description from the acclaimed author William Gibson is such an example; a relevant place (topic) to visit in order to produce possible design, because it already is a projection (and, maybe, a prediction).

Gibson is best known in digital culture as the father of the subgenre Cyberpunk, and coiner of the popular term and notion of Cyberspace – from the novel *Neoromancer* (1983). One of Gibson's later and lesser-known achievements is *Virtual Light* (1993), a novel set in a decaying California at the beginning of the twenty-first century. While Gibson's early conception of Cyberspace and Virtual Reality was that of an immersive 3D environment, extended by stereoscopic vision and movement-tracking, creating a virtual space where people – or rather their representations – could meet and interact *Virtual Light* presents an alternative version of a related technology, what we today call augmented or mixed reality.

The story in the novel revolves around a pair of 'virtual light' glasses ('shades'), which give the wearer a special view of the world:

> Rydell noticed the weight as he slid them on. Pitch black. Then there was a stutter of soft fuzzy ball lightning, like what you saw when you rubbed your eyes in the dark, and he was looking at Waraby. Just behind Waraby, hung on some invisible wall, were words, numbers, bright yellow. They came into focus as he looked at them, somehow losing Waraby, and he

saw that they were forensic stats. 'Or,' Freddie said, 'you can just be here *now*–'. And the bed was black, sodden with blood, the man's soft, heavy corpse splayed out like a frog. That thing beneath his chin, blue-black, bulbous. (Gibson 1995: 134)

The detective in the story is here viewing a crime scene in two different modes. First, he is actually there and perceives the room as real, but with the glasses on he can also view the room as it was when the police documented the scene earlier. He can see the bed *both* as a real bed *and* as it looked with the murder victim on it. In addition, he has access to the forensic reports from 'some invisible wall'. In this model, two spaces merge: the real and the recorded/digital 3D version. More description of the functionality represented by these glasses is found in another passage:

Friend of mine, he'd bring a pair [the shades] home from the office where he worked. Landscape architects. Put 'em on you go out walking, everything looks normal, but every plant you see, every tree, there's this little label hanging there, what its name is, Latin under that .... (1995: 127–8)

Again, there is the doubling of spaces and mixing of realities: the real world of plants and objects and the digital representations showing their names. In 1993 this was clearly fiction – today it still is. But we are rapidly getting closer. Under the headings of *augmented reality* and *mixed reality* this combining or convergence of representational modes is being explored in numerous research laboratories (Biber and Raskar 2005). Most of the technology needed is available: wireless, GPS, motion tracking, and multimodal databases of any kind and topic. Gibson's literary example is a complete *design*, in fact two designs of this composite technology exemplifying all the fields in our grid. Some of the features are technologically far into the future, but similar designs could be achieved based on today's available technology.

Consequence: Future Imaginings of History

Let us put Gibson's technology in a more common setting; imagine a walk in the Roman Forum of today. On your way up the Via Sacra towards the Triumphal Arch of Septimus Severus facing the Capitol, you pull out your latest GPS-enabled broadband phone. Prior to arriving in Rome, you downloaded relevant software for your visit to the Forum, or you just access it there and then. Just before the Arch you stop and activate the device, hold it up in front of your face; not to take a picture of the present scenery, but to look through it and into the Forum Romanum of antiquity. You may even choose which version of the Forum you might want to access; for instance, the late republic or Imperial Rome. As you pan and tilt the device, the Forum of old is revealed. To the left and behind the Arch you see the complete versions of the Temples of Vespasian and Concoria Augusta, and behind them the Tabularium. In front, you see golden statues and people standing on the Rostra, the platform where the orator and rhetoricians once made their famous speeches in defence of clients, or to promote a political decision. Slide the epoch selector to republican times and pan the device towards the old senate building and the old Rostra. Here you may hear and see Marcus Tullius Cicero deliver one of his famous speeches. The written versions of these are of course also available if you want to examine them more closely – as well as verbal audio information on all the objects of interest visible on the screen. It is obvious that such a use of the technology should not be limited to leisure time, but also play an integral part in learning at all levels.

Topic 2: Hyperspace and Real Space

Localization gives us an opportunity to revisit the concepts of navigation and move-ment in hypertext theory that could prove relevant for our task. In the pre-web days of hypertext research, prior to Tim Berners-Lee's first public presentation of his World Wide Web at Hypertext '91 in San Antonio, Texas, a primary focus was on *navigation* and *browsing*, and the differences between the two (McAleese 1989). The radical potential was identified as being in the free, non-*author*itarian travers-ing of the hypertext networks of nodes and links. However, the more this freedom of browsing was given to the user, the more difficult it became to navigate and find one's way around in the multilinear textual space. Often the user found herself 'lost in hyperspace' (Nielsen 1995), a position from where orientation was difficult and the significance of the information context became next to meaningless.

To prevent this loss of positioning, it was necessary to always furnish the user with three important pieces of information by providing answers to the following questions: (1) Where have I been? (2) Where am I?, and (3) Where can I go from here? Well-known hypertext systems such as *Intermedia* at Brown University found excellent solutions to these problems in the functionality of the so-called 'Web View-window' (Landow 1992).

With hypertext, after the emergence of the World Wide Web, this problem has diminished because of the less-radical hypertext structures and the more common use of the one-windowed browser, as opposed to multiple windows in most pre-web hypertext systems. Today, the Web provides us with the opportunity to access (in principle) any kind of information from (almost) anywhere on the planet. We are free to move according to the networked system of links and nodes inside this hypertextual space. We ourselves, however, remain relatively stationary, or to put it another way: our position is predominantly irrelevant (except in the cases where advertizing i involved) to how we access or receive the information we choose or are confronted with.

With positioning systems such as GPS, WiFi- and GSM-triangulation, this changes dramatically. The convergence of mobility, localization and networked hypertext structures creates a situation where any kind of information is available to anyone, anywhere, and with relevance to the context of positioning. With hypertext, the problem was getting lost in hyperspace. With localization technology, the subject always knows where he/she is (in the real world). In addition, because the system knows the relevant information or topics linked to that place (*topos*) the position of the user is easily accessed and provided. Consequently, the two patterns of structure and movement mirror and support each other: the network of link and nodes and the network of possible positions in real space.

Topic 3: Convergence of Cartography and the Encyclopedia

The new is often intimately connected to the old; the current reality of databases, hypertext, mobility and positioning has been prefigured by older technologies. Two particularly relevant information technologies had their breakthrough more than 200 years ago. These are both relevant to the current development. In the eighteenth century, European cartography made a major breakthrough with printed maps of increased accuracy, due to the systematic method of triangulation. Among the prominent developers were the male representatives of the Cassini family in France (Headrick 2000). The emergence of precise cartography and printed maps coincided with the invention of the modern encyclopedia, first edited and printed by the French philosopher Denise Diderot in the second half of the century.

Maps and encyclopaedias (including dictionaries) are examples of print- and paper-based information technologies developed and designed for different, but also related and combined uses. Maps are used as mobile devices to orient and navigate in real space. In addition, maps are integrated into books to display geographical positioning and relationships. Written texts (in the genre of dictionary entries) have frequently been embedded in maps to increase the density of information and meaning for various uses.

Both maps and encyclopaedias are multimodal texts (Kress and van Leeuwen 2001). The maps and encyclopaedias of Cassini and Diderot have distinct contexts of use; the former predominantly figurative and mobile, the latter stationary and dominated by written text. It is obvious that many of the conventions and interface solutions provided by these technologies should be studied carefully for the possible adaptation to digital contexts.

Topic 4: Travel and Guides

With the evolution of the practical travel guide in the nineteenth and twentieth centuries, we have experienced a continual convergence between maps and encyclopaedias. Current travel guide books (for instance the exemplary designs from the UK publisher Dorling Kindersley) show increased integration between the two traditions mentioned above; combining maps and encyclopaedic entries with drawings, photographs, computer-generated 3D-models, layering (transparent pages etc.) and random access by colour codes visible in closed-book mode.

A particular sub-genre of travel guides, or guide books, is relevant here. These are a kind of what we might call the 'now and then' genre. They use the technique of juxtapositioning to compare the visual representation of scenes and objects from different points in time; often a current view compared to a reconstruction. A typical tourist publication on ancient Rome combines real photography of today's remains of antique buildings and transparent reconstructions of its original shape (Archeolibri 2007). This layered solution is a parallel to, and a precursor of, the double descriptions of augmented reality as described by Gibson. Other, more recent examples may not need graphic reconstructions but may benefit from the availability of older photographs (Yenne 2007).

Topic 5: Online 3D Worlds and Shared Simulations

While hypertext systems provide the discontinuous movement ('jumping') between information nodes (of various textual material), dynamic and navigational 3D spaces provide continuity in time and space. Online 3D worlds like *Active World* and *Second Life*, and MMORPGs like *Everquest* and *World of Warcraft,* are simulated worlds that can be shared by thousands of users, each represented by their own avatar, and, maybe more importantly, their own individual point of view. There are as many subjective perspectives in online graphic environments as there are individual active users. Any member of the 3D-community (or game), wherever he or she is placed on the web, may access this shared world and generate a point of view into this virtual world, based on a dynamic version of the central perspective.

In the case of real space and hyperspace, we described an analogy (or mapping) between navigation and movement between the two. With real space and dynamic 3D environments, the analogy becomes a shared-features set. Virtual environments are often designed to share the physical laws of the real world: gravity, light and shadow, aerial perspective etc. (Some 'laws' however can be neglected, like flying in *Second Life*).

Subjective and individual perspectives in virtual worlds are as many as there are individual users and respective avatars. These perspectives exist in addition to our real perspectives. In mixed reality solutions they are combined.

Potential Genre Designs *Positioned Simulations*

Given the full integration of the necessary hardware and software ingredients, we are waiting for the multimodal discourses and services these platforms will enable. Which, then, are the digital genres that will emerge from this technology, and how do we influence this process for the benefit of, for example, learning and leisure? This is a rhetorical question. The answer, however, is to be found in rhetorical practice as design; that is, *genre design.*

In our current genre design experiment, taking multimodality, mobility and positioning as the situation of exigency, we are proceeding from the simple to the complex;

from the linear to the multilinear and interactive. The material that follows concerns two potential genre designs. How do we proceed when we intend to conduct digital designs within the context and domain of meaningware? The chosen procedure in this particular project is to start with a sequential perspective on the user's actual use and experience of the system under design. The next stage is to extend the sequence to an interactive mock-up, where the actual features of the interface are combined with the context and topic of the prototype. A third stage in this design procedure is to create *in situ* examples, using pre-recorded material as opposed to real-time generated sequences based on real positioning. When these three stages are finalized, evaluated and revised, real implementation can begin. Furthermore, the designs of the two first stages now serve as designs for further implementation and testing.

Cases of 'Positioned Simulations'

We have visited a series of examples and practices, all tentatively related to multi-modality, mobility and localization. All of these examples are designs, past present or future. And they may all be analysed according to our six-celled grid. The designs we are particularly looking for in this context are the ones which may 'meet' the exigency caused by the convergence of multimodality, mobility and positioning, and their relationship to the description and analysis of the examples above.

By combining and experimenting with the features found in the described examples and the emergence of the new hardware and software features, we will close this chapter by presenting two examples of work in progress with possible designs for a potential genre, here called *Positioned Simulations*. These designs are in their early phases, that is, they have not yet been technically and practically implemented – only simulated. There is also the purpose to create the design at the level of meaningware *before* it is technically realized, rather than the other way around.

There are few limitations for the areas in which situated simulations may be used. They all concern combining the real perspective of the user with the 'same' perspective derived from a simulated version of the same world. While the real is always the *then* and *there* of the user's position, the simulated model may represent that which is absent or unavailable, whether it is past, present or future. It could be: (a) what a place, space or object once looked like, or (b) what a place or object might hide, or (c) what may take place in the future. The two designs presented below are both historic reconstructions of past objects and events.

Case 1: Past + Present – The Oseberg Viking Ship and Its Gravemound

The most famous and beautiful of the known Viking ships is the Oseberg ship, excavated in 1904. Today it is on display as a full reconstruction in The Viking Ship

Fig. 6.1 Double perspectives on the Oseberg gravemound

Museum in Oslo, Norway. The grave mound where the ship was found is also reconstructed. But it is empty. With situated simulations we will be able to compensate for this. By constructing a 3D version of the ship and all its belongings the way it looked when the burial took place and when the mound was raised on top of it, we can, once more, place the ship inside the mound. By applying the real world coordinates to the 3D version, it will be possible to 'see' the ship inside the mound through your mobile phone when visiting the real place. The position of the object is defined and the positioning software on your terminal knows your position. The server then sends the view of the ship from exactly that position to your phone/terminal (see Fig. 6.1). If you walk to the other side of the mound you will see the other side of the ship through your phone. And if you walk on top of the mound you can look down into the ship from above.

The challenge of genre design in this case is not just to make this technically possible, and to provide the graphic view of the simulation that matches your position, but, in addition, to combine the various visual channels with information provided by other textual types: audio narration, written text, pictures, drawings etc. It is also a question of telling the story of this ship and its use in the Viking age; the burial event and ceremony; the excavation; the conservation and reconstruction etc. The simulation is not, of course, limited to displaying the ship as it was when it was buried, but could also display the history of the ship inside the mound, up until the day it was excavated.

Case 2: Past + Present – The Battle of Pharsalus

In June, 48 BC, the Roman Civil war reached its climax in the decisive battle between Julius Caesar and Pompeius Magnus, which took place on the plains of

Fig. 6.2 Double perspectives and views on the battlefield of Pharsalus

Thessaly in Northern Greece, near the town of Pharsalus. Today the site shows signs of this historic event. However, given the combination of the computer game strategy genre (*Rome Total War*), GPS-positioning, broadband services and innovative interface designs, the battle can be re-enacted as a *positioned simulation* including the historical documents, describing the battle and the events leading up to it, from Caesar himself, Cicero, Appian, and others. If the historic battle-version of the Pharsalus battle in *Rome Total War* was put on the server as an event, a mobile phone user could visit the real battle field, climb the nearby hill and watch the whole (reconstructed) battle unfold from the same perspective and position as he or she actually is. As shown in Fig. 6.2, the user can also change view (not position), that is, zoom in on particular parts of the event. In this battle, the turning point is when Caesar's infantry force Pompeius' cavalry into retreat. This particular phase (and place) of the battle could thus be seen in close-up. Again, the design challenge is not just to provide the simulation 'correctly', but rather to combine the visual information with other text types in order to tell the story of this battle in a way that makes it informational, entertaining and relevant to the possible choices of the user. Julius Caesar describes the battle over 10 pages in his comments on the Civil War. Possibly, his narrative could be used as one of several choices of narration.

These two tentative and sketchy designs have been generated in the process of reflecting upon the technological potential of mobility, broadband and positioning systems in comparison with Gibson's futuristic and fictional design, navigation and orientation in hypertext systems, the traditions and conventions of cartoghraphy, encyclopedias, various kinds of travel guides and historical publications, and online graphic computer games. In the survey so far there are some features that have been given more attention than others. This is particularly so concerning the factual documentation found in travel guides (maps, pictures, perspective drawings and writing), which is primarily context-dependent, that is, for use at a certain location – the location of the user/reader (the traveller) using the guide, and the individual and subjective, simulated perspective of player/participants in virtual worlds. However, other features from the visited topics may also make it to the final designs.

It has been the purpose of this chapter to show the relevance of some humanistic perspectives in digital design. From the point of view of the humanities, the computer is a communicational device, a vehicle for mediation of multimodal textuality, meanings and messages. In the current hardware- and software-dominated development, the level of meaningware needs more attention. In this context, the long and rich traditions of communication and textual theories may serve, not only as analytical perspectives, but also as rules for construction, and as inspiration and sources for designs and invention in innovative digital textuality.

References

Archeolibri S.R.L. (2007). *Rome reconstructed*. Texts by G. Coletta, drawinigs by A. Tosolini. Rome: Archeolibri.
Bernstein, M. (1998). Patterns of Hypertext. In Shipman, F., Mylonas, E., & Groenbaek, K. *Proceedings of Hypertext '98*. New York: ACM. Also available at http://www.eastgate.com/patterns/Print.html
Biber, O., & Raskar R. (2005). *Spatial augmented reality: Merging real and virtual worlds*. Wellesley, MA: A. K. Peters Ltd.
Bürdek, B. E. (2005). *DESIGN. History, theory and practice of product design*. Boston, Basel & Berlin: Birkhäuser.
Chatman, S. (1990). *Coming to terms. The rhetoric of narrative in fiction and film*. Ithaca: Cornell University Press
Gibson, W. (1995). *Virtual light*. London: Penguin Books.
Headrick, D. R. (2000). *When information came of age. Technologies of knowing in the age of reason and revolution, 1700–1850*. Oxford: Oxford University Press.
Kay, A. (1989). Predicting the future. *Stanford Engineering*, 1(1), 1–6. Also available at www.ecotopia.com/webpress/futures.htm.
Kress, G., & van Leeuwen, T. (2001). *Multimodal discourse. The modes and media of contemporary communication*. London: Arnold.
Landow, G. P. (1992). *Hypertext: The convergence of contemporary critical theory and technology*. Baltimore: Johns Hopkins University Press.
Liestøl, G. (2006). Conducting genre convergence for learning, *International Journal of Continued Engeneering Education and Lifelong Learning*, 16(3/4), 255–270.
Liestøl, G. (2009). Situated Simulations: *A Prototyped Augmented Reality Genre for Learning on the iPhone in International Journal of Interactive Mobile Technologies* (iJIM), 3 - Open access.
Liestøl, G. (in press). PowerPoint beyond hardware and software. In A. Morrison (Ed.), *Inside multimodal composition*. Cresskill N.J: Hampton Press.
McKeon, R. (1987). *Rhetoric. essays in invention and discovery*. Woodbridge: Ox Bow Press.
McAleese, R. (1989). Navigation and browsing in hypertext. In R. MacAleese (Ed.), *Hypertext: Theory into practice* (pp. 5–38). Exeter: Intellect Books.
Ulmer, G. (1994). *Heuretics. The logic of innovation*. Baltimore: Johns Hopkins University Press.
Yates; J., & Orlikowski, W. J. (2001). Genre systems: Chronos and kairos in communicative interaction. In R.M. Coe, L. Lindgard & T. Teslenko (Eds.), *The Rhetoric and ideology of genre: Strategies for stability and change* (pp. 103–121). Cresskill, N.J.: Hampton Press.
Yenne, B. (2007). *San Francisco. Then and now*. San Diego: Thunder Bay Press.

7

Unreal Estate: Digital Design and Mediation in Marketing Urban Residency

Andrew Morrison and Synne Skjulstad

Mediating Real Estate

Fig. 7.1 Digitally rendered interior of unbuilt apartment in Oslo

In the Nordic countries, web-based simulations are now widely used as an addition to the print-based marketing and exchange of domestic properties. Our interest in this chapter is to analyse how domestic dwellings are mediated online via digital representations. These representations draw on a range of digital tools and simulations of their professional uses in architecture, urbanism and web design. We approach these representations as mediating artefacts that clearly ask consumers to engage in an imaginative rendering of the unbuilt. The digitally designed and digitally mediated artefacts project not simply visions of the unbuilt, but envision what is to be built. In many cases they also include properties as having been sold prior to physical construction. We situate our analysis within the practices of buying and selling real estate. The digitally mediated exchange of such properties falls within the ambit of advertising discourse. This is a discourse that has persuasion as its primary aim. It seeks to draw and direct the activity of users towards the pre-purchase of future dwellings; an activity that is not merely a material one but also imaginary.

We refer to such mediation as *unreal estate* (Morrison et al. 2007). By this we mean the digital projection of property that is yet-to-be-built. Where digitally

I. Wagner et al. (eds.), *Exploring Digital Design: Multi-Disciplinary Design Practices*,   189
Computer Supported Cooperative Work, DOI 10.1007/978-1-84996-223-0_7,
© Springer-Verlag London Limited 2010

Fig. 7.2 Property portal showing entry with explicitly digitally rendered constructions. 'Tool palette' (*left*) remediated to provide alternate views on the projected property. Main image (*right*) shows oblique street elevation

designed dwellings remain to be built, they are already constructed online via a blend of technology enhanced mediation that is hyperreal (Eco 1986; Baudrillard 1995). We discuss this term below, but it is visible in Fig. 7.1, in which the user meets a seemingly realistic view of an apartment space clad with contemporary furnishings, with a view out onto the urban world. This space is navigable in a 360° view, further suggesting it is an actual space and thereby further augmenting the user's 'willing suspension of disbelief' (Coleridge 1817). Yet these are spaces that are clearly digitally constructed: they are composed via software, they blend a variety of visual representations, and they are accessible and navigable online (Fig. 7.2).

This digitally mediated domain of online advertising and the marketing of domestic property is at the same time projected as an intermediary between the planning sketches and Computer Aided Design (CAD) drawing boards of urban planners and architects. It also includes the embedding of digital photographs of 'real' settings and simulated collages of these various elements on the part of web designers. 3D illustrations are employed to generate a sense of an imagined future, while at the same time luring potential buyers through persuasive moves between the written and the visualized. The digital material used in such online advertising consists precisely of a medley of co-ordinated visualizations from planning, designing and visualizing by architects, property developers and marketers (Schmidt and Wagner 2004). In a commercial context, it may be seen as part of an emerging 'dot.com urbanism' (Ross 2004), one that has been widely circulated on television shows about home improvement (Lorenzo-Dus 2006) and property assessment and upgrading that employ digital visualizations. These digital adverts are part of a wider public digital culture in which relations and connections between media, architecture and urban spaces are fashioned (e.g. McQuire 2008; Klingmann 2007).

Exploratory Discourse

It is the interplay between the digitally pictured and the proxemically persuasive that we investigate as digitally mediated communication design (see Chapter 3). Our approach is one that sees web texts as emergent cultural forms (e.g. Rivett 2000). We include selected visual material along with links to them so that readers may navigate the representations themselves dynamically, and view them in colour. Our chapter is also written as a visual essay, with textual analysis as its main approach. We present a phenomenon whose articulation is made possible through digital design tools and processes. However, the field of online advertising has seldom been studied at the level of mediation where the texturing and techniques employed to persuade consumers are analysed as persuasive, digital design. It is this that we address.

Our essay, therefore, is inductive and exploratory rather than declarative. As humanists, we adopt a critical view on the challenge to interpretation posed by new media (Bolter 2003; Strain and van Hoosier-Carey 2003). We study this web phenomenon of mediating and selling unreal estate as a self-knowing form of advertising and marketing. Consumers know the mediations are simulations – they relate to them because of their own experiences of being in the world, and because of their capacities to extrapolate from what is projected back into the world (Fig. 7.3).

Selection of Sites

As background to the analysis it is important to refer to our own experience and position. Over a 2-year period we regularly accessed websites that advertise domestic properties in our home city. We familiarized ourselves with the tactics used by established property sellers in marketing regular, already completed

Fig. 7.3 Distinctly CAD
rendered abstract representation[1]

properties, some relatively recent and others from across the span of the residential history of the city.

We selected the main online portal for the presentation of properties in the city (www.finn.no) and we visited all the links to properties still to be built or in development but nevertheless appearing online and marketed as attractive invest-ments prior to their completion. We chose a number of sites that illustrate the main features present in many of the representations, ensuring that we chose material from different estate agents and from different parts of the city. We then made selected screengrabs.

On Communication Design

We situate our overall approach within Communication Design, a term we prefer to interaction design and its legacy in Human Computer Interaction (HCI) that until recently has largely focused on functionality and usability. For us, Communication Design is an under-investigated aspect of digital design research. Frascara (2004) has argued that it also needs to be seen in relation to the development

---

[1] http://www.finn.no/finn/realestate/object?finnkode=8794024&sid=14aKWV03oE392159&pos= 180&tot=null

of visual design competencies and expressions. Helfand (2001) has also argued that we connect the potentially disparate elements of graphic design, 'new media' and visual culture. A socio-cultural approach to design allows such connections. These too need to be linked to information systems design, and to the design of communicability and affordances for users' engagement that stretch further than a functionalist approach to use relations. Their overall intent is to shift activity into situated meaning making that is realised from assembled semiotic resources (Skjulstad & Morrison 2005).

Outline of Chapter

In the section below, called 'Contexts of Mediation', we present aspects of the emerging domain of online advertising. This is a domain of digital design that is surprisingly under-researched in terms of the symbolic and persuasive in the construction of cultural expression. We link this to a Communication Design perspective (see Chapters 2 and 3) and draw on earlier studies we have carried out that analyse ways in which consumers are implicated in the branding and exchange of commercial products and services (Morrison and Skjulstad 2007; Morrison and Skjulstad forthcoming). We argue that, along with attention to design processes and to user activities, close analysis of what consumers meet and how it is conveyed to them online may be studied via multimodal discourse theory and as mediated discourses of design. These discourses increasingly inscribe digital tools and conventions of use as part of their textualisation of the persuasive as part of our day-to-day digital communication practices.

In 'Contexts of Mediation' below, we next address questions of context in the mediation of unreal estate. In the next section, we cover a number of core concepts that provide some means of addressing the phenomenon of projected persuasion. This is followed in section entitled 'Hyperrealism', by an analysis of imagined and projected domestic spaces, both interiors and exteriors, via hyperrealist visualizations. The next section is labelled '3D Visualization'. Here we analyse ways in which the marketing portal and the websites of estate agents incorporate and co-ordinate images from architects and 3D views from graphic and web design professionals as part of a persuasive online discourse. The section 'From Visiting to Moving In', discusses the findings of the analysis and relates these findings back to the notion of unreal estate. We close with a discussion of the shift towards greater user participation in building unreal estate that is generated via our activity and not simply by our accessing or visiting given representations of the digital home. We argue that this has implications for understanding the processes, products and performative participation in the digital design domains that it is moving in. First, though, we examine what does exist, as it were, in the emerging domain of online advertising.

Contexts of Mediation

Marketing and Mediating Unreal Estate Online

Persuasion is the name of the game in this form of interactive advertising (Sundar and Kim 2005). It is an advertising that takes place online and draws on well-established traditions in print and electronic media. However, the marketers of unreal estate draw on digital and non-digital styling as a means of creating a sense of veracity. Hand-drawn lines and figures are blended with clearly visible computer-generated textures. Together these display these sites as digitally mediated constructions designed to engage customers. The representations are also housed within the formal business sites of known and reputed estate agents. A sense of veracity – both in relation to reputation and the vision of a future dwelling – is partly achieved by the placing of the unreal estate alongside already existing built properties (Kalay and Marx 2006).

Below, we examine a selection of representations of domestic apartments on the web in one Scandinavian capital city, Oslo. We see this as part of the analysis of a wider, emerging web-mediated discourse that is concerned with persuasion. Similar discourses were widely addressed in the area of print advertising, and even relationships between art and advertising (Gibbons 2005), but have not received much mention in the effluvia of writings on 'new media' and digital culture. Neither have they been much studied in terms of visualization (Barnard 1995). Much of the analysis of digital advertising is cast in terms of consumer tracking and purchasing patterns.

However, online advertising employs a variety of well-tried techniques from print and television advertising and remediates these for the dynamic digital domain of the web while introducing new persuasive turns that digital technologies allow (Fagerjord 2003). One such remediation (Bolter and Grusin 1999) is to link products with lifestyles well covered in analyses of advertising in print and for film and television (e.g. Dyer 1982; Vestergaard and Schrøder 1985; Williamson 1994).

It is both in print and online that there has been an expansion in the mediation of domestic properties. We see a variety of visual–verbal adverts for properties in mainstream and local newspapers, in weekend supplements and in the prospectuses of estate agents. Great attention is paid to layout and to photography, and this has clearly been influenced by improved digital cameras and means of rapid composition. Online we see a diversity of representations, from floor plans to CAD-developed illustrations and photographs of the surrounding area, as well as illustrations of the 'actual': the dwellings to be built. Navigating unreal estate sites involves visitors in their own embodied building of the imagined through the processing of techniques of simulated layering. It also involves them in using a reflexive blend of media and representation types in the mediation of properties that have not been built. Already we see how architecture and public space is peppered with screen-based mediations (Slaatta 2006), and with strategic architectural communication in brand building, as part of what Klingmann (2007) refers to as 'brandscapes'. Consumers are persuaded through a medley of digital mediation that, in total, is designed to offer them a dependable and attractive representation of a future home. This can be seen in Fig. 7.4, in which a dense view of downtown apartment block is shown along with the more pastoral tones and spaces of a suburban semi-detached residence with its accessibility and affluence symbolized by the latest car model, the A8 from Audi. Lifestyle is clearly being projected here, and two luxury cars and underground parking mark this out. Projected is potential comfort and affluence, but also a sense of the exclusive location of a hillside property. One *imagines* the view.

Fig. 7.4 Two renditions of the unreal estate of downtown and suburban domestic property. 'Consept urban base' (sic) (*left*); 'Truly your dream on Oslo's roof' (*right*)

A Socio-Cultural Perspective

The main features of a socio-cultural perspective to design have been outlined earlier in the book (see Chapter 3). It is important, however to reiterate that this perspective approaches design and its related communication in terms of contexts of situation and mediated action. The intersecting relations between tools and signs and contexts of production and consumption are seen as being realized in and through multimediational artefacts that may transverse multi-sites and media. Our concern is with the situatedness of mediating artefacts; that is, as part of web-based communication.

However, we take this approach to communication an additional step and argue that these artefacts are more than mere textual representations. They are the representational embodiments of design processes and products in their own right. The adverts for unreal estate occur within a formally functioning business portal; they are not autonomous and disembodied texts, but parts of wider discourses. These texts that project future properties are grounded in the context of the 'real'; they are markedly reflexive in their inscription of digital design tools, professional practices and modes of representation afforded via digital compositional technologies; motivated users meet them in an established property portal and re-appoint them in relation to existing physical structures and being in the world.

Where there has been much written on 'new media' from humanistic perspectives, such as on narrative and gaming, analyses of online advertising rarely discusses relationships between tools and signs in digital mediation. A socio-cultural approach to digital design pays attention to such relationships. The mediating artefact, a concept drawn from Wartofsky (1979), is an analytical construct situated in a contextualized process of technologically mediated meaning making. Often in terms of mediated meaning making, focus moves to the analysis of interaction, as is the case with studies in education that concern the uses of online learning environments by students and processes of meaning making (Wertsch 1991). However, the specifically design-oriented communicative artefacts embodied in any digital interface also need to be analysed in terms of the design of media and communication. Their very textual nature, affordances and constraints impact on how we conceptualize wider communicative acts; in this case the search, selection and purchase of a domestic property.

In the context of unreal estate, we may ask what is mediated by whom and who is mediating what. In answering these questions, we look at two levels, one macro and one micro. Connected to the notion that communication occurs in contexts of situation, at the macro level we refer to the notion of the mediating artefact. We use this concept to access matters of the imagined and the simulated as they are realized in the online articulations of the unbuilt. At the micro level, we investigate how specific types of diagrams and illustrations are incorporated within renditions of unreal estate. We inquire into how these articulations are themselves topiaries, or shaped forms, to borrow a metaphor from formal gardening.

Fig. 7.5 *Split screens* showing location, lifestyle irony, viewing times and front elevation

At a textual level, these diverse and connected systems and representations are similar to those identified by the Russian literary linguist Mikhail Bakhtin (1981, 1984, 1986). Bakhtin advanced several concepts that are at the centre of the notion of dialogical communication, as well as its social situatedness. These concepts are useful in accounting for the level of articulation, that is the mediated as utterance. Bakhtin developed speech genres to account for the diversity of socially situated modes of utterance. He also theorized the notion of speaking positions that are wedged within inherited genres and realized through 'social languages' that are themselves in flux. This diversity of expression also relates to speaking positions and the concept of addressivity. Developed further through the works of speech act theorists, discourses in different, overlapping and intersecting modes may be viewed as being enacted through and in action (e.g. Norris and Jones 2005).

In the case of 'unreal estate' persuasive utterances are realized through the online mediation and concatenation of a diversity of digital design drawing and illustration tools that are applied within the persuasive enactment of advertising. In the material we study we see that a variety of professionally generated representations are housed within a property portal. They are the result of diverse design activity by different actors, yet they are co-assembled as persuasive online discourse (see also Morrison and Skjulstad 2006; Morrison and Skjulstad forthcoming). Such mul timodal assemblages are gathered in one linked environment through which we are also able to compare various renditions.

In the section on text analysis we go into detail as to how mediating artefacts are themselves articulated via digital tools and media. This focus on articulation has received less attention in the predominant domains in which a socio-cultural perspective has been developed, namely, learning and work. In media and cultural studies, the term was taken up by Stuart Hall to refer to ways in which power is voiced within mediated discourse (e.g. Hall 1997). In a communication design view on digital design and its discourses, articulation refers to actual means of voicing via multimodal mediation. It includes attention to intertextual and interpersonal relations in communication, whether narrative, expository or persuasive. The design of multimodal affordances becomes critical. Multimodal affordances may be said to include the ways digital environments are designed to engage participants to take up cultural resources and to collaboratively contribute those of their own. Mediation is central to the 'translation' of these affordances within and across modes of discourses (spoken, visual, written, auditory, kinetic, etc.) (Skjulstad 2007; Morrison and Eikenes 2008). We have addressed this, for example, in an analysis of how a leading global mobile phone manufacturer literally brands the ease of video production (multiliteracy) via its site as a means to motivating consumers to take part in a globally mediated advertising campaign in which 'user-driven content' is circulated by producer-consumers themselves (Morrison and Skjulstad forthcoming).

Our interest in mediation is to do with the ways in which digital designs in the form of websites are drawn up to anticipate customer interests, while also persuading them to follow them through. This is to extend studies of media, power and positionality in print and televisual advertising into digital domains and the ways they implicate consumers in co-creating the environments and processes of their own need and desire.

Mediating Artefacts

Artefacts are widely discussed in design research. Here we refer to one approach to them that deals especially with the level of the imaginative within a representation. Wartofsky (1979) developed his concept of the mediating artefact in a view that situated perception as part of action. This action may be seen to move from the literalism of the construction and use of the primary artefact such as a hat (as seen in Fig. 7.5), to the modes of representation and re-articulation of traditions and skills in secondary ones (the genre of the website shown in Fig. 7.5). The abstract and the imaginative are what make up what Wartofsky labelled tertiary artefacts, such as the hyperrealist 3D rendering seen in Fig. 7.4 of an apartment block superimposed on a photographic sky.

These tertiary artefacts are ones that do not bear direct representations to the here-and-now of the material world as a given. In the case of unreal estate this is to do with projections of designed apartments that can only be mediated as coherent texts through the multiple, co-articulated visualizations that are possible via digital media. Yet these tertiary artefacts are patently unreal: we are invited to engage with them as idealized versions of what domestic dwelling may be, and in many cases consumers are warned that these images cannot legally be held as facsimiles of what is still to be built. While the importance of prior or historical knowledge and influences is acknowledged in socio-cultural theory, and plays a part in Wartofsky's conceptualization of mediating artefacts, concerning the tertiary artefact, space is given to the imaginative (Wartofsky 1979: 209). This is not an abstract and undefined space, however. It refers to embodied representations. What is important in this view is that the creative, imaginary and the perceptually innovative are embodied in artefacts themselves. Here the artefacts are the persuasive adverts realized via digital design professionals; co-ordinated but also embodied via a property portal. We have also studied this with respect to the online mediation and marketing of luxury waterfront apartments (Morrison et al. 2007).

There is an additional dialectic in Wartofsky's model and this is that these embodied imaginaries may in turn influence our perception of the here-and-now and the ways in which we think about it, act in it and, in turn, conceptualize the 'real world' further. It is this 'representation of possibilities which go beyond present actualities' (Wartofsky 1979: 209) that we see as one of main reasons to concentrate on the textualization of online artefacts such as sites selling properties still to be built. We see what is designed, planned, projected and persuasive. The adverts make us look at real estate anew.

A Blend of Visualizations

In the shaping of this mediated experience for potential buyers, there is often a blend of modes for representing physical locales and contexts, planning sketches, completed architectural drawings and web mediations. The web becomes a repository for the convergence of a range of design activities and their passages of articulation via CAD tools and Web interface design, including vrml type features, taking us from walk-throughs to 'immersive space' (Bowman 1996). Alongside this medley of modes, digital communication design is being extended into the shaping of hybrid or mixed reality environments that increasingly call for participants to not only engage with textual representations but also to physically move aspects of the mediated into new configurations. These are ones that are realised symbolically and communicatively, not only in terms of a structural or functional 'interaction' design.

The sites analysed here suggest how some of the representations of professional practice and features and functions of digital tools are incorporated within commercial property marketing sites. Textually, we see a range of tools and their textual contexts of application, from drawing and planning, to interior architecture, and visual projections of new urbanism, and allusion to other domains of online advertising. In a sense, this is an extension into online persuasion of visual, spatial and temporal features of digital discourses of architecture and urbanism (e.g. Crysler 2003) that knowingly make use of digital tools and textualisations that link 'new' media, architecture and urban studies (e.g. McGrath and Shane 2005; McGrath and Gardner 2007). We also see this as the marketing of co-operative work from projects in urbanism, architecture and interior design where digital mediation is used to market a built and interior lifestyle aesthetic. We now turn to the way in which hyperrealism is constructed in a selection of sites.

Hyperrealism

From Reality TV to Hyperrealistic Representation

Developments in digital imaging software and distribution have had a major effect on photography (e.g. Jenks 1995; Darley 2000; Wells 2004). The photographic image is now digital: it may be re-rendered, manipulated and adjusted. Along with CAD and desktop software tools, there has arisen a desire on the part of digital designers to reach for hyper-real representations of the photographic. For some, the greatest achievement is to compose a digital image that is seemingly photographic, just as painters have toyed with extreme realism and its micro details. Paradoxically, where photography has become more malleable, digitally drawn images have become more hyperreal. They are simulations of the real.

In the diversity of digital mediations now available in games and online discourses, representational realism has become a widespread mode. Prior to the popularization of the internet and digital tools and technologies, Baudrillard advanced the concept of the simulacrum as an object that exists on its own, without a model upon which it is based, but nonetheless a copy. Baudrillard (1994) argued that 'the real no longer exists' meaning that the significations and representations in a simulated version of the real come to overshadow the representations and circulations of the real. Referring to a story on mapping by Borges, Baudrillard (1994: 1) wrote that:

> Abstraction today is no longer that of the map, the double, the mirror or the concept. Simulation is no longer that of a territory, a referential being or a substance. It is the generation

by models of a real without origin or reality: a hyperreal. The territory no longer precedes the map, nor survives it. Henceforth, it is the map that precedes the territory – precession of simulacra – it is the map that engenders the territory....

In an increasingly mediatized world, 'reality' is realized through signs, and these create our sense of existence and influence our access and responses to it that include the digital.

However, as we discuss below, technologically enhanced mediations circulate in social and cultural contexts and ultimately have a bearing on the built environment and lived spaces.[2] In 'unreal estate', the use of hyperrealistic photography is not a case of the copy replacing the original as Baudrillard argued. Instead we see a simulation of a reality to-be-built. We are therefore interested to see how the 'objects' are defined by the 'code': here the code is an online semiotic mediation constructed via digital design tools and expressions. The hyperrealistic coherence is created by the co-ordination of a range of digital tools. This may be seen in the construction of a virtual city, for example, in the positioning of designers as avatars and populations as agents in an investigation of new ways to deconstruct and plan urban spaces (Batty and Hudson-Smith 2005).

In our current study, this is to link reality in unreal estate, a communicative space that is already designed and it has been designed through digital tools, now themselves mediationally inscribed within websites. The original is a digital representation designed for a real building site. This representation is aimed to persuade actual consumers towards the purchase of a dwelling not yet built. The websites we analyse are also marketed inside the finn.no portal that sells existing real estate alongside the projections of the to-be-built. It is the mediatized design of this unreal estate that consumers encounter and within which they are persuaded to engage.

On Remediation and Hypermediacy

Bolter and Grusin (1999) have argued that the refashioning, uptake and reorientation of developments of successive media may be understood through the concept of remediation. While this approach may be critiqued as promoting a componential analysis of different media in digital mediations (Skjulstad 2007), it points to the issue of articulation of different media types as part of change processes. Their concepts of immediacy and hypermediacy are pertinent to the analysis of representations of unreal state and the reach therein for forms of visual realism.

Bolter and Grusin (1999: 53) write that '... digital hypermedia seek the real by multiplying mediation so as to create a feeling of fullness, a satiety of experience, which can be taken as reality.' Bolter and Grusin (1999) refer to visual representations

---

[2] http://www.fxnetworks.com/shows/originals/niptuck/

that explicitly point to the medium itself as hypermediacy; as users we pay close attention to acts and procedures of mediation, especially visual ones that involve us in seeing how that mediation is crafted via other media types and conventions. By focusing on hypermediacy as we do here, we are able to move inside representations of the physical world as simulations of the real and see how digital tools and artefacts are part of these picturings. In this process, the act of mediation is made transparent so that the gap between sign/signifier and the resulting signification is homogenized and the user believes that the representation is the object, with the result that the medium sits in the background.

Selling the Planned and Projected

Fig. 7.6 Exterior of apartment complex, with ground floor terrace, walkway and summer blossoms. Frydenberg project[3]

One of the problems facing sellers of property is how best to show it to prospective buyers. As advertising developed as a field, brochures or prospects were compiled

---

[3]Frydenberg exterior: http://www.finn.no/finn/viewimage?finnkode= 8840103&reference= 3/884/010/3_1375009088.jpg&adheading=FRYDENBERG+-+Salgsstart+nytt+byggetrinn+30 +november+fra+1800-2000%21++3-%2C+4-%2C+og+5roms+leiligheter&sid= 14aFM74x s 322516&pos=1&adTypeId=9

so as to show both exteriors and interiors. Drawings, paper models, site photographs and pictures of similar buildings were used to present planned projects as well as properties in development. Photographs of properties included in prospects handed to potential buyers then moved onto being mediated via direct mailings, freely distributed local print papers, and the press. With the spread of digital photography, images became included in both print and online representations. In marketing unreal estate, agents need to persuade buyers that still-to-be-built properties are on a par with those that are already built, and may even supersede them in their aesthetics and amenities. Hyperrealism – part of a design strategy for mediation of property online – is employed in many of the online representations of new residences in Oslo, especially apartments.

In the example of Frydenberg, shown in Fig. 7.6, a card index interface metaphor from the *finn.no* portal is visible. In the vertical menu, different thumbnail visualizations are housed. As a whole, this menu bar provides an overall view of the representations, mixing tertiary artefacts in the form of 3D renderings with photographic realizations, supported by a map and plans. Most of the unreal estate featured in the portal has links to project sites from the estate agent and developer. Frydenberg is marketed as an ideal purchase, suitable for all ages, and especially suited to children, the young and the urban.[4] It is described in the accompanying written text as being green and quiet as well as maximizing the possible capacity per unit. In addition, the 600-apartment complex is marketed as being within reach of both the city and the forest that frames the urban area. Furthermore, it has views over the city as well as adjoining a park.

Verbal–Visual Coherence: Exteriors

In these adverts, verbal description is mirrored visually (Kress 1998). In Fig. 7.6 we have selected one of the images that shows the wider context of the apartment complex. Although a series of geometrically arranged, five storey blocks are presented, this is done on a diagonal axis with a flowering tree and natural low hedge in the foreground. The elevation up the slope with a hill in the background suggests that the apartments look south and westwards towards the fjord. This is a summery scene; children are playing with a ball or balloon on a ground floor terrace and two adults accompany them. To the left, a couple walks past on a path that threads its ways through the leafy space between the blocks. The apartments have large windows and spacious terraces. Pastel tones are offset by the perfumed lilacs typical of summer in Scandinavia, adding to the sense of a known and friendly urban outdoors. In terms of Experience Design (McCarthy & Wright 2004), multiple sensory messages are signified in this image, with the result that the property may be seen as an accessible, digital instance of a potentially desirable dwelling.

---

[4] On Fredenberg: http://www.bolig.skanska.no/sok-bolig/Projects/Frydenberg/Om-projektet/

Fig. 7.7 Interior views. Perspective from interior of a ground floor apartment with flowers, child's tricycle and playground (*above*); Terrace apartment view, full sunlight, and open door, with flatscreen television, Italian dining chairs and occupant on terrace (*below*); Frydenberg project[5]

The scene is hyperreal in that it is manifestly a blend of the photographic or photograph-like (the people, tree and bushes) and the digitally rendered (the façades). Together these images constitute unreal estate: this environment is not built, but it is situated in a palette to the left of the screen that contains images of

[5]Frydenberg interior: http://www.finn.no/finn/viewimage?finnkode= 8840103& reference=3/884/010/3_1375009088.jpg&adheading=FRYDENBERG+-+Salgsstart+ nytt+ byggetrinn+30.+november+fra+1800-2000%21++3-%2C+4-%2C+og+5-roms+leiligheter&sid= 14aFM74xts322516&pos=1&adTypeId=9 and http://www.finn.no/finn /viewimage ?finnkode =8840103&reference=3/884/010/3_1375009088.jpg&adheading=FRYDENBERG+-+Salgsstart+ nytt+byggetrinn+30.+november+fra+1800-2000%21++3-%2C+4-%2C+og+5-roms +leiligheter &sid=14aFM74xts322516&pos=1&adTypeId=9

the actual world. This also applies to the interior views, which are related to the sunny outdoor images and the approach from the exterior. The image menu bar reminds us that this is constructed space and leads us to acknowledge that the elements are instances of hypermediacy, as Bolter and Grusin (1999) argue. We are meant to look inside them and to know that they are constructed, but the intention is that we trust them as 'accurate' simulations.

Inside Looking Out

Figure 7.7 shows images of interiors, looking into corners that maximise internal and external views (reminding us of the 3-point turns in QuickTimeVR). In the upper image, an additional scene of summery living is presented. The wooden floors and contemporary furnishings, drawn from or simulating a 3D furniture library, are complemented by a vase of lilies. These blossoms are picked up in the distance in the form of two flowering cherry trees that lead the eye along the diagonal from the clean interior and large windows out through the open door. On the terrace are a table and chairs; a child's bicycle and teddy bear lean against a supporting post. This is clearly a child-friendly property. To the right a picture window shows a scene of urban tranquillity as a father watches children playing on the swings. Two people walk along the main path, their gaze drawn in the other direction suggesting additional action, though in no way threatening.

In contrast to this image of life on the ground floor, in the lower image sun streams through an open terrace door into an upper apartment and onto the wooden floor and occasional table, upon which sits a bowl of apples. These pick up the tone of the dining chairs and drapes. That this is a living room is suggested not only by the sofa and flat screen TV but by the variegated hosta plant in the foreground, and by the vista over the city that we see as a similar view to that of the man standing on the terrace, hands in pockets. Hyperrealism is further apparent in the extent to which light is represented: this is shown in the glass on the terrace door and via the visualization of reflection in the TV panel. The overall effect is of a modern, functionally furnished apartment, with contemporary furniture in the form of sofa, designer chairs on the terrace and dining room (by Catifa), and the accoutrements of the digital urban lifestyle, symbolized by the TV.

These details are more than descriptive: they indicate how the textual result of digital rendering processes in which 3D tools have been applied to generate hyperrealism may be seen as shaping a sensorized experience on the part of consumers. Contemporary styles and objects from interior design are inscribed through reference to other print mediations of furniture and related web sites that use clip art libraries. Dillon (2006) has argued that clip art libraries are infused with categorizations based on common sense; here, in contrast, we see the professional importation of specialist furnishings into a simulation of contemporary Scandinavian urban interior design. As Darley (2000: 193) reminds us, such images are aestheticized.

The overall digital image is a blend of tools and articulations, signifying a whole-some lifeworld that can now be hypermediated to the extent that we absorb its mediation as 'naturalized' (Gitelman 2006) while knowingly observing it through a 'virtual window' (Friedberg 2006). In the context of immersive virtual reality, Morse (1998: 221) observes that '… although a virtual environment is an invention and a simulation that is prepared in advance, we (and even its designers) cannot fully anticipate what it means to experience that realm until we are "inside".' This would seem pertinent to a fuller textual analysis of how we are persuaded to enter unreal estate, and ultimately, as we show later, how to begin to construct it ourselves.

Linking Real and Unreal Estate

In the same panel of images on the left (the menu in finn.no; see Figure 7.6) one can also see two wider views of the context within which this apartment complex is situated. The digital images of the unreal are constructed so that they play off photographs of existing urban vistas. They appear in the same overall context, even if they are given a category of 'new' developments. Figure 7.8 shows how hyper-realism is created by linking the digitally rendered with the photographic. This double articulation simultaneously accesses the 'real' and realizes the virtual. It thereby alerts consumers to the very constructedness of unreal estate.

The adverts are presented as knowingly constructed. These articulations may be seen as a move in chains of representations that, ultimately, will lead to additions to the built environment. McCullough (2004) has described how architecture is being linked with pervasive computing such that our notions of the built are being extended. In architecture, we also see the growth of interest and studies in the 'immaterial', but we follow the broad approach of Hill (2006: 3) in seeing this not so much in terms of the actual absence of matter but more the 'perceived absence of matter' and a necessary linkage on the part of the participant to transversing the material and immaterial. Digital representations and users' participation need to be joined; the digital design of this discourse asks that we draw selectively on both representational and performative approaches to digital design while avoiding a fetishization of communication itself.

In the upper image a view, presumably from one of the higher terraces, shows an autumnal scene looking towards the city centre and southwards down the Oslo fiord. The second image, below, shows the projected image of a development in the nearby park. Real fiord and digitally generated lake both suggest that these apart-ments are connected to wider open spaces and activities. In the park we see a small jetty, a floating platform and a young couple with a pram beside a fountain that rises out of the concrete surface. There are lights around the lake, perhaps suggesting we imagine them reflected in the water at night. These contrasting modes of represen-tation engage us in acts of comparative and differential seeing. We build our fuller sense of the potential site and its surroundings through the imaginative passage between the photographic and the digitally drawn. This contrasts with our readings

Fig. 7.8 Contrasting images of locale, autumn colours and fiord in photograph (*above*), digital drawing of park development with small lake (*below*).[6] Frydenberg project

of adverts in the press where single images are provided of properties prepared for filming, or their presentation online as finished and 'furnished' entities. In unreal estate, the user in invited into a persuasive arena in which the communication design is geared towards also making space for their own conceptions of a future property. This is more than a simulated persuasion; it is a move to act.

Making the Connections

In some instances, this blend of the digitally drawn 3D environment is even more marked in its use of CAD images and close-up photographs. This can be seen in the site for a suburban apartment complex called Holmen/Makrellbekken. In Fig. 7.9, we have composed a collage of some of the images from the image palette to the

---

[6]http://www.finn.no/finn/viewimage?finnkode=8840103&reference=3/884/010/3_ 1164095435671. jpg&adheading=FRYDENBERG+-+Salgsstart+nytt+byggetrinn+30.+november+fra+1800-2000%21++3-%2C+4-%2C+og+5-roms+leiligheter&sid=14aFM74xts 322516&pos=1&adTypeId=9

Fig. 7.9 Extracts from 'palette' of urban apartments showing photographic and CAD representations

left of the main screen for this site, as seen in Fig. 7.2. Larger versions of these images do not co-occur but replace one another in the main window of finn.no. The effect of selecting them one after another is to build a sense of the imagined inside the real, so that the leafy numbered street with its apple blossoms are a part of the 3D landscape and its angular structures and seemingly floating kitchen. There is an 'architectural' confidence to these simulations and the offer of their imagining. The whole context is not shown but suggested. Digital persuasion may be realized through the interstitials between the online spaces, now pollenated now pixellated, co-present yet alternating.

In looking at this site the tertiary artefact seems most powerful. It is a concept that helps explain renderings and reverberations between the real and the imagined. Wartofsky (1979: 209) conceived of tertiary artefacts as '… a domain in which there is free construction in the imagination of rules and operations different from those adopted for "this-worldly" praxis.' These views of unreal estate are imagined, yet they are also planned, detailed and integral to a wider digital design project that moves material property through digitally-assisted design processes and finally on into the electronics of the financial property sector.

Wartofsky saw representations as embodied in artefacts and this is clearly the case here. Somewhat uncannily for us reviewing the mediated persuasion of unreal estate, Wartofsky (1979: 209) observed that 'Once the visual picture can be "lived in", perceptually, it can also come to color and change our perception of the "actual" world, as envisioning possibilities in it not presently recognised.' This would seem to be precisely what the architects and estate agents would wish to achieve through their projection of a digitally designed future lifeworlds alongside that of familiar flora and fauna. We do not see what cannot be seen, but we are able to visualize in our own minds' eyes that which will be realized. Prior to the web, it was not possible to toggle between these representations that, online, give users multiple affordances to conceptualize their lived futures by way of different co-ordinated views.

3D Visualizations in 3D

Transposing CAD Tools and Representations

These co-ordinated views are also achieved through the inclusion of visualizations that incorporate features and functions of different digital tools. CAD tools have been used in architecture and other domains of dimensional design since the 1980s. As tools have improved along with storage space and rendering speeds, we have nevertheless seen on the web a continuation of simulated 3D in 2D space, such as in vrml. 3D visualisation produced in applications such as 3D StudioMAX may be understood as compositions that can involve a range of software, plug-ins and imports that are threaded together so as to create a global illusion. Furniture and props may be added; animated elements and correspondences between them may be realized in Flash (Burk 2005); 3D video footage may be included in an overall site. As a result, a variety of renderings may be related to one another in a mediational environment that is also digital.

However, as Lunenfeld (2000) has argued, the 'snap to grid' function in such tools is not a simple matter of aligning a function with a cultural representation via a Cartesian grid, but rather a process of finding relationships between form and function that are inflected with critical theory. Significations are realized through such tools, and these influence modes of representation communicatively (McCullough 1996; Manovich 2003). Yet, at an additional level, the tools become part of the semiosis of digitally-rendered representations – they are inscribed at the level of articulation, they are part of the digital texturing of the representation and their functions are simulated onscreen for our limited kinetic use.

As we have already mentioned, many of the sites contain line drawings in the box of images on the left. Some online sites advertising unreal estate have features that link aspects of photorealistic renderings to the inscription of CAD drawings of interiors and floor plans. This can be seen in one of the sectors of the Frydenberg site.[7] It offers a different view from that of other sections seen above, this time including a map that is clearly drawn with digital tools. In addition, though, this

---

[7] See: http://www.finn.no/finn/realestate/object?finnkode=8936380&sid=14a07pxyAC 954859&pos=1&tot=10; and http://www.finn.no/finn/realestate/object?finnkode=8840103 &sid= 14a07pxyAC023253&pos=2&tot=10

section also includes a zoomable aerial photo, thereby 'grounding' imagined or unreal estate to the actual land upon which it is to stand.

These websites are typically composed by web design companies that co-ordinate different media elements in the wider design and development process. Images of floor plans and cutaways are included from material drawn by architects as well as by companies involved in developing 3D visualizations specifically designed to provide mediations of the unbuilt. According to PLACEBO EFFECTS, based in Oslo, 'The 3d models depicting a whole floor plan complete with furniture, materials and lighting but without a ceiling, have become a product of its own – the shoebox (3dBOX).'[8] This refers to isometric views in CAD.

Many of the perspectives we see in the 3D visualisation on the web portal are presented via isometric views. These are views that are a variant of a parallel perspective: all the sides are shown as spatially parallel in the view. The angles of the sides are 30° but this may vary slightly; right angles are shown as such. The result is that the dimensions given may be read as 'true'. In the 3D illustrations discussed below we see a further variant which is the twisting of this parallel perspective and its realization as an isometric perspective: the view is from above. This gives the user a unique position that is itself an announcement that digital visualizations can provide a point of view for potential buyers. These are buyers who would otherwise not be able to see through the 2D representations of the unbuilt to 3D realizations of their imagined and planned construction. This is extended in the use of trimetric perspective in the representations of the interiors.

Cutaway to the Bedroom

Examples of this use of isometric views can be seen in the images which follow. In Fig. 7.10, the main window shows a highlighted 3D cutaway accompanied by two floorplans. Both make use of colour to augment a line drawing. To the left is a photograph of an actual and fully furnished bedroom that is in the mode of an interior design magazine image. In terms of the tertiary artefact, the juxtaposition-ing of these images suggests a possible shift in the potential buyer's attention to the modular construction of the apartment as planned, and projects a potentially achievable result in the very private space of the bedroom. This is further signalled in the image of a woman holding the back of her dress, a suntan line clearly visible, which, at the same time, suggests the leisure, and perhaps the finances, to travel to warmer zones subsequent to an actual investment in the property. Similar to other domains of advertising, sensory allusions and connotations are achieved through the juxtapositioning, here the corporeally 'marked' and the mapping of the body of the apartment.

---

[8]http://www.placebo-fx.com/projects.html

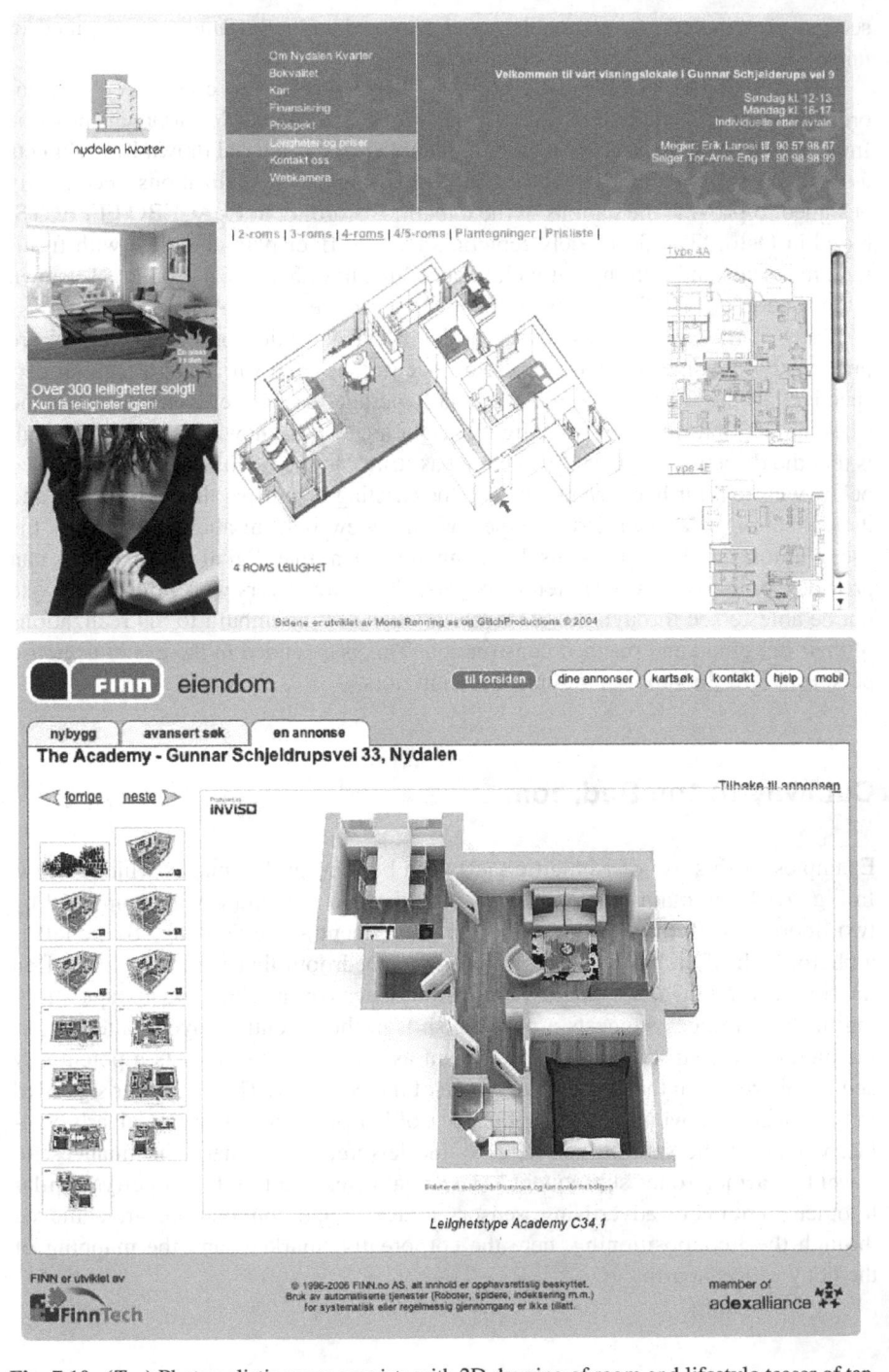

Fig. 7.10 (*Top*) Photorealistic room coexists with 2D drawing of room and lifestyle teaser of tan line, and (*bottom*) Multiple choices for user try-out and viewing of detail

Seeing Inside the 'Set'

Figure 7.11 is a clear example of the shoebox; it presents no external walls as is the case in Fig. 7.10. In addition, a library of furniture and textures appears to have been applied. This set-like view appears to be more lived-in than the one above it, suggesting a quickly readable scale of furnishings to floor area.

Fig. 7.11 Screengrab of detailed 3D 'shoebox' visualization of luxury apartment[9]

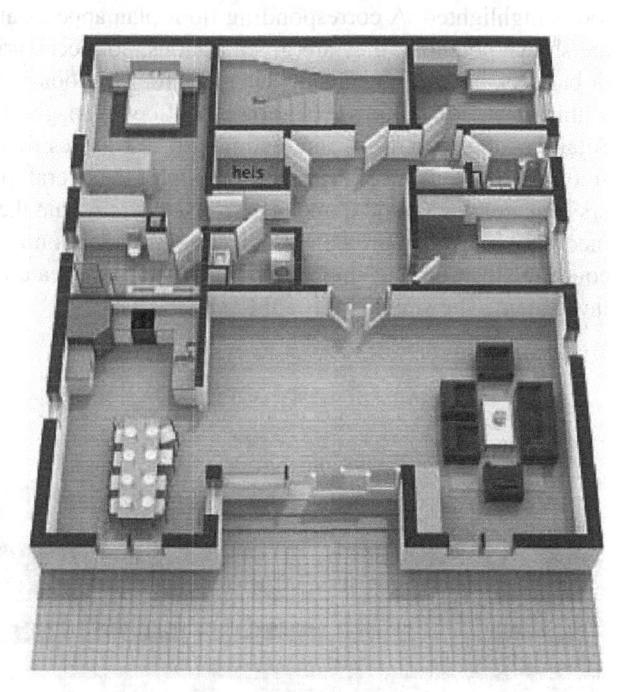

Some sites include even larger representations of the planned space and, further, suggest an option for its furnishing. However, this is shown schematically, without much detail or flair, although for example we can see plates on the dining room table and red dots on the black stove top. Like the geometry of the space, the kitchen fittings and the lounge furniture are angular and modular. Shadows are used to further simulate that this is to be an actual space, though this is achieved with a single light setting from above, not visible to the screen viewer, and showing no variation or apparent hyperrealism in comparison with the interiors discussed earlier.

---

[9]http://www.finn.no/finn/viewimage?finnkode=8194230&reference=0/819/423/0563553957 .jpg &adheading=Elegante+leiligheter+p%E5+Nordstrand&sid=10a4bmjSDD986393&pos=3&adTy peId=9

The Simulated as Sold

Two further examples indicate variation in new apartment complexes by position, size and cost. In 'The Academy' (Fig. 7.12), the entire complex is shown in a small navigational block drawing to the top left. Block B has been selected by the user and this is highlighted. This block is then shown in larger scale below it, with floors and individual apartments presented. The user has selected an apartment and this too is highlighted. A corresponding floor plan appears at the bottom right. Buyers are shown potential; they are given options, not necessarily fitting their own needs or budgets, but they are able to see plans for neighbouring apartments and variation within them. The short text above the floor plan gives the size and some main details of the apartment. Interestingly, it also states that the apartment is already sold, creating a sense of the marketability of the overall property, encouraging buyers to search for unsold unreal estate elsewhere within the complex. Here the imagined may in turn effect the real, shifting our attention and action from the level of conceptualization and into practice, but it does create a sense of activity and of investment. The simulated is sold.

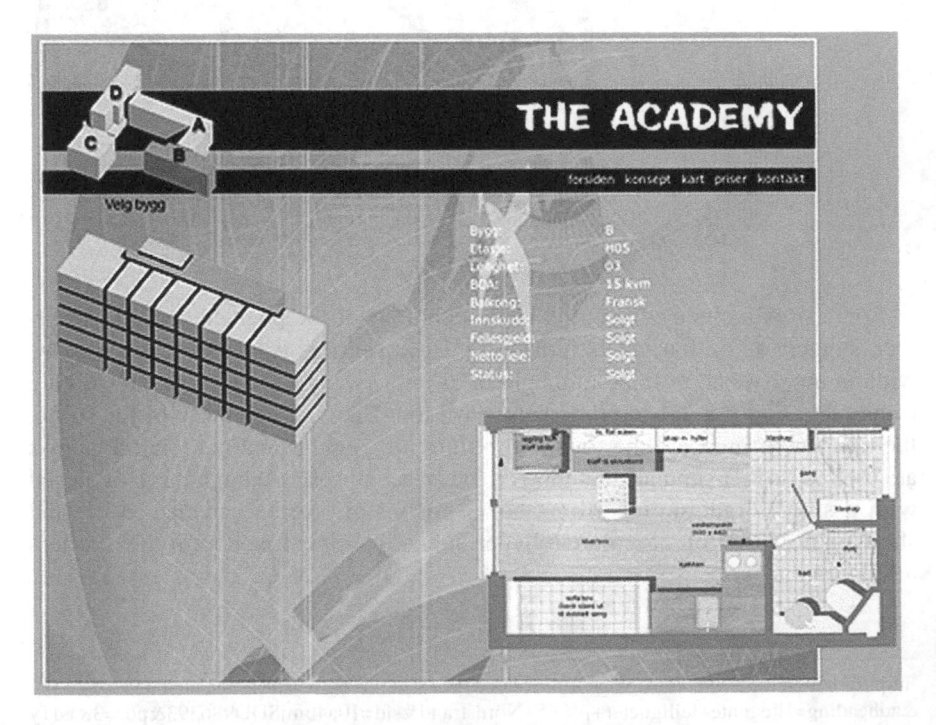

Fig. 7.12 Three concurrent menus and one floor plan displayed in detail

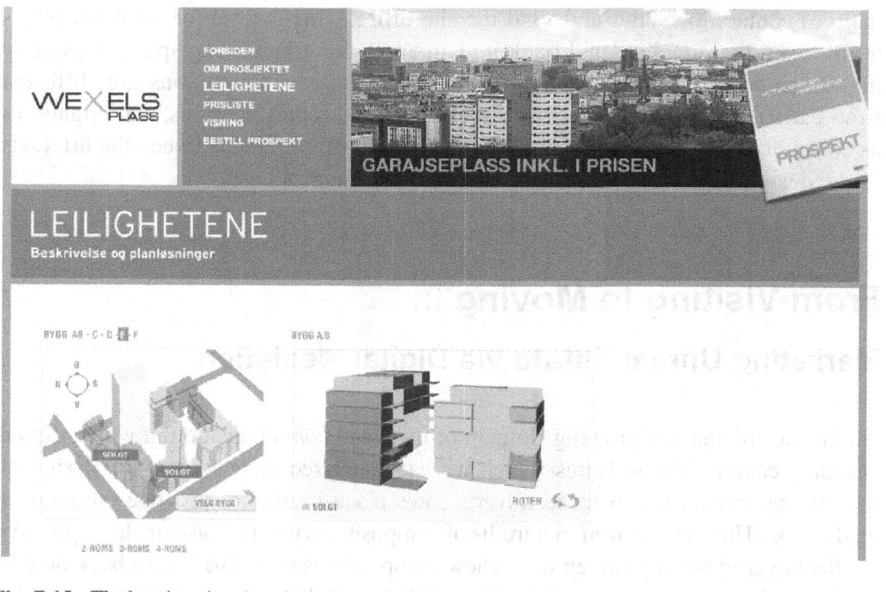

Fig. 7.13 Flash animation (*top left*) shows building selected from apartment block complex; with floor plan (*bottom left*) and detailed illustration with properties (*right*)

The Full Picture

This technique is also apparent in several in sites for properties that are linked from within the property portal to the real estate developer's full site. This also allows potential buyers and interested viewers a fuller view of apartments already planned and in construction. Visualizations of urban design and development meet online marketing. For several new large developments, we encounter a blend of more detailed planning views of the wider area and its aerial elevations, as well as a more visually developed portfolio of individual buildings and specific apartments within them.

In Fig. 7.13, an apartment complex is first shown as a set of differently coloured blocks.[10] A selected apartment may be rotated, adding an additional simulated turn from the CAD toolbox, and greater use is made of colour and opaque markings. It is possible to zoom in on floor plans, at which point fuller details are provided about each apartment. Taken together, these features further suggest that the artefact is more than an imagined and conceptual construction, but a complex mediation of information system and semiotic (Bødker and Bøgh Andersen 2005) that, for the average buyer, is trustworthy.

The mediations we see online here are themselves digital designs. They are part of a wider communication design strategy to provide visitors and buyers with seemingly rich contextual information that would ultimately also, perhaps, persuade

---

[10]http://www.wexelsplass.no/

them to contact the seller and visit the site office. This is to move, in Wartofsky's terms, from the imagined and back into an emerging urban living space marked by its contemporary architecture and aesthetics. These visualizations are different from earlier ones in that they inscribe professional representations, and engage us as consumers in moving through unbuilt properties onscreen, between the artefacts of the designers and marketers and our own built homes.

From Visiting to Moving In

Marketing Unreal Estate via Digital Mediation

Online advertising is a growing domain of mediated communication in which digital design is central. The websites which we have analysed indicate how the design of mediational persuasion in these adverts takes place inside not just one medium or media type. They are realized in a trellis of compositions that now also includes involving the buyer in activity-driven use. These compositions may also in turn back on one another and borrow communicative features that cross the different domains of professional design work, documentation and publication (Schmidt and Wagner 2002).

In the property portal examined above, we see numerous examples that draw together urban design, planning and development with visual mediations of the digitally drawn and designed. There we see that digital imaging tools are being transposed from sites of professional work to the online mediation of projected properties. We have coined the term 'Unreal Estate' to cover the digital mediation of the unbuilt involving a co-ordination of CAD tools and hyperreal illustrations. We have presented a textual analysis of selected adverts in a city-wide portal (but one that spans the country) that encompasses such digital illustration as part of its marketing of new properties. We have shown that simulations of future reality do indeed project desires, as Baudrillard asserts. We do not suggest that this is part of 'a contagious hyperreality', but we see that such media projections are part of an expanded and wider urban design process that is to do with capital, prime locations and processes of investment in projects as part of their realization (Morrison et al. 2007).

Furthermore, we see that there is an important articulation of the projection of exterior and interior design, linking the un/built environment with movement into virtual interiors of domestic spaces. We have shown that online advertising is moving from print and filmic genres and convention to online, kinetic and 3D representations, and offering users spaces to imagine their futures, in some cases through leaving elements incomplete. Here we referred to the role of artefacts in connecting the emerging visual, spatial and kinetic phenomena of online advertising to the inscription of tools and signs in the signification of digital artefacts in wider contexts of 'habitation'.

Our approach has been to see this online mediation in terms of persuasive public commercial discourse that is highly purposive in its intent to communicate what is desirable through acts of visualizing it and by way of engaging users in making better informed choices. We have acknowledged that such creation and marketing of unreal estate, using properties from the project-driven domains in which it is designed, needs to be connected to wider social and economic contexts. The adverts to which we have pointed also have fairly limited potential for visitors in terms of expressing their personal interests and wishes. What is shown is a projection on the part of sellers. However, this is only one part of how unreal estate is being embodied. What we also now see are applications that are directed into the hands of potential buyers so that they adopt some of the illustrative, envisioning and communicative roles earlier taken by web marketing and property developer concerns.

Making 'Home Pages'

In the popular game series, *The SIMS*,[11] players may develop intricately designed domestic spaces and related amenities in wider contexts of residency. Concerning 3D environments and socio-cultural views on design, Flanagan (2003) sees the SIMS as a site for the enactment of transformative activities that may be analysed as engendered, but also allows for the playing out of social change. While Lemke (2005) shows that this game is about relations between time and place, the game is not connected to the players' actual worlds. This is what is being taken up by several sectors of both the marketing of the built environment and interior design.

We see this as an instance of making 'home pages'. This is an activity that extends beyond the largely presentational focus of the sites we have featured and discussed to offering affordances for users to take up and apply to their own interior designing. This is further stretched to multi-level marketing in which digital representations are circulated back to print and into storage media other than the web. Online users may also buy a set of DVDs to install, such as 3D Home Designer.[12] The global interior design and product company IKEA provides tools to enable consumers to customize their homes, especially kitchens.[13]

We see here that professionally designed visualization tools and processes may engage users in generating images of their own unreal estate. In contrast to the examples discussed earlier in the chapter, this unreal estate is personalized to the user's taste. In performing their own designs of unreal estate interiors, users activate their own mediating artefacts. These are realizations of imaginative renderings embodied through given tools sets, and with the potential for shared meaning making through their circulation online

---

[11] http://www.thesims2.co.uk/products.view.asp?id=46&page=1&movie_id=126&movies_nav_page=1&movie_q=hi#mp

[12] http://astore.amazon.co.uk/thedictionofcell/detail/B0009JHTXS/026-0691026-0063607

[13] IKEA: steps to your new kitchen:http://www.ikea.com/ms/en_GB/complete_kitchen_guide/planner_tool/download/index.html

Sharing Design Performances

Where the explicit aim of the sites that market future properties is to project a wide yet specific representation of the potential selections, we encounter online a digital discourse that is about the projection of design as already 'drawn'. However, as web developers build their own digital mediations online, users are invited to enact some of the co-ordinating activities involved in an integrated design. The inscription of digital design tools and their features online, such as sliding scales, remains a simulation in that the actual tools are not in the hands of the consumers, and their participation is encapsulated with in a commercial subscription site.

Textual analyses of emerging design phenomena do have an important place alongside explorations of performative use. Digital design research needs to continue to investigate the role of participation in the development and use of processes and products that are linked to our envisioning and actual building of lived environments. In the related domain of electronic art there are debates about shifting publics from spectators to visitors. As Jacucci and Wagner (2005) stress, hard divisions between designers and users no longer hold when users become performers – their participation in mixed reality environments is crucial to the completion of digital design. This is already seen in mixed reality installation arts where digital design is geared towards participants' generative performativity between the given and the enacted (Morrison and Sem 2008; Morrison et al. 2010). This applies equally to online advertisers, so that visiting a website is extended to completing an activity by participation, based on need, interest and choice. In making such a move, online advertisers now also face the mediational activity of external and multiple makers of meaning in which more critical voices may be present.

Here we are already beginning to see how advertisers incorporate the discourses of social networking and their primary sites such as *MySpace,* and draw consumers into new relations of production and consumption (Morrison and Skjulstad 2007). Further, design performances created and shared by consumers may also be easily linked to commentary and critique in social networking sites (see Chapter 8). There may be tensions between design companies' orientation of users via their appealing yet nevertheless pay-to-participate tools, and the actions of users circulating their designed residences and commenting on them in the discourses of co-ordination that are not those of networks and chains of work by design professionals. Concerning unreal estate, the notion of the mediating artefact may be linked to the coordination of discourses as enacted via online artifacts (Morrison et al. 2007).

Already, the electronic foundation stones of web-based mediation of unreal estate may be said to be persuasively cast. Whose unreal estate comes into being and in relation to which commercial constraints is a paradox. Unreal estate as digital, cultural simulation will be constructed via online via consumers' performances. Yet, the mediational design and discursive performativity may diverge in relation to what arises from the earth and joins the built environment and what circulates in the wireless worlds that we activate above and across it, and, importantly, project back into and onto it.

Acknowledgements

Thanks to our fellow authors in this volume, to colleagues at InterMedia (University of Oslo) and to Birger Sevaldson and Peter Hemmersam (AHO, Oslo) for suggestions and comments.

References

Jacucci, C., Jacucci, G., Wagner, I., & Psik, T. (2005). A manifesto for the performative development of ubiquitous media. In O.W. Bertelsen, N.O. Bouvin, P.G. Krogh & M. Kyng (Eds.), *Proceedings of the 4th decennial conference on critical computing: between sense and sensibility*, Aarhus, Denmark (pp. 19–28). New York: ACM Press.

Bakhtin, M. (1981). *The dialogic imagination: Four essays by M.M Bakhtin*. In M. Holquist (Ed.), C. Emerson & M. Holquist (Transl.). Austin: University of Texas Press.

Bakhtin, M. (1984). *Problems of Dostoevsky's poetics*. In C. Emerson (Ed. & transl). Minneapolis: University of Minnesota Press.

Bakhtin, M. (1986). *Speech genres and other late essays*. In C. Emerson. & M. Holquist (Eds.), V. McGee (Transl.). Austin: University of Texas Press.

Barnard, M. (1995). Advertising: the rhetorical imperative. In C. Jenks (Ed.), *Visual culture* (pp. 26–41). London: Routledge.

Batty, M. & Hudson-Smith, A. (2005). Urban Simulacra: London. *Architectural design* [Special Issue], 75(6), 42–47.

Baudrillard, J. (1994). *Simulacra and simulation*. In S. Glaser (Transl.). Ann Arbor: The University of Michigan Press.

Baudrillard, J. (1995). *The gulf war did not take place*. In P. Patton (Transl). Bloomington: Indiana University Press.

Bødker, S. & Andersen, P-B. (2005). Complex mediation. *Human-computer interaction*, 20(4), 353–402.

Bolter, J. (2003), Critical theory and the challenge of new media. In M. Hocks & M. Kendrick (Eds.), *Eloquent images: word and image in the age of new media* (pp.19–36). Cambridge, MA: MIT Press.

Bolter, J. D. & Grusin, R. (1999). *Remediation: understanding new media*. Cambridge, MA: MIT Press.

Bowman, D. (1996). Conceptual design space: beyond walk through to immersive space. In D. Bertol (Ed.), *Designing digital space* (pp. 225–236). New York: Wiley.

Burk, Y. (2005). Teaching new perspectives: digital space and flash interactivity. *Digital creativity*, 16(3), 140–152.

Coleridge, S. (1817). Biographia Literaria. In H. Jackson (Ed.) (1985). *Samuel Taylor Coleridge*. OUP: Oxford.

Courchesne, L. (2002). The construction of experience: turning spectators into visitors. In M. Resier, & A. Zapp (Eds.), *New screen media* (pp. 256–267). London: BFI.

Crysler, C. (Ed.) (2003). *Writing spaces: discourses of architecture, urbanism and the built environment, 1960–2000*. New York: Routledge.

Darley, A. (2000). *Visual digital culture*. London: Routledge.

Dillon, G. (2006). Clipart images as commonsense categories. *Visual communication*, 5(3), 287–306. Available at: http://vcj.sagepub.com/cgi/content/abstract/5/3/287

Dyer, G. (1982). *Advertising as communication*. Methuen: London.

Eco, U. (1986). *Travels in hyperreality: essays. 1st edition*. San Diego, CA: Harcourt Brace Jovanovich.

Fagerjord, A. (2003). Rhetorical convergence: studying web media. In G. Liestøl, A. Morrison, & T. Rasmussen (Eds.), *Digital media revisited: theoretical and conceptual innovation in digital domains* (pp. 293–325). Cambridge, MA: MIT Press.

Flanagan, M. (2003). SIMple & personal: Domestic space and The Sims. Paper presented at *the Melbourne DAC, the fifth international Digital Arts and Culture Conference,* Melbourne, Australia. Available at: http://hypertext.rmit.edu.au/dac/papers/

Frascara, J. (2004). *Communication design.* New York: Allworth.

Friedberg, A. (2006). *The virtual window: from Alberti to Microsoft.* Cambridge, MA: MIT Press.

Gibbons, J. (2005). *Art and advertising.* London: I.B. Tauris.

Gitelman, L. (2006). *Always already new: media, history and the data of culture.* Cambridge, MA: MIT Press.

Hall, S. (Ed.) (1997). *Representation: cultural representations and signifying practices.* London: The Open University Press.

Helfand, J. (2001). *Screen: essays on graphic design, new media, and visual culture.* New York: Princeton Architectural Press.

Hill, J. (2006). *Immaterial architecture.* London: Routledge.

Jacucci, G., & wagner, I. (2005). Performative uses of space in mixed media environments. In E. Davenport, & P. Turner (Eds.), *Spaces, spatiality and technologies* (pp. 191–216). London: Springer.

Jenks, C. (Ed.) (1995). *Visual culture.* London: Routledge.

Kalay, Y. & Marx, J. (2006). Architecture and the internet: designing places in cyberspace. *First monday.* Special Issue #5: Virtual Architecture at State of Play III, 6–8 October 2005. Available at: http://firstmonday.org/issues/special11_2b/kalay/index.html

Klingmann, A. (2007). *Brandscapes: architecture in the experience economy.* Cambridge, MA: MIT Press.

Kress, G. (1998). Visual and verbal modes of representation in electronically mediated communication: the potentials of new forms of text. In I. Snyder (Ed.), *Page to screen* (pp. 53–79). New York: Routledge.

Lemke, J. (2005). Place, pace & meaning: multimedia chronotopes. In S. Norris & R. Jones (Eds.), *Discourse in action: introducing mediated discourse analysis* (pp. 110–112). London: Routledge.

Lunenfeld, P. (2000). *Snap to grid: a use's guide to digital arts, media, and cultures.* Cambridge, MA: MIT Press.

Manovich, L. (2003). The poetics of augmented space. In A. Everett & C. Caldwell (Eds.), *New media: theories and practices of digital textuality* (pp. 75–92). New York: Routledge.

McCarthy, J. & Wright, P. (2004). *Technology as experience.* Cambridge, MA: MIT Press.

McCullough, M. (1996). *Abstracting craft: the practiced digital hand.* Cambridge, MA: MIT Press.

McCullough, M. (2004). *Digital ground.* Cambridge, MA: MIT Press.

McGrath, B. & Gardner, J. (2007). *Cinemetrics: architectural drawing today.* London: Wiley.

McGrath, B. & Shane, G. (Eds.) (2005). Introduction. *Architectural digest* [Special Issue], 75(6), 5–15.

McQuire, S. (2008). *The media city: media architecture and urban space.* London: Sage.

Morrison, A. & Sem. I. (2008). Stretching multiliteracies: production-based education & new media. *Digital Kompetanse/Nordic Journal of Digital Literacy,* No. 3/2008, 180–201.

Morrison, A. & Eikenes, J.O. (2008). 'The times are a-changing in the interface'. *Multimodality and Learning. An international conference.* Institute of Education, University of London. 19–20 June.

Morrison, A., Sem, I. & Havnør, M. (2010). Behind the wallpaper: performativity in mixed reality arts. In A. Morrison (Ed.), *Inside multimodal composition.* Cresskill, NJ: Hampton Press.

Morrison, A. & Skjulstad, S. (2006). Mediating hybrid design: a study of the projection of automotive innovation on the web. In *Proceedings of Wonderground – the 2006 Design Research Society International Conference,* Lisbon, Portugal.

Morrison, A. & Skjulstad, S. (2007). Talking cleanly about convergence. In T. Storsul & D. Stuedahl (Eds.), *Ambivalence towards convergence* (pp. 217–335). Göteborg: Nordicom.

Morrison, A. & Skjulstad, S. (forthcoming). Laying egs in other people's pockets. In B. Gentakow, E. Skogseth, & S. Østerud (Eds.), *Literacy – technology – cultural techniques. How does communication technology mediate culture?* Cresskill, NJ: Hampton Press.

Morrison, A. Skjulstad., S., & Sevaldson, B. (2007). Waterfront development with web mediation. *Proceedings of design inquiries. 2nd Nordic design research conference.* Konstfack, Stockholm, 27–30 May 2007.

Morse, M. (1998). *Virtualities: television, media art and cyberculture.* Bloomington: Indiana University Press.

Norris, S., & Jones, R. (2005). (Eds.). *Discourse in action: introducing mediated discourse analysis.* London: Routledge.

Penny, S. (2004). Representation, enaction, and the ethics of simulation. In N. Wardrip-Fruin & P. Harrigan, P. (Eds.), *First person: new media as story, performance, and game* (pp. 73–84). Cambridge: MIT Press.

Rivett, M. (2000). Approaches to analysing webtext: a consideration of the web site as an emergent cultural form. *Convergence,* 6 (3), 34–60.

Ross, A. (2004). Dot.com urbanism. In N. Chouldry & A. McCarthy (Eds.), *Mediaspace: place, scale and culture in a media age* (pp. 145–162). London: Routledge.

Schmidt, K., & Wagner I. (2002). Coordinative artifacts in architectural practice in M. Blay-Fornarino, A.M. Pinna-Dery, K. Schmidt & P. Zaraté (Eds.), *Cooperative systems design: a challenge of the mobility age. Proceedings of the fifth international conference on the design of cooperative systems (COOP2002),* Saint Raphaël, France (pp. 257–274). Amsterdam: IOS Press.

Schmidt, K., & Wagner, I. (2004). Ordering systems: coordinative practices and artifacts in architectural design and planning. *Computer supported cooperative work,* 13(5–6), 349–408.

Skjulstad, S. (2007). Communication design and motion graphics on the web. *Journal of media practice,* 8(3), 359–378. Doi: 10.1386/jmpr.8.3.359_1

Skjulstad, S. (2010). What are these? Designers' websites as communication design. In A. Morrison (Ed.), *Inside multimodal composition.* Cresskill NJ: Hampton Press.

Skjulstad, S. & Morrison, A. (2005). Movement in the interface. *Computers and composition,* 22(4), 413–433. Doi:10.1016/j.compcom.2005.08.006

Slaatta, T. (2006). Urban screens: towards the convergence of architecture and audiovisual media. *firstmonday.* Special Issue #4: Urban Screens: Discovering the potential of outdoor screens for urban society. Available at: http://www.firstmonday.org/issues/special11_2/slaatta/index.html

Strain, E., & van Hoosier-Carey, G. (2003). Eloquent interfaces: Humanities-based analysis in the age of hypermedia. In M. Hocks & M. Kendrick (Eds.), *Eloquent images* (pp. 257–281). Cambirdge: MIT Press.

Sundar, S. & Kim, J. (2005). Interactivity and persuasion: influencing attitudes with information and involvement. *Journal of interactiver advertising,* 5(2). Available at: http://www.jiad.org/vol5/no2/sundar/index.htm#sundar

Vestergaard, T. & Schrøder, K. (1985). *The language of advertising.* Oxford: Blackwell.

Wartofsky, M. (1979). *Models: representation in scientific understanding.* Dordrecht: D. Reidel.

Wells, L. (2004). *Photography: a critical ntroduction. 3rd edition.* London: Routledge.

Wertsch, J. (1991). *Voices of the mind. a sociocultural approach to mediated action.* Cambridge: Harvard University Press.

Williamson, J. (1994). *Decoding advertisements: Ideology and meaning in advertising.* London: Marion Boyars.

8

Whisperings in the Undergrowth: Communication Design, Online Social Networking and Discursive Performativity

Andrew Morrison, Even Westvang, and Simen Svale Skogsrud

Introducing Contexts for Communication Design

The Phenomenon Social Software

...Stumbleupon Sixdegrees, Orkut, Friendster ... Metafilter, Synchronicity, Livejournal, ... TagWorld, Cyworld, flickr ... LinkedIn, Bebo, FaceBook, Hatebook ... Reddit, MySpace, YouTube ... UpComing, Jaiku, *Underskog* ... Zoomer, MeetMoi, Twitter ... iLike, OKCupid, delicious...

This string of names indicates some of the many social networking sites and applications now available. Since the dotcom demise one of the emerging features in digital design has been the collaborative shaping of such social networks online. The scores of applications facilitate encounters, linkages, memberships and exchanges in shared online sites and services. These related but varied sites and services typically fall under the banner of social networking, also labelled social software, and social computing. In contrast to the burgeoning spread of social networking tools and sites, and the immense volume of their hourly messagings across media types, few studies give voice to their genesis as designs for collaborative articulation. Fewer make the connection between designers' and participants' discourses. Fewer still situate their understanding of digital designing in relation to multimodal discourse theory and frames of socio-cultural activity theory in which mediated action and activity are central. In terms of Communication Design, digital design research rarely strays into the discursive design of affordances for distributed communication: most studies concern digitally mediated discourse as discoursed, either as product or process.

However, these discourses come into being by way of their realizing discourse potential that is inscribed within applications or artefacts designed to facilitate communication. Links between applied discourse theory and socio-cultural perspectives on digital design offer some means for unpacking the design for discursive performativity on the part of participants to collaborative online communication sites and services. In this context, performativity is seen as a reflexive, and recursive activity that oscillates between the designers of an emergent, multi-genre online discourse

I. Wagner et al. (eds.), *Exploring Digital Design: Multi-Disciplinary Design Practices*, Computer Supported Cooperative Work, DOI 10.1007/978-1-84996-223-0_8, © Springer-Verlag London Limited 2010 domain and the discursive enactments and requests for the design of additional communicative needs on the part of participants. This 'dialogical' activity may be understood through concepts from Activity Theory, especially relations between the object (goal) of the activity and acts of mediated meaning making.

Our interest in discursive performativity is to do with repositioning this concept in relation to the those of the utterance, meta-discourse moves and semiosis. This shifts a positioning of self as voiced firmly within alterity and resistance to dominant codes and conventions, towards situated articulations within critical, contexts of collaborative communication (e.g. Ellis & Bochner; 1999, Markham 1998, Hine 2000 on virtual ethnography). In designing the affordances for such communication, difference may be heard within community. The design challenge is how to create sites and spaces for multiple mediation and expression that not only enable but motivate for performativity on the part of participants.

In order to account for this, we take up the notion of expansive design. We show how an unfolding design process is connected to its own discursive enactment: various features of social networking and software tools and systems were woven together in the system that was developed so as to enable communication to occur. In this sense it incorporated features of blogs, wikis, photo-sharing, book-marking and calendaring services to allow for participation in one linked environment, an environment that not only made it possible to build a network of discourse but which was adapted and improved through its users' understanding and needs. We refer to this as the shaping of an innovative communication community in which designers' and participants' performative discourses are intertwined in processes of communication design and designing for communication.

On *Underskog*

We present and analyse the dynamics of the design of a web-based social calendaring service, *Underskog* (meaning undergrowth in Norwegian). *Underskog* was designed for use in one capital city in Scandinavia. In 2005 *Underskog* was conceived of as a small, invitation-only service. In 2008 it hosts around 13,000 users in a variety of online configurations and discourse communities. *Underskog* was devised in 2005 and attempted to converge a number of functions and features already present in emerging forms of online social networking software. In this sense, it had as its object the coordination of a range of tools and mediations in pursuit of a shared activity. At the same time, it was an experiment in which the design of a shared online service would emerge through the activities or discoursing afforded by its mediation. *Underskog* drew together a range of tools and approaches we encountered in other social network sites and services. It is this syncreticism that is one core feature of *Underskog*. A second feature is that it was designed incrementally and informed via users' views.

On the part of the designers and researcher, Communication Design was primarily to do with designing for participation. *Underskog* was aimed at enabling

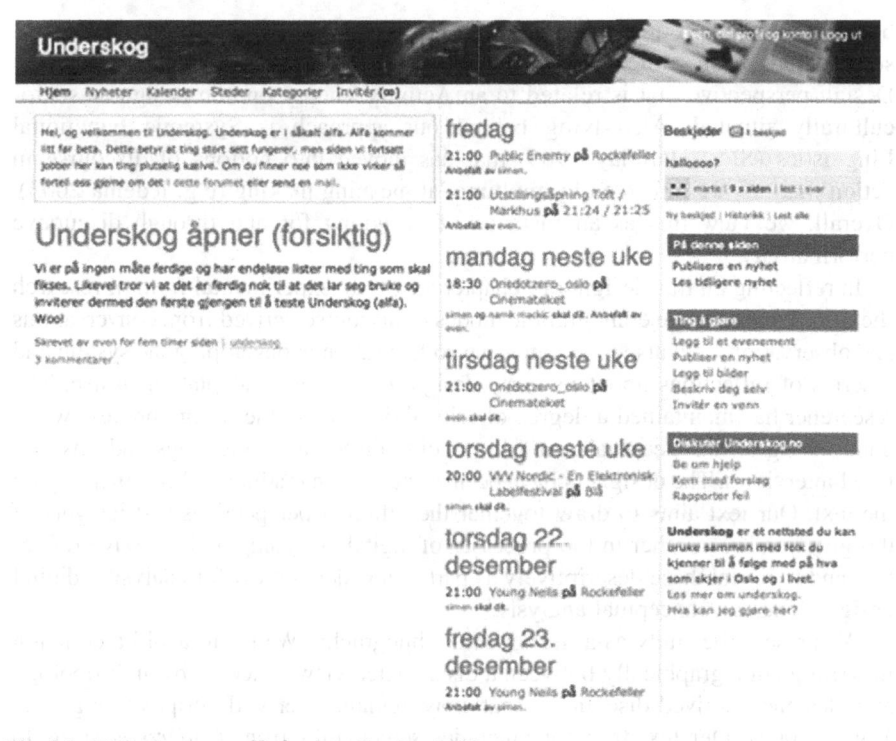

Fig. 8.1 Early front page *Underskog*, October 2005

social interaction in the physical capital city itself, as well as providing an online discussion space. The system was co-designed by a team of three colleagues in the small Oslo-based digital media company Bengler. The design drew on more than a decade of shared work that ranged across media types, software and systems. *Underskog* was built without formal financing and between other ongoing and new projects. It is an example of a highly motivated experiment that aims to meet a potential shared communicative need and ongoing engagement. In early use, the design of *Underskog* was influenced by the expression of needs and wants of users. As the network grew, features were improved and others were added (Fig. 8.1). At the same time, an iterative design process was enriched through participants' emerging contributions to the service and by their suggestions about its transformation.

On Our Research Approach

In drawing out aspects of the design dynamics that have been part of the multimediational digital design of *Underskog*, our focus in this chapter is on the collaborative or co-design (Sanders and Stappers 2008) in the intersections of discourses between a design group, a researcher, and users of *Underskog*. Overall, these intersections have been framed within what we argue may be labelled a Communication Design perspective that is related to an Activity Theory one on design as socioculturally situated. Also lying behind our approach is Systemic Functional Linguistics (SFL; Halliday 1985) that has moved into notions of discourse in action that too are informed by multimodal meaning making (e.g. Iedema 2003). Overall, we view this as an instance of designing for and through discursive performativity.

In reflecting on this design, our chapter adopts an experimental form of research rhetoric. We interleave ethnographic modes of discourse derived from conversations and observations, but also from intensive collaboration in developing the system and a series of reflections about its early design and ongoing adaptation in use. The researcher has maintained a degree of critical distance in the design process while contributing to it conceptually and in ongoing discussions, meetings and unstructured interviews. The designers have been co-authors in reading and commenting on the text. Our text aims to draw together the different perspectives and insights of designers and researcher in the processes of digital designing and reflexive reflection and to reveal these descriptively as part of a wider context for analysing digital design alongside conceptual analysis.[1]

We present the study as a multimodal ethnography. We try to avoid a collision in writing ethnographically between a distanciated view inflected by anthropology and designer derived-discourses that may remain overly descriptive (e.g. van Veggel 2005). Our text therefore includes screengrabs from *Underskog* so as to illustrate an ongoing process, albeit one which initially aimed to provide a service to a circle of friends. The chapter slips between discourses around social and participative media that are en vogue while offering some material about how a shared communicative space might be realized from conception through to performative use. We toggle between modes of writing as suggested at the start of the chapter. 'Montage' is part of our rhetoric in communicating about an unfolding process and its relations and connections to theory both on the way and in retrospect. Theoretical-analytical and contextual-narrative material is demarcated by different sections. All-in-all, we hope to show that inquiry into digital design may also include aspects of designers' own creative and experimental digital discourses inthe-making, together with the pressures and wishes of users and participants in social software environments.

---

[1]Rhetorically, the account is presented through the interplay of collaborative ethnographic material developed through dialogues between the designers and a researcher, and visual material drawn from the social software environment itself and logs of *Underskog* in use. The text has images, charts and tables, quotes, narrative and expository text. We shift between these modes of providing a reflexive account of a multi-level, iterative design process. However, in this text we limit ourselves to the interplay between designers and the researcher, and to selections from *Underskog* that illustrate our argument. This study may then be expanded in a later one that makes fuller reference to a user-based analysis.

Getting to Grips with Social Networking and Software

> Networks are the extension of our social world; they also act as its boundary. We may use the network to extend the range of people we can contact; we may use it to limit the people who can contact us. Most of the networking sites so far are designed to grow networks, not limit them. Yet costs and limits can add value. The expenditure of energy to maintain a connection is a signal of its importance and of the benefits it bestows. (Boyd 2004: 81)

Affordances for Collaborative Enactment

'Social software' is one of the terms that has come to the fore in the growth of what has loosely been called Web 2.0; not merely hypertext (Millard and Ross 2006), but the emergence of a more participatory, collaboratively produced online discourse involving applications that allow for user-generated content and communication. Spanning blog and wiki tools, global video-rich sites such as *YouTube* and spaces for the sharing of processes and multimodal and multimediational content, 'social software' points to both the underlying applications, but also the enactment of collaborative discourses online.

> Social networking sites are on-line environments in which people create a self-descriptive profile and then make links to other people they know on the site, creating a network of personal connections. Participants in social networking sites are usually identified by their real names and often include photographs; their network of connections is displayed as an integral piece of their self-presentation. (Donath and Boyd 2004: 72)

The related term 'Collaborative commons' highlights the public sphere aspects of these discourses and principles that lie behind them of open systems, non-hierarchical information and participation structures that champion collaborative authorship and knowledge building in the public domain.[2] Attention has been given at the same time to the spread of social movements and their self-organizing qualities (e.g. Melucci 1996; Chesters and Welsh 2005).

In keeping with such an ethos, in Wikipedia, social software is currently presented according to a medley of related matters of connecting tools, services and the shared meaning making activities that linked users enact.[3] Social networking services now also become entwined as part of virtual communities of one kind or

---

[2] In many ways the communicative groundwork for social software and social networking was laid by way of the emerging discourses of earlier online networks, such as the WELL (Rheingold 2000). In the 1990s, user groups, net forums and online chat each saw the emergence of online discursive exchanges that were enabled through the design of software that afforded both synchronous and asynchronous communication across time and space. These forms of computer-mediated communication have been widely studied, less in terms of their underlying communication design and more in terms of their situated uses, for example, information exchanges, threaded conversations, gendered power plays and virtual identities (e.g. Turkle 1995)

[3] http://en.wikipedia.org/wiki/Social_software

another, as well as being related to cross media communication (from TV and wikis to SMS and blogs) and wider collectives and activities in online gaming. Social calendaring services allow for linked users to trawl and select from listed events and share their intentions and reflections.

Social networking as design and collaborative enactment may also be positioned in relation to an emerging literature on the creative industries (Hartley 2005) and 'convergence culture' in which tensions, ambivalences and interplays occur between corporate media interests and 'prosumers' who increasingly mediate their own meaning making participatively, not only acting as consumers of mediated media (e.g. Deuze 2006; Jenkins 2006). Studies are beginning to examine how advertizers incorporate consumers' participative discourses into their corporate persuasion. Here textual analyses have an important role to play in unpacking how such persuasion is crafted (Morrison and Skjulstad 2007, 2010).

However, little research has moved into the dialogical aspects of the digital design of social software and networking environments for communicative collaboration as part of the cultural and communicative design and expression (on 'taste' see Liu et al. 2006).[4] Beer (2008) argues that approaches to framing and defining social network sites, such as the recent potentially benchmark article by Boyd and Ellison (2007), miss the important commercial and consumer-oriented aspects of widely-available applications and by-pass their functions in a capitalist digital communication ecology. In this chapter, our research into digital design and social network/ing sites and services specifically looks into a context where non-commercial interests drive the unfolding of a digital design process, artefact and articulation by participants.

Production-Based Inquiry

In the autumn of 2003, Even begins to study at the local university. Keen to formalize his knowledge and at the same time develop a sharper critical vocabulary to analyse it, he finds that an old acquaintance, Andrew, is still beavering away at production-based digital design research, now within and across several projects at the interdisciplinary research centre InterMedia. It's almost a decade since Even and Andrew met at the Department of Media and Communication where Even now studies. They recall their lively making of connections between two CD-ROM research and development projects led by Gunnar Liestøl (see this volume) connected to mediating Norwegian cultural history; the first on the voyages of Thor Heyerdahl and the second on the Vikings. Even soon inspires him with accounts of the diverse work he has done with Simen at Bengler.

Even and Andrew soon fall into frequent discussions about contemporary digital media and design that includes a project on multimodal discourse that Andrew leads (Morrison 2010). In time, Andrew invites Even into this project. Simultaneously they debate ways of understanding, building and analysing the rapid emergence of

---

[4] see e.g. http://www.thefacebookproject.com/

online software and networking applications and functionalities, such as *Livejournal*, *flickr*, and *del.cio.us*. It is these applications that Even and Simen also investigate and that Andrew draws into a commissioned journal article on multimodal discourse and multiliteracies (Morrison 2005). It's not long too before Andrew and Simen, who've met briefly, also reconnect and find that they have a shared interest in narrative (Morrison 2003).

After months of solitary authorial devotion, in the autumn of 2004 the first novel by Simen is published in Oslo, Norway (Skogsrud 2004). To work as the single-minded author of a fictional work, Simen took time out from his usual collaborative new media design practice with colleagues at the Oslo-based digital design collective Bengler. Collaboration's been central to Bengler's design work, especially between Simen and Even who've worked together on numerous projects over a decade.

Relations Between Artefacts and Objects

The tools now available for online social networking move earlier linking activities between individuals and groups from otherwise dispersed home pages on the web to databases of linked categories that appear in personal profiles, friends of friends, identification of shared interests and the online processing of common memberships and events. These tools have grown exponentially in the past 5 years, from early adaptors in special interest communities to millions of college student users and broadband subscribers in homes and workplaces (Boyd 2004).

Added to this has been the growth of mobile technologies. These have helped shift networking as an activity off desktop computers and into a kinetics of pervasive and ubiquitous computing that links linking with physical location as well as shearing it from identity and action locked only to place. Not only has this been possible in the uber-networked cities and special interest communities, for example San Francisco and New York, it has spread to diverse groups, settings and societies, including Asia in particular, and to handheld devices such as mobile phones and PDAs.

What is common to these social networking applications and environments is that they are realized through the performance of participants in a lattice of tools, artefact and mediations. There is, then, an ongoing unfolding discourse, or a process of co-creation or poiesis.

Designing Design

9 December 2004. The social software seminar.[5] This is an important event for us – a platform for discussing an emerging digital design phenomenon. A range of local and international speakers all arrive and we have a lively day of presentations and

---

[5] http://imweb.uio.no/projects/designingdesign/social_software.html

discussions: news and views from New York city; from inside collaborative gaming; a sociologist looking to theories of networking; a mashup of sorts between emerging practices and prior conceptualizations. Even gives a talk too and, as the coordinator of the event, he finds plenty to connect to. We discuss themes such as relations between online and face-to-face networks. Tagging, the emergence and activities of photo-sharing services such as flickr are presented alongside work from doctoral research into young Norwegians' use of mobile phones. We looked at the ACM library for these papers, we've tried to gather together knowledge from a participant at the BBC and from a diverse audience that includes not only university staff and students and related research projects at InterMedia and the University, but also colleagues and students from interaction design at the Oslo School of Architecture and Design. And we manage to get all the video up the same day, reinforcing the shared meaning making we put into play in our first Designing Design seminar into research rhetoric.

Plenty of seminar discourse, but how to situate it in applied discourse theory, how to design for distributed communication? A social networking site that would have the design for performative enactment as part of media ecology, a process of iterative design in and through multimodal discourse. More coffee, more connecting the emerging digital designs as communication to existing theories on collaboration and multimodal discourse. Later Even comments that without this seminar it'd have been much harder to conceptualize *Underskog*. 'You were right, and right at the start, to talk about collaborative discourse,' he tells Andrew (who's pleased to hear this but has to ask what he means when much of the talk in process has necessarily been about building functions; and a likeable venue in which to communicate).

Cross-mediations

The software applications involved in the spread of social networking include blog tools, wikis, and social calendaring and linking services, as suggested in the only partial list given at the chapter's start. Blogs and wikis have emerged as important components in the expansion of the web and its collaborative articulation. Blogs have reinvigorated individual written authorship on the web, a range of linking devices allowing for cross-post connections and feedback loops (e.g. Morrison 2005). Less common are multiply-composed blogs that have a shared communicative object, a feature that is also prevalent in wikis which, as tools, make for flatter structures and spaces for collaborative and transmutational and participatively emergent discourse. Identifying shared interests and their discursive threads in a variety of media types contributes to the purposive mediation via such tools.

Shaping the Shaping

It's a week or so after the seminar and Even and Andrew meet at the university again. It's not necessary to talk details about the seminar – that happened the night out with the participants. Now we're down to a meta discussion about multimodal discourse, back to the notions of discourse performance and competence, to speech act theory, to the notion of discursive performativity, post Judith Butler. Again and again we return to utterance and Bakhtin (1981, 1986). We centre on a cross media design, on the importance of providing for communication, of linking aspects present in other systems, but connected to the thinking of Pragmatics, of discourse in action, of the system being realized in and through its emergent communication, or the need to build iteratively.

We discuss the discourse theories in applied and critical linguistics, socio-cultural theories of learning and communication, there's a fluid and helpful meta frame in the room, but we find it hard to locate in the research literature. Even though CMC and its accompanying research field had a good 20 years of history the reaches of the writable web and the constant mutations of its means of distribution and mediation seemed difficult to address within existing theory.

Social Networking Expands

Interconnected blogs as a form of hypertext allow us to see how communities are composed (Chin and Chignell 2006). Social network analysis, used by these authors, is also applied elsewhere in marking measures of community construction online. The study of dynamic, complex and emergent systems has also been taken up as part of the study of relationships between individuals and groups (e.g. Sawyer 2005). The social activity of blogging has also been studied (Nardi et al. 2004a, b; Morrison and Thorsnes 2010). This has also extended to the creative constructions of the 'blogosphere' in the form of blogs and wikis (Tacchi 2004; Quiggin 2006).

In all of these applications and the user-based performative discourses that ensue and are circulated, collaboration and community building are central. At the time of writing, *Facebook* is the most widely-known social networking application. It specifically allows personal profiles to be shared and cross-cut with others, connecting the old and given relations with the emergent and the new. Originating as a tool or platform for connecting ivy-league college students in the US and now widely used *Facebook* is now a global communication phenomenon. It has been widely adopted in Norway. A glossy magazine detailing how it functions is now on sale in major British airport bookstores (Dennis Publishing 2007).

Affordances for Communities of Interest

Other such services have been closely studied in the ways they have been used to generate communities of interest, such as the ethnographic accounts of *Friendster* published by Boyd (2004, 2008). These communities have not remained static; as participants have come to understand the mechanics and mediative potential of the sites (e.g. Boyd 2006), so too have the machinations of diverse interests and indeed irony surfaced. Boyd (2008) refers to how 'Fraudsters' surfaced in *Friendster* as a ludic and expressive element of the building of online personas and mediated identity.

In *Underskog*, the intention was to provide affordances for social networking online via new design and discursive configurations that would move from designers' intentions to a collaborative community space that would include a diversity of interests and events. The service and site was aimed to offer an alternative to corporate and commercial concerns in connecting collaboration and consumption. It would make for the threading of shared cultural, professional and personal interests situated in one urban zone. In digital design terms, *Underskog* was devised through a process that engaged participants in its use as contributors to an iterative design activity that factored their interests and needs into the communicative functionalities of the system through use.

A Sociocultural Approach to Communication Design

Digital Design Matters

Broadly, we approach communication design in a sociocultural perspective that has mediated meaning making (Wertsch 1991) as its primary concern. Theoretically, the chapter draws on perspectives from applied discourse studies in linguistics. The title of the chapter refers to discursive performativity in terms of emergent and rhizomatic properties and processes at the level of utterance and social language after Bakhtin (1981, 1986). However, we argue that approaches to performance and performativity in design research may be extended to encompass the enactment of participants in building designs for communication and in realizing communication through design (e.g. Kazmierczak 2003). This is grounded in notions of participatory design in and through dialogue (e.g. Luck 2003) and disclosure (e.g. Newton 2004), where the dialogical is framed as means and mediation (Wells 2007). For Shotter (2003) discourse may be understood as chiasmatic, that is realised in its dynamic and interpersonal unfoldings. In terms of discursive investigations, Shotter and Billig (1998) argue for an approach that seeks to realize relational-responsive understanding in favour of that which is representational-referential. These approaches may be applied to mediated discourse and especially to the co-design of social network environments where activity between designers and participants contributes to discourse that is simultaneously embodied and embedded in the materialities of the physical here-and-now and the digitally enacted.

Unlike much design research, adopting such views on mediated discourse and meaning making places weight on multimodal discourse and its roles in Communication Design (Morrison 2010). Conceptual frameworks from Activity

Theory are included, with emphasis on design. The chapter further references recent literature on 'social software' that is both ethnographic in character and also located in the field of Human Computer Interaction (HCI). Concerning digital design, this multi-level analysis is concerned with both the interplay of designers' and analysts' discourses and an approach to digital design research that engages with the unfolding and emergent.

Core Concepts

In short, in terms of Activity Theory, *Underskog* is an instantiation of relations between software tools and semiotic objects. It is through these relations that mediated meaning making at the level of digital design for discursive performativity occurs. This is achievable through emergent joint action between designers and users, and ultimately between users themselves. An approach to discourse as action (Norris and Jones 2005) is realized by multimodal discoursing that transverses previous tool-genre sets such as blogs and bookmarking. In this sense as Wells (2007) argues, action is not only object oriented; it is also structured and structures emerging discourse genres, or multimodal genres.

'Designing a Great Party'[6]

Having marshalled character and events into print, Simen holds a memorable book launch party. In his droll style, says Even, Simen comments that it's the type of small, but interesting event he'd typically have missed himself. Simen recognizes that there is a need to connect to current events in the city and that this might offer a 'site' for sharing information. Mcdia may have cinema listings and cultural events of a certain scale, but many of the most interesting events are difficult to find and the dissemination of information about them is mostly word of mouth or through badly coordinated mailing lists. He registers the domain *underskog*.no, thinking it may perhaps be a group blog on topical affairs in Oslo.

On Expansive Design

We converge the various theoretical perspectives in relation to Communication Design by way of reference to social semiotics that situates technical system and mediational design and the ensuing articulations by users in relation to developmental

---

[6] With Synchronicity Caterina Fake also uses the same metaphor which she says is something they discovered when making social MMO, the precursor to flickr: http://www.christine.net/2006/08/caterina_fake_a.html

and transformational processes of mediated meaning making. This is framed within an Activity Theory (AT) perspective that places activity at the centre. In the case of *Underskog*, this activity may be conceptualized in an approach Engeström (2006) labels expansive design. Referring specifically to interaction design, a domain of digital design we see as related to the wider Communication Design, Engeström (2006: 3) argues that it needs to be located in the activity system of the products and services produced and used. Importantly these refer to not only products but also relations and seeds of future activity. An expansive design approach to interaction and communication also produces integrated instrumentalities. For Engeström (2006: 3), 'Expansive interaction design is best performed jointly by producer-practitioners and their key customers, supported by interventionists.' Building on his earlier work on developmental learning, he further argues that this approach needs to be linked with implementation and learning, especially where these are also longitudinal, and where we encounter resistance and turning points, negotiation and appropriation by users (Engeström 2006: 18ff).

Expansive design draws explicitly on his model of expansive learning (Engeström 1987, 2001) that includes in its overall transformational approach the activity system as the unit of analysis, multi-voicedness, historicity, contradictions, and expansive transformations. Engeström (2001) envisages stages in cycles of transformation: (1) questioning existing practices; (2) analysing existing practices; (3) collaboratively building new models, concepts and artefacts for new practices; (4) examining and debating the created models, concepts and material and immaterial artefacts; (5) implementing these; (6) reflecting on and evaluating the process; and (7) consolidating the new practices.

In terms of expansive design, similar stages may be said to occur in the design of *Underskog*, though through iterative moves and in working with the malleability of digital materials these stages may be conceived of as a flexible helix rather than a sequence of cycles. We do not go into the underlying Activity Theory in detail in this chapter. We conceptualize communication design in an AT frame and the ways it may be realized online and how web-based communication influences the design of the service (e.g. Barab et al. 2004a, Barab et al. 2004b).

However, we see this approach as enabling recognition of the preceding systems, tools, knowledge and practices, that is historically, and in terms of a their more recent activation, in processes of iterative and performative design; that is one in which participants to an unfolding design for communication, are involved in a process of refinement through discursive use. This is, in a sense, the two-way building of a community of practice and practices of community (Wenger et al. 2002). Much of the literature on emergence in developmental studies of learning and work refers to the building of innovative knowledge communities. In a parallel move that frames this in a model of expansive learning to expansive design, we argue that what is also needed is a further move from a focus on knowledge to one of innovative communication communities.

On Performativity and Digital Design

Overall, we adopt the notion of discursive performativity: our digital design inquiry is about designing for communication through the realization of which communication on the design then contributes to moderations and modifications of it. Recently, performativity has begun to feature in digital design research publications. In these publications there is also an overlap in reference to performance, the performative and performativity, not always with reference to their disciplinary genesis nor to the trans-disciplinary relations between these discipline-based origins and practices.

How we engage with digital tools and technologies – and indeed with one another online or on the move – is often cast in terms of performance that hails from theatre studies and the performing arts. There is a focus on performance in literary and cultural studies that extends beyond the stage and metaphors of theatre to encompass a mode of enactment. In design terms, this enactment is about designing for and through performativity by participants. Performativity refers to shared production of the framing and enactment of multimodal collaborative discourse online. It draws on the notion of discursive performativity developed by Butler (1993) with reference to gender and positionality in deconstructing '… how the connections between certain acts and certain forms of speech, habitually enacted together, come to constitute a compulsory performance (an embodiment) of heterosexuality' (Threadgold 2003: online) (see Chapter 3). However, our notion of a multimodal collaborative and expansive design of discursive performativity is to do with the mediated emergence of a discursive or mediating artefact and an artefact of mediation over time. It is to do with relations between 'writing' technology, enabling and responding to 'utterances' and an ecological understanding of mediated meaning making and processes of mediatization in constituting performative discourse.

In this sense, our view is aligned with the argument by Threadgold (1997) that we need to attend to poesis, or discourse in the making. While we acknowledge Butler's important contribution to unmasking position, hegemeony and alterity in discourse, we focus on the building of a collaborative digital discourse environment and its performative moves in and through design by designers with participants. This situates discourse production and critique of its production in relation to developments in Critical Discourse Analysis (CDA) (e.g. Wodak 2001). It extends that frame into the domain of discursive performativity, that is, the activity of making anew. This is to engage in an ecological and mediatized enactment of design and utterance in shared meaning making. Boucher (2006) argues that Butler does not give adequate attention to the level of utterance. It is important that this emergent, ecological activity includes design, not separates it from the generation and performativity of socially situated online collaborative discourse.

The performative digital discourse design of *Underskog* was chiefly a matter of developing three intersecting design tracks that relate also to cycles of transformation in expansive learning: (1) the development of a conceptual framework for the Communication Design of the system; (2) system design and programming; and (3) allowing for ongoing adaptations, adjustments, redesign and refinement in and through use.

We take up these intersecting design tracks in shifts between two modes of written text: the first formal and analytical; the second more journalistically phrased and situated in contexts of use, including an array of screengrabs from *Underskog*. Our motivation is to draw together our shared and diverse knowledge from practice and theory and to realize it via a reflexive account of the various and iterative relations and intersecting common and distinct activities in digital design research where ecological and emergent knowledge is being articulated. Following the work of the media sociologist Roger Silverstone (1994), this is a question of double articulation between the technical and the symbolic (Livingstone 2007).

Changes While Building

'We matured our understanding of the site through the process of building it,' says Even. 'We were surprised we could design in such a way.' We had intentions and plans but needed to let things unfold, to let the nature of *Underskog* arise from the process itself. It was possible to change visual design, adjust functionality, the phrasing, to adapt, to translate. In the late 1990s we were engaged as consultants to build a variety of applications, for example games for mobile phones. In the design process a system was first envisioned and then realized as a specification. The specification was exhaustive and could then be implemented by parties without prior knowledge of the project. Given the rigidity of the process, one's ability to judge the future needs of the user was critical, but also extremely error prone.

Underskog, on the other hand, was built 'in vivo', in active collaboration with the participants. A minimal set of useful functions resting on the top a powerful web framework (Ruby on Rails) was established in weeks and then people were invited onto the building site to give feedback. This is not only a good thing in terms of ensuring that one builds what is actually needed, but also makes feedback real in the sense that suggestions are likely to be taken up and deployed on the site; often within hours.

Further into the 'Forest'

On *Underskog*

Underskog is a web venue for people interested in how the 'undergrowth' of Norwegian cultural life can help one another find what's valuable in the city and in life.

The main aim of *Underskog* was to develop a site, or a mediatized space, where existing social bonds in the physical world could be further connected, shared, investigated, and traversed online (see Fig. 8.2). In short, the aim was to design affordances for discursive performativity, that is to provide a site with multiple intersecting communicative affordances that would allow users to actively and collaboratively engage in building a form online, and unfolding, yet linked public discourse.

With shared and process-driven online communication at its core, *Underskog* was designed to enable participants to enact their social relations and networked calendaring around city-wide events. This was intended as a means for mediating the sharing of common interests, for building social cohesion, and enabling the expression of identity and membership. In time, this would extend to the specification of broad and specific interests and their various performances by participants, and revisions and extensions to the underlying social network. The digital medium in this sense became its own discursive message.

Sketching on Rails

October 2005. Work starts on *Underskog*. Simen and Alex at Even's flat in Tøyen, Oslo, drawing data models on sketch-pad paper. It's been three late nights and some evenings. Evolving design as the object becomes clearer. Still not much of a tight plan. The basic building blocks of *Underskog* are articles, events, venues and comments. Having used services like flickr, which use social networks to flow information according to social proximity, it seemed that implementing similar features might be useful. It gradually dawns on us that events can have participation and that we can use the social graph to build calendars that could show you what your friends are up to. Seeing who is going to an event can be more engaging and receiving a daily mail from the system listing what your friends are doing today can both save you many phone conversations and lead you to new experiences. We also build a system for personal messages that updates in real-time, striking a balance between instant messaging and asynchonous messaging like mail.

Where many similar services have a global front page of editorialized content or the user's own profile page as their starting point, *Underskog* starts people off on the front page after logging in. The front page shows bulletins in reverse chronological order, like a blog, and upcoming events and their participation. Alex comes up with a row of icons, wee stylized men, to represent participation to events. The participation of your friends is shown in green.

The software development of *Underskog* adheres closely to the patterns of the framework we were learning – the web development framework 'Ruby on Rails' – and it certainly does help us along. Two of us had never built a database-backed web site before. Designing while designing, says Andrew referring to discussions with Doug Engelbart here in Olso in the early 1990s and in the Bay Area, California.

9 November 2005 *Underskog* is deployed to a spare server and switched on. We decided to release *Underskog* as a closed beta with the premise of making it public as it reached production grade. Day 0 is counted from the time of our first message: 'Får

Fig. 8.2 *Underskog* today – even Westvang's front page (new comments in my conversation threads, my friends are discussing, bulletins from forums I subscribe to, what people are doing in Oslo the next 3 days, my messages, my circle online now)

vi se noen events snart, ell?' (Should we have some events soon, or?). First steps: from user 1, Simen to user 2, Even! In the excitement of actually having got this far we see ourselves looking at each other, wondering if the system will ever be used by anyone!

Voice and Language

Building for a specific audience of friends and acquaintances also means we can voice *Underskog* in vernacular Oslo dialect. In this specificity lies many cultural markers which may attract and repel. Having worked for years as professional communicators, it felt liberating to be crafting a piece of software for ourselves and our friends without the usual constraints in making something for certain age groups of target audiences.

Looking back on this is interesting in terms of the origin of current popular online social networking spaces. Many of them, such as *Myspace* and *Facebook*, have come from similarly situated origins in being crafted by small teams of individuals attempting to satisfy needs they themselves had. Many services rely on an ethos of inclusivity and sharing as a premise for generating the content consumed there and it would seem that such an ethos may be difficult to establish for someone with a clearly visible marketing plan. It is also surprising how resilient the original premises of such sites are when these sites are bought and sold. It would seem that the many minute design considerations made as a site matures imparts a specific unerodable texture to the user experience.

Connecting the Dots

Back to the coding. We attempt to anticipate, designing affordances with useful constraints, tools with an understandable specificity that have leeway for expression. What matters is that this is designing through. It's about designing with participation in and through use, with inputs of people, their expressions of needs, and wants. Early on we thought we'd separate the calendar and the discussion, now

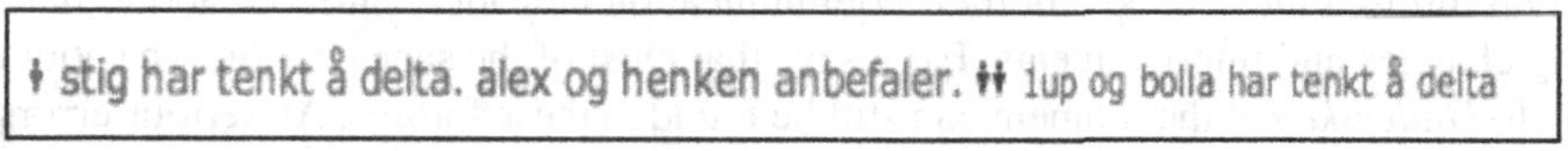

> ✝ stig har tenkt å delta. alex og henken anbefaler. ✝✝ 1up og bolla har tenkt å delta

Fig. 8.3 Event participation your friend Stig will attend, Alex and Henken are recommending, and two other people you don't know will attend

they're integral to one another (Fig. 8.3). Usage patterns emerge; with some people engaging in discussion, while others use it to signal their plans.

'What was successful was what came out of the fabric of making it' (Even Westvang).

A year later Even would comment: 'We had no faith in corporate media, we wanted to build something that was a social entity, that linked digital design with people's lifeworlds, yet made something new, that would unfold in the process of its making.'

Being Through 'Language'

Even is reflecting on the overall discursive connection between features and language. Some of the following features were innovations at the time of implementation and have very much to do with designing *Underskog* as a place for being through language: 'social conversations' [as secluded space], 'kudos' [as intimate acts of appreciation and support], 'forums/moderation' [multiplicity of voice, enlargement of space], 'kudos, event participation and friend connection' [as non-verbal acts], 'starring' [following of conversations – which means that conversations never die in *Underskog* – The thread 'What are you listening to right now?' has 11,141 comments and 'what are you doing right now has' 11,050. It also means that communities of interest may form around a thread and meet there sporadically to discuss as they will all be alerted to new activity once someone says something there].

Requests Rolling in

Autumn 2005. Moving from concepts to communication. It's a time of responding to people's needs, letting them voice their concerns to enact what a growing group of people request to meet their needs, to see these growing in and through use.

In August 2007 Andrew asks Even again about this period when people helped each other to learn the system. It's interesting how much people will put up with if the motivation is there. User experience is much more than just usability. In the first few months of *Underskog* we integrated with *flickr* for all aspects of image uploading. This also included profile pictures, something which meant that setting your picture entailed the arduous process of opening a *flickr* account and then tying it to *Underskog*. We watched in amazement as novice internet users helped each other jump through these hoops. In their communication new ideas surfaced about making changes and improvements. Even says that most of the sane changes we should do to *Underskog* at the moment can still be found in these forums. All serious errors have long since been reported there and so have suggestions for improvement. He continues, 'In communicating the design of *Underskog* we've never been able to say, "We'll talk to those on the implementation end, those who do the actual programming". This gives people a different relationship to designers. This is where technical design and making meets communication design: there are no other "technicians" to whom we can defer responsibility.' But back to Autumn 2005.

Almost all the early talk on *Underskog* has to do with the service itself. It ranges from bug reports in the registration form, to availability (invitations and cities listed), feature requests (RSS and ICAL feeds needed) to reactions to design choices. For example, we initially only explicitly listed the participation of your friends while anonymizing the names of others. This was done in respect of people's privacy, but turned out to be mostly a source of irritation. Someone pointed this out to us and we could correct it quickly. We're seeing how the mix of suggestions, co-operatively given with this shared object in emergence. It's the knowing engagement in the transformational activities, in their discursive performativity, that also gathers a momentum of its own. The consolidation of any shared space should start with a discussion of its outer parameters and workings.

Yet it was also unclear what public discourse would be interesting for those present in *Underskog* and it therefore felt risky for anyone to walk onto the empty stage

Fig. 8.4 Early screen grab of calendar

i dag

17:00 Litteraturquiz med special guest Ruth Lillegraven på Dattera til hagen

17:00 bleed must be destroyed. på Grafill Galleri
| ✝✝ stig og even skal dit.

18:50 Oslo filmfestival: Me and You and Everyone We Know på Cinemateket

19:00 Banjoland på Spasibar
| ✝ namik skal dit.

19:00 Forfatteraften: Nils-Øyvind Haagensen og Geir Gulliksen på Bokcaféen - Chateau Neuf

19:00 Mirrormask på 21:24 / 21:25

21:15 Enron - The Smartest Guys in the Room på Cinemateket
| ✝✝ simen og alex skal dit.

of the front page and speak out to everyone. We knew of a few good group weblogs, like *BoingBoing*, and the user driven news site *Metafilter* with its strong codex of short stories sprouting dozens of links, and would like to see similar genres of writing being developed in *Underskog*. But whereas the calendar provided a straightforward use-value (see Fig. 8.4), developing the space for discussion would prove much more difficult.

It's 25 November 2005. Here's an entry from the Oslo School of Architecture and Design (see Fig. 8.5); images and tags already a lively feature of the multimodal composition of *Underskog*.

Flurries and Dips

After the flurry of activities this autumn, the Christmas 2005 break is greatly needed. Simen spends the holiday writing in support of *open conversations*. By the

AHO

Også kjent som Arkitektur- og designhøgskolen i Oslo. Det innhegnede, veldig kule bygningskomplekset mellom Maridalsveiens mest støvete parti og Kuba.

■ **By:** Oslo

■ **Mer informasjon:** http://www.aho.no

■ **Adresse:** Maridalsveien 29, 0175 Oslo.

Lagt inn av stian fredag 25. november 2005 kl 05 | arkitektur, design, forelesning, hage, interaction design, party, studier, utstilling, vitenskap

Relaterte bilder

Fig. 8.5 A flavour of AHO in *Underskog*, description, tags, link, contextual images

first of December, the number of posts the front page counted was 65 while the number of events stood at 290. People still weren't talking much in public. *Open conversations* established a liminal, semi-public, space for discussions which could run along the links of the social network. Open conversations are visible on the front page, but only in a list of conversations your friends are engaged in and could therefore travel along the social network announcing themselves only to friends of those engaged. Open conversations are also a good example of how we change the typology of *Underskog* to suit different kinds of expression and being within the space. Even builds support for filtering the calendar by city after pressure from the Bergen community.

Anonymity, Accountability and Discussion

The ways in which a social website lets you display your identity speaks volumes about the intentions of its designers. We've gone with encouraging the use of real names in addition to a handle. This as *Underskog's* purpose is to connect with the flow of events and discourse in the society in which it is embedded. Anonymity is also often the enemy of useful and tempered discussion. Similarly, knowing that everyone can see who you know and may connect them to real life persons adds gravity to the act of uttering. In keeping with this, we also added a field on the profile page showing who you were invited into the service by.

Further, the *Profile page* also provides a list of every utterance someone has made. This is also valuable for people in appraising others. Online discourse often has an oral patterning in its informality, yet misses many important contextual clues such as gesture and tone of voice, which could help in disambiguation. Quickly checking that the person angrily facing you is a repeat offender in unjustly attacking anyone can be a great help in formulating a reply.

Reflecting on Studies of Social Networking

The name is not the thing named, the idea of the pig is not the pig (Bateson 2000: 177).

In contrast to the now vast media coverage of social software and the close, qualitative accounts of their memberships and expression and signalling of youthful and special group identity (e.g. Donath and Boyd 2004; Hertzberg Kaare et al. 2007), few studies are about the design processes and connections between the designed and the used. For example, research articles cover the use of *flickr* and *Friendster* but much of the coverage of the design process is taken up in more journalistic accounts. In contrast, ethnographic studies are often located in the expression of identity and the trajectory of a community and multiple memberships (e.g. Boyd and Heer 2006). Clearly these are important studies and they shed light on how it is that we have come to graduate from earlier performative discourses in Usergroups, online discussion threads and comments to static webpages. Studies tend to centre on the building of a group and its mediated discourses. In writing on the design of social software, attention is often given to the needs of community over those of individuals.

> Thinking of the platform as social software entails designing it with characteristics that have a certain social-science or psychological model of interactions of a group, and building the platform's affordances in order to enhance the survivability and efficacy of the group, even if it sometimes comes at the expense of the individual user's ease of use or comfort. (Benkler 2006: 373–4)

At an additional level, few studies have tracked the design of social software applications and the relationships between the shaping of affordances for communication and the responses of communities and individuals to these affordances in and through their own discursive performativity. This is what we have focussed on.

This current publication does not trace or tabulate tracts or threads of online discourse inside a social software site. It attends to issues of the digital design of the application, and its transformations through use. The focus then is on the iterative design of an application and service informed by its uses but not a study of the mediated online discourses as discourse analysis. As we have discussed elsewhere (Morrison 2010), such discourses online need to be deconstructed as multimodally mediated, not only in terms of language, foundational as this may be to understanding computer mediated communication.

Fora for Debate

During the winter of 2006 the nature of *Underskog* as one public space becomes increasingly problematic. As the front page starts to function and gain momentum as a space of discussion consensus on its purpose is an increasingly problematic aspect of public performativity, not in agreement but in modes of engagement in one's discourse being co-present. Reference becomes critical. Most services implementing social networks solve the problem of dissonance between people by dissolving public space entirely through filtering by social relevance, giving each user their own viewpoint into the service based on who they know. *flickr's* opening screen is a good example: it starts with your own images, then lists those of your friends. Last comes everyone else's pictures. This component has the prominent function to hide it in the future. This works on the assumption that social proximity codes for relevance. *Underskog*, given its limited, interconnected user- base, has not needed to hide 'everyone else', but there are daily disagreements on what the purpose of *Underskog* is and what topics are deemed appropriate for discussion.

Kudos

The giving and marking kudos or appreciation is now an established feature of some social networking sites. The first kudos in *Underskog* is from March 2006. We're very happy with the implementation. Often kudos is signalled publicly, for example through global lists of 'most appreciated' or points displayed by utterances. This, though, undermines the value of the social action of giving kudos. Often the action of giving kudos to an utterance is anonymized as they also come in negative flavours. *Underskog* tells you who appreciated your comment, but keeps it from others. This makes kudos an intimate act of appreciation between those engaged in discussion and is often a way of giving someone support in heated debates.

Crossing the Applications for Networking

Facebook was designed to facilitate information flow in social networks, but it quenches sites of dissent and publicly-held discussion (unless you specialize in it, discussion is only a problem for a service). So you actually would want to design away sites of public exchange of opinion. It is not about discourse as such, but rather the diffusion of non-publicly actionable signals'

There are two strains of sites which have social networks. Those which foreground the social network while decentring discourse and activity *(friendster, orkut, Facebook)*. And those which employ social networks as a device in order to enable activity in a shared creative space. As *flickr's* contacts are contextual/situated in the sense that they are used only for 'flowing' images to your 'Contacts' page. *Flickr* is about sharing images and that sharing is enabled through contacts (some contacts are friends and that is used for access control). They may also be semiotic markers for who you know, but not in the degree of the systems mentioned earlier.

Indeed this distinction is often mirrored in the implementation detail: the former have reciprocal friendships certified by both parties whereas the latter often use bonds which are one-way. *Underskog*, we believe, tries hard to be in the second category and enables conversation and event dispersal using social affinity as a relevance criterion. *Underskog uses* a social network, but would loathe to *be* one.

In the Papers

It's day 110. Monday 27th February 2006. *Underskog's* in the press for the first time.[7] While this is exciting, it's flagged as an e-mail list for gossiping celebs! There's also a surge in traffic on the site. 'I just looked at the spike in activity and it is on the exact day of the story in *Dagbladet*,' writes Even. Clearly the media function in legitimizing an 'outgroup' by misunderstanding it fundamentally. Gossiping celebs? When the roving eyeball has recognized you, you know that you are seen by those who cannot see in and that contribution/performance may appear on other 'stages' as well.

Performativity and Practice-Led Research Revisited

Writing out of the dynamics of practice-led research, Haseman (2006) encourages a turn to performative inquiry (Lincoln and Denzin 2003). He argues that performativity has a bearing towards fields other than the arts, such as its uses in theatre studies, and that it enables research to be conducted across cultural and creative sectors. Practice-led research allows for the composition of messy texts and their revisions and adaptations in and as practice. Such research may include discipline-specific forms and modes of articulation that are presentationally rich and are articulated in multiple media types. However, as Haseman (2006) goes on to argue, while attending to symbolic forms in art, performative research at the same time needs to pay attention to how strategies related to performativity are phrased methodologically.

We take this further to include multimodal articulation in a wider performative design view. We argue that performativity may also refer to the activities of

---

[7] http://www.dagbladet.no/kultur/2006/02/27/459136.html

collaboratively shaping and sharing socially networked discourses together with their multiple and multimodal articulations. Earlier research into online collaborative discourse typically did not include a focus on design, nor digital design. Neither was its core interest the iterative and recursive design of social software, as the interplay between such software and its polyphonic and transmorphic articulations could not be phrased online. In short it was not possible technically, in the form of an integrated, self-commenting and loggable system, to both simultaneously hear about needs and write their affordances into the 'conversation' in code.

In an Activity Theory frame, it is now possible for the mediating artefact and the artefact of mediation to be linked. This has been extended, in the context of mixed reality arts, to include artefacts of performance and performative artefacts (Morrison et al. 2010).

Co-construction and Performativity

In 'A manifesto for the performative development of ubiquitous media', Jaccuci et al. (2005) draw on approaches from media studies, computing, anthropology and theatre studies in continuing discussion of the role of performance in design research, and its role in setting agendas for interaction in ubiquitous computing environments, including art installations. Their manifesto (Jaccuci et al. 2005: 27) conceives of design interventions that involve people in the creative and exploratory co-construction of imagined works. It argues for understanding of the blends of content and form, not their separation. Finally, it proposes we develop further approaches to the mediating aspects by examining performed actions, generative roles and participative authorship.

Developing Multiple Spaces

It's late Spring 2006. *Underskog* is drowning in noise. Too many people are contained within just one public scope and one semi-private. We sit down to build *Underskog 2.0* which has forums which may be subscribed to or hidden. Concurrently moderation is increasingly becoming a problem. As hosts for this 24/7 party of discussion and argument, we are increasingly being called on to step in and uphold standards. We are uncomfortable with this role as, presumably, benevolent dictators and want to disperse the power to moderate and delete unsuitable utterances to people. Posts in *Underskog 2.0* would therefore have the forum they were posted in listed along with the names of those responsible: an attempt at making them feel personally responsible for the actions of others, much like we feel responsible for everything said in *Underskog*.

Given an agreement with the art criticism website kunstkritikk.no, we also design it so that multiple forums may be edited by one editorial board. Some forums may then be published to sites on external domains. Through this system, kunstkritikk.no may use *Underskog* as an editorial office and concurrently publish to their own site and to members of *Underskog*.

In summer 2006 there is another development around thresholds for uttering and the private- public relationship. Participants are no longer wary of posting presumably irrelevant topics. In fact those posting most often have the least to say. Being present was what was important for participants. There is again, in a sense, too much noise; everyone is now contributing to one space. Finishing version 2.0 of *Underskog* becomes urgent.

Deeper into Modes of Inquiry and Reflection

To compose an account of *Underskog* that will give readers a reliable version of the processes of making connections. Of moving in and between modes of designing and development. To convey some of the key moments of re-design. And, especially, to provide a sense of the influence and inputs of users of *Underskog* in communicating their needs and interests to the designers, and the manner and extent to which these could be effected. To devise an account that has to meet the boundaries of a book chapter and that also, above all, relates design practice to the analysis of a collaborative design process. To be aware, too, that ours is rendition that is selective, yet one influenced not only by our transdisciplinary interests and work. It's also infiltrated by the use of the web as a medium as part of a wider discourse of qualitative inquiry involving digital tools and technologies (Dicks et al. 2006).

Into Ethnography

Andrew's sitting in the summer house. It's autumn 2006. An uninterrupted weekend ahead with a variety of books and articles on ethnographic research. Time to take stock. To look further into how to write ethnographically, to give a reflexive and developmental account of an unfolding digital design-related process. This is something that's arising in several projects that involve digital tools, collaborative contexts of use and their related communication design (e.g. Morrison and Thorsnes in press). Techniques used in other domains of digital discourse such as the multi-voiced writings of on composition and rhetoric – but not present much in design research

Andrew's reading about the medley of versions of the self in the modes of reporting in the domain of autoethnography. He finds a mix of literary and expository styles (Bochner and Ellis 2002). Sitting late into a night of quiet, a stream of different written voices echo from the pages. There's concern in these accounts with selfhood yet also the relations of one's self to others. To a certain extent this matters in the 'scripting' of a multi-voiced account that involves reflexivity (e.g. Hertz 2001; Haskell et al. 2002).

Yet, many of the autoethnographies are centred on overcoming a degree of personal difficulty – they do not address issues of the unfolding complexity in collaborative design processes. There's also room for influence from collaborative ethnography (e.g. Lassiter 2005a, b) and collaborative accounts (e.g. Lather 1991; Richardson 1994). How to link the different mediations, textually, in a research account, to bring forth the interplay of the designers' views and his own, to situate these as well in a wider discourse on social networking and the characterizing of Web 2.0.

Andrew recalls the dialogical qualities of the account by Bruno Latour of a failed public transport system cast in the switching between the inquisitive text of a young engineer and a series of factual reports and texts in *Aramis, or The Love of Technology* (Latour 1996). Andrew remembers an inspirational representation from the field of rhetoric and composition studies that involved a group of teacher-researchers in investigating their own collaborative and distributed electronic literacies, in the 'hivemind' (Byrd and Owens 1998).

Finally, v. 2.

Day 234, 2 July 2006. We release *Underskog 2*. Marius Watz snaps this picture (Fig. 8.6) of the front page in the small hours (before breakfast, after deleting stray kudos).

We release 2.0 and there seems to be a collective sigh of relief. *Underskog* sprouts new forums daily. The posting and reposting of esoteric *YouTube* clips

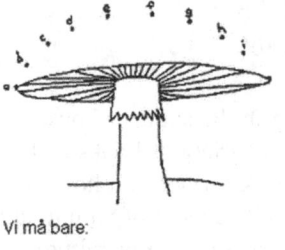

En skog på vei.
Vi oppgraderer. Smør deg med tålmodighet og vent; nettleseren din vil automatisk prøve på nytt om ett minutt.

Vi må bare:

- ikkno
- Skru av skogen
- Skru på "Vi oppgraderer" siden
- Backe opp databasen
- Backe opp filer i stable
- Sette affinities til 1 month
- Installere memcached
- Flytte tonull til trunk
- Installere tonull koden
- Kjøre migrasjoner (Yeah. Affinities ferdig.)
- Gi bulletin 295 en lfrontpage-tag
- Teststarte
- Stikke bort på åpent bakeri og kjøpe frokost
- Slette faderløs kudos
- Konfigurere SSL
- Teste kjøp av sesongkort
- åpne

Fig. 8.6 'Progress mushroom for the launch of the revamped social networking system' (screen capture by Marius Watz); http://flickr.com/photos/watz/180464229/

moved off to a separate forum, as do posters seeking or wanted to rid themselves of concert tickets.

Though strangely it seems the need is not so much to hide these topics as the knowledge that you are able to do so. So the actual use of the feature becomes less important as it being there legitimizes a plurality of esoteric topics, without a need for the recurring meta-discussion on whether this post was warranted. Forums are also given an option to be 'shy' where they are only visible to those who actively have subscribed to them, and thereby function much like the *open conversations* mentioned previously: semi-public spaces within the enclosed space of *Underskog*.

Finding Relationships Between Publication and Participation

Relationships between publics and organizations are interesting for us. The long-standing and internationally known electronic music and sound festival held in Oslo every autumn, called Ultima, is a good example. Ultima asks *Underskog* if it can host the online parts of the festival. And – we say no. Not because it's not part of the events that we list. But we do not want to represent an organization that already has its many spaces. 'Be yourself' – one of our mottos – means be a person not an organization. Calendar listings for the festival run, of course, as members place them into the events list. Ultima too! But in short, every event needs a 'venue'. Ultima has a venue a decade old. Affiliation through users is fine, laterally linked. Often people take time to articulate their own needs. And we need to hold this space open for them.

This is the case with linking *Kunstkritikk*, an online art review and networking site that moves into *Underskog* as well as being openly accessible on the web. The tone and extent of a formal long discourse of art review and interpretation does not produce much comment. A journalist begins to write differently for the medium, to seed issues, questions, argument rather than produce reflected, completed, considered review as product. The aim is to get readers to contribute! Clearly, discourse communities need processes: the need to summarize, to invert the order of discourse. It's important to open editing processes. It would seem that setting up an online discussion would have a lot to do with the distinction between a public meeting and someone giving a speech. Getting people to engage with a well researched, verbose, balanced and closed text is difficult. This is interesting, as it has ramifications for journalistic practice where involvement is wanted. Then there are parties... (Fig. 8.7).

Shared Object of Activity

'It's all a bit like a social reactor' (Simen Skogsrud).

Having a shared object of activity has spawned volumes of detailed discussion and seemingly banal phatic exchanges that together weave a fabric of emergent, daily

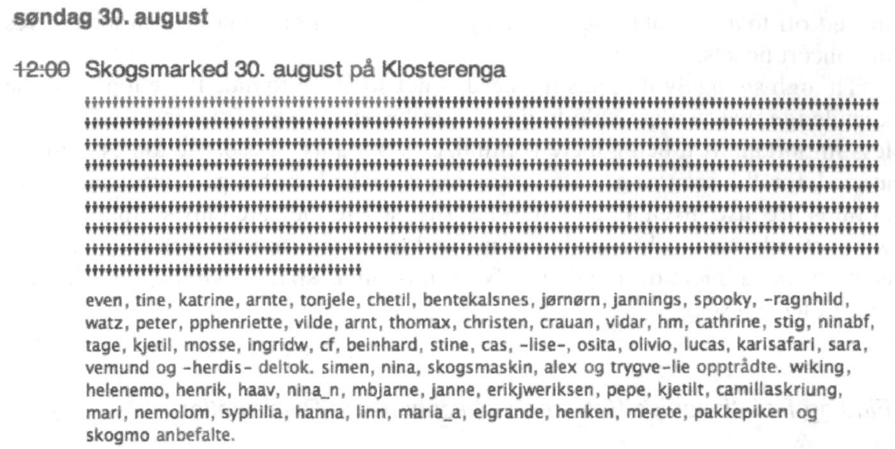

søndag 30. august

~~12:00~~ Skogsmarked 30. august på Klosterenga

‡‡‡
‡‡‡
‡‡‡
‡‡‡
‡‡‡
‡‡‡
‡‡‡
‡‡‡
‡‡‡

even, tine, katrine, arnte, tonjele, chetil, bentekalsnes, jørnørn, jannings, spooky, –ragnhild,
watz, peter, pphenriette, vilde, arnt, thomax, christen, crauan, vidar, hm, cathrine, stig, ninabf,
tage, kjetil, mosse, ingridw, cf, beinhard, stine, cas, –lise–, osita, olivio, lucas, karisafari, sara,
vemund og –herdis– deltok. simen, nina, skogsmaskin, alex og trygve-lie opptrådte. wiking,
helenemo, henrik, haav, nina_n, mbjarne, janne, erikjweriksen, pepe, kjetilt, camillaskriung,
mari, nemolom, syphilia, hanna, linn, maria_a, elgrande, henken, merete, pakkepiken og
skogmo anbefalte.

Fig. 8.7 'Little green men'. Day 373, Sat. 18 November 2006. It's our 1st birthday party (event nr. 11029). *Underskog* members have organized the event. Bands play for free. Some 500–600 people show up to party. Press coverage appears in *Universitas, Bergens Tidende* and *Aften Aften*. The figure is a screen grab from the event of participants

communication online. Finding out what is at issue, where action is, and who is mediating it in what ways, has become a part of 'new' media that is a far cry from the earlier concerns of print and film based culture. Popular cultural communication has moved off the gritty photocopied pages of limited number issues of fanzines, as it were, onto the widest shared communicative medium ever encountered. Where attention is given to shared meaning making, especially in contemporary educational practices and studies, it is often concerned with formal settings and structured tasks. Research is underway, however, to open out the study of wiki-based learning and its pedagogical participatory design and enactment by learners (e.g. Lund and Smordal 2006; Lund 2008; Morrison et al. 2010).

Yet, much of the burgeoning body of online collaborative discourse occurs in a popular cultural public sphere where earlier Habermasian gentility is cross-hatched with the edginess of contemporary urban aesthetics, flurries of mixed registers and a huge variety and assertion of self-expression. As has been noted elsewhere (e.g. Morrison and Skjulstad 2007), advertisers have been astute in co-opting these dynamics and their 'currencies' as part of embedding user-driven content within wider commercially-centred persuasive discourses (see also Uricchio 2004).

2M and Counting...

While Bengler are occupied, elsewhere the 'forest' spins merrily on at 2m pageviews per month. Yesterday (11 March 2007) a journalist in *Dagbladet* (a national daily and online paper) dedicated another full page to *Underskog*, now in their leisurely Sunday supplement.

Moving between Modes

So much to discuss with Even and Simen, Andrew says out loud, knowing their time is precious, knowing too (as Even's repeatedly reminded him) that going over what has been done and what's being planned provides an important shared space for reflection, especially by the designers. That this discussion is qualitatively different – repeats Even – because of Andrew's inputs into the overall communication design of *Underskog*. To link these reflections to digital design research and to notions of discursive performativity in designing for communication and communicating through discursive design. To search for a form that will give readers ways of accessing what is a multimodal ethnography (Dicks et al. 2006).

Aha, says Andrew, thinking back to the volume by Clifford and Marcus (1986), the writings of van Maanen (1995) and subsequent debates about ethnographic and anthropological discourse (e.g. Cheater 1999). Ours needs to be a *reflexive, multimodal ... authnography,* he laughs. To include, he later reflects, both the multimodal representations and mediations of several design actors and references to the requests of users. There'll be plenty of room for an additional paper focusing on the participants' views in more detail. This time we'll need to focus on what, in his new book, Krippendorf (2006) calls the semantic turn in design and design research. Yet we'll need to bear in mind that we are also interested in the co-ordination of the various actors and activities as Pelle Ehn (2007) reminds us in a review of that book. Co-ordination of actors, activities and articulations. Discursive. Discursive performativity.

From Whisperings to Rumblings

'In *Underskog,* isn't it all a question of performing the events?' (Andrew Morrison)

Designing for Performativity

As a reflexive design and design research process, *Underskog* was explicitly informed by theories of digitally mediated communication; it was also enriched by critical reference to related design practice and to the analysis of other social networking systems and services. As digital design research, we focus on designing for performativity (Morrison et al. in press). Performatively, the character of this environment that we report on, and its unfolding as multimodal discourse, has emerged through the expressive activities and interchange of needs and wants between the participants to the service and its designers.

Our focus on performativity was not simply to enable participation in the iterative loops of a digital design process or the inputs of users to a product or service, important and present as these indeed were. It was to connect the potential for discursive enactment from the informed use and construction by digital designers to the hands of linked members of the environment. Through this collaborative, unfolding activity, our challenge was to decide on what were suitable suggestions about the Communication Design and further modes of activity of the site and system, and translate these into live services for users, thereby hopefully extending their own performative discourses. In this sense, as an experiment in enacting an interdisciplinary digital design process and product, *Underskog* was anticipatory, participatory and performative.

'Facing Up'

'It's all in who uses it and why. You can make all the infrastructure you want, but it's not like the much ridiculed 90s adage, that you build it and they simply will come' (Even).

After the release of *Underskog 2.0* we iron out the resulting bugs and take half a step back. The service is feels well-rounded in that the implied functionality exists and is easily navigable. We give out a few thousand invitations and the people who show up mesh well with the existing populace without straining the public space. When graphing the activity on the site, we see blue lines of new friendships appearing every Monday, as people who have found out about each other during the weekend settle in front of their machines. Still it's most important to put what people react to at the front. To put the speech acts first: actionable content. To enable an expansive design and discourse at the level of utterance, to be able to act on information shown, to avoid a closed echo chamber yet be linked to locale, to numerous topics and issues not linked to the city space alone. So we've been concerned to design for representing persons, a *MySpace* homepage angle, indicating scarity and difference and what is currency versus exchange; that you're alive in your social meaning, realised discursively through flickr-ish views. That the service gives emphasis to your actions, reading and writing yourself, but interdiscursively. Not as a separate text, but a view related to others, to accrue social body, Even says. The trick has been to design it so that at a glance a person can see what you're about. There's a non-verbal element to this. You implicitly assemble body through exploratory interaction. What seemed novel about social software was in the ways it allowed for the accrual of links and tags in 'building a social body, a representation through verbal and non-verbal action'. What was also important, writes Even after the discussion, was how the trajectory of this presence delineates the individual narratives of members in such services. The story of their emergence into the space. Without the underlying expansive design and performative discursive stance and enactment 'assembly' would be far harder. Familiar strangers ...

We've tried our best to respond to requests from people for improvements. By mid-January 2008 there have been 338 posts where people have suggested changes. Big, small, very specific, others already in our list. We've read them all, discussed most of them, some we've left for participants to answer. 'Yea, we've also had personalization. You know, a request to allow people to change the appearance of their profile pages, pimping as it's known.' We said that we wouldn't offer this and then Øystein Wika found a way of doing exactly what you wanted to your page and Martinj offered a guide to others as to how to do it. Searching *YouTube* for *Underskog* will bring screencasts of people demonstrating to others how to carry out tasks. This has been a shift on our own expansive design activity; to leave the 'interpretation' of need to the discursive design and performativity to people themselves.

Non Fatum Est...

Enactment, designing for discursive enactment, reflexivity on that discursive enactment that is in and via digital discourse through social software redesign. This is not Butler's level of articulation. It's not the software and system that is the object of communication, but it allows for a wider communication design complex to be collaboratively, collectively discoursed online and to reflexively speak about its own communication design back to the designers. This, therefore, is not a case of what fatefully comes to pass (fact as fate, as it were) but a matter of recursively mediated meaning making coming into being through processes of performativity on and through the discourses of the designed. In closing a chapter on *Friendster*, Boyd (2008) argues that 'Digital social structures disrupt the boundaries that define social communities, but the reassessment of context and performance that accompanies it is endlessly generative.'

From Ideals to Activity

In a café. Another breakfast meeting. June 2006. Time stolen between other projects. We're talking about how the system was developed, the ad hoc beginnings, how far it's all shifted.

'This is a system that was made in our spare time and without financing,' notes Even.

'Yea, it was kind of ... Utopian,' says Simen....

It's now January 2008, and, looking back on the project, Even comments, 'in sense the design was of fairly soft artefacts. They needed to be adapted in use and from the inputs of users with communicative purposes.'

Revisioning Expansive Design

The model of expansive learning we referred to earlier seems to apply well to the iterative and plastic design process involved in developing *Underskog*. In an abductive move, we have termed the cycles and shifts in transformation 'expansive design'. We began by questioning existing practices in light of our own uses of a variety of social networking applications. We analysed these in terms of collaborative, cooperative digital discourse enactment and developed a schema of sorts for coordination of some of these artefacts into a shared object of activity centred on social calendaring. A fully functioning online artefact was then built as a broad model that embodied our core concepts and opened out for the discursive performativity of participants in new practices. Next, we examined and debated these at three intersecting levels of activity: in the design team; between the communication design researcher and the team; and with users as the system was put into operation.

Here the model of expansive learning might be expanded to include a set of micro loops or reflexive turns within stages of implementation and review, based on emergent use and importantly, the practices of users. In other words, in designing for discursive performativity in digital domains, the performative discourses of participants may in turn influence the design of affordances, services, functions and discourse events that enable that discourse. Here the relations between the overall object of the wider activity system and the semiotic artefacts develops an intertwined character that indicates that there are, in effect, multiple layers of mediation and meaning making in emergence, via transformations in which practices of users become part of digital designers' discursive 'material'. Reflection and evaluation of the process has been threaded into this 'knotworking' as Engeström has called it. As the system grew in volume of users and messages, a community of practice also came into being through which layers of participation and discourse moves between participants took on some of the guidance, management and interpersonal structuring of a dynamic digital discourse environment and communicative artefact.

Finding and Designing Coherence

It's summer 2006 and Simen, Andrew and Even are once again meeting to discuss *Underskog*. Breakfast coffee before other project research and *Underskog* coding.

'Places have different ways of developing their own discussions, and,' says Even, 'it's a matter of how to see the arc: the excitement and potential of new republics, an idealism, a potential, not techno-determinism, not socio-determinism, but emergence.'

Andrew suggests, with a wry laugh, that it's how not to impose voices, or volumes.

'Exactly', says Even. 'It's a question of how to make publics, to allow for participation, yet to explode space to allow for different ways of saying. You know, Grice's principles of co-operation you mentioned so early on.'

'Ah,' says Andrew, 'Design conversations, different structures and modes of discourse co-joined.'

January 2008. Even's looking back on *Underskog*. 'One of the encouraging features that emerged was the move from our original provision of helping people from day 1 to the situation where people deal with this between themselves. The system is stable; the discourses of use and assistance feed and nurture one another.'

Removal and Deletion

1 February 2006. The first instance of a member asking for their account to be removed. When building a system in your spare time one aims not at feature completeness according to a specification, but, rather, something interesting for someone to share. Of course if one allows account creation, someone is bound to also request deletion.

Towards Discursive Performativity

'The performance of social relations is not equivalent to the relations themselves, or even to an individual's mental models of them' (Boyd 2008).

As shared and emergent compositions, the ecologies of social networking sites are generated through their underlying technical and communication design. Here we refer to the notion of digital media ecologies proposed by Fuller (2005). However, as digital discourse, these ecologies are also realized through the performative enactments of their participants.

In summary, we might say that our approach is also to do with the expansive design of discursive performativity in shaping and critiquing an emerging artefact and an artefact of emergence in the domain of social networking sites and services. This takes us back to the notion of corporeality, the body in and as discourse (as argues Butler and as Foucault championed). However, this is a 'body' in transformation, a multimodal and multi-planar 'text' that is very much to do with mediational materiality that is collaboratively enacted. Again this points to Threadgold (2003: online), who, referring to Wodak on extending CDA to what mediated relations between text and context, queries how much context to include and how to do this.

The politics of writing, writing the body, critical discourse analysis and cultural studies, all of these are different to politics which intervene in corporeal and othered spaces, but as Butler's and others' struggles with language and discourse show, they can never be entirely separate. That is why we must do more work on the relationships between the two, more work on understanding how much context matters, more work on making the languages in which we do it accessible to those who need them, and more work on learning how to see the world from other places than the privileged ones we tend to occupy. Only then will the worlds we inhabit change our theories and methods to the point where they may actually produce the social change they theorise and to which they make claim (Threadgold 2003: online).

In terms of digital design research, what interests us is to explore the juncture between the design of social software applications and the performative discourses of their users in an ongoing process of design refinement. 'Pitching for performativity' thus enables us to attend to both the design of the software and to its iterative design though performative ecologies of socially mediated use.

New Forests

January 2008. Bengler's been busy building and trialling a new environment inspired by the development and uses of *Underskog*. The 'forest' has been growing on its own without the repeated attention to new functionality needed. There is of course moderation to be done, we follow the discourse. But much of our time has been spent on designing and coding and developing the more elaborate system *Origo* that is open to everyone, not the invite-only and urban calendaring character of *Underskog*.

Origo is an attempt at offering everyone their own *Underskog*, a place of internal and external debate and collaboration. It also ties in with the 40 Norwegian local newspapers and their web-based publishing, thereby offering established publics to those who seek attention for their cause. We also supplement the relevance criteria of social proximity and group membership with spatial proximity. What is happening near where I live? At the same time we attempt to add the same gravity to discussion. People need to register through their mobile phone so we can guarantee stable identities. Local politicians may verify their roles and organizational affiliations and chose what role they want to with which to comment on news stories. It is an attempt at taking all we've learned through *Underskog* and also it itself to other communities to provide places of collaboration, discussion and action.

From Whispers to Roars

'Alone among all the animals, we suffer from the future perfect tense' (Margaret Atwood 2007:5).

In this chapter we have given an account of a digital design initiative in which the object, in Activity Theory terms, is one of designing for discoursing in an online domain. The overall communicative aim in developing *Underskog* has been to facilitate the mediation of joint action online. This action is projected as being potentially realized through a variety of media and tools so as to enable multimodal meaning making by and between participants. This is digital design for discursive performativity. Theories of discourse in action are 'prescripted' in the design of semiotic affordances for online meaning making. This shifts conceptions of discourse in action – still largely contained in linguistic analyses, even within multimodal discourse (Morrison 2010) – to the design of digital discourse potential that may be folded back on itself through the performative engagement of online users in an emergent design process.

This unfolding of design in discursive performativity is possible because of the character of the digital: a multisemiotic environment has designers and participants in relations of co-presence, with their enacted discourses largely visible in an integrated discourse environment. Potential for action is realized in the design of this multimodal semiotic object, and in its discoursing about its design. In this instance, it is not only object-oriented, that is geared towards a communicative goal as the production of discourse (Shotter 2003). It is also realized in emergent mediated meaning making. Where this is 'housed' in a reflexive, iterative, dialogical interplay of coded 'scripts' that are designed to enable digitally mediated performative discourse, this is complemented by a discursive performativity that is central to all layers of its digital design. Relations between artefacts and objects may thereby be framed in terms of emergent, expansive and multimodal digital designing for mediated meaning making. This is not simply a matter of Schön's 'backtalk' of materials or having a conversation with materials (Dearden 2006). It is a matter of making material the co-design of an online site for social networking and its interlinked and mediated semiois through performative participatory discourses that are an emergent, reflexive and dynamic constituent of digital designing.

This is what the team from Bengler who designed *Underskog* has aimed to do in the design of a new, related, but different environment. Called *Origo* (http://www.origo.no/), this environment serves, supports and hopefully enables the interests and needs of local democracy and related community newspapers beyond the wireless zones and criss-crossings of multimodal 'language games' and social activity in the capital city. May the roar begin.

Acknowledgements
Underskog would not have been possible without the third member of the design team, Alex Staubo. Our thanks also to the participants in *Underskog*, to fellow contributors to this volume and to Synne Skjulstad, Ole Smørdal and Marika Luders for suggestions and comments.

References

Atwood, M. (2007). Everybody's happy now. *The Guardian*. Review. 17 November, 5–7.
Bateson, G. (1979/2000). *Mind and nature: A necessary unity*. Cresskill N.J.: Hampton Press & the Institute for Intercultural Studies.
Bakhtin, M. (1981). *The dialogic imagination*. University of Texas Press: Austin. Minneapolis: University of Minnestota Press.
Bakhtin, M. (1986). *Speech genres and other late essays*. Emerson, Caryl. & Holquist, Michael. (Eds.). McGee, Vern. (trans.). Austin: University of Texas Press.
Barab, S., Schatz, S., & Scheckler, R. (2004a). Using activity theory to conceptualise online community and using online community to conceptualise activity theory. *Mind, Culture & Activity*, 11(1), 25-47.

Barab, S., Thomas, M., Dodge, S., & Newell, M. (2004b). Critical design ethnography: Designing for change. *Anthropology & Education Quarterly*, 35(22), 254–268.

Barad, K. (2003). Posthumanist performativity: toward an understanding of how matter comes to matter. *Signs: Journal of Women in Culture and Society*, 28(3), 801–831.

Benkler, Y. (2006). *The wealth of networks*. New Haven: Yale University Press.

Beer, D. (2008). Social network(ing) sites...revisiting the story so far: a response to danah boyd & Nicole Ellison'. *Journal of Computer-Mediated Communication*, 13(2), 516–529.

Bochner, A., & Ellis, C. (2002). (Eds.). *Ethnographically speaking: Autoethnography, literature and aestehtics*. Walnut Creek, Alta Mira Press.

Boucher, G. (2006). The politics of performativity: a critique of Judith Butler. *PARRHESIA: A Journal of Critical Philosophy*, No. 1, 2006, 112–141. Available at: http://www.parrhesia-journal.org/issue1.html

Boyd, D. (2004). Friendster and publicly articulated social networks. In E. Dykstra-Erickson, M. Tscheligi (Eds.), *Proceedings of the SIGCHI conference on human factors in computing systems (CHI '04)*. Vienna, Austria (pp. 1279–1282). New York: ACM Press. 1279–1282.

Boyd, D. (2006). Friends, Friendsters, and top 8: Writing community into being on social network sites. *First Monday*, 11(12). Available at: www.firstmonday.org/issues/issue11_12/boyd/

Boyd, D. (2008). None of this is real: identity and participation in Friendster. In J. Karaganis (Ed.), *Structures of participation in digital culture* (pp. 132–157). New York: Social Science Research Council.

Boyd, D., & Ellison, N. (2007). Social network sites: definition, history, and scholarship. *Journal of Computer-Mediated Communication*, 13(1), 210–230. DOI: 10.1111/j.1083-6101.2007.00393.x.

Boyd, D. & Heer, J. (2006). Profiles as conversation: networked identity performance on Friendster'. In *Proceedings of the 39th Annual Hawaii International Conference on System Sciences (HICSS'06) Track 3*, Kauai, Hawaii (pp. 59c). Washington, DC, USA IEEE Computer Society.

Butler, J. (1993). *Bodies that matter: On the discursive limits of "sex"*. New York: Routledge.

Byrd, D., & Owen, D. (1998). Writing in the hivemind. In R. Taylor, R. & I. Ward, I. (Eds.), *Literacy theory in the age of the Internet* (pp. 47–58). New York: Columbia University Press.

Cheater A. (Ed.). (1999). *The anthropology of power*. London: Routledge.

Chesters, G. & Welsh, I. (2005). Complexity and social movement(s). *Theory, Culture & Society*. 22(5), 187–211.

Chin, A., & Chignell, M. (2006). A social hypertext model for finding community in blogs. In *Proceedings of the seventeenth conference on hypertext and hypermedia (HYPERTEXT '06)*, Odense, Denmark (pp. 11–22). New York: ACM Press: New York.

Clifford, J., & Marcus, G. (Eds.) (1986). *Writing culture: The poetics and politics of ethnography*. Berkeley: University of California Press.

Dearden, A. (2006). Designing as a conversation with digital materials. *Design Studies*, 27(3), 399–421.

Dennis Publishing. (2007). *The independent guide to facebook*. Dennis: London.

Deuze, M. (2006). Collaboration, participation and the media'. *New Media & Society*, 8(4), 691–698.

Dicks, B., Soyinka, B., & Coffey, A. (2006). Multimodal ethnography. *Qualitative Research*, 6(1), 77–96.

Donath, J., & Boyd, D. (2004). Public displays of connection. *BT Technology Journal*, 22(4), 71–82.

Ehn, P. (2007). Review of the semantic turn: a new foundation for design. *Artifact*, 1(1), 56–59.

Ellis, C., & Bochner, A. (1999). Composing ethnography: alternative forms of qualitative writing. *Social Forces*, 77(3), 1236–1237.

Engeström, Y. (1987). *Learning by Expanding: An activity theoretical approach to developmental research*. Helsinki Orienta-Konsultit.

Engeström, Y. (2001). Expansive Learning at Work: toward an activity theoretical reconceptualization. *Journal of Education and Work*, 14(1), 133–156.

Engeström, Y. (2006). Expansive design and activity theory. In S. Bagnara & G. Crampton Smith (Eds.), *Theories and practices of interaction design* (pp. 3–23). Mahwah, N.J: Lawrence Erlbaum Associates Inc.

Fuller, M. (2005). *Media ecologies: Materialist energies in art and technoculture*. Cambridge: The MIT Press.

Halliday, M. (1985/1994). *Functional grammar*. 2nd edition. London: Edward Arnold.

Hartley, J. (Ed.) (2005). *Creative industries*. Blackwell: Malden.

Haseman, B. (2006). A Manifesto for Performative Research. *Media International Australia* (incorporating Culture and Policy), Theme issue 'Practice-led Research'. No. 118, February. 98-106. Available: http://www.emsah.uq.edu.au/mia/issues/miacp118.html. http://eprints.qut.edu.au/archive/00003999/01/3999.pdf

Haskell, J., Linds, W., & Ippolito, J. (2002). Opening spaces of possibility: the enactive as a qualitative research approach. *FQS*, 3(2). Available at: http://www.qualitative-research.net/fqs/fqs-e/inhalt3-02-e.htm

Hertzberg Kaare, B., Bae Brandtzæg, P., Heim, J. & Endestad, T. (2007). 'In the borderland between family orientation and peer culture: the use of communication technologies among Norwegian tweens.' *New Media & Society*. Vol. 9, No. 3. 603–624.

Hertz, R. (2001). *Reflexivity and voice*. London: Sage.

Hine; C. (2000). *Virtual ethnography*. London, Thousand Oaks, New Delhi: Sage Publications.

Iedema, R. (2003). Multimodality, resemiotization: extending the analysis of discourse as multi-semiotic practice. *Visual Communication*, 2(1), 29–57.

Jacucci, C., Jacucci, G., Wagner, I., & Psik, T. (2005). 'A manifesto for the performative development of ubiquitous media'. In *Proceedings of the 4th Decennial Conference on Critical Computing: between Sense and Sensibility*. Aarhus, Denmark, August 20–24, 2005. (Eds). W. Bertelsen, W, Bouvin, N., Krogh, P. & Kyng, M. New York: ACM Press. 19–28.

Jenkins, H. (2006). *Convergence culture: Where old and new media collide*. New York: New York University Press.

Kazmierczak, E. (2003). Design as meaning making: from making things to the design of thinking. *Design Issues*, 19(2), 45–59.

Krippendorf, K. (2006). *The semantic turn: A new foundation for design*. Boca Raton FL: CRC Press.

Lassiter, L. E. (2005a). *The Chicago guide to collaborative ethnography*. Chicago: The University of Chicago Press.

Lassiter, L. E. (2005b). Collaborative ethnography and public anthropology. *Current Anthropology*, 46(1), 83–106.

Lather, P. (1991). *Getting smart: Feminist research and pedagogy with/in the postmodern*. New York & London: Routledge.

Latour, B. (1996). *Aramis or the love of technology*. Cambridge: Harvard University Press.

Lincoln, Y., & Denzin. N. (Eds.) (2003). *Turning points in qualitative research. Tying knots in a handkerchief*. Walnut Creek: AltaMira Press.

Liu, H., Maes, P., & Davenport, G. (2006). Unraveling the taste fabric of social networks. *International Journal on Semantic Web and Information Systems*, 2(1), 42–71.

Livingstone, S. (2007). On the material and the symbolic: Silverstone's double articulation of research traditions in new media studies. *New Media & Society*, 9(1), 16–24.

Luck, R. (2003). Dialogue in participatory design. *Design Studies*, 24(6), 523–535

Lund, A. (2008). Wikis: A collective approach to language production. *ReCALL*, 20(1), 35–54

Lund, A., & Smordal, O. (2006). Is there a space for the teacher in a Wiki? *2006 International Symposium on Wikis*, August 21–23, Odense, Denmark.

Markham, A. (1998). *Life online: Researching real experience in virtual space*. Lanham: AltaMira Press.

Melucci, A. (1996). *Challenging codes: Collective action in the information age*. Cambridge, Cambridge University Press.

Millard, D., & Ross, M. (2006). Web 2.0: hypertext by any other name? In *Proceedings of the seventeenth conference on Hypertext and hypermedia (HYPERTEXT '06)*, Odense, Denmark (pp. 27–30) New York: ACM Press.

Morrison, A. (2003). From oracy to electracies: hypernarrative, place and multimodal discourses in learning. In G. Liestøl, A. Morrison, & T. Rasmussen (Eds.), *Digital media revisited:*

Theoretical and conceptual innovation in digital domains (pp. 115–154). Cambridge, Mass.: The MIT Press.

Morrison, A. (2005). Inside the rings of saturn. *Computers and Composition*, 22(1), 87–100.

Morrison, A. (Ed.) (2010). *Inside multimodal composition*. Cresskill N.J.: Hampton Press.

Morrison, A., Sem, I., & Havnør, M. (2010). Behind the wallpaper: performativity in mixed reality arts. In A. Morrison (Ed.), *Inside multimodal composition*. Cresskill N.J.: Hampton Press.

Morrison, A., Smørdal, O., Lund, A., & Moen, A. (2010). Multiple activity-multiple mediation'. In A. Morrison (Ed.), *Inside multimodal composition*. Cresskill N.J.: Hampton Press.

Morrison, A., & Skjulstad, S. (2007). Talking cleanly about convergence. In T. Storsul, T. & D. Stuedahl, D. (Eds.), *Ambivalence towards convergence* (pp. 217–335). Göteborg: Nordicom.

Morrison, A., & Skjulstad, S. (2010). Mediating hybrid design: imaginative renderings of automotive innovation on the web. In A. Morrison (Ed.), *Inside multimodal composition*. Cresskill N.J.: Hampton Press.

Morrison, A., & Thorsnes, P. (2010). Blogging the emphemeral. In A. Morrison (Ed.), *Inside multimodal composition*. Cresskill N.J.: Hampton Press.

Nardi, B., Schiano, D., Gumbrecht, M., & Swartz, L. (2004a). Why we blog.*Communications of the American Association for Computing Machinery*, 47(12), 41–46.

Nardi, B., Schiano, D., & Gumbrecht, M. (2004b). Blogging as social activity, or, Would you let 900 million people read your diary? In J. Herbsleb & G. Olson (Eds.), *Proceedings of the 2004 ACM conference on computer supported cooperative work (CSCW '04)*, Chicago, Illinois, USA (pp. 222–228). New York: ACM Press.

Norris, S., & Jones, R. (Eds.) (2005). *Discourse in action: Introducing mediated discourse Analysis*. London: Routledge.

Newton, S. (2004). Designing as disclosure. *Design Studies*, 25(1), 93–109.

Nuria Lorenzo-Dus, N. (2006). 'Buying and selling: mediating persuasion in British property shows'. *Media, Culture & Society*. Vol. 28, No. 5. 739–761.

Quiggin, J. (2006). Blogs, wikis and creative innovation. *International Journal of Cultural Studies*, 9(4), 481–496.

Rheingold, H. (2000). *The virtual community: Homesteading on the electronic rontier.* Cambridge, MA: The MIT Press.

Richardson, L. (1994). Writing: a method of inquiry. In N. Denzin & Y. Lincoln (Eds.), *Handbook of qualitative research* (pp. 516–529). Thousand Oaks: Sage.

Sanders, E., & Stappers, P. (2008). Co-creation and the new landscapes of design. *CoDesign*, l(4), 5–18.

Sawyer, R. (2005). *Social emergence: Societies as complex systems*. New York: Cambridge University Press.

Shotter, J. (2003). Real presences: meaning as living movement in a participatory world. *Theory & Psychology*, 13(4), 435–468.

Shotter, J., & Billig, M. (1998). A Bakhtinian psychology: from out of the heads of individuals and into the dialogues between them. In B. Mayerfield Bell & M. Gardiner, M (Eds.) *Bakhtin and the human sciences* (pp. 13–29). London: Sage.

Sirc, G. (2004). Box logic. In A. Wysocki, J. Johnson-Eilola, C. Selfe & G. Sirc (Eds.), *Writing new media* (pp. 111–146). Logan: Utah State University Press.

Skogsrud, S. (2004). *Pragma*. Oslo: Tiden.

Silverstone, R. (1994). *Television and everyday Life*. London: Routledge.

Tacchi, J. (2004). Researching creative applications of new information and communication technologies. *International Journal of Cultural Studies*, 7(1), 91–103.

Threadgold, T. (1997). *Feminist poetics: Poiesis, performance, histories*. London: Routledge.

Threadgold, T. (2003). Cultural studies, critical theory and critical discourse analysis: histories, remembering and futures' *Linguistik Online*, 14(2). Available: http://www.linguistik-online. de/14_03/index.html

Turkle, S. (1995). *Life on the screen: identity in the age of the internet*. New York: Simon & Schuster.

Uricchio, W. (2004). Beyond the great divide: collaborative networks and the challenge to dominant conceptions of creative industries. *International Journal of Cultural Studies*, 7(1), 79–90.

van Veggel, R. (2005). Where the two sides of ethnography collide. *Design Issues*, 21(3), 3–16.

van Maanen, J. (1995). An end to innocence: the ethnography of ethnography. In J. van Maanen (Ed.), *Representation in ethnography* (pp. 1–35). Thousand Oaks: Sage.

Wells, G. (2007). The mediating role of discoursing in activity. *Mind, Culture, & Activity*, 14(3), 160–177.

Wenger, E., McDermott, R., & Snyder, W. (2002). *Cultivating communities of practice*. Boston: Harvard Business School Press.

Wodak, R. (2001). What CDA is about – a summary of its history, important concepts and its developments. In R. Wodak & M. Meyer (Eds.), *Methods of critical discourse analysis* (pp. 1–13). London: Sage.

Wertsch, J. (1991). *Voices of the mind: a sociocultural approach to mediated action*. Cambridge, MA: Harvard University Press.

9

Designing for Sustainable Ways of Living with Technologies

Christina Mörtberg, Dagny Stuedahl, and Pirjo Elovaara

Digital media have placed a focus on sustainability in terms of long-term digital preservation of societal memories and cultural heritage. There is also discussion about technological issues, such as flexible infrastructures, standards and formats, which are explored in relation to how to build sustainable systems (Braa et al. 2004; Byrne 2005; Byrne and Sahay 2007). Further, while there already exists a body of knowledge about standards, classification, and category work (e.g. Star 1991; Bowker and Star 1999; Verran et al. 2007), it is also important to relate these standards, formats and routines in digital design to social and cultural sustainability, and not just durability.

We discuss here sustainability as related to digital design, and pay particular attention to social and cultural sustainability, arguing that the challenges of establishing principles for sustainability are related to alignments between materiality and human practices, with a focus on durability and the re-use of digital material, as well as issues of identity, values, and creation of meaning. Cultural sustainability is a supplemental issue in general discussions of sustainability and also how to integrate sustainability in digital design. The aim here is to relate sustainability to both design and the use of digital means, with a focus on standard, formats and routines, using examples from projects and practices. The examples will be analysed in order to reveal the variety of aspects of sustainability and the challenges involved in integrating these in design principles that can be applied. Understanding how sustainable digital design is part of change and continuity is investigated by addressing the question: How is it possible to anchor cultural and social sustainability as a principle inside design practice? Considering digital design as sociomaterial practice, our argument on cultural sustainability addresses a notion of situatedness beyond the social (Haraway 1997; Suchman 2007).

Empirical material from two research projects: *From government to e-government: gender, skills, technology and learning* and *Research Narrative and Mediation* (RENAME) will be used in the discussions of sustainability. The first project explores the transformation in the Swedish public sector described by the overall concept of e-government. Modernization of the Swedish public sector, where rationalisation, efficiency and effectiveness are explicit elements, is a dominant

I. Wagner et al. (eds.), *Exploring Digital Design: Multi-Disciplinary Design Practices*, 261
Computer Supported Cooperative Work, DOI 10.1007/978-1-84996-223-0_9,
© Springer-Verlag London Limited 2010

discourse. Strong political hopes are also expressed in the creation of a good service society by the use of IT, a so-called 24-h authority or 24/7 agency (Elovaara 2004; Elovaara et al. 2006; Ekelin 2007). The project's focus is on employees' perspectives, how their working conditions will change, and what kind of qualifications will be needed in the future, depending on the transformation from government to e-government. We use examples from civil servants' activities and doings in their day-to-day work, related to standards, formats and routines.

The second case is a communication design project related to the reconstruction of a Viking boat in Norway. Fragments of three boats were found together with a Viking ship in 1880. The resulting Gokstad excavation was one of the largest archaeological findings of Viking times in Norway. The fragments of one of the three boats were left in the storeroom of the Museum of Cultural History at the University of Oslo. In 2003 an ethnologist started a reconstruction of the boat, based on discussions of current traditions of wooden boat building as well as on research of the sailing competences skills of the Vikings. The reconstruction project is a comment on the communication of cultural historical research as such, and Viking history specifically (Planke 2003, 2005). The design project is related to finding ways of using cultural, historical, digital, empirical data from the reconstruction process for communication (Stuedahl and Smørdal in press) in ways that engage young exhibition visitors. Questions related to the standards used for archiving and mediation of the empirical material from the reconstruction project will be the focus point for the discussion of cultural sustainability. The empirical material is used in online as well as in mixed-media exhibition, and invites visitors to get involved in activities on the visitor's blog, during and after the exhibition visit. Sustainability makes visible questions related to the development of standards, taxonomies and concepts that can be sustained across different communities and institutions – as well as it addresses new uses of media and cultural heritage content.

In the next section of the chapter we discuss the notion of sustainable development and sustainable design and, in the following section, we work through the cases. We begin with examples from an exploration of e-government where civil servants are dealing with standards and routines. The second case is related to the politics of categorization in digitization of museum objects in order to preserve them for future society. Finally we discuss the re-visits and how to bring in sustainability as a way of thinking in digital design.

Sustainable Development and Its Relationship to Design

Sustainable development was given its public definition in the report Our Future Common (1987) from the so called Brundtland Commission (Braidotti 2006). Liveable futures and 'a development that meets the needs of the present without compromising the ability of future generations to meet their own need' were underscored in the report (Our Common Futures 1987). The Commission thus extended the concept to focus not only on ecological but also social and economic dimensions. Twenty years after the Brundtland Commission, sustainability became of great importance in public discussions once more when the Intergovernmental Panel on Climate Change (IPCC) released their 4th assessment report, February 2, 2007. Sustainability in this context is dominated by environmental or ecological aspects. Ecological responsibility, economic health or viability and social equity have, though, been in focus in a variety of projects on local and global arenas. Cultural sustainability in particular has emerged from social sustainability, emphasizing cultural vitality in terms of well-being, creativity, diversity and innovation (Hawks 2001). This dimension is thus interlinked with environmental responsibility, economic health and social equity.

Sustainablity in Design ...

Ecological and environmental aspects have been given particular attention through green or sustainable design in architecture and urban planning, industrial development and development of energy systems. The core focus is on physical and technological principles: environmental and health impacts based on parameters such as choices of low-impact materials, energy efficiency, quality and durability; reuse and recycling; as well as service substitution, standardization and modularity. At the same time, several diverging alternative movements propose different focuses and different frameworks for design. The slow design movement, for example, approaches the issue of sustainability by way of slow activism, which includes a philosophy of ways of alternative living, and establishing alternative commercial processes. Design is then a way to reduce the use of human, economic and ecological resources.

Sustainability also becomes a serious issue in design of information systems (IS), with, primarily, a focus on durability (Braa et al. 2004; Byrne 2005; Byrne and Sahay 2007). Braa et al. (2004) argue that durable interventions in local practices (design and implementation of IS) are achieved by extending the network of action both horizontally and vertically, and by facilitating the learning processes through scaling the systems for a number of sites. Further, Elaine Byrne (2005) emphasizes participation and culture as important dimensions to be included in IS design in order to ensure sustainability. IS researchers' main focus is on durability (Braa et al. 2004; Byrne 2005); Eli Blevis' (2006, 2007) focus is on the reduction of materials in interaction design, and in participatory design, sustainability is included in the following way:

> [Accordingly,] IT usage is regarded sustainable to the extent that it contributes to a balance in the development, use, and protection of a company's resources. This should be done in ways that accommodate the company's existing goals and needs, without jeopardizing its future development potentials (Bødker et al. 2004: 54).

The notion of sustainability has evolved and is used in a variety of ways and settings and, hence, there is no common understanding of sustainability (Eichler 1999). Further, the notion has been criticized, particularly in its relation to development. The critique, of the report Our Common Future pays attention to how the development is built upon Western rationality and a continuous exploitation of the Third World (Visvanathan 1991; Escobar 1995). Another argument is that sustainable development has lost its potential and focus because it has become a guideline for policy makers (Sachs 1999). Although the concept is messy, there are some links between the various usages; for example, to create or sustain enduring and viable futures for present and future generations. We will pay particular attention to social, but primarily cultural, sustainability and, therefore, expand the discussion of cultural sustainability in the next section

... and Cultural Sustainability in Digital Design

Most projects related to cultural sustainability are connected with community development and artful activities, where culture is understood as a key element in the creation of sustainable communities. The cultural dimension is, in this chapter, closely related to engagement, expression and dialogue and stresses values, aspirations, diversity, creativity, and participation in recreation (Duxbury and Gillette 2007). Sustainable design is understood as a component of cultural sustainability, by its 'active force in [...] reflecting and representing the respective peoples and places in which it is working' (Blankenship 2005: 24).

The issue of culture related to sustainability is a challenge in digital design, that is designing connections that can retain existing communities and practices, as well as being part of building new practices. Our point of departure is that designing for sustainable ways of living with technologies has to focus on what Bødker et al. (2004) call 'a balance' between development, use and institutional practices. That is, identity, values and norms, as well as a cultural–historical perspective of knowledge, need to be taken into consideration by the institutions, the collective and the individual in order to build a deep understanding of a balance between design and use. A focus on existing knowledge-traditions and practices is suggested, which paves the way to approach the cultural aspects in design projects related to well-defined values of practices (Stuedahl 2004; Mörtberg et al. 2010).

Culture is one way to extend the discussions of alternative approaches to sustainability (Hawks 2001). Central to such a development is that culture is not understood in a conservative meaning, as an instrument that sustains or excludes process of change but, rather, that culture is the feature by which multiple aspects of a development process connects and gives it a direction. The Danish anthropologist Kirsten Hastrup (1988) argues that culture addresses the systems of relations, where the production of meaning is understood as intertwined with the relations between people, material and immaterial artefacts, actions and social processes.

These relations are implicit, comparative and stand in contrast to each other. It is these differences and heterogeneities that make it possible to describe and identify cultures. Culture is actually constituted and made visible in the elements and moments of difference; where it becomes visible that what one culture represents is what another does not. Culture is therefore an analytical implication that focuses on systems of relations identified by differences (Hastrup 1988).

Values are the ideas of what seems important and filled with meaning, and stand in relation to norms or the expectations of behaviour that people in a culture constitute and negotiate about in their lives. Values are also intertwined with the design of digital artefacts and are understood as the ideas and norms of a culture embedded in material objects. All are part of cultural translations and transformation processes. Institutions generalize these norms and values that are produced individually and collectively, and structure them as patterns in society. The values, norms, materiality, institutions, thought and action, as well as the historical dimension, make a whole that is embedded in cultural practice.

To understand culture in this way also provides a perspective on meaning-production that is relevant for digital design. Meaning production is a human activity that is entangled with symbols, materiality, thought and action in the past and in the present. Culture is therefore a relational practice that challenges, recreates and transforms meaning (Hastrup 1988). That is, culture as a relation between identity, meaning, values and norms negotiated collectively, is constituted in the performed relational practices. This will be the departure point for our argument of cultural sustainability.

Cultural sustainability includes norms, values, multiplicity and heterogeneity compared with social sustainability that puts attention on power relations and equity related to ethics, justice and human dignity (Cheney et al. 2004). Further, how to create maintenance and continuity between the past and the present are important aspects to be considered when one explores cultural sustainability and the question is how to go about designing the connectedness. In this chapter, cultural sustainability will be discussed in relation to standards and practices.

Cat's Cradle: An Actor-Network-Theory

Susan Leigh Star (1991) focuses on categorization and standards in her discussion of how power relations are intertwined in networks between humans and nonhumans. Her discussion is based on her allergy to onions and also on a story of a student's ambiguous identities (being in a high tension zone between two categories; woman/man). To be in the margins between standards and categories, Star argues, is what needs to be considered when one starts the analysis of a network; that is, to make visible invisible work as well as conventions and standards that stabilize networks for many, but not for all. Star (1991: 52) writes: 'Power is about whose metaphor brings worlds together, and holds them there'. Networks, standards and categories are not given but created in negotiations and translations between various actors and these are made visible and invisible, dependent on where boundaries are drawn. That is, where one starts the network is also a process where things are sorted in and out (Bowker and Star 1999).

Donna J. Haraway (1997) another feminist scholar also emphasizes the relationship between humans and nonhumans, and how they are constituted in material-semiotic practices. Haraway asks, though, for whom and how hybrids of human and nonhuman work; for example how gender and other asymmetrical power relations are intertwined with networks of humans and nonhumans. Haraway also argues that knowledge is not comprehensive but partial because knowledge, like categories or standards are not static or frozen 'there are always more things going on than you thought; maybe less than there should be, but more than you thought!' (interview with Lykke et al. 2000: 55). Partiality and situatedness can also be illustrated by the metaphor or figuration of the cat's cradle (Haraway 1994).

Haraway's (1994) use of cat's cradle as her actor-network theory is built on cultural studies; feminist, multicultural, and antiracist theory/projects; and science studies. Cat's cradle is a string game that has been played in numerous cultures and settings. Other such games are known as mosquito, green monkey, Siberian hut, carrying wood and Jacob's ladder. Cat's cradle is a collective string game, in contrast to most other (Ackers Johnson 1993, 1995). One player starts with a string figure that is handed over to the next player who creates a new figure based on the original. The play continues with the creation of these figures, going back and forth between the players, thus inviting collaboration Transferred to the production of knowledge, it indicates that knowledge is not universal because people's embodied knowledge differs, is situated and located in place, time, context; that is, built on physical, social and cultural experiences over time. Knowledge is not once-and-for-all given but rooted somewhere, and dependent on where it is produced in practices where history, culture and places intersect in negotiations and translations. Haraway emphasizes embodiment, and that bodies matter in relations between humans and nonhumans. This takes us to Judith Butler and her gender performativity.

Gender performativity is another part of the string used in this chapter (see also Chapter 2 about performativity). Performativity is not theatrical but it is a 'becoming' that takes place through repeated activities or ongoing actions and doings. Judith Butler underlines that '[i]f gender is performative, then it follows that the reality of gender is itself produced as an effect of the performance' (Butler 2004: 218). The performance is a practice, citational practice, where existing norms are reproduced, reworked or are questioned. The 'result' of ongoing performances or what does or does not emerge is dependent on re-iterations of norms and values. Although existing norms are cited (reproduced) they are also exceeded or reworked. The subject, but also the materiality of the body – the sexed body, is produced in the performance. That is, subjects and objects do not pre-exist but are dependent on ongoing intra-actions (Barad 2003).

Sustainable or Unsustainable Standards and Formats?

Sustainability, feminist technoscience and gender performativity constitute the frame of reference in this chapter. We use the game of cat's cradle as 'collaborative practices for making and passing on culturally interesting patterns' (Haraway 1994: 70). Further, we use it in the analysis of the empirical material when we explore standards and formats and how these are, or are not, sustainable. Hence the cat's cradle is used in our mapping of various layers of actors or stories about standards and formats. We now look at the first project and at Jill's narratives.

Behind the Scenes: The Performance of Sustainability in Day-to-Day Activities

The stage is set and everything is in play in order to start the game. The first string figure is created by the civil servants and the researchers in the research project *From government to e-government: gender, skills, technology and learning,* conducted in the county of Blekinge in the southeast of Sweden. The county has been dependent on the metal industry, fishing and the military; forms of employment that have undergone huge transformations or have disappeared. Politicians and administrative officers, both at county and municipality level, have developed strategies to adapt to the transformations and to find ways for more sustainable futures. Consequently, a variety of measures and IT projects have been conducted at a county and municipality level e.g. in schools, libraries, spatial planning, and the health care sector (Ekdahl et al. 2000; Elovaara 2004; Ekelin 2007). The municipalities' efforts to create sustainable futures continue, but the primary focus, however, is on the modernization of the public sector; that is, on creating e-government. The research project, *From government to e-government: gender, skills, technology and learning,* has placed a special focus on civil servants' participation, experiences and knowledge in the transformation process. We use empirical material from this project in our discussions of sustainability.

Civil servants from four municipalities participated in the project and a variety of methods were used, such as cartographic exercises, scenarios, walk-throughs with disposable cameras, in-situ interviews, informal interviews, and Digital Storytelling. These games thus took place in various workshops and informal interviews. In this chapter, the focus is on one of the players, Jill, and her string figures; other civil servants were also involved but not always visible in the game. Jill has worked since 1987 in a municipality accounts department. Consequently, she has experiences of changes in terms of organizational changes, new governance regimes, technology innovations, and implementations of IT systems. At the time of the research she was responsible for tasks related to the municipal invoicing process.

Cash Payment or Not: Sustainable Routines

One session or string game started with a look at the photos the civil servants had taken when they walked through their work place with disposable cameras. After browsing through them, the civil servants chose and placed some photos on the map, created in the cartographic exercise, photos they thought would serve as good illustrations of their day-to-day work. The cat's cradle came into play when we, the researchers (Christina and Pirjo), asked them to consider the relationships between the people and technologies they had illustrated on their maps; relationships that were reinforced by the photos. When it was Jill's turn to play, she did so with a wonderful story. She talked about a woman who was behind with the fee payments for the day nursery. One day this woman showed up in Jill's office with cash in order to pay her bill. Jill had to inform the woman that payment by cash was no longer accepted. The story or the game could have ended here, but as Haraway (1994: 70) emphasizes, 'one does not "win" at cat's cradle; the goal is more interesting and more openended than that'. The string was taken over by Jill, a considerate, creative and innovative person, who navigates between possibilities and obstacles. That is, she created a new pattern when she suggested that, in order to pay the day nursery bill, the citizen should use the Svensk Kassaservice (Swedish Cashierservice) located near the municipality office. They went to the bank, the citizen paid the bill, she handed over the receipt to Jill, and back in her office, Jill registered the payment. The game had no single winner, but many: the citizen has paid the amount that she owed, thereby not risking being put on the dept collection register, a consequence of the municipality's measure; Jill was able to do her tasks and get in the fees; and the municipality got their money. Here, the cat's cradle ended on one layer but continued on another. We, the researchers, continued the creation of new patterns by starting a discussion of the possibilities of offering e-services to the citizens, for example to check their fees and payments on the municipality's web page: a self service municipality. The cradle went back and forth between the participants with suggestions of various services, but suddenly Jill's colleague sitting beside one of us (Pirjo) said very, very quietly: 'but then Jill will become unemployed'; a cut was created (see also Elovaara et al. 2006).

The cut or the frozen string figure – risk of unemployment – emerged out of the intra-action. E-services offered to citizens might result in situations where the citizens are undertaking tasks that civil servants were doing before the implementation of IT. We address such questions as: Is the design sustainable enough if people are replaced by technologies? Do IT-systems and services automatically replace people? We move back to Jill and another session or cat's cradle game.

Standard Identifiers: Disciplining Technologies

Some prevailing string figures or patterns of Swedish e-government games are rationalization and efficiency. Other string figures are also at play, for example the citizen's involvement in the transformation process as well as the provision of digital services for citizens. Digital services are created through Internet portals and public web pages. These string figures consist of how to find information about the municipality and its services; interactions with politicians; how to apply for day nursery; ask question directed at digital assistants; and so forth. Hence the services are relatively simple but they shed light on how civil servants will be replaced by citizens or technologies. In an informal interview, conducted in June 2007, we talked about the future and future e-services. Jill emphasized that there will always be tasks for civil servants like her, however new IT systems and services are implemented. Her explanation was that new services also create new tasks and Jill gave examples of how citizens' Internet payment creates new tasks. The invoice for, for example, day care nursery has identifiers such as an account number and an OCR (Optical Character Reading) number. The account number identifies the organization, and the OCR number identifies the payee. Banks offer services that give organizations opportunities to block payments registered without an OCR number or an incorrect OCR number. The payer then receives the message 'You have to register the OCR number' or 'The registered OCR number is wrong'. But not all organizations have adopted this service. Further, this functionality does not cover all user mistakes. Jill told how, when they pay bills with internet banks, citizens can make mistakes depending on whether they are using the OCR number for a month other than the current one. The transactions transferred from the bank are controlled electronically at the municipality; a payment with an incorrect identifier, OCR number, appears on a log for incorrect transactions. Jill, who is responsible for tasks related to the payments, has to figure out why the transactions failed. Due to her thoughtfulness and her ability to correct the wrong transaction, she diagnoses the errors, and adjusts and registers the actual OCR number. Jill solves citizens' inaccurate use of OCR numbers and prevents them from getting demands on the bills. Yet she does not succeed in pinpointing all problems. One episode she talked about was when a man showed up at the municipality office, telling her how his wife had received demands for her trade union fee that she thought she had already paid. It was paid, the account number was right but the OCR number used belonged to the municipality. The payment was thus on Jill's log list. Hence he solved her problem, and she paid back the money.

Jill acts and intervenes behind the scenes; she corrects the failures that citizens have created, and she invents solutions that make her work more smoothly. Her activities are also rooted in a citizen-oriented way of acting when she takes responsibility for them. Her stories illustrate how the citizens, the civil servant, the technologies, account numbers, OCR number, software, banks, log lists are all enrolled in the network; it is obvious how the actors are 'associated in such a way that they make others do things' (Latour 2005: 107). The cat's cradle starts with the citizen's internet payment where s/he creates a pattern that is handed over to many hands, humans as well as nonhumans, in order to continue the cradle, and finally Jill puts her hands on the string pattern, sometimes to create a whole new one or, at other times, to deal with partial patterns.

Weaving Together Unsustainable Standards and Routines

It is obvious how Jill creates meaning in her everyday work, not only for herself but also for the citizens. Her actions are based on particular values of accountability such as creativity, unconventional solutions, correction, and helping hands in the wings. Jill creates continuity in the network and the cat's cradle is kept alive despite the partial patterns (e.g. wrong OCR numbers); she creates new ones by unconventional solutions. Governance is an aspect Hawks (2001) includes within cultural sustainability. Governance, and particularly good governance, is used in e-government research to underscore participation and involvement. Jill's doings and activities are examples of good governance. Further, her day-to-day activities are sites of knowledge production (Haraway 1991).

The municipality had standardized their routines by removing the possibility of paying in cash. The majority of citizens have adapted to existing routines but not the woman Jill talked about. Jill's story was unclear about the reasoning behind the municipality's decision not to deal with cash. A not-too-unusual argument is to eliminate the risk of keeping cash in the offices. Another is the ambition to create standard routines: that payments be transferred electronically by services provided by external banks or post offices. This standard or routine did not work for the citizen who wanted to pay with cash. Jill, the civil servant, cared about the citizen and wanted to help her. Equity and dignity are aspects included in social sustainability. Jill's caretaking, responsibility and creativity in order to facilitate the citizen's everyday life are interpreted as expressions of social sustainability. That is, Jill had an ambition to act in order to treat all as equal in such a way that the citizen could keep her self-respect.

Sustainability in terms of economic aspects can also be discussed with the presented examples of this cash payment: the municipality gets their money when the fee for the day-care nursery is paid; the citizens does not have any debts; the citizen is not registered in the dept collection file, and the municipality save resources since there is no need to send a demand. It became obvious how thoughtfulness is embodied in Jill's way of dealing with various tasks. The existing standards or routines were not adapted to cover all citizens but, depending on Jill's actions, social sustainability in terms of equality was constituted. Hence her activities and her accountability are aspects that give social sustainability meaning.

Citizens have to live with standards like the OCR numbers despite the fact that they are not self-sustainable, that is, one has to register the exact OCR number. Banks offer services to control the standard but they are not generally used. OCR numbers like other categories or classification systems are created in negotiations and translations where things are sorted in and out (Bowker and Star 1999) but as Donna Haraway underscores 'there are always more things going on than you thought' (interview with Lykke et al. 2000:55). Citizens register both right and wrong OCR numbers. Jill has to deal with all occurrences related to the numbers, that is, the log is what enrols her in the network or the partial pattern created by the citizen that are transformed by a variety of players (actors) before she takes over the string figure. Jill adjusts inadequate string figures, created by a system that is not sufficiently sustainable, thereby enabling a continuity of the endless game or dance. Further, Jill is also doing category work (Bowker and Star 1999; Gane 2006) when she acts in the wings and corrects the payment logged on the error list in order to make the system more sustainable than it is. The OCR game is an example of an e-service that is not sustainable without humans intra-acting in the wings; in the creation of sustainable patterns.

An IT system is usually used in a changing environment. If this is not integrated in the design, and in design principles, it might limit those who use the system. At first it was obvious how the system limited Jill, but on the other hand she found ways to deal with an incomplete system through her creativity and unconventional ways of acting, thus, her agency seemed not to be restricted by the technology; she found sustainable ways of living with it. Jill is not unique in terms of dealing with technologies but what is obvious in her narratives is how her thoughtfulness is embodied in everything she does. That is, norms, values and ideals that are cited in her enactments are based on accountability (Butler 1993, 2004). The cradle does not end here since other norms or values are also cited and reproduced in the performances; norms and values that also govern Jill's doings and activities. Jill takes responsibility, is creative, and innovative but she is still one of the lowest paid administrative officers in the municipality. Hence the gendered division of labour in the municipality, as well as in Swedish society, is included in her everyday activities; the ongoing performances. The Swedish public sector is the dominant labour market for women, civil servants are predominantly women, and generally they are low-paid. Gendered values and norms of how to evaluate Jill's work are entangled in the performances. Following Butler (1993), it is clear that a connection between gender and the materialization of the sexed bodies exists (see also Barad 2003).

Performing identity, meaning, values and norms but also creativity, diversity and governance are components in cultural sustainability. Governance in terms of good governance was obvious in Jill's relating of her day-to-day activities, or in her continuity of the game. Strings of creativity and innovation were also woven in Jill's narratives/figures, values that created meaning in her day-to-day activities. The string game of standard and formats continues with additional iterations with a particular focus on cultural heritage and cultural sustainability.

Standards for Digital Cultural Heritage

Cultural heritage and the institutions involved in its preservation and communication, such as archives and museums, profoundly illustrate issues of sustainability in their change-processes related to digitization. Museums and archives are cultural institutions that can help people negotiate social and cultural boundaries and borders that are fluid and changing in relation to historical and societal development. Hence they are able to 'provide opportunities for critical, even conflicted exchanges between communities to articulate and mediate a sense of separate as well as shared space. This requires more proactive and interactive approaches rather than the tried ways of expressing collective memory and identity selectively' (Isar 2006: 223). The proactive and interactive cultural heritage communication that is addressed here also focuses on the relation between users and producers of cultural heritage communication, actualizing questions about such issues as who have the power to define the heritage – and how this relates to cultural changes in society. The issue of the sustainability of cultural heritage institutions points to cultural changes in society that also have to be taken into consideration. For example, social software such as Flickr, MySpace, Facebook, etc., represent a clear example of changing practices of public media communication, as well as of people's expectations of participation in public discussions (Beer and Burrows 2007). This has also been assimilated by cultural institutions that use Facebook, for example, to share art from the museum's collections with others (Stuedahl 2008).

Museums, cultural and natural heritage collections and archives are clear examples of this change – as collections and archives are resources for reflection upon cultural diversity, cultural identity, and cultural heritage, professionally represented according to current societal norms. While technologies, standards and formats are discussed and explored within cultural heritage institutions, relating to the structures of collection management inside such cultural heritage institutions, less attention has been paid to the societal and collective memories of the public outside. Lately, attention has turned to how to relate social memories, vivid in society, to the categorization work within the institutions and archives (Russo et al. 2006; Trant 2006; Chan 2007). This growing opportunity for cultural heritage institutions to build digital meeting places for public and institutional cross-communication, as well as between multiple groups and cultures, calls for attention to the sustainability of the infrastructure, i.e. the criteria that are to be used for establishing the meeting points.

Taking departure from the overall vision that archives of cultural heritage will be publicly accessible in the future, as several of the current main European projects in cultural heritage argue (EPOCH, MICHAEL), the design challenge in the case described here is related to the CIDOC CRM standard, which is a metadata standard developed for archiving digital representations of cultural heritage objects. The claim of the CIDOC CRM standard is to provide a wider presentation of cultural heritage objects, with its object-oriented focus on events as a departure point for categorizing into a broader spectrum of classes. The CIDOC CRM ontology is based on connecting objects and events, and is developed for museums and collection management to categorize digital documentation and representations of tangible objects according to its metadata.

The development of the standard is not bound to digitalization only – but also opens up for richer semantics and diverse categories for registering cultural heritage material in general (Ore 2001). Former registration systems for museums collections were poorly developed with regard to diverging needs and interests related to cultural heritage. Digitalization has in itself brought a broader set of categories suitable for heterogeneous users, as well as building users' expectation of access to cultural heritage archives that, before, were closed to the public. The challenge is to make this standard suitable for archiving other types of empirical research material as well, such as digital videos and sound recordings. These types of media representations fall outside the categories of the more usual standard. The CIDOC CRM standard for metadata is made for photo and text material, which broadens the established categories in archives – but which does call for disciplinary expertise to be used properly.

In the design case it was decided to use the CIDOC CRM standard for archiving the research material. The case illustrates the constraints where citational practices and norms are (re)produced, reworked, and questioned (Butler 2004). Developing new standards is reminiscent of the work involved in designing new practices related to existing standards in that it actualizes the issue of who participates in the development of new systems in sorting things out – and who does not.

Knowledge and Practice as Identifiers for Sustainable Standards

It is well known that standards for documentation are important for a durable system in most public institutions. The necessity for standards and formats is to design for sustainability but also 'to determine which (...) traditions are fundamental and sustainable, and which are outdated' (Bødker et al. 2004: 140–1). Addressing the role of traditions for sustainable design implicates a notion of *something given* (Lash 1996), or knowledge that is based on the frameworks that history and culture (Stuedahl 2004) give to the design and use of new technologies. In the described digitization project this is illustrated by an intersection between different traditions of categorization and taxonomies involved in digital design. The design project is focused on the digital communication of the reconstruction of a Norwegian Viking boat, the third Gokstadboat, managed by the ethnologist, Terje, between 2003 and 2005.[1] In the reconstruction project, the ethnologist researcher had several research goals. As it was an external research project of the Vikingship museum, one of the university museums in Oslo, Terje was in a position to use an experimental approach and an explorative perspective was welcomed. The use of CIDOC CRM standard was one of these explorative goals in the project.

---

[1] The third Gokstadboat was originally found in 1880, in one of the largest archaeological findings of Viking times in Norway, the Gokstad excavation. Three boats and the remnants of a ship were found in what is supposed to have been a king's grave at Gokstad near Sandefjord, south of Oslo. The Gokstadship and the boats were found cut into pieces and packed flat in the grave. The Gokstadship and two of the reconstructed boats are exhibited in the Vikingship museum in Oslo, one of the museums of the university, and give an impression of completeness and truth as if there was no doubt about the form and shape of the nine hundred year-old fragments that were found. In the museum storeroom, the third boat from the Gokstad excavation has been stored in approximately two hundred pieces and fragments, as they were found in 1880. The third Gokstadboat was never reconstructed because too many fragments were missing. The fragments of this boat are still conserved in the museum's collection.

During the reconstruction, Terje used digital media to document the process and built a rich resource of documentary material that illustrates how reconstructions are based on interpretations and reflexive processes. Terje's goal in his reconstruction project was to show how the interpretations of the excavated fragments were based upon readings, interpretations and negotiations with current scientific knowledge and discourse (Planke 2001, 2003, 2005).

Terje's use of digital media to document field work documents the process, for example, of how his interpretations of historical phenomena have developed during the collaboration with the traditional boat builder and the meetings and discussions with boat builders from other boat traditions, such as from the northern part of Norway. The reconstruction process is in this way documented as a knowledge-building process, as well as a process of reconstructing objects of the past. All these processes of reflection and negotiation between experts is hidden and silenced when the boat is finished. When the reconstructed objects are exhibited in the museum they do, in general, communicate only one hypothesis – the one that is materialized in the reconstructed object – and the other hypotheses are excluded. Terje's project is to make accessible several of the interpretations that were at stake during the reconstruction.

Connection Between Standards and Individual Practices and Knowledge

The CIDOC CRM standard was used to systematize the empirical research material and to connect the specific material of the reconstruction project with the established cultural heritage archives at the University of Oslo. In the reconstruction project, though, the focus on the reconstruction as a process instead of on the reconstructed artefact alone produced a major conflict with the categories of the CIDOC CRM standard. This was the main reason for the struggle that Terje had when he started tagging his empirical material with the CIDOC CRM system of metadata. The tagging implied a two-step process. Terje had first to use the editing system AVID to digitize the digital video recordings. In this system, the different periods of a recording are sorted visually in sequences with their own text box. Terje started to make some of his empirical analyses in these text boxes by sorting the diverse discussions and activities into themes related to the reconstruction process. Terje also used the textbox in AVID to give reflexive comments on the development of the reconstruction, about his own process of understanding the form of the boat in comparison with the hypothesis of the boat builder. All these analytical comments were related to the process, not only of boatbuilding as such, but also in relation to current research discussions of the sailing characteristics of current wooden boats compared to the possible competencies of the Viking sailors.

Terje's analytical cradle, with the sequences of the video and the framework of the editing program, clearly showed how use of technology and categories really makes a difference for the meaning-making processes related to it. The practicalities of using AVID for tagging the empirical sequences was that, to be able to tag the sequences with text, he had to move the cursor to the bottom of the screen and stop the video, then move the cursor back to the textbox to be able to fill it in. With traditional nondigital transcription equipment, Terje normally used a foot pedal to stop the audio files in order to be able to write while handling the recordings. Terje experienced the cat's cradling between different windows and sequences as time-consuming but he managed to tag most of the 50 h in this way.

Terje's cradle with his digital recordings and the categorizing systems stopped while he tried to use CIDOC CRM to tag metadata to the textboxes that followed the recorded sequences. The level of definition of objects in the analytical textboxes related to the video recordings in AVID was clearly different from the level of definition in the event-based categories of the CIDOC CRM standard. The task of mixing these two was too difficult to cradle and Terje had to give priority to other research tasks. There were several reasons for this: first of all he could not see the extra qualities that CIDOC CRM could give him in his analysis of the material. Categorizing with CIDOC CRM metadata seemed to make additional work rather than giving any new dimensions to the analysis. Secondly it was nearly impossible to identify the point in the video material that could be called an event, since interpretations are long-term developments that build on a variety of issues and that crystallise in a chain of events. Terje's understanding and interpretations built the basis for the reconstruction evolved over time – and it was a rather invisible and intangible process.

Further, interpretations in general have to be articulated and supported by an explanation, as they are not visible. Therefore, the empirical recordings needed additional explanations and contextualization to make the development visible. For Terje's research activities, the focus on events as a mandatory framework for categorizing posed principal questions about his analytical freedom: how should he identify categories that could relate to his proposed arguments about the long-term discussion in the field of Viking boat research? Or how could he define categories that build relations with former understandings the technologies of the Viking boat? All this was part of the text he wrote in the text box – but it was difficult to put in the framework of events and categories. The CIDOC CRM standard caused him trouble because it was too demanding, without offering any real advantage.

Terje's endeavour to translate the CIDOC CRM object-oriented ontology to intangible processes and fluid transformation was an example of how a cat's cradle interaction can stop, because it is too time consuming and demanding. As a solution, the video material was tagged with Terje's own categories, giving tags that are not easy for external users to search.

Archiving the digital documentation of the reconstruction of the third Gokstadboat shows how digitization brings to the forefront the divergence of knowledge, categories and ontologies that lies behind existing systems. The project also demonstrates how digitization in fact represents cultural digitization (Beer and Burrows 2007), where the categorization and archiving challenges existing knowledge-structures embedded in concepts, categories and semantics inside the institutions, as well as in individual expertise. Digitization as such demands multiple layers of categorization (Ore 2001), and in reality, multiple cultural categories are used. For a sustainable system to emerge, it is important to take these cultural categories and values into consideration.

Terje's case also illustrates how digitization work is deeply related to social issues such as social networking and participation (Beer and Burrows 2007) in relation to cultural heritage resources. His lack of motivation for making the extra effort to use the standard can also be understood in relation to the unspoken social and professional framework that remains in the background of his project. The CIDOC CRM standard was not well known or employed in his specific professional connections, either in the boatbuilding community, or in the research of wooden boats.

The CIDOC CRM standard is well suited to archiving of object-based cultural heritage, such as photo material from the reconstruction, and for an approach to cultural heritage artefacts. But CIDOC CRM was less suited for the categorization of interpretative processes and development of arguments, because it involved a different type of modality (Stuedahl and Smørdal 2010) which was not bound to artefacts or events – but to a cumulation of understanding. The CIDOC CRM standard for metadata clearly illustrates our argument for the importance of culture in connection with approaches to sustainable digital design.

Designing for Cultural Sustainability

Designing for cultural sustainability in the context of cultural heritage communication might also allow for participation and interaction where the subject is constituted in the enactment (Butler 1993, 2004) between cultural heritage artefacts and narratives. This is especially relevant for the relation between digital archives, their public use and the individual users. The challenge is to design lucid archiving projects for the multiple and multicultural understandings of the categories and cultural taxonomies and in society.

Based on this, the researchers in the digital archive project decided to experiment with the social taxonomy possibilities that are provided by social media like Flickr. Thus, an additional iteration was discussed as a continuity of the string game, where it was decided that the video material should be published without expert editing or tagging but left open for visitors to tag. The design approach is then based on making a connection between professional and public knowledge, or embodied and situated knowledge, and to create common grounds for multiple ontologies and concepts to meet. This is a process of meaning-making and creation of shared values that is articulated as an important part of cultural sustainable development (Hawks 2001). A sustainable design approach like this is relevant for building a digital design of cultural heritage that can support the communication of multiple collective memories in the future.

Museums need to build sustainable connections between their objects and narratives and society in order to gain a role as knowledge institutions for the future development of sustainable societies. Digitalization requires that such a connected-ness should also imply the connection of professional understanding with public understandings, all the way down to the categories and standards used for searching and archiving. In the design project, the idea was to build a closer connection between researchers and visitor communication. Making empirical research material accessible to the public, though, created challenges related to the non-sustainability of existing categories. This posed considerable questions about the development of a sustainable semantic. For the purpose of archiving empirical research material at the same level as sustainable archiving of museum objects, an extension of the standards of typologies and categories of archiving was needed to integrate the participatory demand of current society to access digital resources and repositories. Further, a reflection upon the standards of typologies and categories used in cultural heritage research was needed – as it became important to argue why cultural heri-tage *research* was in need of categories different from those of cultural heritage *practices*.

Discussion

We have discussed sustainability with a focus on standards and formats in two proj-ects, one dealing with e-government and the other with the mediation of a Viking boat reconstruction. We have argued that the concept of sustainability has evolved, and is used in a variety of ways, but also that all variations have something in com-mon: the necessity to integrate sustainability in the development of viable futures, not only in the development of societies but also in the design of IT systems, prac-tices, and standardization. The question we addressed was whether a system or a practice really is sustainable without relating them to sustainable ways of living. Our argument is to consider the intersection of culture, community, and governance in addition to also integrating these dimensions into design in a way similar Blevis (2006, 2007) in his integration of sustainability in (interaction) design.

We have used the string game cat's cradle in the mapping of layers of actors involved in the examples we have discussed. The use of the string game showed in the first case that the standards and the related IT systems were not sustainable without humans acting backstage. Governance and good governance, elements necessary in the creation of cultural vitality and sustainability, were integrated in the enactments of the civil servants. Further, gendered norms in terms of gendered division of labour in Swedish society were reproduced and intertwined in the net-works. This also shed light on the necessity to integrate social sustainability in IT design in terms of equity in ethics, justice and human dignity. Situated knowledge is also important to identify and include in designing for sustainable ways of living with technologies. We have discussed how a civil servant's day-today activities and doings in the wings are also sites for production of knowledge. It was obvious how this was integrated in the layers of networks in order to keep alive the game that depended on unsustainable design solutions and IT systems. Thus, the civil servant acting in the wings used her previous experience and knowledge to continue the game in order to create a collective surplus value. The worlds (practices) emerging are not comprehensive but are situated, partial and context-dependent (Haraway 1991). The focus on cultural and social sustainability is thus proposed as an addition to the focus on material sustainability.

In the other project reported in this chapter, the Gokstad boat reconstruction, the game stopped because of the extra efforts that the standards caused in terms of time. This was a standard of archiving that was transformed into a standard to be used as a combination between documentation and analysis. The standards did not create additional meaning for the researcher compared with those he usually used. The case illustrated how a cat's cradle in a game about standards must be meaningful for the humans in order for them to act and to sustain the practice. This shed light on the cultural sustainability of IT design in terms of the importance of meaning-making, the values and the connection to well-known practices.

The focus on sustainable design builds attention to these issues in cultural heritage processes. Consequently, we argue sustainability is also germane to long-term preservation, in particular to how to design sustainable digital communication of cultural heritage objects and knowledge. This includes standards, formats, databases, software and hardware in order to preserve cultural heritage in sustainable way – to be able to support future cultural communication and informal learning.

Nevertheless, most of the present systems design research and discussions deal with how IT can support sustainable development of a future society or how IT systems should be durable – and less with how the principles of sustainable development can be embedded in the design of future systems. Braa et al. (2004) argue for a horizontal and vertical expansion of the network of action in order to ensure sustainability. This might be of importance to a higher degree in some applications than others. Further, sustainability can be included in digital design by reducing non-recyclable consumption of materials, as Blevis (2006, 2007) does in his integration of sustainability in interaction design. This will ensure impacts that can certainly be assigned to ecological and economic dimensions. We have, however, extended the discussion by the inclusion of social and cultural dimensions. The consideration of values, norms and meaning-making has shown how standards and routines are unsustainable without a helping hand. This, for us, is also an important part of the creation of livable futures. All these dimensions or assemblages should be identified and included in performances, not only in the development of societies but also in design of IT systems, communities and cultural heritage. Digital design takes place in environments that are changing; some parts are stable and others are unstable. We have argued that designers should be more sensitive to incompleteness as something ongoing in sociomaterial processes.

The analysis builds on actor-network-theory and feminist technoscience positions that underscore the interconnectivity between nature and culture. Further, Alander (2007) argues that it is neither possible nor valuable to separate sustainability in various dimensions, because they intersect in everyday activities. It is thus impossible to know where one dimension starts, where it ends, and where another starts and ends. We agree with her argument and the value of understanding sustainability as empirically and politically entangled in social, economic, environmental and cultural issues. We have, however, focused on various dimensions of sustainability, such as ecological, economic, social and cultural. This can be interpreted as being caught up in an apprehension of culture and nature being separated and we propose to keep the dimensions separated for analytical reasons. We argue that, to be able to understand the design challenges for a sustainable design, the layers of social issues of, for example, equity and justice do have an explanatory dimension that also is cultural. The values and norms of equity and dignity are indeed constituted in repeated doings and actions where they are reproduced or questioned; citational practices (Butler 1993, 2004) are also intertwined with the cultural dimension. In order to be able to design for social and cultural sustainability, the dimensions such as creation of meaning, values and norms have to be understood and taken into consideration.

We have argued that history, culture and places are prerequisites in the development of sustainable design and sustainable ways of living. Such an approach requires a concept of culture that is flexible enough to enhance widely different and multiple social groups and organizations. A conception of culture that focuses on differences (Hastrup 1988) instead of commonality and uniformity (equalness) seems to provide a perspective that invites creation of an understanding of how historical traditions are integrated in people's activities. To understand culture as a system of relations, where materiality, meaning, thought and action build both differences and relationships, means that culture is understood both as an intersubjective category and a context that makes connections and produces continuity (Hastrup 1988).

Future discussions of sustainability will probably also have another focus than the dominant environmentally and ecologically based discussions we have had so far. Social and cultural sustainability require new practices as well as new ways of thinking. In digital design, cultural sustainability builds a relationship between the creation of meaning, values and experiences of multiple users of digital media, IT systems and artefacts that will sustain technical development and progress. The notion of sustainability involves an emerging design methodology that strives to understand the context before designing the system or the product. Long-term sustainable solutions are addressed, based on a concern for designing for future generations (Edelholt 2004). Both e-services/administration and use of cultural heritage archives and collections address user groups and practices that are not well known to designers. The design, therefore, has to direct a multiplicity of values, norms and identities – as well as the continuity of these in multiple future-use situations.

Acknowledgments

This chapter would not have been written without the civil servants, discussions with Terje Planke and Ole Smørdal. Thanks also to our fellow authors in this volume, to Eli Blevis, to participants in the seminar A Matter of Digital Materiality, CMC conference, University of Oslo November 2007, and to Heather Owen.

References

Alander, S. (2007). *Offentliga storkök i det gröna folkhemmet: Diffrakterade berättelser om hållbar utveckling*. [Public restaurants in the green people's home – diffracted stories of sustainable development] Diss. Luleå: Luleå University of Technology.

Ackers Johnson, A. (1993). *Cat's cradle. A book of string figures*. Palo Alto: Klutz.

Ackers Johnson, A. (1995). *String games from around the world*. Palo Alto: Klutz.

Barad, K. (2003). Posthumanist performativity: toward an understanding of how matter comes to matter. *Signs: Journal of Women in Culture and Society*, 28(2), 801–831.

Beer, D., and Burrows, R. (2007). Sociology and, of and in Web 2.0: some initial considerations. *Sociological Research Online*, 12(5), http://www.socresonline.org.uk/12/5/17.html. Accessed 17 April 2007.

Blankenship, S. (2005). Outside the center: defining who we are. *Design Issues*, 21 (1), 24–31.

Blevis, E. (2006). Advancing sustainable interaction design: two perspectives on material effects. *Design philosophy papers,* 04/2006, ISSN 1448–7136. http://www.desphilosophy.com/dpp/dpp_journal/journal.html. Accessed 17 April 2007.

Blevis, E. (2007). Sustainable interaction design: invention & disposal, renewal and reuse. In Begole, B. Payne, S. Churchill, E. St. Amant, R. Gilmore, D. & Rosson M.B. (Eds.), *Proceedings of the SIGCHI conference on Human factors in computing systems (CHI '07)*, San Jose CA, USA (pp. 503–512). New York, NY, USA: ACM.

Braidotti, R. (2006). *Transpositions: On nomadic ethics*. Cambridge: Polity Press.

Braa, J., Monteiro, E., & Sahay, S. (2004). Networks of action: sustainable health information systems across developing countires. *MIS Quartely*, 28(3), 337–362.

Bowker, G. C., & Star, S. L. (1999). *Sorting things out: Classification and its consequences*. Cambridge, Massachusetts and London, England: The MIT Press.

Butler, J. (1993). *Bodies that matter: On discursive limits of 'sex'*. New York: Routledge.

Butler, J. (2004). *Undoing gender*. New York: Routledge.

Byrne, E. (2005). Using action research in information systems design to address change: a South African health information systems case study. Proceedings of the 2005 annual research conference of the South African institute of computer scientists and information technologists on IT research in developing countries SAICSIT '05 (pp. 131–141). White River, South Africa.

Byrne, E., & Sahay, S. (2007). Generalizations from an interpretive study: the case of a South African community-based health information system. *South African Computer Journal*, 38, 8-19.

Bødker, K., Kensing, F., & Simonsen, J. (2004). *Participatory IT Design. Designing for Business and Workplace Realities*. Cambridge, Massachusetts, London, England: MIT Press.

Chan, S. (2007). Tagging and searching – serendipity and museum collection databases. Museums on the web 2007, April 11–14, 2007 San Francisco California. http://www.archimuse.com/mw2007/papers/chan/chan.html

Cheney, H., Nheu, N., & Vecellio, L. (2004). Sustainability as social change: values and power in sustainable discourse. *Sustainability and Social Science, Round Table Proceedings*. The Institute for Sustainable Futures, Sydney and CSIRO Minerals, Melbourne. http://www.minerals.csiro.au/sd/pubs/cheney_et_al_final.pdf. Accessed 19 November 2007.

Duxbury, N., & Gillette, E. (2007). *Culture as a key dimension of sustainability: Exploring concepts, themes, and models*. Working Paper No. 1. Creative City Network of Canada, Centre of Expertise on Culture and Communities. http://www.cultureandcommunities.ca/downloads/WP1-Culture-Sustainability.pdf. Accessed 19 November 2007.

Edelholt, H. (2004). *Design, innovation och andra paradoxer: Om förändring satt i system*. [Design, innovation and other paradoxes: about systematic transformations] Diss. Göteborg: Chalmers tekniska högskola.

Eichler, M. (1999). Sustainability from a feminist sociological perspective: a framework for disciplinary reorientation. In E. Becker & T. Johan (Eds.), *Sustainability and the social sciences: a cross-disciplinary approach to integrating environmental considerations into theoretical reorientation* (pp. 182-206). London: Zed Books and UNESCO.

Ekdahl, P., Gulbrandsen, E., Mörtberg, C., Trojer, L., & Aas, G. H. (2000). *Möten mellan retorik & verkligheter: En samlad processutvärdering av projektet BIT-världshus i Blekinge tätorter.* [Meetings between rethorics and realities: an evaluation of the project BIT cottages in Municipalities in Blekinge] Ronneby: Högskolan i Karlskrona/Ronneby, Enheten IT & Genusforskning.

Ekelin, A. (2007). *The work to make eparticipation work.* Diss. Karlskrona: Blekinge Institute of Technology.

Elovaara, P. (2004). *Angels in unstable sociomaterial relations: Stories of information technology.* Diss. Ronneby: Blekinge Institute of Technology.

Elovaara, P., Igira, F., & Mörtberg, C. (2006). Whose Participation? Whose Knowledge? – Exploring PD in Tanzania-Zanzibar and Sweden. In Wagner, I. Blomberg, J. Jacucci, G. & Kensing, F. (Eds.), *Proceedings of the ninth conference on Participatory design: Expanding boundaries in design - Volume 1* , Trento, Italy (pp. 105–114). New York: ACM Press.

Escobar, A. (1995). *Encountering development: The making and unmaking of the third world.* Princeton, NJ: Princeton University Press.

Gane, N. (2006). When we have never been human, what is to be done? Interview with Donna Haraway. *Theory, Culture & Society*, 23(7–8), 135–158.

Haraway, D. J. (1991). *Simians, cyborgs, and women: The reinvention of nature.* Routledge: New York.

Haraway, D. J. (1994). A Game of cat's cradle: science studies, feminist theory, cultural tudies. *Configurations*, 2(1), 59–71.

Haraway, D. J. (1997). *Modest_witness@second_millenium. Femaleman©_meets_oncomouse™: Feminism and technoscience.* New York and London: Routledge.

Hastrup, K. (1988). Kulturen som analytisk begrep [Culture as analytical concept]. In H. Hauge & H. Horstbøll (Eds.), *Kulturbegrepets kulturhistorie [The culturehistory of the concept culture]* (pp. 120–139). Aarhus: Aarhus Universitetsforlag.

Hawks, J. (2001). *The fourth pillar of sustainability Culture's essential role in public planning.* Australia: The Cultural Development Network.

Isar, Y. R. (2006). Sustainability needs cultural learning. *Museums & Social Issues* ('A Culture of Sustainability'), 1(2), 151–172.

Lash, S. (1996). Tradition and the Limits of Difference. In P. Heelas, S. Lash & P. Morris (Eds.), *Detraditionalization* (pp. 250–276). Oxford: Blackwell Publishers Ltd.

Latour, B. (2005). *Reassembling the social: An introduction to Actor-Network-Theory.* Oxford New York: Oxford University Press.

Lykke, N., Markussen, R., & Olesen, F. (2000). "There are always more things going on than you thought!" Methodologies and thinking technologies. Interview with Donna Haraway, part two. *Kvinder, Køn & Forskning*, 9(4), 52–60.

Mörtberg, C., Stuedahl, D. & Alander, S. (2010) "Why do the orders go wrong all the time?" Exploring sustainability in an e-commerce application in Swedish public school kitchens. *Information, Communication & Society*, 13(1), 68–87.

Ore, C.-E. (2001). *The Norwegian museum project. Access to and interconnection between various resources of cultural and natural history.* http: www.muspro.uio.no/posterecdl.html. Accessed 25 June 2008.

Planke, T. (2001). *Tradisjonsanalyse. En studie av kunnskap og båter* [Analysis of Tradition. A study of knowledge and boats]. Master Thesis. Oslo: Department of Cultural Studies, University of Oslo.

Planke, T. (2003). Reconstructing small boats. Fragments, tradition, intention. *ISBA – International symposium on boat and ship archaeology.* The Vikingship Museum, The National Museum of Denmark.

Planke, T. (2005). Gjenstand, handling og historisitet. Ting, kultur og historie – den materielle utfordringen [Artifacts, actions and historicity. Things, culture and history – the material challenge]. *Seminar for Cultural Studies and Cultural History*, January 2005. University of Oslo.

Russo, A., Watkins, J., Kelly, L., & Chan, S. (2006). How will social media affect museum communication? In *Proceedings Nordic Digital Excellence in Museums (NODEM)*, University of Oslo Dec. 7–9 2006, Norway. http://www.tii.se/nodem/06/

Sachs, I. (1999). Social sustainability and the whole development: exploring the dimensions of sustainable development. In E. Becker & T. Johan (Eds.), *Sustainability and the social sciences: A cross-disciplinary approach to integrating environmental considerations into theoretical reorientation* (pp. 25–36). London: Zed Books and UNESCO.

Sirc, G. (2006). Box Logic. In (Eds.) Wysocki, A., Johnson-Eilola, J., Selfe, C. & Sirc, G. *Writing New Media: Theory and Applications for Expanding the Teaching of Composition.* Logan, UT: Utah State UP. 111–146

Star, S. L. (1991). Power, technologies and the phenomenology of conventions: on being allergic to onions. In J. Law (Ed.), *A sociology of monsters: Essays on power, technology and domination* (pp. 26–56). London and New York: Routledge.

Stuedahl, D. (2004). *Forhandlinger og overtalelser. Kunnskapsbygging på tvers av kunnskapstradisjoner i brukermedvirkende design av ny IKT (Negotiations and persuations. Knowledge building crossing knowledge traditions in user participation in design of new ICT, in Norwegian).* Diss. Oslo: InterMedia, Faculty of Education, University of Oslo.

Stuedahl, D. (2008). Historisk engasjement med digitale medier. *Lokalhistorisk magasin Norsk lokalhistorisk institutt og Landslaget for lokalhistorie*, 19(2), 12–17.

Stuedahl, D. and Smørdal, O. (2010). Design as alignment of modalities. In A. Morrision (Ed.), *Inside multimodal composition.* Cresshill N.J.: Hampton Press.

Suchman, L. (2007). *Human-machine reconfigurations: Plans and situated actions, 2nd Edition.* Cambridge: Cambridge University Press.

Trant, J. (2006). Exploring the potential for social tagging and folksonomy in art museums: proof of concept. *New Review of Hypermedia and Multimedia*, 12 (1), 83–105.

Verran, H., Christie, M., Anbis-King, B., Van Weeren, T., & Yunupingu, W. (2007) Designing digital knowledge management tools with Aboriginal Australians. *Digital Creativity*, 18(3), 129–142.

Visvanathan, S. (1991). Mrs Brundtland lovely non-magical cosmos. *Lokayan Bulletin*, 9(1), January–February 1991, also in *Alternatives*, 16(3), Summer 1991.

World Commission on Environment and Development (1987). *Our common future.* Oxford: Oxford University Press.

Epilogue
A Multidisciplinary Take on Digital Design

Tone Bratteteig and Ina Wagner

Design is about making things and digital design makes *digital* things. Design is about envisioning something that does not yet exist, something for the future. Digital design is about designing environments with digital components, paying attention to the larger context of history, culture, social relations, collective practices, and new public spaces. The digital seems to invite change and it increases the pleasures of changing by inviting people to engage in explorative–experimental ways of doing things. The possibility offered by the 'undo' function to erase experiments with unwanted consequences, together with the effortlessness of change, as well as the simplicity of doing things that formerly required a specialist – all this makes it tempting to explore digital designs. The possibility to connect to others, known and unknown, and contribute to communities that reach beyond the local environment invites more people to be active communicators and citizens.

The aim of this book has been to explore digital design as an area where different traditions meet, and to develop a multidisciplinary approach to digital design research that accounts for the complexities of the relations between design practice and digital things on the one hand, the social and cultural processes of how people appropriate digital designs and participate in their making on the other. People's practices and their lived environments have been central to our approach to digital design.

With this definition of digital design in mind we have engaged in an analysis of the digital – as in informatics – and the socio-cultural – as in the humanities and social sciences – giving a voice to the core disciplines that contribute to digital design.

The informatics aspects of the digital are concerned with the characteristics of digital designs. They are not static – they do things: they transform input to output, they interact with people (and machines) in input–output sequences, and they represent parts of the world through their models of the context, in which they get their input and deliver their output. The humanist perspective takes account of the context, in which digital designs are embedded, producing both, narrative–descriptive and conceptual accounts of practices and relations.

As people increasingly not only use text in interacting with and through digital devices, there is a need to include sound, bodily movement, as well as different (static as well as moving, dynamically changing) visual forms. Knowledge and experience from the humanities and its extensions into the arts, with a focus on multimodal communication, on many-voicedness, narratives, tropes, and genres enrich our understanding of the uses that digital designs have – and can have. The humanities provide an elaborate apparatus for analyzing forms of communicating, for expressing experiences, representing ideas and translating between different media and modalities. Researchers coming from humanist traditions push the boundaries of their disciplines when engaging in translating their analytical concepts to digital forms. Designers need to recognize and understand this rich humanist take on communication in order to benefit from this book and productively use these perspectives for creating better designs.

Designers can also learn something from informatics in this book. Informatics used to focus on information systems that were digital models of (parts of) the world. As we move to develop socially embedded technologies and information environments, modeling can no longer be *the* central activity in the approach to understand the context (Nygaard 1996). The complexities in the context increase as the range of forms of interaction with the digital increase: more interactions are possible; more users can interact; more users contribute and express themselves through the media. The richer user interaction – especially the possibility for consumers to also be producers – encourages a focus on configurable and customizable systems: to 'design for design after design' (Telier et al. (forthcoming). The informatics concern is then to maintain the technical quality and robustness: we like to trust the technology to function in predictable and controllable ways while still being opened up to the users. There is an interesting connection of this concern with the strive for openness, adaptability, flexibility, and sustainability in architecture; and architects have taken up the discourse in informatics on openness and configurability.

The difficulty of opening to other approaches while not losing your own perspective is not untypical of multidisciplinary projects. All authors of this book are part of a hermeneutic tradition, in which the words and concepts we use are always open to different interpretations. It is this flexibility and openness that allows us communicate with strangers, learn and be creative. Wittgenstein's notion of language-games and of 'family resemblances' between games captures this. Creativity relies in particular on this human ability to, in practice in a language-game, follow a rule in a completely unforeseen and still appropriate way, and this is an opening for a multidisciplinary discourse on digital design research. The basis we have in common is that we are all researchers and that design is part of our research. The challenge, however, is in how to productively address our different relations to the digital on the one hand, to the practice of designing on the other. Egon Bittner (1965), in his essay 'The concept of organization', argued that the sense of a concept (common-sense or theoretical) is relative to the practice for which it has been devised. Looking at the digital design researcher, we can say, with Bittner, that for researchers to capture the meanings of the digital and how it is enacted, practices of design and use 'must be discovered by studying their use in real scenes of action by persons whose competence to use them is socially sanctioned' (1969: 247).

Our explorations into digital design have been grounded in a deep commitment to understanding how the digital and the socio-cultural meet in the ways digital designs are made and embedded in human practice. We argue that to arrive at such an understanding a careful analysis of the diversity of digital designs and design practices is needed. The examples of digital design and design research discussed in this book show how engaging with a multiplicity of methods and theoretical frameworks can enrich design practice and design thinking.

References

Bittner, E. (1965). The concept of organization, *Social Research*, 32(3), 239–255.
Nygaard, K. (1996). "Those Were the Days"? Or "Herioc Times Are Here Again"? IRIS Opening speech 10. August 1996. *Scandinavian Journal of Information Systems*, 8(2), 91–108.
Telier, A. (T. Binder, P. Ehn, G. De Michelis, G. Jacucci, P. Linde and I. Wagner) (forthcoming). *Design Things*. Cambridge: MIT Press.

About the Authors

Tone Bratteteig, Ph.D., is associate professor at the Department of Informatics, University of Oslo, where she leads a research group on Design of Information Systems. She was one of the initiators and the coordinator of the multidisciplinary research initiative, Digital Design, at the University of Oslo. Bratteteig is educated as a computer scientist, but her research background and profile is multi-disciplinary and she is involved in several multidisciplinary research projects. Bratteteig has been doing participatory design research from the early 1980s, in later years addressing more general questions concerning design and use of information systems. Her current research focuses on the relations between autonomy and automation when introducing digital technologies that distribute (work) tasks between people and technologies ("Automation and Autonomy", 2009–2013, funded by The Norwegian Research Council).

Pirjo Elovaara, Ph.D., is senior lecturer in Technoscience Studies at the School of Planning and Mediedesign, Blekinge Institute of Technology, Sweden. Her research field is based on feminist technoscience and focuses on design and use of information and communication technology. She is especially interested in the concepts and practices of participation and agency. She has also been involved in a number of local and regional ICT development projects in the region of Blekinge, in the southeast of Sweden. Her latest research project, together with Christina Mörtberg, was about gender, skills, technology and e-government with the title 'From government to e-government: gender, skills, learning and technology' (2005–2007).

Gunnar Liestøl, Ph.D., is professor at the Department of Media and Communication, University of Oslo. He has a magister artium degree in literature and a Ph.D. in media studies on the thesis 'Essays in Rhetorics of Hypermedia Design' (1999). He has designed several hypermedia systems, among them the award-winning 'Kon-Tiki Interactive' (1995). He is the author of numerous articles and books, both national and international, including *Digital Media Revisited* (2003, MIT Press, with A. Morrison and T. Rasmussen). Liestøl is currently head of the project: 'INVENTIO – Theory and Practice on Designing Digital Genres for Learning and Leisure' (2006–2010), funded by the Norwegian Research Council, exploring the convergence of mobility and localization in digital media textuality.

Andrew Morrison, Ph.D., is an associate professor at InterMedia, an interdisciplinary research centre at the University of Oslo and Professor of Interdisciplinary Design at the Institute of Design, Oslo School of Architecture and Design (AHO). His current research is into mixed reality arts, mediatized persuasion in branding and advertising, the collaborative design of a mobile GPS narrative and design and research into digital research rhetoric online. He publishes research and supervises graduate students in these areas at AHO. Andrew co-edited *Digital Media Revisited*

(2003, MIT Press, with G. Liestøl and T. Rasmussen); he has recently edited and co-authored *Inside Multimodal Composition* (2009, Hampton Press), a collection of multidisciplinary design and practice-based research pieces with Communication Design at its core. Morrison heads the Communication Design Research Group at InterMedia and is Leader of Design Research at the Institute of Design (AHO). His earlier research and participatory design has been into academic communication and electronic literacies, critical discourse and HIV/AIDS education and prevention.

Christina Mörtberg, Ph.D., docent/reader, is an associate professor at the Department of Informatics, University of Oslo, Norway and University of Umeå, Sweden. Mörtberg's current research interests can be described in two interrelated areas that link to each other. In the first, systems design, she bases her research on situated perspectives and participatory design approaches and in the second, a theoretical/methodological perspective is in focus where systems design is studied in combination with theory/methodology based on feminist technoscience and science and technology studies. Mörtberg has been involved in numerous national, Nordic, and international research projects throughout the years and has also been one of the founders of several transnational research networks. She has published and continues to publish her research on her own as well as in collaboration with doctoral students and colleagues.

Synne Skjulstad, Ph.D., is engaged in postdoctoral research as a scholar at the Department of Media and Communication, University of Oslo. She is working on a research project on cross-mediated and aestheticized advertising and branding in digital domains, labelled BRANDO. Skjulstad has a background in media studies. She has previously worked with practice-based research relating to digital media expressions, from hypervideo, experimental online research mediation, to digital media in dance performance. Her Ph.D. was an article-based publication that focused on a communication design perspective for textual analysis of multimodal websites.

Dagny Stuedahl, Ph.D. and postdoc at Department of Media and Communication, University of Oslo, has a background in ethnology, history and theatre studies. Her design research focus is related to socio-cultural aspects of participatory design, digital design, communication design – and especially related to design with and for youths. Her background in ethnology brings a concentration on performative interactions between individuals and the collective in media spaces, in which technological artefacts play an important role. Her current research focuses on the interchange between narratives, proximity-based social and personal media and digital environments related to youths' engagement with digital cultural heritage. Stuedahl was coordinator of CMC convergence track, which has initiated and supported this book project financially.

Ina Wagner, Ph.D., is professor for Multidisciplinary Systems Design and Computer-Supported Co-operative Work (CSCW) and Head of the Institute for Technology Assessment and Design, Vienna University of Technology. After completing her Ph.D. in physics she spent the first part of her career in science education, researching into and exploring innovative approaches to learning, before moving to the sociology of work, building cooperative relations with designers. Since then she has edited and written numerous books and authored over 150 papers on a variety of issues, amongst them computer-support of hospital work and of architectural design and planning, with a strong focus on CSCW issues, a feminist perspective in science and technology, as well as ethical and political issues in systems design. In her approach to the design of IT systems she combines ethnographic studies of work with design interventions and user participation. This also engages sociological interest in work and occupations, organization, management and technology. From 1995 to 1997 she was Chair of the Equal Opportunity Commission of the Austrian Ministry of Science, Research, and Culture, and from 1997 to 2000 she was member of the European Group on Ethics in Science and New Technologies. She is member of the Austrian Bioethics Committee, since 2001. From 2005 to 2007 she held a CMC– Professor II position at Oslo University; since 2009 she is adjunct professor in Design of Information Systems, Department of Informatics at the University of Oslo.

Even Westvang, tinkers, designs and develops for digital media, something he has been doing professionally since 1995. Currently he splits his time between the two web services Underskog and Origo. He has worked closely on these and many other projects with Simen Skogsrud, also a co-founder of the innovative Oslo-based digital media and design company Bengler.

Simen Svale Skogsrud, sees himself as a storyteller by way of technology and has worked with an array of media over the last 15 years. He currently tends to the social websites origo.no and underskog.no. His first novel, Pragma, was published in 2004 (Tiden). More about Simen is available at http://origo.no/simen.

Index